A Book of Friendliness

Reprinted by Seton Press
Printed in the United States of America.

Seton Press
1350 Progress Drive
Front Royal, VA 22630

Phone: 540-636-9990
Fax: 540-636-1602

For more information, visit us on the Web at www.setonpress.com
Contact us by e-mail at info@setonpress.com

ISBN: 978-1-60704-011-8

Cover: *The Adoration of the Shepherds* by Le Brun

A Book of Friendliness

A Collection of the Prose and Poetry Which Has Helped to Better the World

By

SISTER MARY CHARLOTTE, R.S.M., M.A.
SISTER MARY BRENDAN, R.S.M., M.ED.
and
MARY SYNON, LL.D.

IN ACCORDANCE WITH THE EDUCATIONAL PLAN OF
RIGHT REVEREND GEORGE JOHNSON, PH.D.
AND
UNDER THE GENERAL SUPERVISION OF
MOST REVEREND FRANCIS J. HAAS, D.D., PH.D., LL.D.
AND
RIGHT REVEREND FREDERICK G. HOCHWALT, PH.D.

GINN AND COMPANY

BOSTON · NEW YORK · CHICAGO · ATLANTA · DALLAS
COLUMBUS · SAN FRANCISCO · TORONTO · LONDON

849.1

Acknowledgments

For kind permission to reprint copyrighted material, acknowledgment is hereby made to the following:

Brandt & Brandt for "American Names," from *Selected Works of Stephen Vincent Benét*, published by Rinehart & Company, Inc. (copyright, 1927, by Stephen Vincent Benét); "Tavern," from *Renascence and Other Poems*, by EDNA ST. VINCENT MILLAY, published by Harper & Brothers (copyright, 1917, by Edna St. Vincent Millay); "Little Gentleman," from *Penrod*, by BOOTH TARKINGTON, published by Doubleday & Company, Inc. (copyright, 1914, 1942, by Booth Tarkington).

Doubleday & Company, Inc., for "Great Discovery," from *Madame Curie*, by EVE CURIE (copyright, 1937, by Doubleday & Company, Inc.); "Gates and Doors," from *Main Street and Other Poems*, by JOYCE KILMER (copyright, 1917, by Doubleday & Company, Inc.); "Rouge Bouquet" and "Kings," from *Poems, Essays and Letters*, by JOYCE KILMER (copyright, 1914, 1917, 1918, by Doubleday & Company, Inc.); "Bivouac on a Mountain Side" and "The Ship Divine," from *Leaves of Grass*, by WALT WHITMAN (copyright, 1924, by Doubleday & Company, Inc.); "L'Envoi," from *The Seven Seas*, by RUDYARD KIPLING (copyright, 1893, 1894, 1896, 1905, 1933 by Rudyard Kipling), and "Roll Down to Rio," from *Just-So Stories*, by RUDYARD KIPLING (copyright, 1902, 1907, by Rudyard Kipling), both poems by Kipling reprinted by permission of Mrs. George Bambridge, The Macmillan Company of Canada, Limited, and Doubleday & Company, Inc.

Harper & Brothers for "White Butterflies," by CHARLES ALGERNON SWINBURNE; "On the African Coast," from *Country of the Dwarfs*, by PAUL DU CHAILLU; "Feast o' Saint Stephen," from *This Way to Christmas*, by RUTH SAWYER; "SOS—Arctic Bay," from *Flying Priest over the Arctic*, by REVEREND PAUL SCHULTE, O.M.I. (copyright, 1940, by Harper & Brothers); Harper & Brothers and Henry William Parker for "Times Were Hard in Pontiac," from *The Lane that Had No Turning*, by SIR GILBERT PARKER (copyright, 1900, by Harper & Brothers; copyright, 1926, by Sir Gilbert Parker).

J. B. Lippincott Company for "Wishes for My Son," by THOMAS MACDONAGH; "Song at Samarcand," from *The Land of the Polish People*, by ERIC P. KELLY (copyright, 1943, by J. B. Lippincott Company); "The Barrel Organ" and "The Highwayman," from *Collected Poems*, Volume I, by ALFRED NOYES (copyright, 1906, by Alfred Noyes); "Helper to Molokai," from *Man of Molokai*, by ANN ROOS (copyright, 1943, by Ann Roos); all reprinted by the permission of the publishers, J. B. Lippincott Company.

The Macmillan Company for "The Scarecrow in the Cherry Tree," from *A Kentucky Cardinal*, by JAMES LANE ALLEN; "Abraham Lincoln Walks at Midnight," from *Collected Poems*, by VACHEL LINDSAY; "Travel Song," from *Selected Poems*, by SISTER M. MADELEVA (copyright, 1930); "How Dark Patrick Saved the Bank of Ireland," from *Dark Patrick*, by SEUMAS MACMANUS; "Sea Fever" and "Roadways" from *Collected Poems*, by JOHN MASEFIELD; "Barter," from *Collected Poems*, by SARA TEASDALE; "The Fragrance of Roses," from *The High Romance*, by MICHAEL WILLIAMS; The Macmillan Company and Miss Pamela Hinkson for "Saint Francis to the Birds," from *Collected Poems*, by KATHARINE TYNAN HINKSON.

Charles Scribner's Sons for "My People Came to This Country," reprinted from *War Songs*, by STRUTHERS BURT (copyright, 1942, by Charles Scribner's Sons); "The Star of Bethlehem," by ALICE CORBIN HENDERSON; "Through the Gates of Castle Garden," reprinted from *From Immigrant to Inventor*, by MICHAEL PUPIN (copyright 1922, 1923, by Charles Scribner's Sons); "The Shepherdess," from *The Poems of Alice Meynell*; Charles Scribner's Sons and Constable and Company, Ltd., for "I Have a Rendezvous with Death," from *Poems*, by ALAN SEEGER (copyright, 1916, by Charles Scribner's Sons; 1944, by Elsie Adams Seeger); all used by permission of the publishers, Charles Scribner's Sons.

The America Press for "A Saint for Monday Morning," by REVEREND LEONARD FEENEY, S.J.

The Athenæum Press

GINN AND COMPANY · PROPRIETORS · BOSTON · U.S.A.

D. Appleton-Century Company, Inc., for "Sister Mary Josephine," by MOTHER MARY ANGELA, from *On the King's Highway*, by Sister M. Eleanore (copyright, 1931, by D. Appleton and Company); "The Vinegar Man," from *Narratives in Verse*, by RUTH COMFORT MITCHELL (copyright, 1923, by D. Appleton and Company); "The Benefit Dance," from *Mrs. Wiggs of the Cabbage Patch*, by ALICE HEGAN RICE (copyright, 1937, by D. Appleton-Century Company, Inc.); all reprinted by permission of the publishers, D. Appleton-Century Company, Inc.

Burns Oates & Washbourne, Ltd., for "Fleet Street," by SHANE LESLIE; "The Shepherdess," by ALICE MEYNELL.

The Catholic World for "Sun-Browned with Toil," by EDWARD F. GARESCHÉ, S.J.

The Christian Century Press for "Christ in Woolworth's," by TERESA HOOLEY, from *Master of Man*, by Thomas C. Clark.

The Commonweal for "Totalitarian State," by MARGARET MÜNSTERBERG.

Dodd, Mead & Company for "The Soldier," by RUPERT BROOKE; "Daisies" and "Triumphalis," from *Echoes of Vagabondia*, by BLISS CARMAN (copyright by Dodd, Mead & Company, Inc.); "A Hymn," by G. K. CHESTERTON; "The Sea Gypsy," by RICHARD HOVEY; "My Financial Career," from *Literary Lapses*, by STEPHEN LEACOCK; "How Pleasant to Know Mr. Lear," from *The Complete Nonsense Book*, by EDWARD LEAR; the poems by JOHN BANISTER TABB, from *The Poetry of Father Tabb* (copyright, 1902, 1923, 1928, by Francis A. Litz); all reprinted by permission of the publishers, Dodd, Mead & Company, Inc.

E. P. Dutton & Co., Inc. for "The Spires of Oxford," from *The Spires of Oxford and Other Poems*, by WINIFRED M. LETTS (copyright, 1945, by Winifred M. Letts).

Forum for "The Infant of Prague," by PAUL CLAUDEL, reprinted by permission of *Forum*, the author, and the translator, Molly A. Haley.

Friends' Peace Committee for "The Christ of the Andes," by ANNA P. HANNUM.

Ginn and Company for "City Colors," by KARLE WILSON BAKER; "Bolívar the Liberator," from *Never Surrender*, by BRASSIL FITZGERALD.

Harcourt, Brace and Company, Inc., for "To Ignace Paderewski," from *McAroni Ballads*, by T. A. DALY (copyright, 1919, by Harcourt, Brace and Company, Inc.); "The Wall of Nanking," from *North to the Orient*, by ANNE MORROW LINDBERGH (copyright, 1935, by Anne Morrow Lindbergh); "The Tropics in New York," from *Harlem Shadows*, by CLAUDE MCKAY (copyright, 1922, by Harcourt, Brace and Company, Inc.); all reprinted by permission of the publishers, Harcourt, Brace and Company, Inc.

Henry Holt and Company, Inc., for "Chores," from *A Goodly Heritage*, by MARY ELLEN CHASE (copyright, 1932, by Henry Holt and Company, Inc.); "Mending Wall," by ROBERT FROST, from *North of Boston* in *Collected Poems of Robert Frost* (copyright, 1930, 1939, by Henry Holt and Company, Inc.; copyright, 1936, by Robert Frost); "Loveliest of Trees," from *A Shropshire Lad*, by A. E. HOUSMAN; "Fog," from *Chicago Poems*, by CARL SANDBURG (copyright, 1916, by Henry Holt and Company; copyright, 1943, by Carl Sandburg); "God Is at the Anvil," by LEW SARETT, from *Tinder and Flint* in *The Collected Poems of Lew Sarett* (copyright, 1941, by Henry Holt and Company, Inc.); all reprinted by permission of the publishers, Henry Holt and Company, Inc.

Houghton Mifflin Company, the authorized publishers for selections from the works of OLIVER WENDELL HOLMES and HENRY WADSWORTH LONGFELLOW; "The Tumbler of Our Lady," from *Mont Saint Michel and Chartres*, by HENRY ADAMS; "Songs for My Mother," by ANNA HEMPSTEAD BRANCH; "Lilacs," from *What's O'Clock*, by AMY LOWELL; "Opportunity" and "The Fool's Prayer," by EDWARD ROWLAND SILL.

Ladies' Home Journal for "The Third Lamb," by ANNE D. KYLE, reprinted by special permission from the *Ladies' Home Journal* (copyright, 1929, the Curtis Publishing Company).

Little, Brown & Company for "The Last Lesson," from *Monday Tales*, by ALPHONSE DAUDET; "The Battlefield," from *Poems of Emily Dickinson*, edited by Martha Dickinson Bianchi and Alfred Leete Hampson; "On the Appian Way," from "*Quo Vadis*," by HENRYK SIENKIEWICZ; Little, Brown & Company and Jacques Chambrun, Inc., for "The Football Game," from *The Varmint*, by OWEN JOHNSON (copyright, 1910, by Little, Brown & Company), reprinted by permission of Little, Brown & Company, the publishers.

Longmans, Green & Co., Inc., for "The Little Waves of Breffny," by EVA GORE-BOOTH.

Lothrop, Lee & Shepard Co., Inc., for "The House by the Side of the Road," from *Dreams in Homespun*, by SAM WALTER FOSS (copyright, 1897).

Maryknoll for "A Thank You to Abu and the Boys," from *Across a World*, by REVEREND JOHN J. CONSIDINE, M.M.; "Antu Christmas," from *Men of Maryknoll*, by JAMES KELLER and MEYER BERGER.

McClelland and Stewart, Ltd., for "The Soldier," from *The Collected Poems of Rupert Brooke*, published by McClelland and Stewart, Ltd.; "Triumphalis" and "Daisies," by BLISS CARMAN; "My Financial Career," by STEPHEN LEACOCK.

Julian Messner, Inc., for "Vineyards in the Sun," reprinted by permission of Julian Messner, Inc., from *Dr. George Washington Carver, Scientist*, by SHIRLEY GRAHAM and GEORGE D. LIPSCOMB (copyright, 1944, by Julian Messner, Inc.).

Oxford University Press for "A Hymn," by G. K. CHESTERTON; "At the Shrine," by RICHARD KENDALL MUNKITTRICK, from *The Oxford Book of American Verse*.

The Pan-American Union for "Song of the Americas," by JULIA COOLEY ALTROCCHI, reprinted from the *Bulletin of the Pan-American Union*.

[Continued on page viii]

Faith and Freedom
LITERARY READERS

Nihil Obstat:

REV. JAMES J. KORTENDICK, M.A., S.T.B., *Censor Deputatus*

Imprimatur:

✠ JOHN M. McNAMARA, D.D., Administrator (s.v.), *Archidiocesis Baltimorensis-Washingtonensis*

BALTIMORAE, DIE 1 JUNII, 1947

COMMISSION ON AMERICAN CITIZENSHIP

THE CATHOLIC UNIVERSITY OF AMERICA

PUBLISHED FOR THE CATHOLIC UNIVERSITY OF AMERICA PRESS
WASHINGTON, D. C.

Preface

The Christian faith is a faith founded on friendliness. A great commandment which Christ gave to His followers bade them to love one another. The example which He gave to them was one of friendliness to all men.

The Christians who listened to the Apostles of Christ learned from them and practiced this creed of friendliness. In time they spread it through many of the countries of the world. Through the ages the tradition of Christian kindliness and courtesy has come down to us.

Friendliness is not exactly the same as friendship. Friendship implies a closer bond between persons than friendliness demands. Friendliness was the spirit of service to others which inspired the Good Samaritan to help the stranger on the road. Although he had never before seen the man whom he helped and probably would never see him again, the Samaritan was, for the time of his service, the other man's friend; but their association was one of friendliness rather than of friendship.

This friendliness may be shown in every relationship of life from the family fireside to the world hearth of the family of nations. It is particularly evident in the time of great Church feasts, such as Christmas and Easter, when people speak the season's greetings to strangers with the same joy they reveal to old friends. But, although the feast days should emphasize the good will of the people of the world toward one another, the practice of friendliness should not be confined to any particular occasions.

One of the best means for the expression of friendliness has been literature. The literature of many lands gleams with shining tales of man's understanding of and man's kindliness toward his fellow man. In English and American literature thousands of noteworthy selections bear witness to the wide practice of the Christian law of love.

Kindliness in action is so widespread that one cannot think of any part of life without it. People in their homes, fellow workers in the towns, wanderers on the highways, soldiers on the march, sailors on the sea, pilots in the air, all have practiced this virtue of charity; and their practices have been recorded either as fact or fiction. This beautiful record of men's good deeds to one another has grown in time into a wealth of literature.

It would be impossible to give recognition to all the writers who have shown their own love of humankind by telling the adventures and emotions of others. All we can do is to choose a few of the many fine selections from literature which portray the friendliness that men have shown one another as they have met upon the highway which is life.

Reynal & Hitchcock, Inc., for "Night Warden," from *Night Flight*, by ANTOINE DE SAINT-EXUPÉRY.

The Rudder for "The Coasters," by THOMAS FLEMING DAY, reprinted from *The Rudder*, Magazine for Yachtsmen.

Saint Anthony's Guild for "Sea-Birds" and "Lady of Lidice," by FRAY ANGELICO CHAVEZ.

Sheed and Ward, Inc., for "Crossroads," from *Priest-Workman in Germany*, by HENRI PERRIN, S.J., translated by Rosemary Sheed (copyright, by Sheed and Ward, Inc., 1948); Sheed and Ward, Gerald Duckworth & Co., Ltd., and the author for "Courtesy" and "Noel," from *Sonnets and Verse*, by HILAIRE BELLOC.

Spirit for "To Each of Four Lost with the *Dorchester*," by ANNABELLE WAGNER BERGFELD; "Steel Worker," by KATHERINE EDELMAN; "Proof," by ETHEL ROMIG FULLER.

The Torch for "My Heritage," by HELEN C. CALIFANO.

Vincentian Foreign Mission Society for "The Divine Office of the Kitchen," by CECILY HALLACK.

A. P. Watt & Son for "A June Night in Russia," and "Harvest in Russia," by MAURICE BARING.

The Wise Book Company, Inc., for "Who Hath a Book," by WILBUR D. NESBIT.

WILLIAM S. BRAITHWAITE for "Rhapsody"; FRAY ANGELICO CHAVEZ for "A Prayer for the Nations," from *Eleven Lady Lyrics*; SISTER MARY JEAN DORCY, O.P., for "Exile"; Mrs. Charles Eastman for "An Indian Boy's Training," from *Indian Boyhood*, by CHARLES EASTMAN (copyright, by Elaine G. Eastman), published by E. M. Hale and Company; REVEREND LEONARD FEENEY, S.J., for "Farewell without Tears"; BRASSIL FITZGERALD for "Bolívar, the Great Liberator," from *Never Surrender*; LOUIS GINSBERG for "A Quiet Street after Rain"; DANIEL WHITEHEAD HICKY for "Who Pilots Ships" and "To an Aviator"; Dr. J. M. Kilgour for "In Flanders Fields," by JOHN MCCRAE; Dr. Francis E. Litz for poems by JOHN BANISTER TABB; Virgil Markham for "A Prayer," by EDWIN MARKHAM; Captain Francis Newbolt for "Lord of the Winds" from *Poems by Mary E. Coleridge*, published by Messrs. Elkin Mathews & Marrot (now Messrs. George Allen & Unwin); BRIAN O'HIGGINS for "Christmas and the Gael"; ODELL SHEPARD for "Home Thoughts"; RABBI ABBA HILLEL SILVER for "America"; Sisters of the Holy Cross for "Travel Song," by SISTER M. MADELEVA, and "Lovely Things," by SISTER M. NOEL, from *Songs of the Rood*; A. W. SMITH for "A Bountiful Providence"; Lorna Gill Walsh for the following poems selected from *Catholic Anthology, the World's Great Catholic Poetry*, edited by Thomas Walsh and published by The Macmillan Company: "At High Mass," by ROBERT HUGH BENSON; "Song to the Virgin Mary," by PERO LOPEZ DE AYALA, translated by THOMAS WALSH; "While to Bethlehem We Are Going," by SISTER VIOLANTE DO CEO, translated by JOHN BOWRING; "This Day, O Father, Give Us Daily Bread," by FRANCIS JAMMES, translated by GEORGE N. SHUSTER; ESTHER BALDWIN YORK for "Stranger at the Peace Table."

For their willing assistance acknowledgment is also made to the Faculty of The Catholic University of America, and particularly to the Director and Staff of the Mullen Library; to Sister Mary Hildegarde, R.S.M., of Our Lady of Cincinnati College for the Choral speech work; and to the Reverend Gerard Sloyan for his translation from the Latin of the Blessings of the Roman Ritual.

The illustrations for this book were made by Ralph Shepherd, Cheslie D'Andrea, Raymond Thayer, and Bruno Frost.

Contents

I. By the Fireside

II. In the Town

III. On the Highways

IV. At Christmastide

V. In Their Own Lands

VI. On the Sea and in the Sky

VII. Among the Nations

VIII. In Christ Our Lord

A Book
of Friendliness

RALPH SHEPHERD

I

By the Fireside

Home is the place of happiness. The deepest joys, the tenderest loves, the greatest pleasures are all to be found beside the family hearthstone.

This happiness does not grow of itself. Like a fire, it needs care—the logs of love, the spark of sympathy. That care is friendliness—the friendliness of parents toward their children, of children toward their parents, of brothers and sisters toward one another, of all within the home toward all who come into it.

You cannot see friendliness. You cannot touch friendliness. It may be silent, for it needs no words, but you can feel friendliness as soon as you enter a home.

In every time and in every land men and women have felt so deeply about happiness in the home that they have written great stories and great poems on the joys of families and friends by the fireside. They have written of smiles and tears, of welcomes and farewells. They have built the best of literature, a collection of writing which lifts the hearts of its readers and leads them into a desire to live in the warm fashion of the happy, friendly people of the printed pages. Their stories and poems are like lighted brands taken from the fire of the true friendliness of life.

Blessing for a Home

Hear us, O Lord most holy, Father almighty, God eternal: and deign to send from heaven Thy holy angel, that he may watch over and cherish, protect, abide with and defend all those who have their dwelling in this house. Through Christ our Lord. Amen.

2 Corinthians v, 1-5

For we know that if the earthly house in which we dwell be destroyed, we have a building from God, a house not made by human hands, eternal in the heavens. And indeed, in this present state we groan, yearning to be clothed over with that dwelling of ours which is from heaven; if indeed we shall be found clothed, and not naked. For we who are in this tent sigh under our burden, because we do not wish to be unclothed, but rather clothed over, that what is mortal may be swallowed up by life. Now he who made us for this very thing is God, who has given us the Spirit as its pledge.

The great English novelist Charles Dickens was a master in writing of many kinds of homes. One of the pleasantest he pictured was the one David Copperfield visited with his nurse, Peggotty, when he went to her home in

The House by the Sea

CHARLES DICKENS

The carrier's[1] horse was the laziest horse in the world, I should hope, and shuffled along, with his head down, as if he liked to keep people waiting to whom the packages were directed. I fancied, indeed, that he sometimes chuckled audibly over this reflection, but the carrier said he was only troubled with a cough.

The carrier had a way of keeping his head down, like his horse, and of drooping sleepily forward as he drove, with one of his arms on each of his knees. I say "drove," but it struck me that the cart would have gone to Yarmouth[2] quite as well without him, for the horse did all that; and as to conversation, he had no idea of it but whistling.

Peggotty had a basket of refreshment on her knee, which would have lasted us out handsomely if we had been going to London by the same conveyance. We ate a good deal, and slept a good deal. Peggotty always went to sleep with her chin upon the handle of the basket, her hold of which never relaxed; and I could not have believed, unless I had heard her do it, that one defenseless woman could have snored so much.

We made so many deviations up and down lanes, and were such a long time delivering a bedstead at a public house, and calling at other places, that I was quite tired, and very glad, when we saw Yarmouth. It looked rather spongy and soppy, I thought, as I carried my eye over the great dull waste that lay across the river; and I could not help wondering, if the world was really as round as my geography book said, how any part of it came to be so flat. But I reflected that Yarmouth might be situated at one of the poles; which would account for it.

1. *carrier:* a porter or teamster. 2. *Yarmouth* (yär′mŭth): a seaport in Norfolk County, England.

As we drew a little nearer, and saw the whole adjacent prospect lying a straight low line under the sky, I hinted to Peggotty that a mound or so might have improved it; and also that if the land had been a little more separated from the sea, and the town and the tide had not been quite so much mixed up, like toast and water, it would have been nicer. But Peggotty said, with greater emphasis than usual, that we must take things as we found them, and that, for her part, she was proud to call herself a Yarmouth Bloater.[3]

When we got into the street (which was strange enough to me) and smelt of fish, and pitch, and oakum, and tar, and saw the sailors walking about, and the carts jingling up and down over the stones, I felt that I had done so busy a place an injustice; and said as much to Peggotty, who heard my expressions of delight with great complacency, and told me it was well known (I suppose to those who had the good fortune to be born Bloaters) that Yarmouth was, upon the whole, the finest place in the universe.

"Here's my 'Am!" screamed Peggotty, "growed out of knowledge!"

Her nephew was waiting for us, in fact, at the public house, and asked me how I found myself, like an old acquaintance. I did not feel, at first, that I knew him as well as he knew me, because he had never come to our house since the night I was born, and naturally he had the advantage of me. But our intimacy was much advanced by his taking me on his back to carry me home. He was, now, a huge, strong fellow of six feet high, broad in proportion, and round-shouldered; but with a simpering boy's face and curly light hair that gave him quite a sheepish look. He was dressed in a canvas jacket, and a pair of such very stiff trousers that they would have stood quite as well alone, without any legs in them. And you couldn't so properly have said he wore a hat as that he was covered in atop, like an old building, with something pitchy.

Ham carrying me on his back and a small box of ours under his arm, and Peggotty carrying another small box of

3. *Yarmouth Bloater:* a large red herring which is smoked and salted at Yarmouth. Thus, people born there were called by the same name.

ours, we turned down lanes bestrewn with bits of chips and little hillocks of sand, and went past gasworks, ropewalks, boatbuilders' yards, shipwrights' yards, shipbreakers' yards, calkers' yards, riggers' lofts, smiths' forges,[4] and a great litter of such places, until we came out upon the dull waste I have already seen at a distance; when Ham said, "Yon's our house, Mas'r Davy!"

I looked in all directions, as far as I could stare over the wilderness, and away at the sea, and away at the river, but no house could *I* make out. There was a black barge, or some other kind of superannuated[5] boat, not far off, high and dry on the ground, with an iron funnel sticking out of it for a chimney and smoking very cosily; but nothing else in the way of a habitation that was visible to *me*.

"That's not it?" said I. "That ship-looking thing?"

"That's it, Mas'r Davy," returned Ham.

4. *ropewalks . . . forges:* all places of business connected with the repair, building, and fitting out of ships. 5. *superannuated:* very old; ready for retirement.

If it had been Aladdin's palace, roc's egg and all,[6] I suppose I could not have been more charmed with the romantic idea of living in it. There was a delightful door cut in the side, and it was roofed in, and there were little windows in it; but the wonderful charm of it was that it was a real boat, which had no doubt been upon the water hundreds of times, and which had never been intended to be lived in on dry land. That was the captivation of it to me. If it had ever been meant to be lived in, I might have thought it small, or inconvenient, or lonely; but never having been designed for any such use, it became a perfect abode.

It was beautifully clean inside, and as tidy as possible. There was a table, and a Dutch clock, and a chest of drawers, and on the chest of drawers there was a tea tray with a painting on it of a lady with a parasol, taking a walk with a military-looking child who was trundling a hoop. The tray was kept from tumbling down by a Bible; and the tray, if it had tumbled down, would have smashed a quantity of cups and saucers and a teapot that were grouped around the book. On the walls there were some common colored pictures, framed and glazed, of Scripture subjects; such as I have never seen since in the hands of peddlers without seeing the whole interior of Peggotty's brother's house again at one view. Abraham in red going to sacrifice Isaac in blue, and Daniel in yellow cast into a den of green lions, were the most prominent of these. Over the little mantelshelf was a picture of the *Sarah Jane* lugger,[7] built at Sunderland, with a real little wooden stern stuck on to it; a work of art, combining composition with carpentry, which I considered to be one of the most enviable possessions that the world could afford. There were some hooks in the beams of the ceiling, the use of which I did not divine then; and some lockers and boxes and conveniences of that sort, which served for seats and eked out the chairs.

All this I saw in the first glance after I crossed the threshold—childlike, according to my theory—and then Peggotty

6. *Aladdin's . . . all:* reference to the wonderful tales told in the *Arabian Nights.*
7. *lugger:* a small boat carrying four-sided sails.

opened a little door and showed me my bedroom. It was the completest and most desirable bedroom ever seen—in the stern of the vessel; with a little window, where the rudder used to go through; a little looking-glass, just the right height for me, nailed against the wall and framed with oyster shells; a little bed, which there was just room enough to get into; and a nosegay of seaweed in a blue mug on the table. The walls were whitewashed as white as milk, and the patchwork counterpane made my eyes quite ache with its brightness. One thing I particularly noticed in this delightful house was the smell of fish, which was so searching that, when I took out my pocket handkerchief to wipe my nose, I found it smelt exactly as if it had wrapped up a lobster. On my imparting this discovery in confidence to Peggotty, she informed me that her brother dealt in lobsters, crabs, and crawfish; and I afterwards found that a heap of these creatures, in a state of wonderful conglomeration with one another, and never leaving off pinching whatever they laid hold of, were usually to be found in a little wooden outhouse where the pots and kettles were kept.

We were welcomed by a very civil woman in a white apron, whom I had seen curtsying at the door when I was on Ham's back, about a quarter of a mile off. Likewise by a most beautiful little girl (or I thought her so), with a necklace of blue beads on, who wouldn't let me kiss her when I offered to, but ran away and hid herself. By and by, when we had dined in a sumptuous manner off boiled dabs,[8] melted butter, and potatoes, with a chop for me, a hairy man with a very good-natured face came home. As he called Peggotty "Lass," and gave her a hearty smack on the cheek, I had no doubt, from the general propriety of her conduct, that he was her brother; and so he turned out—being presently introduced to me as Mr. Peggotty, the master of the house.

"Glad to see you, sir," said Mr. Peggotty. "You'll find us rough, sir, but you'll find us ready."

I thanked him, and replied that I was sure I should be happy in such a delightful place.

8. *dabs:* fish; a kind of flounder.

"How's your ma, sir?" said Mr. Peggotty. "Did you leave her pretty jolly?"

I gave Mr. Peggotty to understand that she was as jolly as I could wish, and that she desired her compliments—which was a polite fiction on my part.

"I'm much obleeged to her, I'm sure," said Mr. Peggotty. "Well, sir, if you can make out here, for a fortnut, 'long wi' her," nodding at his sister, "and Ham, and little Em'ly, we shall be proud of your company."

Having done the honors of his house in this hospitable manner, Mr. Peggotty went out to wash himself in a kettleful of hot water, remarking that "cold would never get *his* muck off." He soon returned, greatly improved in appearance; but so rubicund,[9] that I couldn't help thinking his face had this in common with the lobsters, crabs, and crawfish—that it went into the hot water very black and came out very red.

After tea, when the door was shut and all was made snug (the nights being cold and misty now), it seemed to me the most delicious retreat that the imagination of man could conceive. To hear the wind getting up out at sea, to know that the fog was creeping over the desolate flat outside, and to look at the fire and think that there was no house near but this one, and this one a boat, was like enchantment. Little Em'ly had overcome her shyness, and was sitting by my side upon the lowest and least of the lockers, which was just large enough for us two, and just fitted into the chimney corner. Mrs. Peggotty, with the white apron, was knitting on the opposite side of the fire. Peggotty at her needlework was as much at home with the bit of wax candle as if she had never known any other roof. Ham, who had been giving me my first lesson in all-fours,[10] was trying to recollect a scheme of telling fortunes with the dirty cards, and was printing off fishy impressions of his thumb on all the cards he turned. Mr. Peggotty was smoking his pipe. I felt it was a time for conversation and confidence.

"Mr. Peggotty!" says I.

"Sir," says he.

9. *rubicund:* ruddy. 10. *all-fours:* a game played with cards.

"Did you give your son the name of Ham because you lived in a sort of ark?"

Mr. Peggotty seemed to think it a deep idea, but answered: "No, sir. I never giv him no name."

"Who gave him that name, then?" said I, putting question number two of the catechism to Mr. Peggotty.

"Why, sir, his father giv it to him," said Mr. Peggotty.

"I thought you were his father!"

"My brother Joe was *his* father," said Mr. Peggotty.

"Dead, Mr. Peggotty?" I hinted, after a respectful pause.

"Drowndead," said Mr. Peggotty.

I was very much surprised that Mr. Peggotty was not Ham's father, and began to wonder whether I was mistaken about his relationship to anybody else there. I was so curious to know that I made up my mind to have it out with Mr. Peggotty.

"Little Em'ly," I said, glancing at her. "She is your daughter, isn't she, Mr. Peggotty?"

"No, sir. My brother-in-law, Tom, was *her* father."

I couldn't help it. "Dead, Mr. Peggotty?" I hinted, after another respectful silence.

"Drowndead," said Mr. Peggotty.

I felt the difficulty of resuming the subject, but had not got to the bottom of it yet, and must get to the bottom somehow. So I said: "Haven't you *any* children, Mr. Peggotty?"

"No, master," he answered, with a short laugh. "I'm a bacheldore."

"A bachelor!" I said, astonished. "Why, who's that, Mr. Peggotty?" Pointing to the person in the apron who was knitting.

"That's Missis Gummidge," said Mr. Peggotty.

"Gummidge, Mr. Peggotty?"

But at this point Peggotty—I mean my own peculiar Peggotty—made such impressive motions to me not to ask any more questions that I could only sit and look at all the silent company, until it was time to go to bed. Then, in the privacy of my own little cabin, she informed me that Ham and Em'ly were an orphan nephew and niece whom my host had at different times adopted in their childhood, when they were left destitute; and that Mrs. Gummidge was the widow of his partner in a boat, who had died very poor. He was but a poor man himself, said Peggotty, but as good as gold and as true as steel—those were her similes. The only subject, she informed me, on which he ever showed a violent temper or swore an oath, was this generosity of his; and if it were ever referred to by any one of them, he struck the table a heavy blow with his right hand (had split it on one such occasion), and swore a dreadful oath that he would be "Gormed" if he didn't cut and run for good, if it was ever mentioned again. It appeared, in answer to my inquiries, that nobody had the least idea of the etymology of this terrible verb passive, to be gormed; but that they all regarded it as constituting a most solemn imprecation.

I was very sensible of my entertainer's goodness, and listened to the women's going to bed in another little crib like mine at the opposite end of the boat, and to him and Ham hanging up two hammocks for themselves on the hooks I had noticed in the roof, in a very luxurious state of mind, enhanced by my being sleepy. As slumber gradually stole upon me, I heard the wind howling out at sea and coming on across the flat so fiercely that I had a lazy apprehension of the great deep rising in the night. But I bethought myself that I was in a boat, after all; and that a man like Mr. Peggotty was not a bad person to have on board if anything did happen.

Nothing happened, however, worse than morning. Almost as soon as it shone upon the oyster-shell frame of my mirror I was out of bed, and out with little Em'ly, picking up stones upon the beach.

"You're quite a sailor, I suppose?" I said to Em'ly. I don't know that I supposed anything of the kind, but I felt it an act of gallantry to say something; and a shining sail close to us made such a pretty little image of itself, at the moment, in her bright eye, that it came into my head to say this.

"No," replied Em'ly, shaking her head, "I'm afraid of the sea."

"Afraid!" I said, with a becoming air of boldness, and looking very big at the mighty ocean. "*I* ain't!"

"Ah! but it's cruel," said Em'ly. "I have seen it very cruel to some of our men. I have seen it tear a boat as big as our house all to pieces."

"I hope it wasn't the boat that—"

"That father was drownded in?" said Em'ly. "No; not that one. I never see that boat."

"Nor him?" I asked her.

Little Em'ly shook her head. "Not to remember."

Here was a coincidence! I immediately went into an explanation how I had never seen my own father; and how my mother and I had always lived by ourselves in the happiest state imaginable, and lived so then, and always meant to live so; and how my father's grave was in the churchyard near our house, and shaded by a tree, beneath the boughs of which I had walked and heard the birds sing many a pleasant morning. But there were some differences between Em'ly's orphanhood and mine, it appeared. She had lost her mother before her father; and where her father's grave was no one knew, except that it was somewhere in the depths of the sea.

"Besides," said Em'ly, as she looked about for shells and pebbles, "your father was a gentlemen and your mother is a lady; and my father was a fisherman and my mother was a fisherman's daughter, and my uncle Dan is a fisherman."

"Dan is Mr. Peggotty, is he?" said I.

"Uncle Dan—yonder," answered Em'ly, nodding at the boathouse.

"Yes. I mean him. He must be very good, I should think?"

"Good?" said Em'ly. "If I was ever to be a lady, I'd give him a sky-blue coat, with diamond buttons, nankeen[11] trousers, a red-velvet waistcoat, a cocked hat, a large gold watch, a silver pipe, and a box of money."

I said I had no doubt that Mr. Peggotty well deserved those treasures. I must acknowledge that I felt it difficult to picture him quite at his ease in the raiment proposed for him by his grateful little niece, and that I was particularly doubtful of

11. *nankeen* (năn kēn′): brownish-yellow cotton cloth, originally brought from China.

the policy of the cocked hat; but I kept these sentiments to myself.

Little Em'ly had stopped and looked up at the sky in her enumeration of these articles as if they were a glorious vision. We went on again, picking up shells and pebbles.

"You would like to be a lady?" I said.

Em'ly looked at me, and laughed and nodded "Yes."

"I should like it very much. We would all be gentlefolks together then. Me, and uncle, and Ham, and Mrs. Gummidge. We wouldn't mind then, when there come stormy weather. Not for our own sakes, I mean. We would for the poor fishermen's, to be sure, and we'd help 'em with money when they come to any hurt."

This seemed to me to be a very satisfactory, and therefore not at all improbable, picture. I expressed my pleasure in the contemplation of it, and little Em'ly was emboldened to say shyly, "Don't you think you are afraid of the sea now?"

It was quiet enough to reassure me, but I had no doubt if I had seen a moderately large wave come tumbling in, I should have taken to my heels with an awful recollection of her drowned relations. However, I said "No," and I added, "You don't seem to be either, though you say you are";—for she was walking much too near the brink of a sort of old jetty or wooden causeway we had strolled upon, and I was afraid of her falling over.

"I'm not afraid in this way," said little Em'ly. "But I wake when it blows, and tremble to think of Uncle Dan and Ham, and believe I hear 'em crying out for help. That's why I should like so much to be a lady. But I'm not afraid in this way. Not a bit. Look here!"

She started from my side, and ran along a jagged timber which protruded from the place we stood upon, and overhung the deep water at some height, without the least defense. The incident is so impressed on my remembrance, that if I were a draftsman I could draw its form here, I dare say, accurately as it was that day, and little Em'ly springing forward to her destruction (as it appeared to me), with a look that I have never forgotten, directed far out to sea.

The light, bold, fluttering little figure turned and came back safe to me, and I soon laughed at my fears and at the cry I had uttered; fruitlessly in any case, for there was no one near. We strolled a long way, and loaded ourselves with things that we thought curious, and put some stranded starfish carefully back into the water—I hardly know enough of the race at this moment to be quite certain whether they had reason to feel obliged to us for doing so, or the reverse—and then made our way home to Mr. Peggotty's dwelling.

HELPS FOR DISCUSSION

1. Two rooms of Mr. Peggotty's house are described in the selection. Choose one and tell what David saw. If you wish, make a blackboard drawing to show details. What characteristics of the family are revealed in the house?

2. What were David's impressions of the different members of the family? How did each show friendliness?

3. Contrast the night scene outside and inside the old barge. How does Dickens emphasize the love and humble comfort within?

The common beauties of nature, free to us all, have inspired men to write poems like

To a Skylark

PERCY BYSSHE SHELLEY

Hail to thee, blithe Spirit!
Bird thou never wert,
That from Heaven, or near it,
Pourest thy full heart
In profuse strains of unpremeditated art.

Higher still and higher
From the earth thou springest
Like a cloud of fire;
The blue deep thou wingest,
And singing still dost soar, and soaring ever singest.

The pale purple even
Melts around thy flight;
Like a star of Heaven,
In the broad daylight
Thou art unseen, but yet I hear thy shrill delight.

What thou art we know not;
What is most like thee?
From rainbow clouds there flow not
Drops so bright to see
As from thy presence showers a rain of melody.

Teach me half the gladness
That thy brain must know;
Such harmonious madness
From my lips would flow,
The world should listen then—as I am listening now.

A great English literary movement produced many great poems of nature. One of the best-known of these many fine poems is

The Daffodils

WILLIAM WORDSWORTH

[Choir to be arranged in three voices: high, medium, and low.]

Low I wandered lonely as a cloud
That floats on high o'er vales and hills,
Medium When all at once I saw a crowd,
A host, of golden daffodils,
High Beside the lake, beneath the trees,
High, medium Fluttering and dancing in the breeze.

Low Continuous as the stars that shine
And twinkle on the Milky Way,
Medium They stretched in never-ending line
Along the margin of a bay:
Medium, high Ten thousand saw I at a glance,
Tossing their heads in sprightly dance.

Medium The waves beside them danced; but they
Outdid the sparkling waves in glee:
Medium, high A poet could not but be gay
In such a jocund company:
Low I gazed—and gazed—but little thought
What wealth the show to me had brought.

Medium For oft, when on my couch I lie
In vacant or in pensive mood,
Medium high They flash upon that inward eye
Which is the bliss of solitude;
Low And then my heart with pleasure fills,
All And dances with the daffodils.

White Butterflies

ALGERNON CHARLES SWINBURNE

Fly, white butterflies, out to sea,
  Frail, pale wings for the wind to try,
Small white wings that we scarce can see,
  Fly.

Some fly light as a laugh of glee,
  Some fly soft as a long, low sigh;
All to the haven where each would be,
  Fly.

The Butterfly

JOHN BANISTER TABB

Leafless, stemless, floating flower,
From a rainbow's scattered bower,
Like a bubble of the air
Blown by fairies, tell me where
Seed or scion I may find
Bearing blossoms of thy kind.

Flower in the Cranniied Wall

ALFRED, LORD TENNYSON

Flower in the crannied wall,
I pluck you out of the crannies,
I hold you here, root and all, in my hand,
Little flower—but *if* I could understand
What you are, root and all, and all in all,
I should know what God and man is.

HELPS FOR DISCUSSION

1. How does each poem on pages 16–19 help the reader to prize and remember something that reflects the friendly beauty of nature?

2. Read aloud from the poems lines that present attractive word pictures or that reveal joy in song, in motion, or in color.

3. Find comparisons used by the poets to emphasize beauty. (Example: *like a cloud of fire*). Read lines or stanzas in which the poets refer to clouds, stars, the rainbow, laughter, waves.

4. Each poem suggests a poet's deep thoughtfulness and wonder in the presence of natural loveliness. Read lines or stanzas that show desire to learn and understand; pleasure in the memory of beauty; quiet acceptance of a good end.

When you grow up, what shall you remember best about your home? Here's what one girl remembered. It made her write

My Heritage

HELEN C. CALIFANO

Because of my father the smell of the sea is perennially exciting. For he had been seventeen when he went away, and for ten years he had moved across stretches of restless waters to lands fragrant with the spices of the Orient or scorched by the breath of the Sahara and had sailed along shores fringed now with date trees, now with pine. At some time during those years, he had come to regard the great universe about him as a comrade, his life of a sailor as a quest after beauty. One night his ship glided out of the teeming harbor of Calcutta, and Asia had been left behind in the darkness. Another, he had sighted the great Pacific rollers pounding on the beaches of Acapulco.[1] Once again he had rested on the gold and blue strand of Sorrento.[2] That was home, the place where he had been born.

At the age of twenty-seven, he had met my mother, then a girl of twenty-two, in the city of Philadelphia. Shortly after, he had married her. So he had become a family man, a father of seven children of whom I was the youngest. He never forgot, however, that during that period of his life when the world was unfolding before him on mammoth pages of blistering blue skies and enchanted green waters, he had stood in the public places of the ports of the world and had sated his soul with the wonder and the romance of human existence. My childhood memories are dominated by ships, shining gray battleships at anchor in the Philadelphia Navy Yard, merchantmen unloading their varied precious cargoes in a mixed atmosphere of poetry and bilge along the Delaware, tramp steamers coming up from Brazil, ocean liners, fussy little tugs, brigs, oil tankers. My tiny hand in father's strong one, I followed him, shared with him this colorful exciting world of boats and wharves, of meticulous uniforms, of weatherbeaten faces, of straining cables, of picturesque jargon. I felt the lure of far-away places and glimpsed now and then a way of life which rendered me dreamy and which left me breathless. And now that many years have slipped away, in the manner that years come and go, I still stand guard along the coast and watch the thick rain slanting to the sea, or strain to sight a distant shore black and with a blurred outline in the moonlight, or merely sit on a sun-soaked beach dazzled by the shine of breakers creaming at my feet and by my own unbridled dreams of forest-clad islands and coral reefs. I hear voices that are mournful and restless, tormented and compassionate, faint and immense but always touched with that elusive quality which is God. The scream of a sea gull stirs my spirit like a bugle even while it wounds dully like an unrequited love. And the sight of

1. *Acapulco* (ä'kä po͞ol'kō): a seaport in Mexico. 2. *Sorrento* (sôr rĕn'tô): a seaport on the Bay of Naples in Italy.

Chinese coolies squatting elbow to elbow on a deserted dock, smoking, talking, dipping long-handled spoons into dark food pots can halt me like a thrust of hot pain.

Because of him, I tread the earth with music in my heart. He couldn't distinguish a quarter note from a half, nevertheless he was a musician who found in his gift his greatest comfort. His instrument was a battered accordion which had accompanied him on his voyages. He had played it under southern skies fermented by a blazing sun; he had wrenched melody from it in black gulfs of solitude more isolating than bereavement. He carried it with him through life because he had no other alternative. Music was the sum and substance of his existence. I remember him best sitting before the fire, playing and singing old sea chanties, Italian street ballads, snatches from the operas, American folk songs. Thus it was inevitable that when I was old enough to hold an accordion he placed one in my little hands and bade me play. It was just as inevitable that when I had learned to read, he and mother bought me a fine piano and promptly engaged a teacher for me. The absence of much that has long since developed the appearance of necessity was never lamented. I had music, so I had all. Thus when most girls were coveting that armful of flowers so emphatically youth's very own in the shape of a party dress or dance pumps, I was waiting in long patient queues,[3] often in drizzle and snow, to hear Paderewski,[4] or Rachmaninoff[5] or de Pachmann[6] in Philadelphia's old Academy of Music. I haunted churches blessed with distinguished organists. I made a trip to New York to hear Fritz Kreisler.[7] My first colossal extravagance when I began to earn money was to procure a season ticket to the Philadelphia Orchestra. I have known few moments greater than those I experienced, when, for the first time, I saw the great orchestra assemble, and under the baton of Leopold Stokowski[8]

3. *queue* (kū): a waiting line, as of persons before a ticket window. 4. *Paderewski* (pȧ dĕ rĕf'skē): a Polish pianist and composer. 5. *Rachmaninoff* (räκ mä'nē nôf): a Russian pianist, composer, and conductor. 6. *de Pachmann* (dĕ păκ'măn): a Russian pianist. 7. *Kreisler* (krīs'lẽr): an Austrian violinist. 8. *Stokowski* (stō kôf' skē): one of the greatest orchestra conductors of the twentieth century.

approach Beethoven's Fifth Symphony. Life can take from me, and has done so, many enthusiasms and blur a vision once crystal bright, but so long as I breathe it can never deprive me of the solace and of the rich joy of music. As it was with father, so it is with me. I have something for which I did not pay, a world of brightness burning madly in the deepening mists of the agitating years, a wondrous sense of forever coming upon the still apparition of a strange city at dawn. Thus when living becomes a trifle and the hours just so much weariness, a chord masterfully executed or a phrase from Chopin[9] whipped across my spirit can snatch me from tedium and hold me inexhaustibly. So it will always be, for it is my inescapable heritage.

Because of him, the world of books is my special kingdom. When other children were singing Mother Goose Rhymes in rote, I was thrilling to the adventures of some of the great works, of Ivanhoe, and of many others. Now and then when the printed page drifted beyond my depth, father met the

9. *Chopin* (shō'păɴ'): a famous composer.

difficulty with a period of storytelling, but for the most part, he read aloud that I might know at first hand the hypnotic beauty of words strung into place like so many gems in a pleasing pattern. So I learned to love language, to catch fire in its hard jewel-like flame, to search for lifted horizons that set the spirit free in books, to find the answers to plaintive questions on pages of honey hue. I walked with reverence in libraries ancient and dim and through college halls made holy by man's search after truth and goodness. Always there was the joy of discovery and the subtle gratification in the knowledge that this was a voyage of discovery without end. And as I moved about the realms of literature I became aware that an illimitable future lay before me. A nervous exciting light quivered over the world and over every creature and object that covered the earth's surface and grew more fervently glowing with every new literary experience. Life became another Camelot[10] which I viewed with "all her spires and gateways in a glory like one pearl." Led by this feverish inquisitiveness of spirit and mind, I have come through many years of enforced leisure with the certainty that my life has been uninterrupted. Midst many pines and to an unutterable stillness the best which has been thought and said in the world, all the matters which concern mankind have come to me from out of the mist and silence of the centuries. It has drifted through the air that I have breathed, suffusing it and penetrating it with the substance of maturity and of companionship. So, like Henry David Thoreau[11] on the shores of Walden, I have grown "like corn in the night."

Because of him a garden is a corner of heaven and the simplest flower is a breathless miracle. During the years of my childhood and early girlhood, I lived in a section of Philadelphia which, whatever else it possessed, was dismal for lack of garden plots and trees. High wooden fences separated one sprawling shabby yard from another. Back bedroom windows peered gloomily down upon cement blocks and bar-

10. *Camelot* (kăm'ĕ lŏt): the place where King Arthur had his palace and his court.

11. *Thoreau* (thō'rō): an American philosopher and writer. He built a little cabin on the shores of Walden Pond, near Concord, Massachusetts, where he lived alone for several years.

ren earth as hard as weathered hickory. Our backyard was the only exception. Here, each spring, an extravagant dream of color and of blossom sprang to life according to father's plan. Fleshy vivid magnolias gazed endlessly upon trailing cherry blossoms fragilely lavender and shy with an oriental reticence. Dogwood turned wondering platelike eyes of pink to the sky, unaware that a vast host of violets slumbered in purple sleep at their feet. All summer there were roses, some tall and aloof like the aristocrats that they were, some huddled in intimate clusters. There were zinnia beds and petunias, pansies, larkspur and hollyhock, and in the twilight there were always people seeking refuge from the grime of the street. There were other gardens too, that father taught me to love: walled gardens in old Philadelphia, centuries old and serene, at whose grilled gates we stood; the public gardens in the city parks geometrically conceived and precisely opulent; secret gardens in damp spicy woods where thrushes sang notes of unspeakable loneliness against the somber loveliness of laurel, against aisles of lichen and the jadelike canopies of trees.

By stepping into a garden I move out of one world into the calm quiet heart of another. I find in a garden free of human traffic and of human stirring a leveling influence which tempers both ecstasy and despair. Particularly when I am in trouble, I find the soft wind in the trees easing, the fragrance of mingled rose and honeysuckle composing. In moments of woe and of spiritual loneliness, when memories hurt and the present seems unendurable, I enter the garden as I would a holy place. Here, in the half luminous light of evening, the old tangled threads of sorrow and bitterness begin to straighten out again. As the garden and I dissolve into the night, I know an ever-reviving sense of kinship with all growing things and with the Power in Which every atom of life has its being. All these things were on the earth before me and will be here after me, and in some inexplicable way I am joined with them. And thus in a measure I am comforted.

Because of my father all animals are my friends, a song

sparrow pouring out a wealth of melody on the barberry hedge, a melancholy spaniel on his way home in the rain, a black cat dozing before the fire, a rabbit poised under the lilac bush, a plume-tailed squirrel hoarding his treasure. We were never without pets, those which were in our special keeping and those which father brought in from the street or alley where they had been forsaken. In days when veterinarians were few and their skill largely allocated to the healing of horses, father nursed many a sick bewildered creature back to health and sent it on to a home where it was wanted and was well received. All life was precious to him, its every form noble in its own right. He gazed upon every throbbing, pulsating thing, each living organism that shines and sings with the conviction that all were part of a harmonious unity governed by unalterable and eternal laws. He was proud to be part of this magnificent plan, eager to keep the light of life burning in eyes of slighter creatures.

By his example I learned to love the humbler occupants of our planet and befriend them and to learn from them lessons in patience and courage. Thus today, I enjoy a vast friendship beyond that which links me so tenderly and so conclusively to my fellows—chipmunks peering at me as I pass through the woods, sluggish spotted salamanders stirring at the foot of a stump where I pause to rest, sandpipers skirting the water's edge as I stride along a clean summer beach, friendly dogs thrusting their cold rough noses in the cup of my hand. It is my sorrow that, like father, I cannot leave an animal to its pain. It is also my joy. For with every piteous impulse realized I know a great quiet such as that which settles in a valley filled with night; for every kindness rendered I glimpse something that I seek in life for both myself and for him I call friend.

Constrained by this sense of universal brotherhood that is so all embracing and all inclusive, I can never lose sight of an implied Fatherhood. Everywhere as soft veiled eyes look at me from the field, and sky, and sea, I recognize fellow voyagers to whom it is my great privilege to lend a helping hand. All this because of him.

HELPS FOR DISCUSSION

1. "My Heritage" is divided into sections by the expressions *Because of my father* or *Because of him.* Find the main divisions of the selection and explain the five heritages.

2. Read aloud and discuss sentences which tell how each heritage enriched the author's life with friendly and beautiful interests. (Example: First heritage,—sentence beginning, "I felt the lure of far-away places").

3. Find expressions presenting vivid word pictures. Describe what they help you to see.

4. How did the author's love of her father inspire her to a greater love of her Father in Heaven?

William Shakespeare, greatest of English dramatists, spoke through the characters of his plays both wisely and well. It was good advice which he gave when he wrote the speech of

Polonius to His Son

WILLIAM SHAKESPEARE

Give every man thy ear, but few thy voice;
Take each man's censure, but reserve thy judgment.
Costly thy habit as thy purse can buy,
But not express'd in fancy; rich, not gaudy;
For the apparel oft proclaims the man.
Neither a borrower nor a lender be;
For loan oft loses both itself and friend,
And borrowing dulls the edge of husbandry.
This above all—to thine own self be true,
And it must follow, as the night the day,
Thou canst not then be false to any man.

HELPS FOR DISCUSSION

1. Polonius offers five pieces of advice for keeping on friendly terms with other people. Express each precept in your own words.

2. Shakespeare wrote these lines over three hundred years ago. Which of these rules of good conduct do you think we should still try to follow? Give reasons for your opinion.

3. Write a list of your own resolutions based upon this advice of Polonius to his son.

Two storied towns, Shalott and Camelot, are associated with the legends of King Arthur's Court. Out of these legends Tennyson wrote the poem from which these verses are taken:

The Lady of Shalott

ALFRED, LORD TENNYSON

Willows whiten, aspens quiver,
Little breezes dusk and shiver
Thro' the wave that runs for ever
By the island in the river
    Flowing down to Camelot.
Four grey walls, and four grey towers,
Overlook a space of flowers,
And the silent isle embowers
    The Lady of Shalott.

There she weaves by night and day
A magic web with colors gay.
She has heard a whisper say,
A curse is on her if she stay
To look down to Camelot.
She knows not what the curse may be,
And so she weaveth steadily,
And little other care hath she,
The Lady of Shalott.

When the soldier-poet receives word of the birth of his son, he writes

Wishes for My Son

THOMAS MACDONAGH

Now, my son, is life for you,
And I wish you joy of it—
Joy of power in all you do,
Deeper passion, better wit
Than I had who had enough,
Quicker life and length thereof,
More of every gift but love.

Love I have beyond all men,
Love that now you share with me—
What have I to wish you then
But that you be good and free,
And that God to you may give
Grace in stronger days to live?

For I wish you more than I
Ever knew of glorious deed,
Though no rapture passed me by
That an eager heart could heed,
Though I followed heights and sought
Things the sequel never brought:

Wild and perilous holy things
Flaming with a martyr's blood,
And the joy that laughs and sings
Where a foe must be withstood,
Joy of headlong happy chance
Leading on the battle dance.

For I found no enemy,
No man in a world of wrong,
That Christ's word of Charity
Did not render clean and strong—
Who was I to judge my kind,
Blindest groper of the blind?

God to you may give the sight
And the clear, undoubting strength
Wars to knit for single right,
Freedom's war to knit at length,
And to win, through wrath and strife,
To the sequel of my life.

But for you, so small and young,
Born on Saint Cecilia's Day,
I in more harmonious song
Now for nearer joys should pray—
Simple joys: the natural growth
Of your childhood and your youth,
Courage, innocence, and truth:

These for you, so small and young,
In your hand and heart and tongue.

THINGS TO DO

1. Each stanza in "The Lady of Shalott" creates a word picture. Draw or paint an illustration for one stanza.

2. Design a birth card for the infant son of the soldier-poet Thomas MacDonagh. Print your favorite stanza from "Wishes for My Son."

Who Hath a Book

WILBUR D. NESBIT

Who hath a book
  Has friends at hand,
And gold and gear
  At his command;
And rich estates,
  If he but look,
Are held by him
  Who hath a book.

Who hath a book
  Has but to read,
And he may be
  A king, indeed;
His kingdom is
  His inglenook[1]—
All this is his
  Who hath a book.

1. *inglenook: ingle* comes from a Scotch word meaning "fire." Thus, chimney corner.

Out of the memory of humble, everyday tasks has come much great literature. A good writer has made a good story out of her memory of her

Chores

MARY ELLEN CHASE

To lovers of the long and intricate history of language the disuse and final death of certain words is a matter of regret. Yet every age bears witness to the inevitableness of such loss. One cannot, for instance, without a smile speak of gasoline as *fodder* or refer to the replenishment of one's kitchenette during National Canned Goods Week as the buying of *provender*. Since modesty is no longer a "candle to merit," as it was in the mind of Fielding,[1] what need have we for such adjectives as *comely* and *demure*? And how can one with any sense either of perspective or of humor who lies under his automobile and dickers with its works refer to his occupation as a *chore*?

Specialists in dialect tell us that *chore* is largely an American word. In England, where it is limited to an unenviable class of society, it is usually spelt and pronounced with an *a*. They tell us, too (one trusts sadly), that here it has become colloquial, relegated to rural communities which find it a necessary adjunct to common speech. Gone are the days when Emerson suggested the doing of *chores* as an assistance to the seclusion and the reflection of the would-be scholar!

But thirty years ago the word was in reputable, indeed, indispensable use among all families of average means, both rural and urban. Just as reputable and indispensable were the chores themselves, those little, odd, miscellaneous pieces of business which must be performed if the wheels of family life were to turn freely. Indeed, in ours, as in all other families which we knew, chores were part of the accepted routine of the day. Like the talents of the parable they were allotted to each of us according to his several abilities, and remonstrances were not anticipated.

"May we coast in Dr. Grindle's field this morning?" we were wont to ask at a January breakfast.

1. *Henry Fielding* (*1707–1754*): an English novelist and dramatist.

"It will be time to settle that matter," said my mother, "when your chores are finished."

Now the essence of chores lay in their co-operative character. In this they were sharply distinguished from jobs of all kinds. One was paid for a job but never for a chore. The performance of the former connoted agreement and consent; the performance of the latter, participation and partnership. For example, my driving of Constancy, the family cow, to and from her distant pasture twice a day, from April to November, in all weathers was a job. I was paid five dollars for it on the first of every November. The money was mine to use as I liked, and, although I was generally impelled by the attitude and example of my parents to put it in the savings bank, I was never actually constrained to do so. On the contrary, my feeding of the pig was a chore. Its fulfillment required no unreasonable amount of time or effort and was regarded simply as a portion of my share in the comfort and expediency of family life.

My other morning and evening tasks about the barn, for which I ever had a greater predilection[2] than for tasks about the house, were chores—the feeding of the horses, the bedding of the cow, the weekly sweeping of the floor when I became large and strong enough to wield the broom. The carrying of a morning quart of milk to a neighbor, the daily fetching of a dozen eggs (at ten cents a dozen!) from Mrs. Douglass on the hill, the filling of the wood-boxes in kitchen, library, and bedrooms, the piling of wood and the splitting of it, when axes became safe instruments, the shovelling of snow, the fall gathering of apples—these, too, were chores, to be performed by one or another of us cheerfully and without question. Often the assignment of these was varied month by month; sometimes we enjoyed the dramatic device of drawing for them on slips of paper shaken in a hat. But the idea that they were more than our just and due service never once occurred to us. Nor could we be stirred to any possible rebellion by our associates, for every child we knew contributed in precisely the same manner to the well-being of his own household.

2. *predilection* (prē dĭ lĕk'shŭn): preference.

Indoors, a large and growing family with at most one "hired girl" necessitated other and less interesting chores. Lamps must be filled and cleaned, the black wicks, disagreeable alike to nose and fingers, cut in a circular fashion to insure a steady light, and the polished chimneys covered with brown paper bags and arranged in an orderly row upon the shelf above the kitchen sink. Dishes, an interminable number, must be dried with no dampness and with no breakage; beds must be made. Dust cloths must follow the intricacies of Victorian table legs and the small, triangular shelves of whatnots.[3]

Ruleless babies multiplied chores in an almost incredible fashion, even before they began to be peripatetic[4] and hence to demand active and ceaseless guardianship from some older sister or brother. Up to a year old, in those days before Dr. Emmett Holt[5] revolutionized their nurture, their daily naps were a matter of deepest concern and anxiety, for upon such naps depended the even life of the family. It is safe to say that ninety per cent of the infant population of the nineties was swung or rocked in cradles. One, indeed, is given to wondering if the aversion felt by many middle-aged persons to syncopated music might not have been unconsciously engendered by those longer, smoother rhythms to which they were daily accustomed in their infancy!

To one chore made necessary by the presence of five brothers and sisters younger than I at the age of fifteen, I shall always be grateful. On Saturday mornings and on week days during the long winter vacations, which because of municipal poverty were given us from February to April, I was stationed at nine o'clock in the library before the baby's cradle. My task was simple. By judicious swayings of the cradle I was to keep the baby asleep surely for two and, if possible, for three hours, while in the kitchen beyond things continued on their wonted and orderly way. I was never

3. *whatnot:* a light open set of shelves used for the display of small pieces of china or glass and other interesting objects. 4. *peripatetic* (pĕr ĭ pȧ tĕt'ĭk): walking about. 5. *Holt:* the author of a book on the raising of children which has had great influence all over the United States.

averse to this chore; in fact, it became so coveted that in order to secure its allotment I was willing to resort to bribery. For in those long, slow hours I could read, exempt from any charge of idleness which sometimes fell upon those who devoured books during working time.

I prepared for the graduate school by that cradle. Today when college freshmen confess to an ignorance of the Waverley novels[6] or *Scottish Chiefs*,[7] *Lorna Doone*[8] or *Great Expectations*,[9] I am lenient, remembering that their brothers and sisters were never rocked. My parents were wise enough to prohibit few books, only seeing to it that nothing on our family shelves was inadvisable or harmful. When I had exhausted our none too abundant store, I borrowed from every house in town, from the Ladies' Social Library, and from the few rather pious volumes lent every week by the Superintendent of the Sunday School. I read Shakespeare, Thackeray, George Eliot; William Black, Dickens, and the Brontës; Hawthorne, Cooper, and Robert Louis Stevenson. I do not remember that I was conscious of any difference in treatment

6. *Waverley novels:* a series of historical novels by Sir Walter Scott. 7. *Scottish Chiefs:* a historical novel written by Jane Porter. 8. *Lorna Doone:* a romantic novel by R. D. Blackmore. 9. *Great Expectations:* one of the later novels by Charles Dickens.

between *Bleak House*[10] and *Little Women,* between George Eliot[11] and Sophie May,[12] that I regarded one as duller than the other, more difficult to "get into." They were all stories. If they took me into a different world and kind from the one I knew, I glorified in the swift and certain transference; if they related experiences I had had, I felt a pleasurable sense of companionship and sympathy.

One set of books, now doubtless passed out of circulation, I recall with especial pleasure, the biographies and historical sketches of J. S. C. Abbott. These, much to my regret, we did not own; but I borrowed them volume by volume, covered each with the brown paper we were required to wrap about all borrowed books, read and reread before a reluctant return. Probably these were inaccurate and sentimental; it is difficult, indeed, to credit such a prolific writer as Mr. Abbott with both accuracy and objectiveness; but they opened doors to me into new periods and civilizations—Greece and Rome, the Renaissance, Spain, the French Revolution—and I shall never forget them.

Mr. Abbott, too, possessed an added value in that the perusal of his books pleased my father. When he tiptoed in at noon, if perchance the baby had been induced to sleep so late, and looked over my shoulder as he invariably did, I was sure to receive a more reassuring nod than that provoked by *Five Little Peppers.* I was, in point of fact, more than once guilty of a swift substitution at the eleventh hour. Seeing him walking up the driveway and being desirous for one reason or another of his heartiest approval, I often hastily hid *Jo's Boys* beneath the chair cushion and became engrossed in Creasy[13] or Froissart[14] or John Fiske,[15] gentlemen without the charm, exuberance, and vivacity of Mr. Abbott or of Charles Dickens in *A Child's History of England.*

Much, of course, of the morning's absorption depended upon the baby; and many were the savage impulses I re-

10. *Bleak House:* a novel by Dickens. 11. *George Eliot:* under this pen name Mary Ann Evans wrote a number of novels. 12. *Sophie May:* a writer for juveniles. 13. *Sir Edward Creasy:* an English historian. 14. *Froissart* (froi'särt): an early French chronicler and poet. 15. *Fiske:* an American historian.

strained when he or she woke at the wrong moment and demanded attention. Thus the sight of *The Lay of the Last Minstrel*[16] will ever be attended by a feeling of exasperation, for the child in question refused to sleep longer precisely at the moment for the opening of the grave of Michael Scott in Melrose Abbey and the rash seizure of the Mighty Book by William of Deloraine! I remember only once in those years of reading when I woke the baby myself, desperate in the great silent room for company. That was upon the occasion of my completion of *Wuthering Heights*,[17] which Stevenson calls "that powerful, miserable novel." And, indeed, I confess to that same desire for company more than once in later readings of that miraculous book, written—how could she have done it?—by a half-crazed girl of twenty-four.

Another chore made necessary by the ever-present baby was the nightly putting him to bed at six o'clock. This was in no sense so delightful as sitting by his cradle, and I recall it only because of its recurrence over a period of many years. Perhaps, too, the participation therein of every member of the family, except my father, caused it to partake generously of the inherent nature of a chore.

The procession started in the kitchen, the baby having been undressed and swathed in night clothes and blankets by the kitchen stove. My mother bore her youngest. She was preceded by my oldest sister who, as attendant acolyte, and by reason of her age entrusted before the others of us, carried a lamp, lighted in winter, in summer ready for lighting. I followed my mother with a large pan, which contained the baby's bottles, his milk, and a small tin cup for heating the same over the lamp in question. A sister, two years my junior, grasped in one hand a creosote burner and in the other a tiny bottle of creosote against the croup, which might make its insidious appearance without the slightest warning. My brother brought up the rear of the line with an armful

16. *The Lay of the Last Minstrel:* a long narrative poem by Sir Walter Scott.
17. *Wuthering Heights:* a novel by Emily Brontë. It is laid on the lonely moors of Yorkshire where the author lived. The story is based on the dreadful hate of a man for his neighbors and friends.

of extra blankets and diapers. We stopped for a moment in the library for my father to look with pride and approbation upon the baby and then went our way up the long, curving stairs. We did not think it strange that my father took no part in the evening rite. Early we took it for granted that he, like the other fathers we knew, was supposed to be manually ineffective so far as life indoors was concerned.

As the years went on, the procession changed character, my brother being released as soon as a younger sister was old enough to take his place. In those days the work of women and the work of men were in more distinct categories than they are today. Only I continued with my chores in the stable, my mother consenting on the ground that I was of less service in the house. But without or within we did our share toward the common weal.

Chores overreached themselves in their by-products. In our family, as in all others, each child was made to feel himself necessary to a larger group. If he went away for an infrequent visit, we saw to it that the performance of his chores was well arranged for before his departure. Although his individuality was not stressed as it is today, although in the average family he was seldom regarded as singular or problematical, his co-operative value was tacitly admitted and encouraged. His assistance was taken for granted, and his willingness as well. In some rare cases it may have happened that children were over-worked, that they were made to feel a responsibility incompatible with their years. But at all events selfishness did not flourish under such a system. As for me, recalling Mr. J. S. C. Abbott and realizing that in those years between eight and seventeen I did fifty per cent of all the reading of my life, I can only return thanks for the chores that were required of me and for their inestimable by-products.

HELPS FOR DISCUSSION

In the author's mind, what were the differences between jobs and chores? How did performance of chores develop family spirit? What chores are duties of children in homes today?

Songs for My Mother

ANNA HEMPSTEAD BRANCH

I. *Her Hands*

My mother's hands are cool and fair,
  They can do anything.
Delicate mercies hide them there
  Like flowers in the spring.

When I was small and could not sleep,
  She used to come to me,
And with my cheek upon her hand
  How sure my rest would be.

For everything she ever touched
  Of beautiful or fine,
Their memories living in her hands
  Would warm that sleep of mine.

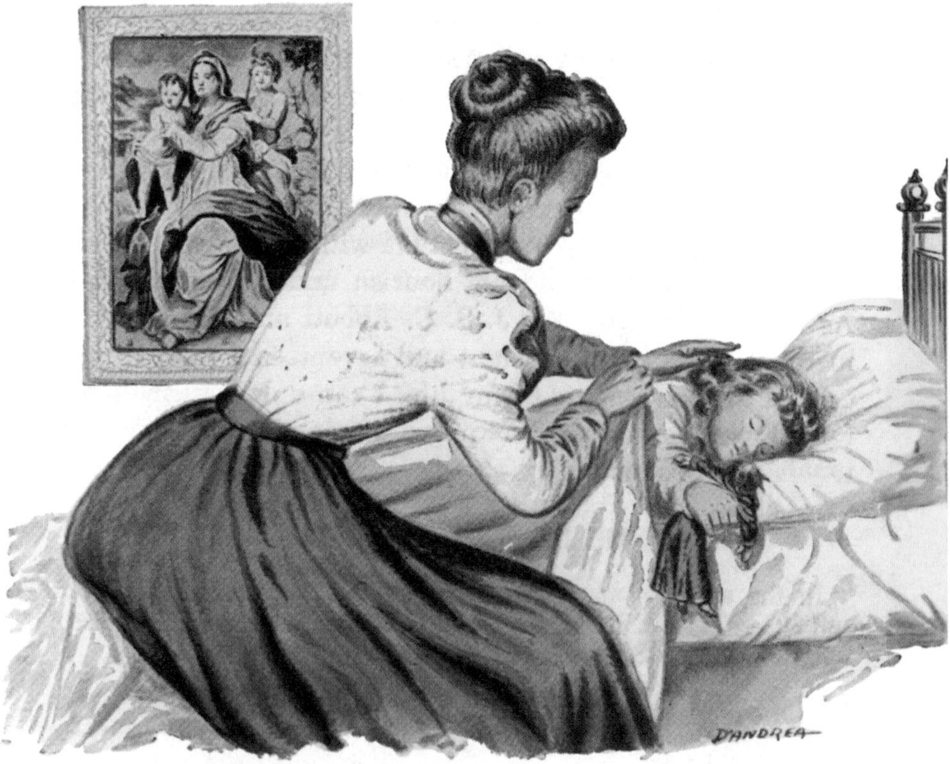

Her hands remember how they played
  One time in meadow streams,—
And all the flickering song and shade
  Of water took my dreams.

Swift through her haunted fingers pass
  Memories of garden things;—
I dipped my face in flowers and grass
  And sounds of hidden wings.

One time she touched the cloud that kissed
  Brown pastures bleak and far;—
I leaned my cheek into a mist
  And thought I was a star.

All this was very long ago
  And I am grown; but yet
The hand that lured my slumber so
  I never can forget.

For still when drowsiness comes on
  It seems so soft and cool,
Shaped happily beneath my cheek,
  Hollow and beautiful.

II. *Her Words*

My mother has the prettiest tricks
  Of words and words and words.
Her talk comes out as smooth and sleek
  As breasts of singing birds.

She shapes her speech all silver fine
  Because she loves it so.
And her own eyes begin to shine
  To hear her stories grow.

And if she goes to make a call
  Or out to take a walk
We leave our work when she returns
  And run to hear her talk.

We had not dreamed these things were so
  Of sorrow and of mirth.
Her speech is as a thousand eyes
  Through which we see the earth.

God wove a web of loveliness,
  Of clouds and stars and birds,
But made not anything at all
  So beautiful as words.

They shine around our simple earth
  With golden shadowings,
And every common thing they touch
  Is exquisite with wings.

There's nothing poor and nothing small
  But is made fair with them.
They are the hands of living faith
  That touch the garment's hem.

They are as fair as bloom or air,
  They shine like any star,
And I am rich who learned from her
  How beautiful they are.

PICTURES OF HOME AND FIRESIDE

All great artists have portrayed man's love of home. They have painted with lasting skill the simplest phases of home life—the hearth, the kitchen, the garden. Among some of these pictures are *The Apple Peeler*, by DE HOOCH; *Homework*, by CARRIÈRE; *The Kitchen Maid*, by CHARDIN; *An Old Lady with a Book*, by REMBRANDT. With sublime artistry they have also painted pictures of the Blessed Virgin, who is the symbol of home. Perhaps you know the *Madonna of the Rose Garden*, by FRANCESCO; *The Immaculate Conception*, by MURILLO; *The Mother of Our Lord*, by GOODALL; *Virgin Writing the Magnificat*, by BOTTICELLI; *The Alba Madonna*, by RAPHAEL.

"God walks among the pots and pans," said Teresa of Avila, one of the great saints. Around her words a poet has written

The Divine Office of the Kitchen

CECILY HALLACK

Lord of the pots and pipkins,[1] since
I have no time to be
A saint by doing lovely things and
Vigiling with Thee,
By watching in the twilight dawn,
And storming Heaven's gates,
Make me a saint by getting meals,
And washing up the plates!

Lord of the pots and pipkins, please,
I offer Thee for souls
The tiresomeness of tea-leaves
And the sticky porridge bowls!
Remind me of the things I need,
Not just to save the stairs,
But so that I may perfectly lay
Tables into prayers.

Accept my roughened hands
Because I made them so for Thee!
Pretend my dish mop is a bow,
Which heavenly harmony
Makes on a fiddle frying pan; it
Is so hard to clean,
And oh, so horrid! Hear, dear Lord,
The music that I mean!

Although I must have Martha hands,
I have a Mary mind,
And when I black the boots, I try
Thy sandals, Lord, to find.

1. *pipkins:* pans.

I think of how they trod our earth,
  What time I scrub the floor.
Accept this meditation when I
  Haven't time for more!

Vespers and Compline come to pass
  By washing supper things,
And mostly I am very tired; and
  All the heart that sings
About the morning's work is gone
  Before me into bed.
Lend me, dear Lord, Thy tireless
  Heart, to work in me instead!

My Matins are said over night to
  Praise and bless Thy name
Beforehand for to-morrow's work,
  Which will be just the same;
So that it seems I go to bed still
  In my working dress.
Lord, make Thy Cinderella, soon
  A heavenly Princess.

Warm all the kitchen with Thy Love,
  And light it with Thy peace!
Forgive the worrying and make
  The grumbling words to cease.
Lord, Who laid breakfast on the shore,
  Forgive the world which saith,
"Can any good thing come to God
  Out of poor Nazareth?"

The Shepherdess

ALICE MEYNELL

She walks—the lady of my delight—
  A shepherdess of sheep.
Her flocks are thoughts. She keeps them white;
  She guards them from the steep;
She feeds them on the fragrant height,
  And folds them in for sleep.

She roams maternal hills and bright,
  Dark valleys safe and deep.
Into that tender breast at night
  The chastest stars may peep.
She walks—the lady of my delight—
  A shepherdess of sheep.

She holds her little thoughts in sight,
  Though gay they run and leap.
She is so circumspect and right;
  She has her soul to keep.
She walks—the lady of my delight—
  A shepherdess of sheep.

Millions of boys and girls
have read the stories Louisa M. Alcott wrote.
Only a few ever saw

The Play Louisa Gave

CORNELIA MEIGS

The Alcott family was moving. It was not the first time, nor yet the last; for, in the first twenty-eight years of Louisa's life, this household was to achieve the record of twenty-nine moves. Scars on the mahogany and walnut dressers bore witness, now, of perhaps a dozen upheavals through which they and the Alcotts had gone together. Louisa, standing on the threshold and watching the low-posted beds and the horsehair sofas come staggering in, was now thirteen years old.

Moving had never ceased to be an adventure with the Alcotts, and it was invariably a gay occasion. The rambling brown house, which was now to be their home, resounded with cheery voices all along its dark passages. Louisa's spirit thrilled to the adventure of taking up life in a new place, in a storybook old dwelling with a pine-covered hill behind it, and with a gate opening upon the Concord-to-Lexington highroad. Down that road Paul Revere had galloped; over the pine-covered hill had marched a company of redcoats to take part in the first battle of the Revolution. The family was glad to come back to Concord, the peaceful, pleasant town with its square white houses and with its neighbors who were all friends.

The house had eight outside doors, so that, as they were settling to the table, or to read about the lamp in the low-ceilinged sitting room, a rap somewhere would send every member of the family flying, each one to a separate door, to admit the arriving friend. It was there, with a great deal of flurry and fluttering, that the household sat down at last, that evening of the moving-in. Anna had been busy in the kitchen; Louisa had kindled crackling fires in the numerous fireplaces. The smaller children were washed, and Bronson came out from the congenial task of unpacking his books.

Around the table there began a hilarious account of the adventures of the day, each person having her own joke to tell of the absurd mishaps which go with moving, of the things which were lost and broken, of the lack of things which could not be had in a household where money was still as scarce as good spirits were abundant.

In Louisa's eyes, the two great assets of the new abode were the little room in the wing and the barn. The Alcotts never kept a horse, although the girls often dreamed of galloping down the shady Concord roads, as did the more fortunate members of their acquaintance. There are, however, a hundred good uses for a roomy barn, other than those intended by the original builder. As everyone knows, barns are particularly well suited for dramatic purposes.

The drama, at that time, was Louisa's ruling passion. It is probable that before she slept that night, she was already busy outlining plots wherein beautiful heroines were rescued from dungeons, and princesses, disguised as slaves, won the hearts of disillusioned kings. As soon as the little room was in order, very bare and neat, with the scent of dried herbs in the closet, Louisa sat herself down to the table and fell to creating. Thus were born not only Duke Roderigo, but Duke Roderigo's boots.

Some little time later the Alcotts' Concord friends were invited to witness the first, and possibly the only performance, of a drama in three acts by Louisa Alcott, enacted, from the hero and the villain down to the page boy who brings in the cup of poison, by the four Alcott girls: stage manager and mistress of costumes, Louisa Alcott. She was good at creative dressmaking and knew just what her characters should wear. The hero was of the extravagantly noble kind, full of splendid motives and manly virtues. It was absolutely impossible to portray him without a slashed doublet, a sash, and tall, romantic boots. Louisa, with her vigorous mixture of fanciful and practical energy, made not only the hero, but the boots as well.

Somewhere she laid hands upon some skins of tanned leather and cut out crude profiles of what she imagined a nobleman's boots to be. These she sewed together, over and over, as a less enterprising young person sews patchwork. The result was truly magnificent. To walk any distance in the boots would have been quite impossible; but noblemen of Louisa's kind did not walk, fortunately; they strode a few paces to the rescue of captive maidens. Louisa trod the boards of the barn theater through her first play, in a blaze of glory. The curtain went down to applause which shook the old barn rafters. Some of the acclaim was for Anna, who was a really gifted actress, some of it was for Louisa; and a great deal of it was, deservedly, for the boots.

Excited and delighted by her first success, Louisa worked away in the little room, writing more and more dramas of the same sort. So many plots came crowding to her brain that from plays she overflowed into stories of the same grandiloquent sort. They were cut out, as the boots had been, by the pattern of what she imagined the life of the high nobility to be, and they were put together with the same industrious ingenuity.

Between the stories and plays she dreamed long dreams of the great things she hoped to do. "Am I going to be an actress," she wondered, "or a playwright, or a story writer?" She had no idea which it was to be.

Whatever it was, she was going to be it with all her might. Yet underneath her soaring fancies there lay a firm foundation of practical resolution. She saw plainly that her father, though recovered now, had very little real knowledge of the jostling world about him, that her mother was worn and worried over the problems of living. She could see that her sister Anna was as ambitious as herself, that Elizabeth was not strong, and that little May was growing up with a beauty-loving nature of passionate intensity. No children ever loved one another and their parents more than did the Alcotts. The way in which Louisa adored them all, as the years passed, could never be put into words,—the way she loved them and intended to take care of them.

There in the little room she made what she called the plan of her life and vowed to herself that she would give these beloved ones what each one needed. There was to be security for her father, peace and comfort and "a sunny room" for her mother, opportunity for Anna, care for Beth, education for May. One of the most interesting tales in the world is the record of how resolutely Louisa kept that promise and how, no matter what things went against her, she always refused to be beaten.

THINGS TO DO

1. Louisa Alcott knew what she wanted to do when she grew up, and why she wanted to do it. Write a brief description of what you should like to do, giving the reasons why you have chosen this particular lifework.

2. When Louisa grew up she became a story writer. Her best-loved book is *Little Women*, the story of her own family. In Chapter II she describes a play that is given by the "little women." Get a copy of the book from the library and compare the two versions—the one described by Miss Meigs, which you have just read, and the incident as it appears in *Little Women*.

Poets have sung in praise of the Mother of God ever since Saint Luke set down the noblest song of womanhood in.

The Magnificat

LUKE I, 46-55

My soul magnifies the Lord,
  and my spirit rejoices in God my Savior;
Because he has regarded the lowliness of
    his handmaid;
  for, behold, henceforth all generations shall
    call me blessed;
Because he who is mighty has done great things
    for me,
  and holy is his name;
And for generation upon generation is his mercy,
  to those who fear him.

He has shown might with his arm,
he has scattered the proud in the conceit of their heart.
He has put down the mighty from their thrones,
and has exalted the lowly.
He has filled the hungry with good things,
and the rich he has sent away empty.
He has given help to Israel, his servant,
mindful of his mercy—
Even as he spoke to our fathers—
to Abraham and to his posterity forever.

Mother of God

EDGAR ALLAN POE

At morn, at noon, at twilight dim,
Maria! thou hast heard my hymn!
In joy and woe, in good and ill,
Mother of God, be with me still!
When the hours flew brightly by,
And not a cloud obscured the sky,
My soul, lest it should truant be,
Thy grace did guide to thine and thee;
Now, when the storms of fate o'ercast
Darkly my present and my past,
Let my future radiant shine
With sweet hopes of thee and thine!

The Virgin

OLIVER WENDELL HOLMES

Is thy name Mary, maiden fair?
Such should, methinks, its music be;
The sweetest name that mortals bear
Were best befitting thee;
For she to whom it once was given
Was half of earth, and half of heaven.

Exile

SISTER MARY JEAN DORCY, O.P.

She would have loved a tiny house
With modest rows of shining ware,
And plants upon the window sill,
Where she could see them at her prayer.

She must have planned the nursery
And cupboard space for Joseph's tools:
A woman always needs a home,
An ordered place with quiet rules.

But one must haste to Bethlehem,
For tyrants' laws are cruelly blind—
The sturdy cradle Joseph made
Is stored away and left behind.

One cannot take a thousand things
When one is fleeing in the night
From wrath too terrible to name.
One never learns the art of flight.

Home is the dear One in her arms,
And home is Heaven to all at last:
But still, her wistful glance would stray
To lighted windows as she passed.

Our Lady of the refugees,
Who knows so well an exile's tears,
Light us a window when we come
Homeward beyond the reach of years!

Town
OFFI
1 HR
RALPH I. SHEPHERD

III

In the Town

The highest praise which any stranger can give to a community is the declaration that it is a friendly place. For this means that its people greet one another and the newcomer with courtesy and kindliness, expressing in their speech and manner the virtue of charity. By their continuing practice they build up a reputation for their community which makes its friendliness a local tradition.

In this tradition writers of both prose and verse find material for literature. Some of the finest novels, short stories, and poems are based upon the desire of writers to set down in words the fine feeling of a friendly town, either at work or at play. In this literature they have shown how friendliness is a recognition of the dignity of the individual as a child of God. They have stressed the respect and love of men for one another.

Sometimes this respect is presented by showing the evil results of a lack of respect, as it is in the story of Penrod. The humor of Booth Tarkington does not conceal the fact that Penrod has to pay for his departure from his community's friendliness. Tarkington, one of the friendliest of writers, does not condone young Master Schofield's wrongdoing. With a grin he seems to say to his readers, Here is what a boy should *not* do! Even though Penrod offends, the community remains a friendly place.

There is a more solemn note in the literature of a town at work; but it is still the high note of men and women considering one another as they labor, moving forward toward a better time when all mankind will recognize the dignity and the friendliness of labor.

Prayer for the People

O God, whose mercy knows no end and whose goodness is infinite in store: ever suing Thy clemency, we offer thanks to Thy great majesty for endless gifts bestowed; that Thou who grantest Thy petitioners their needs, deserting them not, mayest dispose them well for the reception of Thy further benefits. Through our Lord Jesus Christ Thy Son: who lives and reigns with Thee in the unity of the Holy Ghost, God, world without end. Amen.

I Corinthians xiii, 4-13

Charity is patient, is kind; charity does not envy, is not pretentious, is not puffed up, is not ambitious, is not self-seeking, is not provoked; thinks no evil, does not rejoice over wickedness, but rejoices with the truth; bears with all things, believes all things, hopes all things, endures all things.

Charity never fails, whereas prophecies will disappear, and tongues will cease, and knowledge will be destroyed. For we know in part and we prophesy in part; but when that which is perfect has come, that which is imperfect will be done away with. When I was a child, I spoke as a child, I felt as a child, I thought as a child. Now that I have become a man, I have put away the things of a child. We see now through a mirror in an obscure manner, but then face to face. Now I know in part, but then I shall know even as I have been known. So there abide faith, hope and charity, these three; but the greatest of these is charity.

One of the immortal characters of American literature
is Mrs. Wiggs of the Cabbage Patch; and one of her happiest occasions was

The Benefit Dance

ALICE HEGAN RICE

Notwithstanding the fact that calamities seldom come singly, it was not until the Fourth of July that the Cabbage Patch was again the scene of an accident.

Mrs. Wiggs had been hanging out clothes, and was turning to pick up the empty basket, when Billy precipitated himself into the yard, yelling wildly: "Chris Hazy's broke his leg!"

Mrs. Wiggs threw up her hands in horror. "Good lands, Billy! Where's he at?"

"They're bringin' him up the railroad track."

Mrs. Wiggs rushed into the house. "Don't let on to Miss Hazy till we git him in," she cautioned, snatching up a bundle of rags and a bottle of liniment. "Pore chile! How it must hurt him! I'll run down the track an' meet 'em."

She was breathless and trembling from excitement as she turned the corner at Mrs. Schultz's. A crowd of boys was coming up the track, trundling a wheelbarrow, in which sat Chris Hazy, the merriest of the lot, waving a piece of his wooden leg in the air.

Mrs. Wiggs turned upon Billy.

"I never lied, ma! I said he broke his leg," the boy gasped out as best he could for laughing, "an' you never ast which one. Oh, boys! Git on to the rags an' arniky!"

Such a shout went up that Mrs. Wiggs laughed with the rest, but only for a moment, for she spied Miss Hazy tottering toward them, and she hastened forward to relieve her anxiety.

"It's his peg-stick!" she shouted. "P-e-g-stick!"

This information, instead of bringing relief to Miss Hazy, caused a fresh burst of tears. She sat down on the track, with her apron over her face, and swayed backward and forward.

"Don't make much difference which one 'twas," she sobbed; "it would be 'bout as easy to git another sure-'nough leg as to git a new wooden one. That las' one cost seven

dollars. I jes' sewed an' saved an' scrimped to git it, an' now it's—busted!"

The boys stood around in silent sympathy, and when nobody was looking Chris wiped his eyes on his coat sleeve. Miss Hazy's arrival had changed their point of view.

Mrs. Wiggs rose to the occasion.

"Boys," she said, and her voice had an inspiring ring, "I'll tell you what let's do! Let's give a benefit dance tonight, an' buy Chris Hazy a new peg-stick. Every feller that's willin' to help, hol' up his hand."

A dozen grimy hands were waved on high, and offers of assistance came from all sides. Mrs. Wiggs saw that now was the time to utilize their enthusiasm.

"I'll go right back to the house, an' git Asia to write out the tickets, an' all you boys kin sell ten apiece. Miss Hazy, you kin come over an' help me git the house ready, an' we'll put Chris to cleanin' lamp-chimbleys."

Under this able generalship, the work was soon under way;

the boys were dispatched with the tickets, and the house was being put straight—at least the parlor was. It would have required many days to restore order to the chaos that habitually existed in the house of Wiggs.

"Asia, you help me roll these here barrels out on the porch, an' I'll mop up the floor," said Mrs. Wiggs. "Miss Hazy, you look 'round in the kitchen, an' see if you can't find a taller candle. Seems like I put one in the sugar-bowl—that's it! Now, if you'll jes' cut it up right fine it'll be all ready to put on the floor when I git done."

When the floor was dry and the candle sprinkled over it, Australia and Europena were detailed to slide upon it until it became slick.

"Would you ast ever'body to bring a cheer, or would you have 'em already here?" asked Mrs. Wiggs.

"Oh, le's bring 'em ourselves!" insisted Asia, who had been to a church social.

So a raid was made on the neighborhood, and every available chair borrowed and ranged against the parlor wall.

By noon the boys reported most of the tickets sold, and Mrs. Wiggs received the funds, which amounted to six dollars.

It being a holiday, everybody was glad to come to the dance, especially as the proceeds were to help little Miss Hazy.

At one time there threatened to be trouble about the music; some wanted Uncle Tom, the old Negro who usually fiddled at the dances, and others preferred to patronize home talent and have Jake Schultz, whose accordion could be heard at all hours in the Cabbage Patch.

Mrs. Wiggs effected a compromise. "They kin take turn about," she argued; "when one gits tired, the other kin pick up right where he left off, an' the young folks kin shake the'r feet till they shoes drop off. Uncle Tom an' Jake, too, is a heap sight better than them mud-gutter bands that play 'round the streets."

"Wisht we could fix the yard up some," said Asia, when there was nothing more to be done in the parlor.

"I got a Japanee lantern," suggested Miss Hazy, doubtfully.

"The very thing!" said Mrs. Wiggs. "We'll hang it in the

front door. Billy's makin' a jack-o'-lantern to set on the fence. Fer the land's sake! What's John Bagby a-bringin' in here?"

The grocery boy, staggering under the weight of an ice-cream freezer and carrying something wrapped in white paper, came up the path.

"It's fer you," he said, grinning broadly. John was cross-eyed, so Miss Hazy thought he looked at Mrs. Wiggs, and Mrs. Wiggs thought he looked at Miss Hazy.

However, the card on the freezer dispelled all doubts:

Fer mrs Wiggs on her 50 Birthday
complements of The Naybors.

Under the white paper was a large, white iced cake, with a "W" in cinnamon drops on top.

"How'd they ever know it was my birthday?" exclaimed Mrs. Wiggs, in delight. "Why, I'd even forgot it myself! We'll have the cake fer the party tonight. Somehow, I never feel like good things b'long to me till I pass 'em on to somebody else."

This necessitated a supply of saucers and spoons, and friends were again called upon to provide as many as possible.

The Wiggses were quite busy until seven o'clock, when they stopped to wash their faces.

"Where's Europena?" asked Asia.

Nobody had seen her for some time. Search was made, and she was discovered standing on a chair in a corner of the parlor, calmly eating the cinnamon-drops off the birthday cake. Fingers and mouth were crimson, and the first stroke of the "W" was missing. Billy was so indignant that he insisted on immediate punishment.

"No, I ain't a-goin' to whip her on my birthday, Billy. She's sorry; she says she is. Besides, the cake ain't spoiled; it's jes' a 'N' now, 'stid of a 'W,' an' N stands fer Nancy jes' as good as W stands fer Wiggs!"

The first guest to arrive was Mr. Krasmier; he had paid ten cents toward the refreshments, and proposed to get his money's worth. Mrs. Eichorn came early, too, but for a different reason; she was very stout, and her happiness for the evening depended largely upon the size of the chair she secured.

Half the spectators had arrived before the hostess appeared. Her delay was caused by the loss of her false curls, which she had not worn since the memorable night at the Opera House. They were very black and very frizzled, and had been bought at a reduced price from a traveling salesman some ten years before. Mrs. Wiggs considered them absolutely necessary to her style on state occasions. Hence consternation prevailed when they could not be found. Drawers were upset and boxes emptied, but with no success.

When hope was about abandoned, Asia suddenly darted out to the shed where the children kept their playthings. When she returned she triumphantly displayed a battered doll, armless and footless, but with a magnificent crowning glory of black, frizzled hair.

Mrs. Wiggs waited until all the guests assembled before she made her speech of thanks for the cake and cream. It was a very fine speech, having been written out beforehand by Mr. Bagby. It began, "Ladies and gents, it gives me pleasure—" but before Mrs. Wiggs got half through she forgot it, and had to tell them in her own way how grateful she was. In conclusion she said: "Couldn't nobody be more obliged than what I am! Looks like nice things is always comin' my way. Hope God'll bless you all! The musicianers have come, so we'll begin the party with a Virginer reel."

The young people scampered to their places, and when Mr. Eichorn made a bow to Mrs. Wiggs she laughingly took her place at the head of the line, and at the first strains of "Old Dan Tucker" she went down the middle with a grace and spirit that flatly contradicted the little red fifty on the birthday cake.

Swing yer pahtners, balance all,
Swing dat gal wid a water-fall.
Skip light, ladies, de cake's all dough,
Nebber min' de weather, so de win' don't blow.

Old Uncle Tom was warming up to his work, and the fun waxed furious. Asia, looking very pretty in her new dress, cast shy glances at Joe Eichorn, who had been "keeping company" of late. Billy, for whom there was no room in the reel, let off his energy in the corner by a noisy execution of the "Mobile Buck." Australia and Europena sat in the window with Chris Hazy, and delightedly clapped time to the music.

When the dance ended, Mrs. Wiggs went to the door to get cool. She was completely out of breath, and her false curls had worked their way down over her eyebrows.

Music and laughter came from the house behind her, as she stood smiling out across the moonlit Cabbage Patch.

"Billy's got promoted," she whispered softly to herself, "an' Asia's got a place, an' Chris'll have a new peg-stick. Looks like ever'thing in the world comes right, if we jes' wait long enough!"

HELPS FOR DISCUSSION

1. Reread the first sentence on page 51. How does the Cabbage Patch community deserve this praise? Cite examples from the selection.

2. Explain what Mrs. Wiggs meant when she said, "I never feel like good things b'long to me till I pass 'em on to somebody else."

3. Quote another saying of Mrs. Wiggs's which reveals her character. Explain its meaning.

The Vinegar Man

RUTH COMFORT MITCHELL

[Choir to be arranged in three voices: high, medium, and low.]

All — The crazy old Vinegar Man is dead! He never had missed a day before!
Medium — Somebody went to his tumble-down shed, by the Haunted House, and forced the door.
Low — There in the litter of pungent pans, the murky mess of his mixing place,—
Deep, sticky spiders and empty cans—with the same old frown on his sour old face.

All — "Vinegar-Vinegar-Vinegar Man!
Face-us-and-chase-us-and-catch-if-you-can!
Solo — Pepper for a tongue! Pickle for a nose!
Solo — Stick a pin in him and vinegar flows!
All — Glare-at-us-swear-at-us-catch-if-you-can!
Ketch-up-and-chow-chow-and-Vinegar-Man!"

Medium — Nothing but recipes, worthless junk, greasy old records of paid and due;
Low — But, down in the depths of a battered trunk, a queer, quaint valentine torn in two—
High — Red hearts and arrows, and silver lace, and a prim, dim, ladylike script that said—
Low — (Oh, Vinegar Man, with the sour old face!)—
"With dearest love, from Ellen to Ned!"

All — "Steal-us-and-peel-us-and-drown-us-in-brine!
He pickles his heart in"—*a valentine!*
Solo — "Vinegar for blood! Pepper for his tongue!
Stick a pin in him and"—*once he was young!*
All — "Glare-at-us-swear-at-us-catch-if-you-can!"
"With dearest love"—to the Vinegar Man!

Low — Dingy old books of profit and loss (died about Saturday, so they say)
And a queer, quaint valentine, torn across . . . torn, but it never was thrown away!

High "With dearest love from Ellen to Ned"—"Old Pepper Tongue! Pickles his heart in brine!"

All The Vinegar Man is a long time dead: he died when he tore his valentine.

Mr. Lear

EDWARD LEAR

How pleasant to know Mr. Lear!
Who has written such volumes of stuff!
Some think him ill-tempered and queer,
But a few think him pleasant enough.

His mind is concrete and fastidious,
His nose is remarkably big;
His visage is more or less hideous,
His beard it resembles a wig.

When he walks out in waterproof white,
The children run after him so!
Calling out, "He's come out in his night-
Gown, that old Englishman, oh!"

He weeps by the side of the ocean,
He weeps on the top of the hill;
He purchases pancake and lotion,
And chocolate shrimps from the mill.

He reads, but he cannot speak, Spanish,
He cannot abide ginger-beer:
Ere the days of his pilgrimage vanish,
How pleasant to know Mr. Lear!

HELPS FOR DISCUSSION

Why did children think of the Vinegar Man and Mr. Lear as queer folks? What is hidden beneath the surface in their lives? Why should unthinking dislike of people be avoided?

Even the best of homes sometimes houses a boy who can cause as much trouble as did Booth Tarkington's hero Penrod when he tried to live down his title of

Little Gentleman

BOOTH TARKINGTON

The midsummer sun was stinging hot outside the little barbershop next to the corner drug store and Penrod, undergoing a haircut preliminary to his very slowly approaching twelfth birthday, was adhesive enough to retain upon his face much hair as it fell from the shears. There is a mystery here: the tonsorial processes are not unagreeable to manhood; in truth, they are soothing; but the hairs detached from a boy's head get into his eyes, his ears, his nose, his mouth, and down his neck, and he does everywhere itch. Wherefore he blinks, winks, weeps, twitches, condenses his countenance, and squirms; and perchance the barber's scissors clip more than intended—belike an outlying flange[1] of ear.

"Um—muh—*ow*!" said Penrod, this thing having happened.

"D'I touch y' up a little?" inquired the barber, smiling falsely.

"Ooh—*uh*!" The boy in the chair offered inarticulate protest, as the wound was rubbed with alum.

"*That* don't hurt!" said the barber. "You *will* get it, though, if you don't sit stiller," he continued, nipping in the bud any attempt on the part of his patient to think that he already had "it."

"Pfuff!" said Penrod, meaning no disrespect, but endeavoring to dislodge a temporary moustache from his lip.

"You ought to see how still that little Georgie Bassett sits," the barber went on, reprovingly. "I hear everybody says he's the best boy in town."

"Pfuff! *Phirr*!" There was a touch of intentional contempt in this.

"I haven't heard nobody around the neighborhood makin' no such remarks," added the barber, "about nobody of the name of Penrod Schofield."

1. *flange:* edge.

"Well," said Penrod, clearing his mouth after a struggle, "who wants 'em to? Ouch!"

"I hear they call Georgie Bassett the 'little gentleman,' " ventured the barber, provocatively,[2] meeting with instant success.

"They better not call *me* that," returned Penrod truculently.[3] "I'd like to hear anybody try. Just once, that's all! I bet they'd never try it ag— *Ouch*!"

"Why? What'd you *do* to 'em?"

"It's all right what I'd do! I bet they wouldn't want to call me that again long as they lived!"

"Suppose it was a boy twice your size?"

"Just let him try," said Penrod ominously. "You just let him try. He'd never see daylight again; that's all!"

2. *provocatively:* tending to provoke or anger. 3. *truculently* (trŭk'ū lĕnt lĭ): fiercely; scathingly.

The barber dug ten active fingers into the helpless scalp before him and did his best to displace it, while the anguished Penrod, becoming instantly a seething crucible[4] of emotion, misdirected his natural resentment into maddened brooding upon what he would do to a boy "twice his size" who should dare to call him "little gentleman." The barber shook him as his father had never shaken him; the barber buffeted him, rocked him frantically to and fro; the barber seemed to be trying to wring his neck; and Penrod saw himself in staggering zigzag pictures, destroying large, screaming, fragmentary boys who had insulted him.

The torture stopped suddenly; and clenched, weeping eyes began to see again, while the barber applied cooling lotions.

"Now what," asked the barber, combing the reeking locks gently, "what would it make you so mad fer, to have somebody call you a little gentleman? It's a kind of compliment, as it were, you might say. What would you want to hit anybody fer *that* fer?"

To the mind of Penrod, this question was without meaning or reasonableness. It was within neither his power nor his desire to analyze the process by which the phrase had become offensive to him, and was now rapidly assuming the proportions of an outrage. He knew only that his gorge[5] rose at the thought of it.

"You just let 'em try it!" he said threateningly, as he slid down from the chair. And as he went out of the door, after further conversation on the same subject, he called back those warning words once more: "Just let 'em try it! Just once—that's all *I* ask 'em to. They'll find out what they *get*!"

The barber chuckled. Then a fly lit on the barber's nose and he slapped at it, and the slap missed the fly but did not miss the nose. The barber was irritated. At this moment his birdlike eye gleamed a gleam as it fell upon customers approaching: the prettiest little girl in the world, leading by the hand her baby brother, Mitchy-Mitch, coming to have Mitchy-Mitch's hair clipped, against the heat.

4. *crucible:* a vessel which resists the action of fire. 5. *gorge:* throat.

It was a hot day and idle, with little to feed the mind—and the barber was a mischievous man with an irritated nose. He did his worst.

Meanwhile, the brooding Penrod pursued his homeward way; no great distance, but long enough for several one-sided conflicts with malign insulters made of thin air. "You better *not* call me that!" he muttered. "You just try it, and you'll get what other people got when *they* tried it. You better not ack fresh with *me*! Oh, you *will*, will you?" He delivered a vicious kick full upon the shins of an iron fence-post, which suffered little, though Penrod instantly regretted his indiscretion. "Oof!" he grunted, hopping, and went on after bestowing a look of awful hostility upon the fence post. "I guess you'll know better next time," he said, in parting, to this his antagonist. "You just let me catch you around here again and I'll—" His voice sank to inarticulate but ominous murmurings. He was in a dangerous mood.

Nearing home, however, his belligerent spirit was diverted to happier interests by the discovery that some workmen had left a caldron of tar in the cross street, close by his father's stable. He tested it, but found it inedible. Also, as a substitute for professional chewing gum it was unsatisfactory, being insufficiently boiled down and too thin, though of a pleasant, lukewarm temperature. But it had an excess of one quality—it was sticky. It was the stickiest tar Penrod had ever used for any purpose whatsoever, and nothing upon which he wiped his hands served to rid them of it; neither his polka-dotted shirtwaist nor his knickerbockers; neither the fence, nor even Duke, who came unthinkingly wagging out to greet him and retired wiser.

Nevertheless, tar is tar. Much can be done with it, no matter what its condition; so Penrod lingered by the caldron, though from a neighboring yard could be heard the voices of comrades, including that of Sam Williams. On the ground about the caldron were scattered chips and sticks and bits of wood to the number of a great multitude. Penrod mixed quantities of this refuse into the tar, and interested himself in seeing how much of it he could keep moving in slow swirls.

Other surprises were arranged for the absent workmen. The caldron was almost full, and the surface of the tar near the rim. Penrod endeavored to ascertain how many pebbles and brickbats, dropped in, would cause an overflow. Laboring heartily to this end, he had almost accomplished it, when he received the suggestion for an experiment on a much larger scale. Embedded at the corner of a grassplot across the street was a whitewashed stone, the size of a small watermelon and serving no purpose whatever save the questionable one of decoration. It was easily pried up with a stick, though getting it to the caldron tested the full strength of the ardent laborer. Instructed to perform such a task, he would have sincerely maintained its impossibility; but now, as it was unbidden and promised rather destructive results, he set about it with unconquerable energy, feeling certain that he would be rewarded with a mighty splash. Perspiring, grunting vehemently, his back aching and all muscles strained, he progressed in short stages until the big stone lay at the base of the caldron. He rested a moment, panting, then lifted the stone, and was bending his shoulders for the heave that would lift it over the rim, when a sweet, taunting voice, close behind him, startled him cruelly.

"How do you do, *little gentleman!*"

Penrod squawked, dropped the stone, and shouted, "Shut up, you dern fool!" purely from instinct, even before his about-face made him aware who had so spitefully addressed him.

It was Marjorie Jones. Always dainty, and prettily dressed, she was speckless and starchy white today, and a refreshing picture she made, with the new-shorn and powerfully scented Mitchy-Mitch clinging to her hand. They had stolen up behind the toiler, and now stood laughing together in sweet merriment. Penrod had experienced some severe qualms at the recollection of his last meeting with Marjorie and his Apache[6] behavior; in truth, his heart instantly became as wax at sight of her, and he would have offered her fair speech; but, alas! in Marjorie's wonderful eyes there shone

6. *Apache* (*a* pä′ chā): a once-savage Indian tribe.

a consciousness of new powers for his undoing, and she denied him opportunity.

"Oh, *oh!*" she cried, mocking his pained outcry. "What a way for a *little gentleman* to talk! Little gentlemen don't say wicked—"

"Marjorie!" Penrod, enraged and dismayed, felt himself stung beyond all endurance. Insult from her was bitterer to endure than from any other. "Don't you call me that again!"

"Why not, *little gentleman?*"

He stamped his foot. "You better stop!"

Marjorie sent into his furious face her lovely, spiteful laughter.

"Little gentleman, little gentleman, little gentleman!" she said deliberately. "How's the little gentleman this afternoon? Hello, little gentleman!"

Penrod, quite beside himself, danced eccentrically.

"Dry up!" he howled. "Dry up, dry up, dry up, dry *up!*"

Mitchy-Mitch shouted with delight and applied a finger to the side of the caldron—a finger immediately snatched away and wiped upon a handerchief by his fastidious sister.

" 'Ittle gellamun!" said Mitchy-Mitch.

"You better look out!" Penrod whirled upon this small offender with grim satisfaction. Here was at least something male that could without dishonor be held responsible. "You say that again, and I'll give you the worst—"

"You will *not!*" snapped Marjorie, instantly vitriolic.[7] "He'll say just whatever he wants to, and he'll say it just as *much* as he wants to. Say it again, Mitchy-Mitch!"

" 'Ittle gellamun!" said Mitchy-Mitch promptly.

"Ow-*yah!*" Penrod's tone-production was becoming affected by his mental condition. "You say that again, and I'll—"

"Go on, Mitchy-Mitch," cried Marjorie. "He can't do a thing. He don't *dare*! Say it some more, Mitchy-Mitch—say it a whole lot!"

Mitchy-Mitch, his small fat face shining with confidence in his immunity, complied.

7. *vitriolic:* biting, as with acid.

" 'Ittle gellamun!" he squeaked malevolently. " 'Ittle gellamun! 'Ittle gellamun! 'Ittle gellamun!"

The desperate Penrod bent over the whitewashed rock, lifted it, and then—outdoing Porthos,[8] John Ridd,[9] and Ursus[10] in one miraculous burst of strength—heaved it into the air.

Marjorie screamed. But it was too late. The big stone descended into the precise midst of the caldron and Penrod got his mighty splash. It was far, far beyond his expectations.

Spontaneously there were grand and awful effects—volcanic spectacles of nightmare and eruption. A black sheet of eccentric shape rose out of the caldron and descended upon the three children, who had no time to evade it.

After it fell, Mitchy-Mitch, who stood nearest the caldron, was the thickest, though there was enough for all. Br'er Rabbit would have fled from any of them.

8. *Porthos:* one of the three musketeers in a novel by Dumas. Porthos was famed for performing feats of great strength. 9. *John Ridd:* hero of the novel *Lorna Doone.* He also was noted for his strength and courage. 10. *Ursus:* a kind of grizzly bear. Here it means that Penrod had the strength of a grizzly.

When Marjorie and Mitchy-Mitch got their breath, they used it vocally; and seldom have more penetrating sounds issued from human throats. Coincidentally, Marjorie, quite berserk,[11] laid hands upon the largest stick within reach and fell upon Penrod with blind fury. He had the presence of mind to flee, and they went round and round the caldron, while Mitchy-Mitch feebly endeavored to follow—his appearance in this pursuit being pathetically like that of a bug fished out of an inkwell, alive but discouraged.

Attracted by the riot, Samuel Williams made his appearance, vaulting a fence, and was immediately followed by Maurice Levy and Georgie Bassett. They stared incredulously at the extraordinary spectacle before them.

"Little GEN-TIL-MUN!" shrieked Marjorie, with a wild stroke that landed full upon Penrod's tarry cap.

"*Ooooch!*" bleated Penrod.

"It's Penrod," shouted Sam Williams, recognizing him by the voice. For an instant he had been in some doubt.

"Penrod Schofield!" exclaimed Georgie Bassett. "*What* does this mean?" That was Georgie's style and had helped to win him his title.

Marjorie leaned, panting, upon her stick. "I cu-called—uh—him—oh!" she sobbed—"I called him a lu-little—oh—gentleman! And oh—lu-look!—oh! lu-look at my du-dress! Lu-look at Mu-Mitchy—oh—Mitch—oh!"

Unexpectedly, she smote again—with results—and then, seizing the indistinguishable hand of Mitchy-Mitch, she ran wailing homeward down the street.

" 'Little gentleman'?" said Georgie Bassett, with some evidence of disturbed complacency. "Why, that's what they call *me*!"

"Yes, and you *are* one, too!" shouted the maddened Penrod. "But you better not let anybody call *me* that! I've stood enough around here for one day, and you can't run over *me*, Georgie Bassett. Just you put that in your gizzard and smoke it!"

11. *berserk:* mad with rage.

"Anybody has a perfect right," said Georgie, with dignity, "to call a person a little gentleman. There's lots of names nobody ought to call, but this one's a *nice*—"

"You better look out!"

Unavenged bruises were distributed all over Penrod, both upon his body and upon his spirit. Driven by subtle forces, he had dipped his hands in catastrophe and disaster; it was not for a Georgie Bassett to beard him. Penrod was about to run amuck.

"I haven't called you a little gentleman, yet," said Georgie. "I only said it. Anybody's got a right to say it."

"Not around *me*! You just try it again and—"

"I shall say it," returned Georgie, "all I please. Anybody in this town has a right to *say* 'little gentleman'—"

Bellowing insanely, Penrod plunged his right hand into the caldron, rushed upon Georgie and made awful work of his hair and features.

Alas, it was but the beginning! Sam Williams and Maurice Levy screamed with delight and, simultaneously infected, danced about the struggling pair, shouting frantically: "Little gentleman! Little gentleman! Sick him, Georgie! Sick him, little gentleman! Little gentleman! Little gentleman!"

The infuriated outlaw turned upon them with blows and more tar, which gave Georgie Bassett his opportunity and later seriously impaired the purity of his fame. Feeling himself hopelessly tarred, he dipped both hands repeatedly into the caldron and applied his gatherings to Penrod. It was bringing coals to Newcastle,[12] but it helped to assuage the just wrath of Georgie.

The four boys gave a fine imitation of the Laocoon group[13] complicated by an extra figure—frantic splutterings and chokings, strange cries and stranger words issued from this tangle; hands dipped lavishly into the inexhaustible reservoir

12. *bringing . . . Newcastle:* carrying goods or ideas to a place where there is already a surplus of these goods or ideas. 13. *Laocoon* (lā ŏk'ō ŏn): a figure of classical mythology, who incurred the wrath of the gods. He was destroyed, with his two sons, by two serpents summoned from the sea by the goddess Athena. The Laocoon Group, sculptured in marble, showing Laocoon and his two sons in the coils of the serpents is now in the Vatican.

of tar, with more and more picturesque results. The caldron had been elevated upon bricks and was not perfectly balanced; and under a heavy impact of the struggling group it lurched and went partly over, pouring forth a Stygian[14] tide which formed a deep pool in the gutter.

It was the fate of Master Roderick Bitts, that exclusive and immaculate person, to make his appearance upon that chaotic scene at this juncture. All in the cool of a white "sailor suit," he turned aside from the path of duty—which led straight to the house of a maiden aunt—and paused to hop with joy upon the sidewalk. A repeated epithet continuously half panted, half squawked, somewhere in the nest of gladiators, caught his ear, and he took it up excitedly, not knowing why.

"Little gentleman!" shouted Roderick, jumping up and down in childish glee. "Little gentleman! Little gentleman! Lit—"

A frightful figure tore itself free from the group, encircled this innocent bystander with a black arm, and hurled him headlong. Full length and flat on his face went Roderick into the Stygian pool. The frightful figure was Penrod. Instantly, the pack flung themselves upon him again, and, carrying them with him, he went over upon Roderick, who from that instant was as active a belligerent as any there.

14. *Stygian* (stĭj'ĭ ăn): referring to the Styx, the mythical river of Hades. The word *Stygian* is often used as a synonym for "black."

Thus began the Great Tar Fight, the origin of which proved, afterward, so difficult for parents to trace, owing to the opposing accounts of the combatants. Marjorie said Penrod began it; Penrod said Mitchy-Mitch began it; Sam Williams said Georgie Bassett began it; Georgie and Maurice Levy said Penrod began it; Roderick Bitts, who had not recognized his first assailant, said Sam Williams began it.

Nobody thought of accusing the barber. But the barber did not begin it; it was the fly on the barber's nose that began it—though, of course, something else began the fly. Somehow, we never manage to hang the real offender.

The end came only with the arrival of Penrod's mother, who had been having a painful conversation by telephone with Mrs. Jones, the mother of Marjorie, and came forth to seek an errant son. It is a mystery how she was able to pick out her own, for by the time she got there his voice was too hoarse to be recognizable.

Mr. Schofield's version of things was that Penrod was insane. "He's a stark, raving lunatic!" declared the father, descending to the library from a before-dinner interview with the outlaw that evening. "I'd send him to military school, but I don't believe they'd take him. Do you know *why* he says all that awfulness happened?"

"When Margaret and I were trying to scrub him," responded Mrs. Schofield wearily, "he said 'everybody' had been calling him names."

" 'Names!' " snorted her husband. " 'Little gentleman!' *That's* the vile epithet they called him. And because of it he wrecks the peace of six homes!"

"*Sh!* Yes; he told us about it," said Mrs. Schofield, moaning. "He told us several hundred times, I should guess, though I didn't count. He's got it fixed in his head, and we couldn't get it out. All we could do was to put him in the closet. He'd have gone out again after those boys if we hadn't. I don't know *what* to make of him!"

"He's a mystery to *me*!" said her husband. "And he refuses to explain why he objects to being called 'little gentleman.' Says he'd do the same thing—and worse—if anybody dared to call him that again. He said if the President of the United States called him that he'd try to whip him. How long did you have him locked up in the closet?"

"*Sh!*" said Mrs. Schofield warningly. "About two hours; but I don't think it softened his spirit at all, because when I took him to the barber's to get his hair clipped again, on account of the tar in it, Sammy Williams and Maurice Levy were there for the same reason; and they just *whispered* 'little gentleman,' so low you could hardly hear them—and Penrod began fighting with them right before me, and it was really all the barber and I could do to drag him away from them. The barber was very kind about it, but Penrod—"

"I tell you he's a lunatic!" Mr. Schofield said.

"*Sh!*" said Mrs. Schofield. "It does seem a kind of frenzy."

"Why on earth should any sane person mind being called—"

"Sh!" said Mrs. Schofield. "It's beyond me!"

HELPS FOR DISCUSSION

1. Why do you think Penrod objected to being called a "little gentleman"? What part did the barber play in building up Penrod's dislike of the title?

2. Explain the meaning of the first paragraph on page 64. How do you think Marjorie knew that Penrod would be teased by the title "little gentleman"?

3. Explain your attitude toward Penrod, Marjorie, Georgie Bassett, and Master Roderick.

4. Why are Penrod's parents so puzzled by the episode? Do you think that Penrod will outgrow his anti-social attitudes? Why?

Going Downhill on a Bicycle: a Boy's Song

H. C. BEECHING

With lifted feet, hands still,
I am poised, and down the hill
Dart, with heedful mind;
The air goes by in a wind.

Swifter and yet more swift,
Till the heart with a mighty lift
Makes the lungs laugh, the throat cry:—
"O bird, see; see, bird, I fly.

"Is this, is this your joy?
O bird, then I, though a boy,
For a golden moment share
Your feathery life in air!"

Say, heart, is there aught like this
In a world that is full of bliss?
'Tis more than skating, bound
Steel-shod to the level ground.

Speed slackens now, I float
Awhile in my airy boat;
Till, when the wheels scarce crawl,
My feet to the treadles fall.

Alas, that the longest hill
Must end in a vale; but still,
Who climbs with toil, wheresoe'er.
Shall find wings waiting there.

Reputation

WILLIAM SHAKESPEARE

Good name in man and woman, dear my lord,
Is the immediate jewel of their souls,
Who steals my purse steals trash; 'tis something, nothing;
'Twas mine, 'tis his, and has been slave to thousands;
But he that filches from me my good name
Robs me of that which not enriches him
And makes me poor indeed.

Boys will be boys, especially in a boy's school. In a famous book, *The Varmint,* an American writer described a school large enough to have two houses which opposed each other in

The Football Game

OWEN JOHNSON

The house championships had gone on until the Woodhull and the Kennedy emerged for the final conflict. The experience gained in these contests, for on such occasions Stover played with his house team, had sharpened his powers of analysis and given him a needed acquaintance with the sudden, shifting crises of actual play.

Now, the one desire of Dink Stover, next to winning the fair opinion of his captain, was the rout of the Woodhull, of which Tough McCarty was the captain and his old acquaintances of the miserable days at the Green were members—Cheyenne Baxter, the Coffee-colored Angel, and Butsey White. This aggregation, counting as it did two members of the 'Varsity, was strong; but the Kennedy, with P. Lentz and the Waladoo Bird and Pebble Stone, the Gutter Pup, Lovely Mead, and Stover, all of the scrub, had a slight advantage.

Stover used to dream of mornings, in the lagging hours of recitation, of the contest and the sweet humiliation of his ancient foes. He would play like a demon; he would show them, Tough McCarty and the rest, what it was to be up against the despised Dink Stover—and dreaming thus he used to say to himself, with suddenly tense arms: "Gee, I only wish McCarty would play back of the line so I could get a chance at him!"

But on Tuesday, during the 'Varsity practice, suddenly as a scrimmage ended and sifted open, a cry went up. Ned Banks, left end on the 'Varsity, was seen lying on the ground after an attempt to rise. They gathered about him with grave faces, while Mr. Ware bent over him in anxious examination.

"What is it?" said the captain, with serious face.

"Something wrong with his ankle; can't tell yet just what."

"I'll play Saturday, Garry," said Banks, gritting his teeth. "I'll be ready by then. It's nothing much."

The subs carried him off the field with darkened faces—the last hopes of victory seemed to vanish. The gloom spread thickly through the school; even Dink, for a time, forgot the approaching hour of his revenge in the great disaster. The next morning a little comfort was given them in the report of Doctor Charlie that there was no sprain but only a slight wrenching, which, if all went well, would allow Banks to start the game. But the consolation was scant. What chance had Banks in an Andover game? There would have to be a shift; but what?

The captain, Garry Cockrell, looking indeed very serious, arrived, looked over the group, and called Stover out. Dink, surprised, jumped up, saying: "You want me, sir?"

"Yes."

Cockrell put his arm under Stover's and drew him away.

"Stover," he said, "I've got bad news for you."

"For me?"

"Yes. I'm not going to let you go into the Woodhull game this afternoon."

Stover received the news as though it had been the death of his entire family, immediate and distant. His throat choked, he tried to say something and did not dare trust himself.

"I'm sorry, my boy—but we're up against it, and I can't take any risks now of your getting hurt."

"It means the game," said Dink at last.

"I'm afraid so."

"We've no one to put in my place—no one but Beekstein Hall," said Stover desperately. "Oh, please, sir, let me play; I'll be awfully careful. It's only a house game."

"Humph—yes, I know these house games. I'm sorry, but there's no help for it."

"But I'm only a scrub, sir," said Stover, pleading hard.

"We're going to play you at end," said Cockrell suddenly, seeing he did not understand, "just as soon as we have to take Banks out; and Heaven only knows when that'll be."

Dink was aghast. "You're not going—you're not going—" He tried to speak and stopped.

"Yes, we've talked it over and that seems best."

"Oh, but I'm so light."

The captain watched the terror-stricken look in his face and was puzzled.

"What's the matter? You're not getting shaky?"

"Oh, no, sir," said Dink, "it's not that. It—it seems so terrible that you've got to put me in."

"You're better, my boy, than you think," said Cockrell, smiling a little, "and you're going to be better than you know now. Now you understand why you've got to keep on the side-lines this afternoon. You're too fragile to take risks on."

"Yes, I understand."

"It comes hard, doesn't it?"

"Yes, sir, it does; very hard."

When the Kennedy and the Woodhull lined up for play an hour later, little Pebble Stone was at end in place of Stover, who watched from his post as linesman the contest that was to have been his opportunity. He heard nothing of the buzzing comments behind, of the cheers or the shouted entreaties. Gaze fixed and heart in throat, he followed the swaying tide of battle, imprisoned, powerless to rush in and stem the disheartening advance.

The teams, now more evenly matched, both showed the traces of tense nerves in the frequent fumbling that kept the ball changing sides and prevented a score during the first half.

In the opening of the second half, by a lucky recovery of a blocked kick, the Kennedy scored a touchdown, but failed to kick the goal, making the score six to nothing. The Woodhull then began a determined assault upon the Kennedy's weak end. Stover, powerless, beheld little Pebble Stone, fighting like grim death, carried back and back, five, ten yards at a time, as the Woodhull swept up the field.

"It's the only place they can gain," he cried in his soul in bitter repetition.

He looked around and caught the eye of Captain Cockrell and sent him a mute, agonizing, fruitless appeal.

"Kennedy's ball," came the sharp cry of Slugger Jones, the umpire.

Dink looked up and felt the blood come back to his body again—on the twenty-five yard line there had been a fumble and the advance was checked. Twice again the battered end of the Kennedy was forced back for what seemed certain touchdowns, only to be saved by loose work on the Woodhull's part. It was getting dark and the half was ebbing fast—three minutes more to play.

A fourth time the Woodhull furiously attacked the breach, gaining at every rush over the light opposition, past the forty-yard line, past the twenty-yard mark and triumphantly, in the last minute of play, over the goal for a touchdown. The ball had been downed well to the right of the goal posts and the trial for goal was an unusually difficult one. The score was a tie; everything depended on the goal that, through the dusk, Tough McCarty was carefully sighting. Dink, heart-broken, despairing, leaning on his linesman's staff, directly behind the ball, waited for the long, endless moments to be over. Then there was a sudden movement of McCarty's body, a wild rush from the Kennedy, and the ball shot high in the air and, to Stover's horror, passed barely inside the farther goal post.

"No goal," said Slugger Jones. "Time's up."

Dink raised his head in surprise, scarcely crediting what he had heard. The Woodhull team were furiously disputing the decision, encouraged by audible comments from the spectators. Slugger Jones, surrounded by a contesting, rioting mass, suddenly swept them aside and began to take the vote of the officials.

"Kiefer, what do you say?"

Cap Kiefer, referee, shook his head.

"I'm sorry, Slugger; it was close, very close, but it did seem a goal to me."

"Tug, what do you say?"

"Goal, sure," said Tug Wilson, linesman for the Woodhull. At this, jeers and hoots broke out from the Kennedy.

"Of course he'll say that!"

"He's from the Woodhull."

"Hold up, hold up, now!" said Slugger Jones, more excited

than anyone else. "Don't get excited; it's up to your own man. Dink, was it a goal or no goal?"

Stover suddenly found himself in a whirling, angry mass—the decision of the game in his own hands. He saw the faces of Tough McCarty and the Coffee-colored Angel in the blank crowd about him and he saw the sneer on their faces as they waited for his answer. Then he saw the faces of his own teammates and knew what they, in their frenzy, expected from him.

He hesitated.

"Goal or no goal!" cried the umpire, for the second time.

Then suddenly, face to face with the hostile mass, the fighting blood came to Dink. Something cold went up his back. He looked once more above the riot to the shadowy posts, trying to forget Tough McCarty, and then, with a snap to his jaws, he answered: "Goal."

THINGS TO DO

1. On the blackboard make a co-operative list of rules of good sportsmanship for one team game played by classmates.

2. Read aloud the poem, "Play the Game," page 79. Illustrate its meaning from the selection, "The Football Game."

Play the Game

WILLIAM MAKEPEACE THACKERAY

And in the world as in the school,
  You know how Fate may turn and shift;
The prize be sometimes to the fool,
  The race not always to the swift.
Who misses or who wins the prize,
  Go lose or conquer as you can;
But, if you fall, or if you rise,
  Be each, pray God, a gentleman.

London has many famous streets, but no street has contributed more to English writing than the one where the great newspapers of London are written, and printed, and sent out—

Fleet Street

SHANE LESLIE

I never see the newsboys run
  Amid the whirling street,
  With swift untiring feet,
To cry the latest venture done,
But I expect one day to hear
  Them cry the crack of doom
  And risings from the tomb,
With great Archangel Michael near;
And see them running from the Fleet
  As messengers of God,
  With Heaven's tidings shod
Above their brave unwearied feet.

HELPS FOR DISCUSSION

1. If you have delivered newspapers on a route or sold them on a street corner, tell some of your experiences with weather, customers, money, "extras," and unusual happenings.

2. Explain the importance of the work of newsboys and carriers in a town's life. From the poem, "Fleet Street," quote lines that show appreciation of the newsboys' faithful service.

Rab and His Friends is a work of fiction; but it became so real to millions of readers that tourists to Scotland are shown the street where the dog-fight took place when

Rab Enters Edinburgh

DR. JOHN BROWN

Four and thirty years ago, Bob Ainslie and I were coming up Infirmary Street from the High School. When we got to the top of the street, and turned north, we espied a crowd at the Tron Church. "A dog-fight!" shouted Bob, and was off; and so was I, both of us all but praying that it might not be over before we got up! And is not this boy nature! and human nature too? and don't we all wish a house on fire not to be out before we see it?

Dogs like fighting; old Isaac[1] says they "delight" in it, and for the best of all reasons; and boys are not cruel because they like to see the fight. They see three of the great cardinal virtues of dog or man—courage, endurance, and skill—in intense action. This is very different from a love of making dogs fight, and enjoying, and aggravating, and making gain by their pluck. A boy—be he ever so fond himself of fighting—if he be a good boy, hates and despises all this, but he would have run off with Bob and me fast enough: it is a natural, and a not wicked interest, that all boys and men have in witnessing intense energy in action.

Does any curious woman wish to know how Bob's eye at a glance announced a dog-fight to his brain? He did not, he could not, see the dogs fighting: it was a flash of an inference,[2] a rapid induction.[3] The crowd round a couple of dogs fighting is a crowd masculine mainly, with an occasional active, compassionate woman, fluttering wildly round the outside and using her tongue and her hands freely upon the men, as so many "brutes"; it is a crowd annular,[4] compact, and mobile;

1. *Isaac:* this refers to Isaac Watts, the famous hymn-writer, who wrote the lines, "Let dogs delight to bark and bite, For God hath made them so." 2. *inference:* a conclusion reached by reasoning. 3. *induction:* reasoning from particulars to the general principle. 4. *annular* (ăn′ū lẽr): forming a circle.

a crowd centripetal,[5] having its eyes and its heads all bent downward and inward, to one common focus.

Well, Bob and I are up, and find it is not over; a small thoroughbred white bull terrier is busy throttling a large shepherd's dog, unaccustomed to war, but not to be trifled with. They are hard at it; the scientific little fellow doing his work in great style, his pastoral[6] enemy fighting wildly, but with the sharpest of teeth and a great courage. Science and breeding, however, soon had their own; the Game Chicken, as Bob called him, working his way up, took his final grip of poor Yarrow's throat, and he lay gasping and done for. His master, a brown, handsome, big young shepherd from Tweedsmuir, would have liked to have knocked down any man, if he had a chance; it was no use kicking the little dog; that would only make him hold the closer. Many were the means shouted out in mouthfuls, of the best possible ways of ending it. "Water!" but there was none near, and many cried for it who might have got it from the well at the Blackfriars Wynd.[7]

Still the Chicken holds; death not far off. "Snuff! A pinch of snuff!" observed a calm, highly dressed young buck,[8] with an eyeglass[9] in his eye. "Snuff, indeed!" growled the angry crowd, affronted and glaring. "Snuff! A pinch of snuff!" again observes the buck, but with more urgency; whereupon were produced several open boxes, and from a mull which may have been at Culloden,[10] he took a pinch, knelt down, and presented it to the nose of the Chicken. The laws of physiology and of snuff take their course; the Chicken sneezes, and Yarrow is free.

The young pastoral giant stalks off with Yarrow in his arms, comforting him.

But the bull terrier's blood is up, and his soul unsatisfied. The boys, with Bob and me at their head, are after him; down

5. *centripetal* (sĕn trĭp′ē tăl): pulled toward the center. 6. *pastoral:* pertaining to a shepherd, here, the shepherd's dog. 7. *Wynd* (wīnd): a lane or an alley several miles away. 8. *buck:* a dashing fellow; a dandy. 9. *eyeglass:* a monocle. 10. *mull . . . Culloden:* a small snuff box made of horn, so old that it could have been in use at the battle of Culloden (kŭ lŏd′ĕn) in Scotland in 1746.

Niddry Street he goes, bent on mischief; up the Cowgate like an arrow—Bob and I, and our small men, panting behind.

There, under the single arch of the South Bridge is a huge mastiff, sauntering down the middle of the causeway,[11] as if with his hands in his pockets; he is old, gray, brindled, and as big as a little Highland bull.

The Chicken makes straight at him, and fastens on his throat. To our astonishment the great creature does nothing but stand still, hold himself up, and roar—yes, roar; a long, serious, remonstrative roar. How is this? Bob and I are up to them. *He is muzzled!* The bailies[12] had proclaimed a general muzzling, and his master, studying strength and economy mainly, had encompassed his huge jaws in a home-made apparatus constructed out of ancient leather. His mouth was open as far as it could; his lips curled up in rage, a sort of terrible grin; his teeth gleaming, ready, from out the dark-

11. *causeway:* a raised way over wet or marshy ground. 12. *bailies:* city officers, somewhat like our policemen.

ness; the strap across his mouth tense as a bowstring; his whole frame stiff with indignation and surprise; his roar asking us all round, "Did you ever see the like of this?" He looked a statue of anger and astonishment, done in Aberdeen granite.

We soon had a crowd; the Chicken held on. "A knife!" cried Bob; and a cobbler gave him his knife: you know the kind of knife, worn away obliquely to a point, and always keen. I put its edge to the tense leather; it ran before it, and then!—one sudden jerk of that enormous head, a sort of dirty mist about his mouth, no noise, and the bright and fierce little fellow is dropped, limp and dead. A solemn pause; this was more than any of us had bargained for. I turned the little fellow over, and saw he was quite dead; the mastiff had taken him by the small of the back like a rat, and broken it.

He looked down at his victim appeased, ashamed, and amazed, snuffed him all over, stared at him, and taking a sudden thought, turned round and trotted off. Bob took the dead dog up, and said, "John, we'll bury him after tea." "Yes," said I, and was off after the mastiff. He made up the Cowgate at a rapid swing; he had forgotten some engagement. He turned up the Candlemaker Row, and stopped at the Harrow Inn.

There was a carrier's cart ready to start, and a keen, thin, impatient little man, his hand at his gray horse's head looking about angrily for something. "Rab, ye thief!" said he, aiming a kick at my great friend, who drew cringing up, and, avoiding the heavy shoe with more agility than dignity, and watching his master's eye, slunk dismayed under the cart, his ears down, and as much as he had of tail down too.

What a man this must be, thought I, to whom my tremendous hero turns tail! The carrier saw the muzzle hanging, cut and useless, from his neck, and I eagerly told him the story which Bob and I always thought, and still think, Homer, or King David, or Sir Walter, alone were worthy to rehearse. The severe little man was mitigated,[13] and condescended to say, "Rab, ma man, puir[14] Rabbie!" whereupon the stump of

13. *mitigated:* grew milder.

14. *puir* (pür): Scottish dialect for "poor."

a tail rose up, the ears were cocked, the eyes filled, and were comforted; the two friends were reconciled. "Hupp!" and a stroke of the whip were given to Jess, the horse; and off went the three.

Bob and I buried the Game Chicken that night (we had not much of a tea) in the backgreen[15] of his house in Melville street, No. 17, with considerable gravity and silence; and being at the time in the Iliad,[16] and, like all boys, Trojans, we called him Hector, of course.

THINGS TO DO

1. *Rab and His Friends* is one of the greatest dog stories of English literature. This is only one of its many fine chapters. Read all the book and come to know its splendid characters: James Noble and his wife Ailie; Jess, who drove the cart through the streets of Edinburgh; and the teller of the story, Doctor John Brown himself.

2. Make a bibliography of dog stories. Jack London has one magnificent dog story. Albert Payson Terhune has several dog tales. Richard Harding Davis wrote one. So did Eleanor Atkinson. Read at least one of these stories and compare it with the scene from *Rab and His Friends.*

3. Write a story about a dog. You may show the dog's courage, fidelity to a trust, companionship, ingenuity.

4. Collect from advertisements and mount pictures of dogs, showing as many types as possible. Make drawings if you prefer. Be able to discuss the characteristics of different breeds and the services each renders to man.

PICTURING LIFE IN THE TOWN

Whether you visit the great art galleries abroad or the equally great galleries at home, you will find pictures of city life, ancient and modern. Among these paintings are: *Marriage at Cana,* by VERONESE; *The Boy Christ in the Temple,* by HOFMANN; *Men on the Dock,* by BELLOWS; *The Dancer,* by DEGAS; *Pipers of Balmoral,* by MELCHERS; *The Laundress,* by DOUMIER.

15. *backgreen:* rear lawn. 16. *Iliad:* an epic poem, ascribed to Homer, which relates the story of the ancient siege of Troy, the heroism of the Trojans, and the burial of Hector.

Every great city knows the music of barrel organs; and the poet sings of them all when he sings of London in

The Barrel-Organ

ALFRED NOYES

There's a barrel-organ caroling across a golden street
In the City as the sun sinks low;
And the music's not immortal; but the world has made it sweet,
And fulfilled it with the sunset glow;
And it pulses through the pleasures of the City and the pain
That surround the singing organ like a large eternal light;
And they've given it a glory and a part to play again
In the Symphony that rules the day and night.

And now it's marching onward through the realms of old romance,
And trolling out a fond familiar tune,
And now it's roaring cannon down to fight the King of France,
And now it's prattling softly to the moon,
And all around the organ there's a sea without a shore
Of human joys and wonders and regrets;
To remember and to recompense the music evermore
For what the cold machinery forgets. . . .

Yes; as the music changes,
Like a prismatic glass,
It takes the light and ranges
Through all the moods that pass;
Dissects the common carnival
Of passions and regrets,
And gives the world a glimpse of all
The colors it forgets.

And there *La Traviata* sighs
Another sadder song;
And there *Il Trovatore* cries
A tale of deeper wrong;

And bolder knights to battle go
  With sword and shield and lance,
Than ever here on earth below
  Have whirled into—*a dance*!

Go down to Kew in lilac-time, in lilac-time, in lilac-time;
  Go down to Kew in lilac-time (it isn't far from London!)
And you shall wander hand in hand with love in summer's wonderland;
  Go down to Kew in lilac-time (it isn't far from London!)

The cherry-trees are seas of bloom and soft perfume and sweet perfume,
  The cherry-trees are seas of bloom (and oh, so near to London!)
And there they say, when dawn is high and all the world's a blaze of sky
  The cuckoo, though he's very shy, will sing a song for London.

The Dorian nightingale is rare and yet they say you'll hear
him there
At Kew, at Kew in lilac-time (and oh, so near to London!)
The linnet and the throstle, too, and after dark the long halloo
And golden-eyed *tu-whit, tu-whoo*, of owls that ogle
London.

For Noah hardly knew a bird of any kind that isn't heard
At Kew, at Kew in lilac-time (and oh, so near to London!)
And when the rose begins to pout and all the chestnut spires
are out
You'll hear the rest without a doubt, all chorusing for
London: —

Come down to Kew in lilac-time, in lilac-time, in lilac-time;
Come down to Kew in lilac-time (it isn't far from London!)
And you shall wander hand in hand with love in summer's
wonderland;
Come down to Kew in lilac-time (it isn't far from London!)

My Financial Career

STEPHEN LEACOCK

When I go into a bank I get rattled. The clerks rattle me; the wickets rattle me; the sight of the money rattles me; everything rattles me.

The moment I cross the threshold of a bank and attempt to transact business there, I become an irresponsible idiot.

I knew this beforehand, but my salary had been raised to fifty dollars a month and I felt that the bank was the only place for it. So I shambled in and looked timidly round at the clerks. I had an idea that a person about to open an account must needs consult the manager.

I went up to a wicket marked "Accountant." The accountant was a tall, cool devil. The very sight of him rattled me. My voice was sepulchral.

"Can I see the manager?" I said, and added solemnly, "alone." I don't know why I said "alone."

"Certainly," said the accountant and fetched him.

The manager was a grave, calm man. I held my fifty-six dollars clutched in a crumpled ball in my pocket.

"Are you the manager?" I said.

"Yes," he said.

"Can I see you," I asked, "alone?" I didn't want to say "alone" again, but without it the thing seemed self-evident.

The manager looked at me in some alarm. He felt that I had an awful secret to reveal.

"Come in here," he said, and led the way to a private room. He turned the key in the lock.

"We are safe from interruption here," he said; "sit down."

We both sat down and looked at each other.

"You are one of Pinkerton's[1] men, I presume," he said.

He had gathered from my mysterious manner that I was a detective. I knew what he was thinking, and it made me worse.

"No, not from Pinkerton's," I said, seeming to imply that I came from a rival agency. "To tell the truth," I went on, as if I had been prompted to lie about it, "I am not a detective at all. I have come to open an account. I intend to keep all my money in this bank."

The manager looked relieved but still serious; he concluded now that I was a son of Baron Rothschild.

"A large account, I suppose," he said.

"Fairly large," I whispered. "I propose to deposit fifty-six dollars now and fifty dollars a month regularly."

The manager got up and opened the door. He called to the accountant.

"Mr. Montgomery," he said unkindly loud, "this gentleman is opening an account; he will deposit fifty-six dollars. Good morning."

I rose.

A big iron door stood open at the side of the room.

"Good morning," I said and stepped into the safe.

"Come out," said the manager coldly and showed me the other way.

1. *Pinkerton's:* a well-known private detective agency.

I went up to the accountant's wicket and poked the ball of money at him with a quick, convulsive movement as if I were doing a conjuring trick. My face was ghastly pale.

"Here," I said, "deposit it." The tone of the words seemed to mean, "Let us do this painful thing while the fit is on us."

He made me write the sum on a slip and sign my name in a book. I no longer knew what I was doing. The bank swam before my eyes.

"Is it deposited?" I asked in a hollow, vibrating voice.

"It is," said the accountant.

"Then I want to draw a check."

My idea was to draw out six dollars of it for present use. Someone gave me a check-book through a wicket and someone else began telling me how to write it out. The people in the bank had the impression that I was an invalid millionaire. I wrote something on the check and thrust it in at the clerk. He looked at it.

"What! Are you drawing it all out again?" he asked in surprise. Then I realized that I had written fifty-six instead of six. I was too far gone to reason now. I had a feeling that it was impossible to explain the thing. All the clerks had stopped writing to look at me.

Reckless with misery, I made a plunge.

"Yes, the whole thing."

"You withdraw your money from the bank?"

"Every cent of it."

"Are you not going to deposit any more?" said the clerk, astonished.

"Never."

An idiot hope struck me that they might think something had insulted me while I was writing the check and that I had changed my mind. I made a wretched attempt to look like a man with a fearfully quick temper.

The clerk prepared to pay the money.

"How will you have it?" he said.

"What?"

"How will you have it?"

"Oh,"—I caught his meaning and answered without even trying to think—"in fifties."

He gave me a fifty-dollar bill.

"And the six?" he asked dryly.

"In sixes," I said.

He gave it me and I rushed out.

As the big door swung behind me I caught the echo of a roar of laughter that went up to the ceiling of the bank. Since then I bank no more. I keep my money in cash in my trousers pocket and my savings in a sock.

The city does not always need the brightness of sunshine to make it beautiful. Sometimes the town is loveliest as one looks upon

City Colors

KARLE WILSON BAKER

Blue at dusk and blue at dawn—
It's then I love the city best:
The milkman and the alley-cat,
The pigeon on her stony nest,

They see her open like a flower
Soft-eyed beneath her veil of blue,
And I, cold elbows on the sill,
Lean out to catch her greeting, too.

In the busy light of noon
The flower wilts in drab and black,

In window-stare and pavement-fire
And glare of tin and smudge of stack.

But when the weather-wheel goes round,
And night and darkness come again,
Who would believe the things it does,
The city, on a night of rain?

The gutters run with topaz fire,
The hooded chariots glint and gleam
Between them, spilling melted gold,
And rubies from a caliph's dream,

And amethyst and emerald
Splinter across the fairy lane
That seemed a city street but now,
Before the darkness and the rain.

Then comes again the azure dawn,
And then again the fiery noon,
And then, at last, the in-between,
That waits so long and goes so soon,

The hour that wraps all jagged things
In filmy web or silken husk,
And brings me back my lovely town—
Blue at dawn and blue at dusk!

Fog

CARL SANDBURG

The fog comes
on little cat feet.

It sits looking
over harbor and city
on silent haunches
and then moves on.

A Quiet Street after Rain

LOUIS GINSBERG

Glittering keen, all things appear
Clairvoyant,[1] carved, and crystal-clear.

Happy to watch the raindrops cease,
Houses are honeycombed with peace;

And, dazzling with a blazing show,
Windows are pelting suns below!

Colors are ambushing the sense
With flaming silent eloquence.

Marvelous, too, it is to see
A rosebush dipped in deity.

Nearby a spider has begun
Upon a fence to thread the sun.

The street is hushed, though far-off steals
A powdery, crumbling sound of wheels . . .

Till Time, who loiters by to scrawl
His warning on a garden wall,

Lingers to watch in strange amaze
How quiet loveliness can blaze—

How immortality can be
Familiar as a fence or tree!

HELPS FOR DISCUSSION

The poems on pages 90–92 present pictures of beauty in city surroundings. Choose a stanza that you particularly like. Read it aloud and tell what it helps you to see.

1. *clairvoyant* (klâr voi′ănt): having the power to see things that are not visible.

Ellis Island is now the gateway through which the immigrant **enters the** United States; but for a long time Castle Garden was the point of entry. **Michael Pupin**, who lived to be one of the great inventors of the nation, told the story of how he entered the country

Through the Gate of Castle Garden

MICHAEL PUPIN

He who has never crossed the stormy Atlantic during the month of March in the crowded steerage of an immigrant ship does not know what hardships are. Many a night I spent on the deck of that ship hugging the warm smokestack and adjusting my position so as to avoid the force of the gale and the sharpness of its icy chilliness. All I possessed was the light suit of clothes which I carried on my back. Everything else I had converted into money with which to cover my transportation expenses. There was nothing left to pay for a blanket and mattress for my steerage bunk. I could not rest there during the cold nights of March without much shivering and unbearable discomfort. If it had not been for the warm smokestack, I should have died of cold.

At first I had to fight for my place there in the daytime, but when the immigrants understood that I had no warm clothing they did not disturb me any longer. I often thought of my yellow sheepskin coat and the black sheepskin cap, and I understood more clearly than ever my mother's farsightedness when she provided that coat and cap for my long journey. A blast of the everlasting gales had carried away my hat; and a Turkish fez[1] such as the Serbs[2] of Bosnia[3] wear was the only headgear I had. It was providential that I had not succeeded in selling it in Prague.[4] Most of my fellow immigrants thought that I was a Turk and cared little about my discomforts. But, nevertheless, I felt quite brave and strong in the daytime. At night, however, when, standing alone alongside the smokestack, I beheld through the howling darkness the white rims of the mountain-high waves speeding on

1. *fez:* a form of cap, usually red and having a tassel, once worn as the national headdress of the Turks. 2. *Serbs:* persons belonging to a certain group of the Slavic race. 3. *Bosnia* (bŏz'nĭ *ȧ*): formerly a Turkish province, now a part of Yugoslavia. 4. *Prague* (prāg *or* prä'hȧ): the capital of Czechoslovakia.

like maddened dragons toward the tumbling ship, my heart sank low. It was my implicit trust in God and in his regard for my mother's prayers which enabled me to overcome my fear and bravely face the horrors of the angry seas.

On the fourteenth day, early in the morning, the flat coast-line of Long Island hove in sight. Nobody in the motley crowd of excited immigrants was more happy to see the promised land than I was. It was a clear, mild, sunny March morning; and, as we approached New York Harbor, the warm sun rays seemed to thaw out the chilliness which I had accumulated in my body by continuous exposure to the wintry blasts of the North Atlantic. I felt like a new person and saw in every new scene presented by the New World, as the ship moved into it, a new promise that I should be welcome.

Presently the ship passed by Castle Garden,[5] and I heard someone say: "There is the gate to America." An hour or so later we all stood at the gate. The immigrant ship, *Westphalia*, landed at Hoboken, and a tug took us to Castle Garden. We were carefully examined and cross-examined, and when my turn came the examining officials shook their heads and seemed to find me wanting. I confessed that I had only five cents in my pocket and had no relatives here, and that I knew of nobody in this country except Franklin, Lincoln, and Harriet Beecher Stowe, whose *Uncle Tom's Cabin* I had read in a translation.

One of the officials, who had one leg only and walked with a crutch, seemed much impressed by this remark and, looking very kindly into my eyes with a merry twinkle in his own, said in German: "You showed good taste when you picked your American acquaintances." I learned later that he was a Swiss, who had served in the Union army during the Civil War. He was particularly attentive while I was being cross-examined and nodded approvingly whenever I scored a point with my answers. He whispered something to the other officials, and they finally informed me that I could pass on. I was conducted promptly to the Labor Bureau

5. *Castle Garden:* a circular building on the Battery, in New York City, used as an immigrant depot before Ellis Island.

of Castle Garden. My Swiss friend looked me up a little later and informed me that the examiners had made an exception in my favor and admitted me, and that I must look sharp and find a job as soon as possible.

My first night under the Stars and Stripes was spent in Castle Garden. It was a glorious night, I thought; no howling of the gales, no crashing of the waves, no tumbling motion of the world beneath my feet, such as I had experienced on the immigrant ship. The feeling of being on *terra firma*[6] sank deep into my consciousness, and I slept the sleep of a healthy youth, although my bed was a bare floor.

The early morning saw me at my breakfast, enjoying a huge bowl of hot coffee and a big chunk of bread with some butter, supplied by the Castle Garden authorities at Uncle Sam's expense. Then I started out, eager to catch a glimpse of great New York, feeling, in the words of the Psalmist, "as a strong man ready to run a race." An old lady sat near the gate of Castle Garden offering cakes and candies for sale. A piece of prune pie caught my eye. No true Serb can resist the allurements of prunes. It is a national sweetmeat. I bought it, paying five cents for it, the only money I had; then I made a beeline across Battery Park, at the same time eating my pie.

6. *terra firma* (tĕr′ȧ fûr′mȧ): solid earth.

My first bargain in America proved a failure. The prune pie was a deception; it was a prune pie filled with prune pits, and I thought of the words of my fellow passenger on the immigrant ship who had said, "No matter who you are or what you know or what you have you will be a greenhorn[7] when you land in America." The prune-pie transaction whispered in my ear, "Michael, you are a greenhorn; this is the first experience in your life as a greenhorn. Cheer up! Get ready to serve your apprenticeship as a greenhorn before you can establish your claim to any recognition," repeating the words of my fellow passenger who had served his apprenticeship in America. No prophet ever uttered a truer word.

The old Stevens House, a white building with green window shutters, stood at the corner of Broadway and Bowling Green. When I reached this spot and saw the busy beehive called Broadway, with thousands of telegraph wires stretching across it like a cobweb between huge buildings, I was overawed and wondered what it all meant. Neither Budapest,[8] nor Prague, nor Hamburg[9] looked anything like it.

My puzzled and panicky expression and the red fez on my head must have attracted considerable attention, because suddenly I saw myself surrounded by a small crowd of boys of all sizes, jeering and laughing and pointing at my fez. They were newsboys and bootblacks, who appeared to be anxious to have some fun at my expense. I was embarrassed and much provoked, but controlled my Serbian temper.

Presently one of the bigger fellows walked up to me and knocked the fez off my head. I punched him on the nose and then we clinched. My wrestling experiences on the pasture lands of Serbia came to my rescue. The bully was down in a jiffy, and his chums gave a loud cheer of ringing laughter. I thought it was a signal for general attack, but they did not touch or interfere in any way. They acted like impartial spectators, eager to see that the best man won.

Suddenly I felt a powerful hand pulling me up by the collar; when I looked up I saw a big official with a club in his

7. *greenhorn:* a raw, inexperienced person. 8. *Budapest* (bōō'dȧ pĕst'): the capital of Hungary. 9. *Hamburg* (hăm'bûrg): a city and port in Germany.

hand and a fierce expression in his eye. He looked decidedly unfriendly but, after listening to the appeals of the newsboys and bootblacks who witnessed the fight, he softened and handed me my fez. The boys evidently appealed in my behalf when the policeman interfered. They had actually become my friends.

When I walked away toward Castle Garden with my red fez proudly cocked up on my head, the boys cheered. I thought to myself that the unpleasant incident was worth my while, because it taught me that I was in a country where even among the street urchins there was a strong sentiment in favor of fair play even to a Serbian greenhorn. America was different from Austria-Hungary. I never forgot the lesson and never had a single reason to change my opinion.

HELPS FOR DISCUSSION

What evidences of friendliness did Michael Pupin find on shipboard and in the new country? What unfriendly acts occurred? What did Pupin contribute to his adopted country? What other famous immigrants made notable contributions to the United States?

The Tropics in New York

CLAUDE McKAY

Bananas ripe and green, and ginger-root,
Cocoa in pods and alligator pears,
And tangerines and mangoes and grapefruit,
Fit for the highest prize at parish fairs,

Set in the window, bringing memories
Of fruit trees laden by low-singing rills,
And dewy dawns, and mystical blue skies
In benediction over nun-like hills.

My eyes grew dim, and I could no more gaze;
A wave of longing through my body swept,
And, hungry for the old, familiar ways,
I turned aside and bowed my head and wept.

Saint Francesca Cabrini must sometimes have smiled with joy when, as she walked through New York streets, she saw people who had come from Italy, as had she, in prayer

At the Shrine

RICHARD KENDALL MUNKITTRICK

A pale Italian peasant,
  Beside the dusty way,
Upon this morning pleasant
  Kneels in the sun to pray.

Silent in her devotion,
  With fervent glance she pleads;
Her fingers' only motion,
  Telling her amber beads.

Dreaming of ilex bowers
  Beyond the purple brine,
Once more she sees the flowers
  Bloom at the wayside shrine.

And, while the mad crowd jostles,
  She, with a visage sweet,
Prays where the bisque apostles
  Are sold on Barclay Street.

Bill's Bill

HARRY STEPHEN KEELER

Bill was a Boy Scout. He was a first-class scout, too, and every scout knows what that means. He had stood many tests, but the one I am going to tell about was the severest of all.

Bill longed with his whole heart for a motorcycle. After looking over all the motorcycles in the field, he decided that the Red Dart, which cost $190, was the machine for him. But the price! Only ten dollars less than two hundred—an immense sum, it seemed, for a boy of sixteen to save.

In the first place Bill knew that he had no chance of getting help from his father, whose business was in anything but good condition. But Bill was not dismayed by this fact; he decided to try and make money enough himself to buy that motorcycle. So he went to see Jerry O'Brien, the man who owned nearly all the newspaper routes on the North Side of Chicago.

"Jerry," he said, "I have known several boys who carried papers for you. Can't you give me a job on one of the morning routes?"

Jerry looked at him some time before he spoke.

"Well," he drawled, "I do need a boy for the Dearborn Avenue route in the morning and the Clark Street route in the afternoon. Each one pays a dollar a week. But think it over well, youngster. The morning route means that you've got to rise at half-past four, so as to start at five, and it will be nearly seven when you finish. The afternoon route will take you from four to five-thirty. And don't forget it either—it's cold these winter mornings. You go all the way from Chicago Avenue to North Avenue, which means you'll have to hustle. Think it over. I don't want to teach you the routes and then have you back out in a week or two."

But Bill did not require much "thinking it over." The idea of owning a Red Dart made it seem easy to climb out of bed before daylight on winter mornings, wade through snow-drifts, and lose playtime after school.

"Take me, Jerry," he begged. "I won't back out. I want money for something that costs a lot—and the only way I can get it is to earn it."

Father not only showed no opposition to the plan, but even helped to argue mother out of her objections. So Bill reported to Jerry the next morning to be taught the route.

It was no soft snap. In October the mornings were warm and pleasant. As winter gradually crept nearer, however, all of the boy's will power was needed to pull him out of bed into an ice-cold room. He shiveringly drew on his trousers, flannel shirt, and two sweaters and made his way down the street, in the teeth of a driving gale or a sleety rain, to the alley where his stock of papers awaited him. The load was heavy enough when he started out with it, but, oddly enough, as it grew smaller, it grew more leaden, until by the end of the route it was almost as tiring as at the beginning.

The morning's work over, there followed in rapid succession, breakfast, school, homework, the afternoon route. By the time the afternoon papers were delivered, it was almost suppertime. After supper, it was early to bed with Bill, in order to get sufficient sleep for rising before daybreak next morning. That was the daily round, and no time whatever was left from Monday to Saturday for football, skating, moving-pictures, or any of the other things which Bill delighted in.

There was this consolation, however. Every day brought him just a little nearer to the longed-for motorcycle.

The last snow melted, and the warm spring mornings returned. Spring ran into summer, and summer turned out to be pleasanter, since Bill had plenty of time for baseball, swimming, and other joys, in spite of three and a half hours of carrying papers. But at last only a few weeks remained before school would reopen and the grind begin again—papers, school, papers, bed; papers, school, papers, bed!

Bill tried to keep this out of his mind as much as possible. He preferred to dwell on the ninety dollars snugly laid away. One more year—or fifty weeks—and he would have another hundred dollars and the beautiful "Red Dart."

Then came the astonishing event—the finding of the $100 bill. It happened in this fashion:

One evening Bill saw in the paper a full-page advertisement of the Red Dart Motorcycle Company. It announced that the company had issued a new booklet, which would be given or mailed to anybody interested in motorcycles. Bill, being among those interested, walked all the way downtown the next afternoon to get one of the little books. After feasting his eyes on the wonderful display of motorcycles in the salesrooms, he asked for a booklet.

He opened it as he left the building. At that moment he glanced down at the pavement and saw a yellow folded slip moving in the wind. Bill stooped to pick it up, but the wind whirled it under a wagon standing by the curb of the crowded street. Reaching out quickly, the boy seized the paper. It crackled on unfolding. One long look—and Bill tingled from his head to his toes.

A hundred dollars!

No one in the passing crowd had paid him the least attention, though he felt that all Chicago was looking at him with a thousand eyes.

At last! . . . why, it made up the sum needed for the motorcycle! It saved fifty weeks of work.

As he trudged homeward the boy's mind was in a whirl. Every now and then he drew the bank note from his pocket and read it, as though to make sure that what had happened was real and not a dream. What luck!

Then came other and different thoughts—troublesome thoughts. The loser might advertise. Bill knew that in such an event there was nothing to do but return the money. He might not see the advertisement, however. Or the owner might believe the bill lost beyond recovery and make no effort to regain it. In that case—

All the time the boy was delivering the afternoon papers, he reasoned that if he did not look at the lost-and-found columns for several weeks, he would not see the advertisement, even if an advertisement were printed. In that case he might buy the motorcycle without any stings of conscience.

He could give up the newspaper routes, which left him no time for himself.

As Bill walked the street, a small voice urged him, "Don't look at the lost-and-found column; don't look at the lost-and-found column!"

Bill made more mistakes that afternoon than he had ever made before. Where he should have left copies of the *Evening News*, angry subscribers found the *Post*; and where *Posts* were desired, copies of the *Evening News* were left. Every now and then Bill rested the bundle on his knee and felt his pocket, to make sure that the bill was still there. All the while his mind worked on the problem without rest. He thought that he must look at the lost-and-found column; then he felt that it would be very foolish to look. Should he have the motorcycle at once, without more work? Or should he throw away this splendid chance?

That night at supper Bill ate little. His mother noticed that something was troubling him. His father made no sign, however, that he had seen anything at all, but when the mother left the room, he spoke to the boy.

"Well, Bill," he asked, "are you worried because vacation is nearly over? Or has Jerry O'Brien decided to give your routes to another boy?"

"I'm sorry that vacation is nearly over, but—"

"But what?"

"Will you answer an imaginary question for me, Father?" asked the boy.

"Yes; what is it?"

"Well," Bill began slowly, "if you found something valuable—say money—would you look in the papers to see if it was advertised?"

"It is not polite to answer one question by asking another," the father replied, "but that is what I am going to do. Listen. Father's business is not very good at present, although he manages to make enough to take care of you and your mother, keep you at school, and let you have for your own what money you make out of school hours. Now, if I lost some money—even a little—do you think that the finder should keep it or return it?"

"I suppose your question answers mine," Bill said solemnly. "When you lose anything, you feel that it ought to be returned; and when you find something, the loser feels the same way."

He went to bed without saying another word.

The next morning Bill dressed early and tiptoed from the house. Fifteen minutes later he reached the point where he got his papers—half of them *Tribunes*—half of them *Heralds*.

For several minutes he stared at the papers. All that he had to do, he reflected, was to open one of them quickly, locate the lost-and-found column, and run his eye down it. If he did so, he might come across the owner of the yellow hundred-dollar bill that he had hidden in the bureau drawer. Then he would never be able to rest until he had restored the money. Perhaps, after all, it was best that he should not look. If people were careless, it served them right to lose things. Surely it would be foolish to look. But on the other hand, the loser might be a bank messenger, who would have to make good the loss.

The boy raised the bunch of papers, swung his shoulder strap around it, and started out on his route. Whenever he rolled a paper before tossing it from the sidewalk to a vestibule, his hand paused for a second in the motion. But he always managed to throw the paper from him and go on to the next subscriber's house. Thus *Tribune* after *Tribune* and *Herald* after *Herald* left the bundle, until finally but one paper remained—*Tribune.*

For some time Bill hesitated in front of the last house on the route. Then he lifted the paper to throw it—without having looked at it. At that moment his eye fell on his scout badge, and the first scout law flashed through his mind: "A scout's honor is to be trusted." His arm fell slowly to his side. He seated himself on a doorstep and unfolded the paper.

There was the lost-and-found column. And a moment later his heart dropped down clean through to his shoes! His visions of a motorcycle, a beautiful, glittering Red Dart, vanished into thin air as he read this advertisement:

> LOST: *yesterday; a bill of large denomination; owner can identify it by giving serial number; reasonable reward if returned between 7 and 9 to John Bennet, 1800 Lake Shore Drive.*

Bill went home to breakfast. His heart was light—most happily light—although he was about to lose his treasure. He realized that the tussle he had had with himself, when he held the last *Tribune*, had been a hard one. But, after all, he would not now have that money on his conscience. The coming year could not pass more slowly than the one just closed, and at its end he would have the Red Dart anyway, all paid for by the sweat of his brow. And perhaps the reward for the return of the bill would help a little.

At seven o'clock that evening Bill was on Lake Shore Drive. In a few minutes he had found "1800." He was rather surprised to see a splendid mansion, with a well-kept lawn, a driveway, and other evidences of wealth. After fumbling nervously for a moment at the iron gate, the boy picked up courage enough to walk up the steps and ring the bell. A man in gray livery answered the summons.

"I would like—I would like to speak to Mr. John Bennet," Bill said.

"Step this way," said the servant. "Stand here; I will see if he is busy."

The butler knocked at a door at the end of the hall. It opened slightly. As it opened, Bill caught sight of a little sharp-featured man, with iron-gray hair and small piercing eyes.

"Boy to see you, sir," explained the servant.

"Tell him to come in," said the little man.

Bill did so. Mr. Bennet closed the door.

"Sit down," he invited. "What can I do for you?"

"I have found your money," Bill blurted out.

"Humph!" returned Mr. Bennet. "So you found it?" He paused. "Well, I lost it and my wife inserted the advertisement. She has an old-fashioned notion that everybody is honest. It's all nonsense! It's all nonsense! I lost a hundred-dollar bill. Was that what you found?"

"Yes," Bill answered. "You said in your advertisement that you knew the number. If it's the same number that's on the bill, I will hand you the money."

The little man jerked a notebook from his pocket. He thumbed the leaves a moment.

"Always put down the numbers of big bills, boy," he said. "This is what I always do. It pays in case they get lost. Let me see—here it is. Number M17472447, Series 1902."

"It's your money, then," interrupted Bill.

He laid the crisp yellow note in Mr. Bennet's hand.

"Humph! humph!" snorted Mr. Bennet, staring at Bill as if he were some rare curiosity. "How did you happen to find it? Where did you come across it? What time of day was it? Where do you live? Do you work downtown? What is your name?"

The torrent of questions took away Bill's breath. Then he collected his wits.

"I go to school," he answered. "My name is William Carston and I live at 124 West Center Street. I happened to go downtown yesterday to get a Red Dart motorcycle advertisement—I have been saving money for a long time for a Red Dart. When I came out of the Red Dart office on Madison Street, I looked down and saw the bill, and—"

"Motorcycle!" exploded Mr. Bennet. "Motorcycle! It's all nonsense! It's all nonsense! Do you want to get blown over the moon? I wouldn't ride one of the pesky things for a million dollars. It's all nonsense! Why, if I—"

He was interrupted by a rapping on the door. Mr. Bennet opened it, and the butler said, "Mr. Smith from New York to see you, sir."

With a quick motion of his wrist, Mr. Bennet jerked out his watch and snapped it open.

"Hm-hm-hm!" he mumbled. "Forgot all about my appointment with Smith. Hawkins, show this young gentleman out."

A big figure loomed up behind the servant.

"Is that you, Smith? I forgot all about you. Step in," said Mr. Bennet.

Bill found himself conducted through the hall and heard the door close behind him. He recovered himself as he walked down the cement path to the sidewalk.

"Well, where's the reward?" he said. "If it had been anybody but a millionaire—"

Presently, however, as he walked along homeward, he found his disappointment lightening. A feeling of great relief was coming over him. He was glad to have the bill off his hands.

The next morning Bill came into the dining-room with a

bright face. His mother and father looked at him with curiosity.

"Letter for you, Bill," said his father.

Bill wonderingly tore open the envelope. At first he saw nothing inside; then he found a small white card in one corner. Taking it out, he read with perplexity the words written in red ink on one side:

> *Sales Department: Credit bearer with $100 on purchase of any motorcycle in stock. J. B.*

Quickly he turned the card over. The printed words on the other side read:

> JOHN C. BENNET, *Owner and General Manager*
> RED DART MOTORCYCLE COMPANY
> CHICAGO NEW YORK LONDON

That afternoon the proudest and happiest boy in Chicago came home with the finest motorcycle in the whole world.

Christ in Woolworth's

TERESA HOOLEY

I did not think to find You there—
Crucifixes, large and small,
Sixpence and threepence, on a tray,
Among the artificial pearls,
Paste rings, tin watches, beads of glass.
It seemed so strange to find You there
Fingered by people coarse and crass
Who had no reverence at all.
Yet—what is it that You would say?
"For these I hang upon My cross,
For these the agony and loss,
Though heedlessly they pass Me by."
Dear Lord, forgive such fools as I,
Who thought it strange to find You there,
When You are with us everywhere.

Sing Ye to the Lord

Sing ye to the Lord a new canticle:
because he hath done wonderful things.

His right hand hath wrought for him salvation
and his arm *is* holy.

The Lord hath made known his salvation: he hath revealed his justice in the sight of the Gentiles.

He hath remembered his mercy and his truth toward the house of Israel.

All the ends of the earth have seen the salvation of our God.

Sing joyfully to God, all the earth; make melody, rejoice and sing.

Sing praise to the Lord on the harp, on the harp, and with the voice of a psalm:
with long trumpets, and sound of cornet.

Make a joyful noise before the Lord our king.

Let the sea be moved and the fulness thereof:
the world and they that dwell therein.

The rivers shall clap their hands, the mountains shall rejoice together

at the presence of the Lord: because he cometh to judge the earth.

He shall judge the world with justice, and the people with equity.

Psalm 97

A Christ-Cross Rhyme

ROBERT STEPHEN HAWKER

Christ His Cross shall be my speed!
Teach me, Father John, to read,
That in Church on Holy day
I may chant the psalm and pray.

Let me learn, that I may know
What the shining windows show:
Where the lovely Lady stands,
With that bright Child in her hands.

Teach me letters, A, B, C,
Till that I shall able be
Signs to know and words to frame,
And to spell sweet Jesus' Name.

Then, dear Master, will I look
Day and night in that fair book
Where the tales of saints are told,
With their pictures, all in gold.

Teach me, Father John, to say
Vesper-verse and Matin-lay;
So when I to God shall plead,
Christ His Cross shall be my speed.

The dangers and the dignity of labor are set forth in these three poems:

Song of a Fellow-Worker

ARTHUR O'SHAUGHNESSY

I went forth in the city, and I met a hundred men,
The worker with the chisel and the worker with the pen,—
The restless toilers after good, who sow and never reap,
And one who maketh music for their souls that may not sleep.

Each passed me with a dauntless look, and my undaunted eyes
Were almost softened as they passed with tears that strove
to rise
At sight of all those labors, and because that every one,
Ay, the greatest, would be weaker if my little were undone.

They passed me, having faith in me, and in our several ways,
Together we began today as on the other days:
I felt their mighty hands at work, and, as the day wore through,
Perhaps they felt that even I was helping somewhat too:

And so we toil together many a day from morn till night,
I in the lower depths of life, they on the lovely height;
For though the common stones are mine, and they have lofty
cares,
Their work begins where this leaves off, and mine is part
of theirs.

And 'tis not wholly mine or theirs I think of through the day,
But the great eternal thing we make together, I and they;
Far in the sunset I behold a city that man owns,
Made fair with all their nobler toil, built of my common
stones.

But when the evening comes, indeed, the words have taken
wing,
The thought sings in me still, but I am all too tired to sing;
Therefore, O you, my friend, who serve the world with
minstrelsy,
Among our fellow-workers' songs make that one song for me.

Steel Worker

KATHERINE EDELMAN

Through the ever-rising din
Drive the white-hot rivets in.

On your ledge, a thousand feet
Above a pigmy-crowded street.

Clamp the swinging beams in place,
Sweat and grime upon your face.

Raise the latticed skeleton
Upward to the blistering sun.

Throw your easy, daring strength
Into every measured length.

Whistle—sing—an inch, or two,
Between eternity and you.

God Is at the Anvil

LEW SARETT

God is at the anvil, beating out the sun;
  Where the molten metal spills,
  At His forge among the hills
He has hammered out the glory of a day that's done.

God is at the anvil, welding golden bars;
  In the scarlet-streaming flame
  He is fashioning a frame
For the shimmering silver beauty of the evening stars.

Love for Christ is best shown by the keeping of His commandment "Love one another"; and this love must always include the belief that

There Are No Little People

GEORGE JOHNSON

Few, very few of you will attain unto heights of eminence in this world.

Few, very few of you will be known as outstanding leaders.

Few, very few of you will ever get your picture in the newspapers.

But that is neither here nor there.

The Kingdom of Heaven is like to a leaven which is hid in a measure of meal.

In the days when Tiberius Caesar embodied the glory that was Rome, the world at large was quite unaware of the fact that an obscure individual was wandering through the obscure sections of an obscure land announcing the coming of the Kingdom of God. The purposes of Christ are accomplished for the most part by little people working in little ways.

His power is made perfect in humble homes, in neighborhoods that are not pretentious, by workmen and clerks and stenographers and teachers, by persons who generally are not noticed—not noticed, that is, except for one thing.

They are noticed because there seems to be something different about them, something that is not of this world, something that makes them gentle and kind and good, something that arouses curiosity about the source of their loveliness.

Those who take the trouble to satisfy that curiosity discover that the answer is Jesus Christ.

"There is only one Name under heaven in which men can be saved." This is a fact which remains immutably true. There is only one possible center for the universe of mankind and that center is the Heart of Jesus Christ. The peace that the world can give is at its very best an armistice; lasting peace can be achieved only under the banner of the Prince of Peace. In Him alone will God gather up the things that are scattered. In Him alone can all things be restored.

This Day, O Father, Give Us Daily Bread

FRANCIS JAMMES

Translated from the French by George N. Shuster

This day, O Father, give us daily bread
For without Thee, our wit and goods are sped.

Thou, teaching well, dost superintend the care
Of kneading fingers, crossed as if in prayer,—

And drawest from the breathless worker's sigh
The words of love which halting poets try.

Our Father of Heaven, this humble folk is Thine;
Be for them every one an overseer benign.

Father of harvesters, here is Thy sickle lying—
To Thee like fields of wheat are families, dying.

Father of millers, here is Thy strong mill—
This turning world, the which like grains we fill.

TOWN
of
RALPH SHEPHERD

IIII

On the Highways

A highway is a broad road between one place and another. Here people meet and mingle, move and pass. Perhaps that is why it so often has a look of friendliness. Whatever the reason, a highway greets its wayfarers with an almost challenging gaiety, as if it were saying, "Come with me for a while, and see what a grand time we'll have!"

Some of the earliest English literature tells of this joy of the highway. Geoffrey Chaucer, who wrote the *Canterbury Tales*, knew the pleasantness of highways and the friendliness of people who met upon them. Since his time countless writers have sung happy songs and told vivid stories of the road.

It is in friendliness that the Christian character of the traveler may most readily be seen. The Christian, be he pilgrim, wanderer, or toiler upon the highway, enjoys the road with his fellow men. With them he shares the common experiences of travel and helps them along the way. With them he sees sun, moon, and stars. With them he meets storms. With them he sometimes weeps, but more often he laughs. With them he is twice the man he would be alone.

Nearly all the writers of the road sing of fellowship, for literature portrays, as it should, a vision that shows the highway as something more than a thoroughfare—it tells of a meeting place of pilgrims on their way to eternity.

Blessing for People and Fields

We call upon Thy loving kindness, O God of greatest might, that Thou mayest bathe with the shower of Thy blessing the fruits which, by the tempering of rain and wind, Thou hast deigned to nurture, and grant that this Thy people may always render thanks to Thee for Thy great gifts, that by the fruitfulness of the earth Thou mayest fill with good things running over the souls of those who hunger, and receive from the impoverished one and him who is in need the praise of Thy glorious name. Through Christ our Lord. Amen.

Matthew xiii, 24-30

Another parable he set before them, saying, "The kingdom of heaven is like a man who sowed good seed in his field; but while men were asleep, his enemy came and sowed weeds among the wheat, and went away. And when the blade sprang up and brought forth fruit, then the weeds appeared as well. And the servants of the householder came and said to him, 'Sir, didst thou not sow good seed in thy field? How then does it have weeds?' He said to them, 'An enemy has done this.' And the servants said to him, 'Wilt thou have us go and gather them up?' 'No,' he said, 'lest in gathering the weeds you root up the wheat along with them. Let both grow together until the harvest; and at harvest time I will say to the reapers, Gather up first the weeds, and bind them in bundles to burn; but the wheat gather into my barn.' "

Centuries ago a group of good pious people, driven out of their homeland of Acadia, wandered the highways of the American colonies, seeking new homes. Their tragic story is told in the famous American classic

Evangeline: A Tale of Acadie[1]

HENRY WADSWORTH LONGFELLOW

This is the forest primeval. The murmuring pines and the hemlocks,
Bearded with moss, and in garments green, indistinct in the twilight,
Stand like Druids of eld,[2] with voices sad and prophetic,
Stand like harpers hoar, with beards that rest on their bosoms.
Loud from its rocky caverns, the deep-voiced neighboring ocean
Speaks, and in accents disconsolate answers the wail of the forest.

This is the forest primeval; but where are the hearts that beneath it
Leaped like the roe, when he hears in the woodland the voice of the huntsman?
Where is the thatch-roofed village, the home of Acadian farmers,—
Men whose lives glided on like rivers that water the woodlands,
Darkened by shadows of earth, but reflecting an image of heaven?
Waste are those pleasant farms, and the farmers forever departed!
Scattered like dust and leaves, when the mighty blasts of October
Seize them, and whirl them aloft, and sprinkle them far o'er the ocean,
Naught but tradition remains of the beautiful village of Grand-Pré.[3]

1. *Acadie* (ȧ'kȧ'dē'): the original French name for Nova Scotia. 2. *Druids of eld:* priests of a pagan religious order in ancient Britain. They performed their ceremonies in the forests. 3. *Grand-Pré* (gräɴ'prā'): a village in Nova Scotia.

Ye who believe in affection that hopes, and endures, and is patient,
Ye who believe in the beauty and strength of woman's devotion,
List to the mournful tradition still sung by the pines of the forest;
List to a Tale of Love in Acadie, home of the happy.

In the Acadian land, on the shores of the Basin of Minas,[4]
Distant, secluded, still, the little village of Grand-Pré
Lay in the fruitful valley. Vast meadows stretched to the eastward,
Giving the village its name, and pasture to flocks without number.
Dikes, that the hands of the farmers had raised with labor incessant,
Shut out the turbulent tides; but at stated seasons the flood-gates
Opened, and welcomed the sea to wander at will o'er the meadows.
West and south there were fields of flax, and orchards and cornfields
Spreading afar and unfenced o'er the plain; and away to the northward
Blomidon[5] rose, and the forests old, and aloft on the mountains
Sea fogs pitched their tents, and mists from the mighty Atlantic
Looked on the happy valley, but ne'er from their station descended.
There, in the midst of its farms, reposed the Acadian village.
Strongly built were the houses, with frames of oak and of hemlock,
Such as the peasants of Normandy built in the reign of the Henries.

4. *Basin of Minas* (mī'nȧs): an inlet on the Bay of Fundy in Nova Scotia.
5. *Blomidon* (blŏm'ĭ dŭn): a headland above the Basin of Minas.

Thatched were the roofs, with dormer-windows; and gables projecting
Over the basement below protected and shaded the doorway.
There in the tranquil evenings of summer, when brightly the sunset
Lighted the village street and gilded the vanes on the chimneys,
Matrons and maidens sat in snow-white caps and in kirtles[6]
Scarlet and blue and green, with distaffs spinning the golden
Flax for the gossiping looms, whose noisy shuttles within doors
Mingled their sounds with the whir of the wheels and the songs of the maidens.

6. *kirtles* (kûr′t′lz): women's gowns.

Solemnly down the street came the parish priest, and the children
Paused in their play to kiss the hand he extended to bless them.
Reverend walked he among them; and up rose matrons and maidens,
Hailing his slow approach with words of affectionate welcome.
Then came the laborers home from the field, and serenely the sun sank
Down to his rest, and twilight prevailed. Anon from the belfry
Softly the Angelus sounded, and over the roofs of the village
Columns of pale blue smoke, like clouds of incense ascending,
Rose from a hundred hearths, the homes of peace and contentment.
Thus dwelt together in love these simple Acadian farmers,—
Dwelt in the love of God and of man. Alike were they free from
Fear, that reigns with the tyrant, and envy, the vice of republics.
Neither locks had they to their doors, nor bars to their windows;
But their dwellings were open as day and the hearts of their owners;
There the richest was poor, and the poorest lived in abundance.

Thus, at peace with God and the world, the farmer[7] of Grand-Pré
Lived on his sunny farm, and Evangeline governed his household.
Many a youth, as he knelt in the church and opened his missal,
Fixed his eyes upon her as the saint of his deepest devotion;
Happy was he who might touch her hand or the hem of her garment!

7. *the farmer:* here, Benedict Bellefontaine (bĕl fŏn tăn′), the father of Evangeline.

Many a suitor came to her door, by the darkness befriended,
And, as he knocked and waited to hear the sound of her footsteps,
Knew not which beat the louder, his heart or the knocker of iron;
Or at the joyous feast of the patron saint of the village,
Bolder grew, and pressed her hand in the dance as he whispered
Hurried words of love, that seemed a part of the music.
But, among all who came, young Gabriel only was welcome;
Gabriel Lajeunesse,[8] the son of Basil the blacksmith,
Who was a mighty man in the village, and honored of all men;
For, since the birth of time, throughout all ages and nations,
Has the craft of the smith been held in repute by the people.
Basil was Benedict's friend. Their children from earliest childhood
Grew up together as brother and sister; and Father Felician,
Priest and pedagogue both in the village, had taught them their letters
Out of the selfsame book, with the hymns of the church and the plain-song.
But when the hymn was sung, and the daily lesson completed,
Swiftly they hurried away to the forge of Basil the blacksmith.
There at the door they stood, with wondering eyes to behold him
Take in his leathern lap the hoof of the horse as a plaything,
Nailing the shoe in its place; while near him the tire of the cart-wheel
Lay like a fiery snake, coiled round in a circle of cinders.
Oft on autumnal eves, when without in the gathering darkness
Bursting with light seemed the smithy, through every cranny and crevice,
Warm by the forge within they watched the laboring bellows,
And as its panting ceased, and the sparks expired in the ashes,

8. *Lajeunesse* (lä zhû nĕ̆s′).

Merrily laughed, and said they were nuns going into the chapel.
Oft on sledges in winter, as swift as the swoop of the eagle,
Down the hillside bounding, they glided away o'er the meadow.
Oft in the barns they climbed to the populous nests on the rafters,
Seeking with eager eyes that wondrous stone,[9] which the swallow
Brings from the shore of the sea to restore the sight of its fledglings;
Lucky was he who found that stone in the nest of the swallow!
Thus passed a few swift years, and they no longer were children.
He was a valiant youth, and his face, like the face of the morning,
Gladdened the earth with its light, and ripened thought into action.
She was a woman now, with the heart and hopes of a woman.
"Sunshine of Saint Eulalie"[10] was she called; for that was the sunshine
Which, as the farmers believed, would load their orchards with apples;
She, too, would bring to her husband's house delight and abundance,
Filling it full of love and the ruddy faces of children.

Pleasantly rose next morn the sun on the village of Grand-Pré.
Pleasantly gleamed in the soft, sweet air the Basin of Minas,
Where the ships, with their wavering shadows, were riding at anchor.
Life had long been astir in the village, and clamorous labor

9. *wondrous stone:* a mythical charm. 10. *Saint Eulalie* (û'lȧ'lē'): refers to the superstition that on Saint Eulalie's Day, February 12, a rich harvest of apples would be assured if the sun shone.

Knocked with its hundred hands at the golden gates of the morning.
Now from the country around, from the farms and neighboring hamlets,
Came in their holiday dresses the blithe Acadian peasants.
Many a glad good-morrow and jocund laugh from the young folk
Made the bright air brighter, as up from the numerous meadows,
Where no path could be seen but the track of wheels in the greensward,
Group after group appeared, and joined, or passed on the highway.
Long ere noon, in the village all sounds of labor were silenced.
Thronged were the streets with people; and noisy groups at the house doors
Sat in the cheerful sun, and rejoiced and gossiped together.
Every house was an inn, where all were welcomed and feasted;
For with this simple people, who lived like brothers together,
All things were held in common, and what one had was another's.
Yet under Benedict's roof hospitality seemed more abundant:
For Evangeline stood among the guests of her father;
Bright was her face with smiles, and words of welcome and gladness
Fell from her beautiful lips, and blessed the cup as she gave it.

Under the open sky, in the odorous air of the orchard,
Stripped of its golden fruit, was spread the feast of betrothal.
There in the shade of the porch were the priest and the notary seated;
There good Benedict sat, and sturdy Basil the blacksmith.
Not far withdrawn from these, by the cider-press and the beehives,
Michael the fiddler was placed, with the gayest of hearts and of waistcoats.

Shadow and light from the leaves alternately played on his snow-white
Hair, as it waved in the wind; and the jolly face of the fiddler
Glowed like a living coal when the ashes are blown from the embers.
Gayly the old man sang to the vibrant sound of his fiddle,
Tous les Bourgeois de Chartres,[11] and *Le Carillon de Dunquerque,*[12]
And anon with his wooden shoes beat time to the music.
Merrily, merrily whirled the wheels of the dizzying dances
Under the orchard trees and down the path to the meadows;
Old folk and young together, and children mingled among them.
Fairest of all the maids was Evangeline, Benedict's daughter!
Noblest of all the youths was Gabriel, son of the blacksmith!

So passed the morning away. And lo! with a summons sonorous
Sounded the bell from its tower, and over the meadows a drum beat.
Thronged erelong was the church with men. Without, in the churchyard,
Waited the women. They stood by the graves, and hung on the headstones
Garlands of autumn leaves and evergreens fresh from the forest.
Then came the guard from the ships, and marching proudly among them
Entered the sacred portal. With loud and dissonant clangor
Echoed the sound of their brazen drums from ceiling and casement,—
Echoed a moment only, and slowly the ponderous portal
Closed, and in silence the crowd awaited the will of the soldiers.
Then uprose their commander, and spake from the steps of the altar,

11. *Tous les Bourgeois de Chartres* (tōō lā bōōr zhwȧh′ dē shȧr′ tr): "All the Citizens of Chartres," a popular dance tune. 12. *Le Carillon de Dunquerque* (lĕ kȧ′rē′yôɴ′ dē dûɴ′ kĕrk): "The Bells of Dunkirk," a dance tune.

Holding aloft in his hands, with its seals, the royal commission.
"You are convened this day," he said, "by his Majesty's orders.
Clement and kind has he been; but how you have answered his kindness,
Let your own hearts reply! To my natural make and my temper
Painful the task is I do, which to you I know must be grievous.
Yet must I bow and obey, and deliver the will of our monarch;
Namely, that all your lands, and dwellings, and cattle of all kinds
Forfeited be to the crown; and that you yourselves from this province
Be transported to other lands. God grant you may dwell there
Ever as faithful subjects, a happy and peaceable people!
Prisoners now I declare you; for such is his Majesty's pleasure!"
As, when the air is serene in the sultry solstice of summer,[13]
Suddenly gathers a storm, and the deadly sling of the hailstones
Beats down the farmer's corn in the field and shatters his windows,
Hiding the sun, and strewing the ground with thatch from the house roofs,
Bellowing fly the herds, and seek to break their enclosures;
So on the hearts of the people descended the words of the speaker.
Silent a moment they stood in speechless wonder, and then rose
Louder and ever louder a wail of sorrow and anger,
And, by one impulse moved, they madly rushed to the doorway.
Vain was the hope of escape; and cries and fierce imprecations

13. *solstice of summer:* the longest day of the year, June 21.

Rang through the house of prayer; and high o'er the heads of the others
Rose, with his arms uplifted, the figure of Basil the blacksmith,
As, on a stormy sea, a spar is tossed by the billows.
Flushed was his face and distorted with passion; and wildly he shouted,—
"Down with the tyrants of England! we never have sworn them allegiance!
Death to these foreign soldiers, who seize on our homes and our harvests!"
More he fain would have said, but the merciless hand of a soldier
Smote him upon the mouth, and dragged him down to the pavement.

In the midst of the strife and tumult of angry contention,
Lo! the door of the chancel opened, and Father Felician
Entered, with serious mien, and ascended the steps of the altar.
Raising his reverend hand, with a gesture he awed into silence

All that clamorous throng; and thus he spake to his people;
Deep were his tones and solemn; in accents measured and mournful
Spake he, as, after the tocsin's[14] alarm, distinctly the clock strikes.
"What is this that ye do, my children? what madness has seized you?
Forty years of my life have I labored among you, and taught you,
Not in word alone, but in deed, to love one another!
Is this the fruit of my toils, of my vigils and prayers and privations?
Have you so soon forgotten all lessons of love and forgiveness?
This is the house of the Prince of Peace, and would you profane it
Thus with violent deeds and hearts overflowing with hatred?
Lo! where the crucified Christ from his cross is gazing upon you!
See! in those sorrowful eyes what meekness and holy compassion!
Hark! how those lips still repeat the prayer, 'O Father, forgive them!'
Let us repeat the prayer in the hour when the wicked assail us,
Let us repeat it now, and say, 'O Father, forgive them!' "
Few were his words of rebuke, but deep in the hearts of his people
Sank they, and sobs of contrition succeeded the passionate outbreak,
While they repeated his prayer, and said, "O Father, forgive them!"

Then came the evening service. The tapers gleamed from the altar.
Fervent and deep was the voice of the priest, and the people responded,
Not with their lips alone, but their hearts; and the *Ave Maria*

14. *tocsin* (tŏk′sĭn): an alarm bell or warning signal.

Sang they, and fell on their knees, and their souls, with devotion translated,
Rose on the ardor of prayer, like Elijah[15] ascending to heaven.

Meanwhile had spread in the village the tidings of ill, and on all sides
Wandered, wailing, from house to house the women and children.
Long at her father's door Evangeline stood, with her right hand
Shielding her eyes from the level rays of the sun, that, descending,
Lighted the village street with mysterious splendor, and roofed each
Peasant's cottage with golden thatch, and emblazoned its windows.
Long within had been spread the snow-white cloth on the table;
There stood the wheaten loaf, and the honey fragrant with wild-flowers;
There stood the tankard of ale, and the cheese fresh brought from the dairy;
And, at the head of the board, the great arm-chair of the farmer.
Thus did Evangeline wait at her father's door, as the sunset
Threw the long shadows of trees o'er the broad ambrosial meadows.
Ah! on her spirit within a deeper shadow had fallen,
And from the fields of her soul a fragrance celestial ascended,—
Charity, meekness, love, and hope, and forgiveness, and patience!
Then, all forgetful of self, she wandered into the village,
Cheering with looks and words the mournful hearts of the women,

15. *Elijah:* a prophet of the Old Testament who was carried up to Heaven in a chariot of fire.

As o'er the darkening fields with lingering steps they departed,
Urged by their household cares, and the weary feet of their children.
Down sank the great red sun, and in golden, glimmering vapors
Veiled the light of his face, like the Prophet descending from Sinai.[16]
Sweetly over the village the bell of the Angelus sounded.

(On the fifth day the orders of the king were carried out, and the Acadians were put on transports that would scatter them far and wide over the continent of North America. In the confusion of embarkation families were separated. Gabriel and his father Basil were carried to separate ships, "while in despair on the shore Evangeline stood with her father." That night the village was set on fire, and Evangeline's father, heartbroken, died.

The years passed, and Evangeline, in the company of Father Felician, had wandered far and wide searching for Gabriel, her betrothed. They at last reached Louisiana where they found Basil the blacksmith, only to learn that Gabriel had that very day left on a trapping and trading trip to the west.

Early the next morning Evangeline and Basil departed, hoping to catch Gabriel. On and on they went into the heart of the Indian country, hearing of Gabriel but never catching up with him. At a Jesuit mission the good priest told Evangeline that only six days before Gabriel had sat in the very spot where she was now sitting. He had pushed on to the north, but would return to the mission in the autumn. Evangeline, sad and weary, begged to be allowed to stay at the mission to await Gabriel's return.)

16. *Prophet · · · Sinai* (sī'nī): Moses, the Prophet, who brought down the Ten Commandments from Mount Sinai.

Slowly, slowly, slowly the days succeeded each other,—
Days and weeks and months; and the fields of maize that were springing
Green from the ground when a stranger she came, now waving above her,
Lifted their slender shafts, with leaves interlacing, and forming
Cloisters for mendicant[17] crows and granaries pillaged by squirrels.
Then in the golden weather the maize was husked, and the maidens
Blushed at each blood-red ear, for that betokened a lover,
But at the crooked laughed, and called it a thief in the cornfield.
Even the blood-red ear to Evangeline brought not her lover.
"Patience!" the priest would say; "have faith, and thy prayer will be answered!
Look at this vigorous plant that lifts its head from the meadow,
See how its leaves are turned to the north, as true as the magnet;

17. *mendicant:* begging.

This is the compass-flower, that the finger of God has planted
Here in the houseless wild, to direct the traveler's journey
Over the sealike, pathless, limitless waste of the desert.
Such in the soul of man is faith. The blossoms of passion,
Gay and luxuriant flowers, are brighter and fuller of fragrance,
But they beguile us, and lead us astray, and their odor is deadly.
Only this humble plant can guide us here, and hereafter
Crown us with asphodel[18] flowers, that are wet with the dews of nepenthe."[19]

So came the autumn, and passed, and the winter,—yet Gabriel came not;
Blossomed the opening spring, and the notes of the robin and bluebird
Sounded sweet upon wold and in wood, yet Gabriel came not.
But on the breath of the summer winds a rumor was wafted
Sweeter than song of bird, or hue or odor of blossom.
Far to the north and east, it said, in the Michigan forests,
Gabriel had his lodge by the banks of the Saginaw River.
And, with returning guides, that sought the lakes of St. Lawrence,
Saying a sad farewell, Evangeline went from the Mission.
When over weary ways, by long and perilous marches,
She had attained at length the depths of the Michigan forests,
Found she the hunter's lodge deserted and fallen to ruin!

Thus did the long sad years glide on, and in seasons and places
Divers and distant far were seen the wandering maiden;—
Now in the Tents of Grace of the meek Moravian[20] Missions,
Now in the noisy camps and the battlefields of the army,
Now in secluded hamlets, in towns and populous cities.
Like a phantom she came, and passed away unremembered.

18. *asphodel* (ăs′ fō dĕl): used by early French poets to describe the daffodil.
19. *nepenthe* (nē pĕn′thē): a drug used by the ancients to give forgetfulness of pain or sorrow.
20. *Moravian:* a religious sect of eastern Pennsylvania.

Fair was she and young, when in hope began the long journey;
Faded was she and old, when in disappointment it ended.
Each succeeding year stole something away from her beauty,
Leaving behind it, broader and deeper, the gloom and the shadow.
Then there appeared and spread faint streaks of gray o'er her forehead,
Dawn of another life, that broke o'er her earthly horizon,
As in the eastern sky the first faint streaks of the morning.

In that delightful land which is washed by the Delaware's waters,
Guarding in sylvan shades the name of Penn the apostle,
Stands on the banks of its beautiful stream the city he founded.[21]
There all the air is balm, and the peach is the emblem of beauty,
And the streets still re-echo the names of the trees of the forest,
As if they fain would appease the Dryads[22] whose haunts they molested.
There from the troubled sea had Evangeline landed, an exile,
Finding among the children of Penn a home and a country.
There old René Leblanc[23] had died; and when he departed,
Saw at his side only one of all his hundred descendants.
Something at least there was in the friendly streets of the city,
Something that spake to her heart, and made her no longer a stranger;
And her ear was pleased with the Thee and Thou of the Quakers,
For it recalled the past, the old Acadian country,
Where all men were equal, and all were brothers and sisters.

21. *city he founded:* Philadelphia, founded by William Penn. 22. *Dryads* (drī'-ădz): wood nymphs. 23. *René Leblanc* (rĕ nā' lē blăɴ'): one of the Acadians who had settled in Pennsylvania.

So, when the fruitless search, the disappointed endeavor,
Ended, to recommence no more upon earth, uncomplaining,
Thither, as leaves to the light, were turned her thoughts and her footsteps.
As from the mountain's top the rainy mists of the morning
Roll away, and afar we behold the landscape below us,
Sun-illumined, with shining rivers and cities and hamlets,
So fell the mists from her mind, and she saw the world far below her,
Dark no longer, but all illumined with love; and the pathway
Which she had climbed so far, lying smooth and fair in the distance.
Gabriel was not forgotten. Within her heart was his image,
Clothed in the beauty of love and youth, as last she beheld him,
Only more beautiful made by his deathlike silence and absence.
Into her thoughts of him time entered not, for it was not.
Over him years had no power; he was not changed, but transfigured;
He had become to her heart as one who is dead, and not absent;
Patience and abnegation of self, and devotion to others,
This was the lesson a life of trial and sorrow had taught her.
So was her love diffused, but, like to some odorous spices,
Suffered no waste nor loss, though filling the air with aroma.
Other hope had she none, nor wish in life, but to follow
Meekly, with reverent steps, the sacred feet of her Saviour.
Thus many years she lived as a Sister of Mercy[24]; frequenting
Lonely and wretched roofs in the crowded lanes of the city,
Where distress and want concealed themselves from the sunlight,
Where disease and sorrow in garrets languished neglected.

24. *Sister of Mercy:* the Sisters of this order did not come to the United States until a much later date. Perhaps Evangeline served as a lay worker of mercy in the almshouse in Philadelphia during these later years of exile.

Night after night, when the world was asleep, as the watchman repeated
Loud, through the gusty streets, that all was well in the city,
High at some lonely window he saw the light of her taper.
Day after day, in the gray of the dawn, as slow through the suburbs
Plodded the German farmer, with flowers and fruits for the market,
Met he that meek, pale face, returning home from its watchings.

Then it came to pass that a pestilence fell on the city,
Presaged by wondrous signs, and mostly by flocks of wild pigeons,
Darkening the sun in their flight, with naught in their craws but an acorn.
And, as the tides of the sea arise in the month of September,
Flooding some silver stream, till it spreads to a lake in the meadow,
So death flooded life, and, o'erflowing its natural margin,
Spread to a brackish lake, the silver stream of existence.
Wealth had no power to bribe, nor beauty to charm, the oppressor;
But all perished alike beneath the scourge of his anger;—
Only, alas! the poor, who had neither friends nor attendants,
Crept away to die in the almshouse, home of the homeless.
Then in the suburbs it stood, in the midst of meadows and woodlands;—
Now the city surrounds it; but still, with its gateway and wicket
Meek, in the midst of splendor, its humble walls seem to echo
Softly the words of the Lord: "The poor ye always have with you."
Thither, by night and by day, came the Sister of Mercy. The dying
Looked up into her face, and thought, indeed, to behold there
Gleams of celestial light encircle her forehead with splendor,
Such as the artist paints o'er the brows of saints and apostles,

Or such as hangs by night o'er a city seen at a distance.
Unto their eyes it seemed the lamps of the city celestial,
Into whose shining gates erelong their spirits would enter.

Thus, on a Sabbath morn, through the streets, deserted and silent,
Wending her quiet way, she entered the door of the almshouse.
Sweet on the summer air was the odor of flowers in the garden;
And she paused on her way to gather the fairest among them,
That the dying once more might rejoice in their fragrance and beauty.
Then, as she mounted the stairs to the corridors, cooled by the east wind,
Distant and soft on her ear fell the chimes from the belfry of Christ Church,
While, intermingled with these, across the meadows were wafted
Sounds of psalms, that were sung by the Swedes in their church at Wicaco.

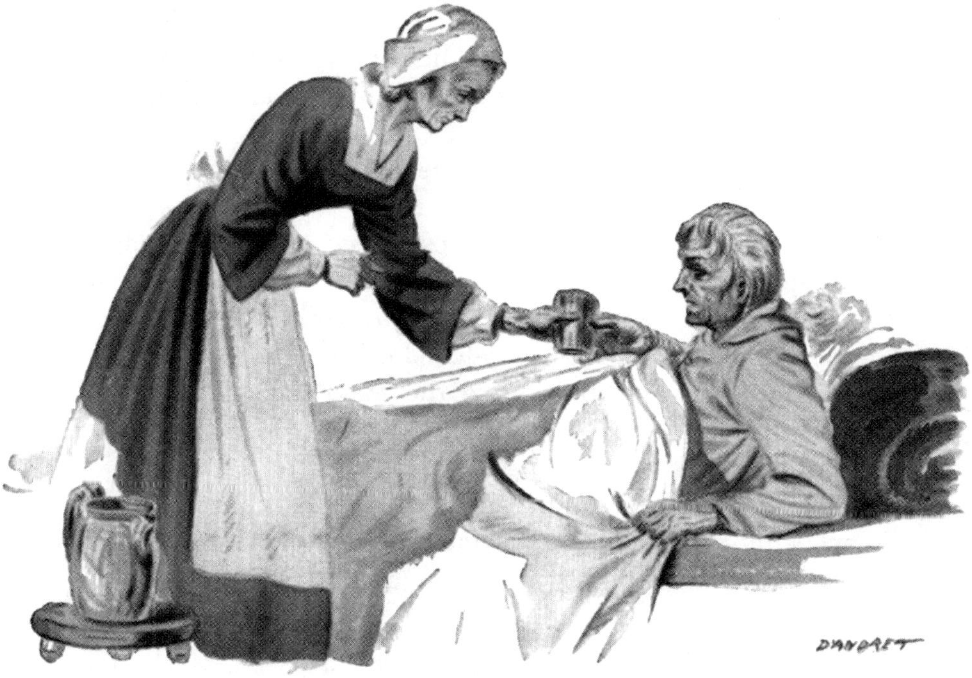

Soft as descending wings fell the calm of the hour on her spirit;
Something within her said, "At length thy trials are ended";
And, with light in her looks, she entered the chambers of sickness.
Noiselessly moved about the assiduous, careful attendants,
Moistening the feverish lip, and the aching brow, and in silence
Closing the sightless eyes of the dead, and concealing their faces,
Where on their pallets they lay, like drifts of snow by the roadside.
Many a languid head, upraised as Evangeline entered,
Turned on its pillow of pain to gaze while she passed, for her presence
Fell on their hearts like a ray of the sun on the walls of a prison.
And, as she looked around, she saw how Death, the consoler,
Laying his hand upon many a heart, had healed it forever.
Many familiar forms had disappeared in the night time;
Vacant their places were, or filled already by strangers.

Suddenly, as if arrested by fear or a feeling of wonder,
Still she stood, with her colorless lips apart, while a shudder
Ran through her frame, and, forgotten, the flowerets dropped from her fingers,
And from her eyes and cheeks the light and bloom of the morning.
Then there escaped from her lips a cry of such terrible anguish,
That the dying heard it, and started up from their pillows.
On the pallet before her was stretched the form of an old man,
Long, and thin, and gray were the locks that shaded his temples;
But, as he lay in the morning light, his face for a moment
Seemed to assume once more the forms of its earlier manhood;
So are wont to be changed the faces of those who are dying.
Hot and red on his lips still burned the flush of the fever,

As if life, like the Hebrew, with blood[25] had besprinkled its portals,
That the Angel of Death might see the sign, and pass over.
Motionless, senseless, dying, he lay, and his spirit exhausted
Seemed to be sinking down through infinite depths in the darkness,
Darkness of slumber and death, forever sinking and sinking.
Then through those realms of shade, in multiplied reverberations,
Heard he that cry of pain, and through the hush that succeeded
Whispered a gentle voice, in accents tender and saintlike,
"Gabriel! O my beloved!" and died away into silence.
Then he beheld, in a dream, once more the home of his childhood;
Green Acadian meadows, with sylvan rivers among them,
Village, and mountain, and woodlands; and, walking under their shadow,
As in the days of her youth, Evangeline rose in his vision.
Tears came into his eyes; and as slowly he lifted his eyelids,
Vanished the vision away, but Evangeline knelt by his bedside.
Vainly he strove to whisper her name, for the accents unuttered
Died on his lips, and their motion revealed what his tongue would have spoken.
Vainly he strove to rise; and Evangeline, kneeling beside him,
Kissed his dying lips, and laid his head on her bosom.
Sweet was the light of his eyes; but it suddenly sank into darkness,
As when a lamp is blown out by a gust of wind at a casement.

All was ended now, the hope, and the fear, and the sorrow,
All the aching of heart, the restless, unsatisfied longing,
All the dull, deep pain, and constant anguish of patience!
And, as she pressed once more the lifeless head to her bosom,

25. *with blood:* symbolic of the slaughtered lamb offered by the Israelites at the time of their exodus from Egypt. Then Moses instructed them to smear the outer door posts of their dwellings with the blood of sacrifice so that the destroying Angel of Death would spare them.

Meekly she bowed her own, and murmured, "Father, I thank
Thee!"

Still stands the forest primeval; but far away from its shadow,
Side by side, in their nameless graves, the lovers are sleeping.
Under the humble walls of the little Catholic churchyard,
In the heart of the city, they lie, unknown and unnoticed.
Daily the tides of life go ebbing and flowing beside them,
Thousands of throbbing hearts, where theirs are at rest and
forever, 409
Thousands of aching brains, where theirs no longer are busy,
Thousands of toiling hands, where theirs have ceased from
their labors,
Thousands of weary feet, where theirs have completed their
journey!

Abridged

HELPS FOR DISCUSSION

1. Why were the Acadians expelled from their own country? When did this occur? Locate on a map the headland of Blomidon above the Bay of Fundy.

2. Describe life in Grand Pre, telling of the men's work, the women's work, the children's schooling, fun and holiday amusements. Read lines from the poem to point your descriptions.

3. Describe the religious life of the Acadians. Read lines to show Father Felician's teachings and his influence over his people.

4. Through what regions had Evangeline journeyed in her search? What must have been the hardships of her wanderings? Where were the lovers reunited?

THINGS TO DO

1. Tell or write an imaginative story of Gabriel's search for Evangeline. If you prefer, compose a stanza in the meter of the poem relating one incident in his wanderings.

2. Make a pictorial map of Evangeline's journeys. Color your map attractively. Leave wide margins in which to write expressions quoted from the poem. Connect these with places on the map.

3. Conduct a quotation quiz. Pupils may quote passages from the poem, asking others to identify scenes and events.

4. Examine the illustrations on pages 119–135. Show what ideas the artist gained from the poem. Sketch an original illustration.

Influences

JOHN BANISTER TABB

Each separate life is fed
From many a fountain-head;
  Tides that we never know
  Into our being flow,
And rays of the remotest star
Converge to make us what we are.

The Bridge

JOHN BANISTER TABB

O that, all strife above,
Strong in the strength thereof
  Man evermore
Built with a broader span
Love for his fellow-man
  From shore to shore!

To a Waterfowl

WILLIAM CULLEN BRYANT

  Whither, midst falling dew,
While glow the heavens with the last steps of day,
Far, through their rosy depths, dost thou pursue
  Thy solitary way?

  Vainly the fowler's eye
Might mark thy distant flight to do thee wrong
As, darkly seen against the crimson sky,
  Thy figure floats along.

  Seek'st thou the plashy brink
Of weedy lake, or marge of river wide,
Or where the rocking billows rise and sink
  On the chafed ocean-side?

There is a Power whose care
Teaches thy way along that pathless coast—
The desert and illimitable air—
Lone wandering, but not lost.

All day thy wings have fanned,
At that far height, the cold, thin atmosphere,
Yet stoop not, weary, to the welcome land,
Though the dark night is near.

And soon that toil shall end;
Soon shalt thou find a summer home, and rest,
And scream among thy fellows; reeds shall bend,
Soon, o'er thy sheltered nest.

Thou'rt gone, the abyss of heaven
Hath swallowed up thy form; yet, on my heart
Deeply hath sunk the lesson thou hast given,
And shall not soon depart.

He who, from zone to zone,
Guides through the boundless sky thy certain flight,
In the long way that I must tread alone,
Will lead my steps aright.

HELPS FOR DISCUSSION

Explain the spiritual message of each of the poems on pages 139-140. Memorize the poem that you like best.

Ichabod Crane! His long, lanky figure has passed before the eyes of countless boys and girls as they have learned of him and his neighbors in the reading of a great American classic,

The Legend of Sleepy Hollow

WASHINGTON IRVING

I. *Sleepy Hollow*

In the bosom of one of those spacious coves which indent the eastern shore of the Hudson, at that broad expansion of the river denominated[1] by the ancient Dutch navigators the Tappan Zee, and where they always prudently shortened sail and implored the protection of St. Nicholas when they crossed, there lies a small market town or rural port, which by some is called Greensburgh, but which is more generally and properly known by the name of Tarrytown. This name was given, we are told, in former days by the good housewives of the adjacent country, from the inveterate propensity[2] of their husbands to linger about the village tavern on market days. Be that as it may, I do not vouch for the fact, but merely advert to it, for the sake of being precise and authentic. Not far from this village, perhaps about two miles, there is a little valley, or rather lap of land, among high hills, which is one of the quietest places in the whole world. A small brook glides through it with just murmur enough to lull one to repose, and the occasional whistle of a quail or tapping of a woodpecker is almost the only sound that ever breaks in upon the uniform tranquillity.

From the listless repose of the place and the peculiar character of its inhabitants, who are descendants from the original Dutch settlers, this sequestered glen has long been known by the name of "Sleepy Hollow," and its rustic lads are called the "Sleepy Hollow Boys" throughout all the neighboring country. A drowsy, dreamy influence seems to hang over the land and to pervade the very atmosphere. Some say that the place was bewitched by a high German doctor during the early days of the settlement; others, that an old Indian chief,

1. *denominated:* named. 2. *inveterate propensity:* habitual inclination.

the prophet or wizard of his tribe, held his powwows there before the country was discovered by Master Hendrick Hudson. Certain it is, the place still continues under the sway of some witching power that holds a spell over the minds of the good people, causing them to walk in a continual reverie. They are given to all kinds of marvelous beliefs, are subject to trances and visions, and frequently see strange sights, and hear music and voices in the air. The whole neighborhood abounds with local tales, haunted spots, and twilight superstitions; stars shoot and meteors glare oftener across the valley than in any other part of the country, and the nightmare seems to make it the favorite scene of her gambols.

The dominant spirit, however, that haunts this enchanted region, and seems to be commander-in-chief of all the powers of the air, is the apparition of a figure on horseback without a head. It is said by some to be the ghost of a Hessian trooper[3] whose head had been carried away by a cannon ball, in some nameless battle during the Revolutionary War, and who is ever and anon seen by the country folk hurrying along in the gloom of night, as if on the wings of the wind. His haunts are not confined to the valley, but extend at times to the adjacent roads, and especially to the vicinity of a church at no great distance. Indeed, certain of the most authentic historians of those parts, who have been careful in collecting and collating[4] the floating facts concerning this specter, allege that the body of the trooper having been buried in the churchyard, the ghost rides forth to the scene of battle in nightly quest of his head; and that the rushing speed with which he sometimes passes along the Hollow, like a midnight blast, is owing to his being belated and in a hurry to get back to the churchyard before daybreak.

Such is the general purport of this legendary superstition which has furnished materials for many a wild story in that region of shadows, and the specter is known at all the country firesides by the name of the Headless Horseman of Sleepy Hollow.

3. *Hessian trooper:* one of the German soldiers hired by the British. 4. *collating:* comparing critically.

II. *Ichabod Crane*

In this by-place of nature there abode, in a remote period of American history,—that is to say, some thirty years since,—a worthy wight[5] by the name of Ichabod Crane, who sojourned, or, as he expressed it, "tarried," in Sleepy Hollow for the purpose of instructing the children of the vicinity. He was a native of Connecticut, a state which supplies the Union with pioneers for the mind as well as for the forest, and sends forth yearly its legions of frontier woodsmen and country schoolmasters. The cognomen[6] of Crane was not inapplicable to his person. He was tall, but exceedingly lank, with narrow shoulders, long arms and legs, hands that dangled a mile out of his sleeves, feet that might have served for shovels, and his whole frame most loosely hung together. His head was small, and flat at top, with huge ears, large green glassy eyes, and a long snipe nose, so that it looked like a weathercock perched upon his spindle neck to tell which way the wind blew. To see him striding along the profile of a

5. *wight:* person. 6. *cognomen:* surname.

hill on a windy day with his clothes bagging and fluttering about him, one might have mistaken him for the genius[7] of famine descending upon the earth, or some scarecrow eloped from a cornfield.

His schoolhouse was a low building of one large room, rudely constructed of logs, the windows partly glazed, and partly patched with leaves of old copy-books. It was most ingeniously secured at vacant hours by a withe[8] twisted in the handle of the door and stakes set against the window shutters; so that, though a thief might get in with perfect ease, he would find some embarrassment in getting out—an idea most probably borrowed by the architect, Yost Van Houten, from the mystery of an eelpot.[9] The schoolhouse stood in a rather lonely but pleasant situation just at the foot of a woody hill, with a brook running close by, and a formidable birch tree growing at one end of it. From hence the low murmur of his pupils' voices conning over their lessons might be heard in a drowsy summer's day, like the hum of a beehive, interrupted now and then by the authoritative voice of the master in the tone of menace or command; or, peradventure, by the appalling sound of the birch, as he urged some tardy loiterer along the flowery path of knowledge. Truth to say, he was a conscientious man, and ever bore in mind the golden maxim, "Spare the rod and spoil the child." Ichabod Crane's scholars certainly were not spoiled.

But when school hours were over he was the companion and playmate of the larger boys, and on holiday afternoons would convoy some of the smaller ones home, who happened to have pretty sisters, or good housewives for mothers noted for the comforts of the cupboard. Indeed, it behooved him to keep on good terms with his pupils. The revenue arising from his school was small, and would have been scarcely sufficient to furnish him with daily bread,—for he was a huge feeder, and though lank, had the dilating powers of an anaconda,[10]—but to help out his maintenance, he was, according

7. *genius:* spirit. 8. *withe:* a flexible twig. 9. *eelpot:* a trap for eels so devised that once the eels enter the trap they cannot escape. 10. *anaconda:* a large snake which can eat tremendous quantities of food.

to country custom in those parts, boarded and lodged at the houses of the farmers whose children he instructed. With these he lived successively a week at a time, thus going the rounds of the neighborhood, with all his worldly effects tied up in a cotton handkerchief.

In addition to his other vocations he was singing-master of the neighborhood, and picked up many bright shillings by instructing the young folk in psalmody.[11] It was a matter of no little vanity to him on Sundays to take his station in front of the church gallery with a band of chosen singers where, in his own mind, he completely carried away the palm from the parson. Certain it is, his voice resounded far above all the rest of the congregation; and there are peculiar quavers still to be heard in that church, and which may even be heard half a mile off, quite to the opposite side of the mill pond, on a still Sunday morning, which are said to be legitimately descended from the nose of Ichabod Crane. Thus, by divers little makeshifts in that ingenious way which is commonly denominated "by hook and by crook," the worthy pedagogue got on tolerably enough, and was thought, by all who understood nothing of the labor of headwork, to have a wonderfully easy life of it.

The schoolmaster is generally a man of some importance in the female circle of a rural neighborhood, being considered a kind of idle, gentlemanlike personage, of vastly superior taste and accomplishments to the rough country swains, and, indeed, inferior in learning only to the parson. His appearance, therefore, is apt to occasion some little stir at the tea table of a farmhouse and the addition of a supernumerary dish of cakes or sweetmeats, or peradventure, the parade of a silver teapot. Our man of letters, therefore, was peculiarly happy in the smiles of all the country damsels. How he would figure among them in the churchyard between services on Sundays! gathering grapes for them from the wild vines that overran the surrounding trees, reciting for their amusement all the epitaphs on the tombstones, or sauntering with a whole bevy of them along the banks of the adjacent mill pond,

11. *psalmody:* the art of singing psalms.

while the more bashful country bumpkins hung sheepishly back, envying his superior elegance and address.

From his half-itinerant life, also, he was a kind of traveling gazette, carrying the whole budget of local gossip from house to house, so that his appearance was always greeted with satisfaction. He was, moreover, esteemed by the women as a man of great erudition, for he had read several books quite through, and was a perfect master of Cotton Mather's[12] *History of New England Witchcraft*, in which, by the way, he most firmly and potently believed.

He was, in fact, an odd mixture of small shrewdness and simple credulity. His appetite for the marvelous and his powers of digesting it were equally extraordinary, and both had been increased by his residence in this spellbound region. No tale was too gross or monstrous for his capacious swallow.

Another of his sources of fearful pleasure was to pass long winter evenings with the old Dutch wives as they sat spinning by the fire, with a row of apples roasting and spluttering along the hearth, and listen to their marvelous tales of ghosts and goblins and haunted fields and haunted brooks and haunted bridges and haunted houses, and particularly of the headless horseman, or galloping Hessian of the Hollow, as they sometimes called him. He would delight them equally by his anecdotes of witchcraft and of the direful omens and portentous sights and sounds in the air which prevailed in the earlier times of Connecticut, and would frighten them woefully with speculations upon comets and shooting stars, and with the alarming fact that the world did absolutely turn round, and that they were half the time topsy-turvy!

III. *Katrina Van Tassel and Her Home*

Among the musical disciples who assembled one evening in each week to receive his instructions in psalmody was Katrina Van Tassel, the daughter and only child of a substantial Dutch farmer. She was a blooming lass of fresh eighteen, plump as a partridge, ripe and melting and rosy-

12. *Cotton Mather (1663–1728)*: a New England clergyman and writer.

cheeked as one of her father's peaches, and universally famed, not merely for her beauty, but her vast expectations. She was withal a little of a coquette, as might be perceived even in her dress, which was a mixture of ancient and modern fashions, as most suited to set off her charms. She wore the ornaments of pure yellow gold which her great-great-grandmother had brought over from Saardam,[13] the tempting stomacher[14] of the olden time, and withal a provokingly short petticoat, to display the prettiest foot and ankle in the country round.

Ichabod Crane had a soft and foolish heart toward the sex, and it is not to be wondered at that so tempting a morsel soon found favor in his eyes, more especially after he had visited her in her paternal mansion. Old Baltus Van Tassel was a perfect picture of a thriving, contented, liberal-hearted farmer. He seldom, it is true, sent either his eyes or his thoughts beyond the boundaries of his own farm, but within those everything was snug, happy, and well-conditioned. He was satisfied with his wealth, but not proud of it; and piqued[15] himself upon the hearty abundance rather than the style in which he lived. His stronghold was situated on the banks of the Hudson, in one of those green, sheltered, fertile nooks in which the Dutch farmers are so fond of nestling. A great elm tree spread its broad branches over it, at the foot of which bubbled up a spring of the softest and sweetest water in a little well formed of a barrel, and then stole sparkling away through the grass to a neighboring brook, that bubbled along among alders and dwarf willows. Hard by the farmhouse was a vast barn that might have served for a church, every window and crevice of which seemed bursting forth with the treasures of the farm. The flail was busily resounding within it from morning to night, swallows and martins skimmed twittering about the eaves, and rows of pigeons, some with one eye turned up as if watching the weather, some with their heads under their wings or buried in their bosoms, and others swelling and cooing and bowing about their dames,

13. *Saardam* (sär'dâm): a town in Holland. 14. *stomacher:* an ornamental bodice. 15. *piqued:* prided.

were enjoying the sunshine on the roof. Sleek, unwieldy porkers were grunting in the repose and abundance of their pens, whence sallied forth, now and then, troops of sucking pigs, as if to snuff the air. A stately squadron of snowy geese were riding in an adjoining pond, convoying whole fleets of ducks; regiments of turkeys were gobbling through the farm-yard, and guinea fowls fretting about it, like ill-tempered housewives, with their peevish, discontented cry. Before the barn-door strutted the gallant cock, that pattern of a husband, a warrior, and a fine gentleman, clapping his burnished wings and crowing in the pride and gladness of his heart, sometimes tearing up the earth with his feet and then generously calling his ever-hungry family of wives and children to enjoy the rich morsel which he had discovered.

The pedagogue's mouth watered as he looked upon this sumptuous promise of luxurious winter fare. In his devouring mind's eye, he pictured to himself every roasting pig running about with a pudding in his belly and an apple in his mouth; the pigeons were snugly put to bed in a comfortable pie and tucked in with a coverlet of crust; the geese were swimming in their own gravy; and the ducks pairing cozily in dishes, with a decent competency of onion sauce. In the porkers he saw carved out the future sleek side of bacon and juicy relishing ham; not a turkey but he beheld daintily trussed up with its gizzard under its wing, and peradventure, a necklace of savory sausages; and even bright chanticleer himself lay sprawling on his back in a side-dish, with uplifted claws, as if craving that quarter[16] which his chivalrous spirit disdained to ask while living.

As the enraptured Ichabod fancied all this, and as he rolled his great green eyes over the fat meadow lands, the rich fields of wheat, of rye, of buckwheat, and Indian corn, and the orchards burdened with ruddy fruit, which surrounded the warm tenement of Van Tassel, his heart yearned after the damsel who was to inherit these domains, and his imagination expanded with the idea how they might be readily turned into cash and the money invested in immense tracts of wild

16. *quarter:* an obsolete word meaning friendly treatment, mercy.

land and shingle palaces in the wilderness. Nay, his busy fancy already realized his hopes and presented to him the blooming Katrina, with a whole family of children, mounted on the top of a wagon loaded with household trumpery, with pots and kettles dangling beneath; and he beheld himself bestriding a pacing mare with a colt at her heels, setting out for Kentucky, Tennessee, or the Lord knows where.

IV. *Brom Van Brunt*

Ichabod's most formidable rival was a burly, roaring, roystering blade[17] of the name of Abraham—or, according to the Dutch abbreviation, Brom—Van Brunt, the hero of the country round, which rang with his feats of strength and hardihood. He was broad-shouldered and double-jointed, with short, curly black hair, and a bluff but not unpleasant countenance, having a mingled air of fun and arrogance. From his Herculean frame and great powers of limb he had received the nickname of "Brom Bones," by which he was universally known. He was famed for great knowledge and skill in horsemanship, being as dexterous on horseback as a Tartar.[18] He was foremost at all races and cock fights; and, with the ascendancy which bodily strength always acquires in rustic life, was the umpire in all disputes, setting his hat on one side, and giving his decisions with an air and tone that admitted of no gainsay or appeal. He was always ready for either a fight or a frolic, but had more mischief than ill-will in his composition, and with all his overbearing roughness there was a strong dash of waggish good humor at bottom. He had three or four boon companions who regarded him as their model, and at the head of whom he scoured the country, attending every scene of feud or merriment for miles around. In cold weather he was distinguished by a fur cap surmounted with a flaunting fox's tail, and when the folks at a country gathering descried this well-known crest at a distance whisking about among a squad of hard riders, they always stood by for a squall. Sometimes his crew would be heard dashing

17. *blade:* a dashing, reckless fellow. 18. *Tartar:* a member of a wild Asiatic tribe whose skill in horsemanship is known over the world.

along past the farmhouses at midnight with a whoop and halloo, like a troop of Don Cossacks[19]; and the old dames, startled out of their sleep, would listen for a moment till the hurry-scurry had clattered by, and then exclaim: "Ay, there goes Brom Bones and his gang!" The neighbors looked upon him with a mixture of awe, admiration, and good-will, and when any madcap prank or rustic brawl occurred in the vicinity, always shook their heads and warranted Brom Bones was at the bottom of it.

This rantipole[20] hero had for some time singled out the blooming Katrina for the object of his uncouth gallantries, and though his amorous toyings were something like the gentle caresses and endearments of a bear, yet it was whispered that she did not altogether discourage his hopes. Certain it is, his advances were signals for rival candidates to retire; insomuch that when his horse was seen tied to Van Tassel's paling on a Sunday night, a sure sign that his master was courting—or, as it is termed, "sparking"—within, all other suitors passed by in despair and carried the war into other quarters. Such was the rival with whom Ichabod Crane had to contend.

Brom, who had a degree of rough chivalry in his nature, would fain have carried matters to open warfare, and have settled their pretensions to the lady according to the mode of those most concise and simple reasoners, the knights-errant of yore—by single combat; but Ichabod was too conscious of the superior might of his adversary to enter the lists against him. He had overheard a boast of Bones, that he would "double the schoolmaster up and lay him on a shelf of his own schoolhouse," and he was too wary to give him an opportunity. There was something extremely provoking in this obstinately pacific system; it left Brom no alternative but to draw upon the funds of rustic waggery in his disposition, and to play off boorish practical jokes upon his rival. Ichabod became the object of whimsical persecution to Bones and his gang of rough riders. They harried his hitherto peaceful

19. *Don Cossacks:* Russians famed for their skill in riding. 20. *rantipole:* wild, rakish.

domains, smoked out his singing school by stopping up the chimney, broke into the schoolhouse at night, in spite of its formidable fastenings of withe and window stakes, and turned everything topsy-turvy, so that the poor schoolmaster began to think all the witches in the country held their meetings there. But what was still more annoying, Brom took all opportunity of turning him into ridicule in presence of his mistress, and had a scoundrel dog whom he taught to whine in the most ludicrous manner, and introduced as a rival of Ichabod to instruct her in psalmody.

V. *The Party at Van Tassel's*

It was toward evening that Ichabod arrived at the castle of the Heer[21] Van Tassel, which he found thronged with the pride and flower of the adjacent country. Old farmers, a spare, leathern-faced race in homespun coats and breeches, blue stockings, huge shoes, and magnificent pewter buckles. Their brisk, withered little dames in close crimped caps, long-waisted short gowns, homespun petticoats, with scissors and pincushions and gay calico pockets hanging on the outside. Buxom lasses almost as antiquated as their mothers, excepting where a straw hat, a fine ribbon, or perhaps a white frock

21. *Heer* (hār): shortened from *Mynheer*, a title of respect.

gave symptoms of city innovation. The sons in short square-skirted coats with rows of stupendous brass buttons, and their hair generally queued in the fashion of the time, especially if they could procure an eelskin for the purpose, it being esteemed throughout the country as a potent nourisher and strengthener of the hair.

Brom Bones, however, was the hero of the scene, having come to the gathering on his favorite steed Daredevil, a creature, like himself, full of mettle and mischief, and which no one but himself could manage. He was, in fact, noted for preferring vicious animals given to all kinds of tricks which kept the rider in constant risk of his neck, for he held a tractable well-broken horse as unworthy of a lad of spirit.

Fain would I pause to dwell upon the world of charms that burst upon the enraptured gaze of my hero as he entered the stately parlor of Van Tassel's mansion. Not those of the bevy of buxom lasses with their luxurious display of red and white, but the ample charms of a genuine Dutch country tea table in the sumptuous time of autumn. Such heaped-up platters of cakes of various and almost indescribable kinds known only to experienced Dutch housewives! There was the doughty doughnut, and the crisp and crumbling cruller; sweet cakes and short cakes, ginger cakes and honey cakes, and the whole family of cakes. And then there were apple pies and peach pies and pumpkin pies, besides slices of ham and smoked beef, and moreover delectable dishes of preserved plums and peaches and pears and quinces, not to mention broiled shad and roasted chickens, together with bowls of milk and cream, all mingled higgledy-piggledy, pretty much as I have enumerated them, with the motherly teapot sending up its clouds of vapor from the midst—Heaven bless the mark! I want breath and time to discuss this banquet as it deserves but am too eager to get on with my story. Happily Ichabod Crane was not in so great a hurry as his historian, but did ample justice to every dainty.

Old Baltus Van Tassel moved about among his guests with a face dilated with content and good-humor, round and jolly as the harvest moon. His hospitable attentions were brief but expressive, being confined to a shake of the hand, a slap on the shoulder, a loud laugh, and a pressing invitation to "fall to and help yourself."

And now the sound of the music from the common room, or hall, summoned to the dance. The musician was an old gray-headed Negro, who had been the itinerant orchestra of the neighborhood for more than a half-century. His instrument was as old and battered as himself. The greater part of the time he scraped on two or three strings, accompanying every movement of the bow with a motion of the head; bowing almost to the ground, and stamping with his foot whenever a fresh couple were to start.

Ichabod prided himself upon his dancing as much as upon his vocal powers. Not a limb, nor a fiber about him was idle; and to have seen his loosely hung frame in full motion and clattering about the room, you would have thought St. Vitus himself, that blessed patron of the dance, was figuring before you in person. He was the admiration of all the Negroes, who, having gathered of all ages and sizes from the farm and the neighborhood, stood forming a pyramid of shining faces at every door and window, gazing with delight at the scene. How could the flogger of urchins be otherwise than animated and joyous? The lady of his heart was his partner in the dance and smiling graciously in reply to all his amorous oglings; while Brom Bones, sorely smitten with love and jealousy, sat brooding by himself in one corner.

When the dance was at an end, Ichabod was attracted to a knot of the sager[22] folks, who, with old Van Tassel, sat smoking at one end of the piazza, gossiping over former times and drawing out long stories about the war.

There was the story of Doffue Martling, a large blue-bearded Dutchman, who had nearly taken a British frigate with an old iron nine-pounder from a mud breastwork, only that his gun burst at the sixth discharge. And there was an old gentleman who shall be nameless,—being too rich a mynheer to be lightly mentioned,—who, in the Battle of White Plains, being an excellent master of defense, parried a musket

22. *sager:* older, wiser.

ball with a small sword, insomuch that he absolutely felt it whiz round the blade and glance off at the hilt; in proof of which he was ready at any time to show the sword, with the hilt a little bent. There were several more that had been equally great in the field, not one of whom but was persuaded that he had a considerable hand in bringing the war to a happy termination.

But all these were nothing to the tales of ghosts and apparitions that succeeded. The immediate cause, however, of the prevalence of supernatural stories in these parts was owing to the vicinity of Sleepy Hollow. There was a contagion in the very air that blew from the haunted region; it breathed forth an atmosphere of dreams and fancies infecting all the land. The chief part of the stories, however, turned upon the favorite specter of Sleepy Hollow, the Headless Horseman, who had been heard several times of late patrolling the country, and, it was said, tethered his horse nightly among the graves in the churchyard.

The sequestered situation of this church seems always to have made it a favorite haunt of troubled spirits. Over a deep, black part of the stream, not far from the church, was formerly thrown a wooden bridge. The road that led to it and the bridge itself were thickly shaded by overhanging trees, which cast a gloom about it even in the daytime, but occasioned a fearful darkness at night. This was one of the favorite haunts of the Headless Horseman, and the place where he was most frequently encountered. The tale was told of old Brouwer, a most heretical disbeliever in ghosts, how he met the Horseman returning from his foray into Sleepy Hollow, and was obliged to get up behind him; how they galloped over bush and brake, over hill and swamp, until they reached the bridge, when the Horseman suddenly turned into a skeleton, threw old Brouwer into the brook, and sprang away over the tree tops with a clap of thunder.

This story was immediately matched by a thrice marvelous adventure of Brom Bones, who made light of the Galloping Hessian as an arrant jockey. He affirmed that on returning one night from the neighboring village of Sing Sing, he had been overtaken by this midnight trooper, that he had offered to race with him for a bowl of punch, and should have won it, too,—but just as they came to the church bridge the Hessian bolted, and vanished in a flash of fire.

All these tales, told in that drowsy undertone with which men talk in the dark, the countenances of the listeners only now and then receiving a casual gleam from the glare of a pipe, sank deep in the mind of Ichabod. He repaid them in kind with large extracts from his invaluable author, Cotton Mather, and added many marvelous events that had taken place in his native state of Connecticut, and fearful sights which he had seen in his nightly walks about Sleepy Hollow.

VI. *The Galloping Horseman*

It was the very witching time of night that Ichabod pursued his travels homeward along the sides of the lofty hills which rise above Tarrytown.

All the stories of ghosts and goblins that he had heard in the afternoon now came crowding upon his recollection. The night grew darker and darker, the stars seemed to sink deeper in the sky, and driving clouds occasionally hid them from his sight. He had never felt so lonely and dismal. He was, moreover, approaching the very place where many of the scenes of the ghost stories had been laid. In the center of the road stood an enormous tulip tree which towered like a giant above all the other trees of the neighborhood and formed a kind of landmark. Its limbs were gnarled and fantastic, large enough to form trunks for ordinary trees, twisting down almost to the earth and rising again into the air. It was connected with the tragical story of the unfortunate André,[23] who had been taken prisoner hard by, and was universally known by the name of Major André's tree. The common people regarded it with a mixture of respect and superstition, partly out of sympathy for the fate of its ill-starred namesake, and partly from the tales of strange sights and doleful lamentations told concerning it.

23. *Major André:* a British spy captured by the Americans in 1780.

As Ichabod approached this fearful tree he began to whistle. He thought his whistle was answered—it was but a blast sweeping sharply through the dry branches. As he approached a little nearer he thought he saw something white hanging in the midst of the tree; he paused and ceased whistling; but on looking more narrowly perceived that it was a place where the tree had been scathed by lightning and the white wood laid bare. Suddenly he heard a groan; his teeth chattered and his knees smote against the saddle; it was but the rubbing of one huge bough upon another as they were swayed about by the breeze. He passed the tree in safety, but new perils lay before him.

About two hundred yards from the tree a small brook crossed the road and ran into a marshy and thickly wooded glen known by the name of Wiley's Swamp.

As he approached the stream his heart began to thump. He summoned up, however, all his resolution, gave his horse half a score of kicks in the ribs, and attempted to dash briskly across the bridge; but instead of starting forward, the perverse old animal made a lateral movement, and ran broadside against the fence. Ichabod, whose fears increased with the delay, jerked the reins on the other side and kicked lustily with the contrary foot. It was all in vain. His steed started, it is true, but it was only to plunge to the opposite side of the road into a thicket of brambles and alder bushes. The schoolmaster now bestowed both whip and heel upon the starveling ribs of old Gunpowder, who dashed forward, sniffing and snorting, but came to a stand just by the bridge with a suddenness that had nearly sent his rider sprawling over his head. Just at this moment a plashy tramp by the side of the bridge caught the sensitive ear of Ichabod. In the dark shadow of the grove, on the margin of the brook, he beheld something huge, misshapen, and towering. It stirred not, but seemed gathered up in the gloom like some gigantic monster ready to spring upon the traveler.

The hair of the affrighted pedagogue rose upon his head with terror. What was to be done? To turn and fly was now too late; and besides, what chance was there of escaping ghost or goblin, if such it was, which could ride upon the wings of the wind? Summoning up, therefore, a show of courage, he demanded in stammering accents, "Who are you?" He received no reply. He repeated his demand in a still more agitated voice. Still there was no answer. Once more he cudgelled the sides of the inflexible Gunpowder, and, shutting his eyes, broke forth with involuntary fervor into a psalm tune. Just then the shadowy object of alarm put itself in motion, and with a scramble and a bound stood at once in the middle of the road. Though the night was dark and dismal, yet the form of the unknown might now in some degree be ascertained. He appeared to be a horseman of large dimensions, and mounted on a black horse of powerful frame. He made no offer of molestation or sociability, but kept aloof on one side of the road, jogging along on the blind side of old Gunpowder. who had now gotten over his fright and waywardness.

Ichabod, who had no relish for this strange midnight companion, and bethought himself of the adventure of Brom Bones with the Galloping Hessian, now quickened his steed in hopes of leaving him behind. The stranger, however, quickened his horse to an equal pace. Ichabod pulled up and fell into a walk, thinking to lag behind; the other did the same. His heart began to sink within him. He endeavored to resume his psalm tune but his parched tongue clove to the roof of his mouth, and he could not utter a stave. There was something in the moody and dogged silence of this pertinacious companion that was mysterious and appalling. It was soon fearfully accounted for. On mounting a rising ground which brought the figure of his fellow traveler in relief against the sky, gigantic in height and muffled in a cloak, Ichabod was horror-struck on perceiving that he was headless! But his horror was still more increased on observing that the head, which should have rested on his shoulders, was carried before him on the pommel of his saddle! His horror rose to desperation. He rained a shower of kicks and blows upon Gunpowder, hoping by a sudden movement to give his companion the slip—but the specter started full jump with him. Away then they dashed, through thick and thin, stones flying and sparks flashing at every bound. Ichabod's flimsy garments fluttered in the air as he stretched his long, lank body away over his horse's head in the eagerness of his flight.

They had now reached the road which turns off to Sleepy Hollow; but Gunpowder, who seemed possessed with a demon, instead of keeping up it, made an opposite turn and plunged headlong downhill to the left. This road leads through a sandy hollow, shaded by trees for about a quarter of a mile, where it crosses the bridge famous in goblin story, and just beyond swells the green knoll on which stands the whitewashed church.

As yet the panic of the steed had given his unskillful rider an apparent advantage in the chase; but just as he had got halfway through the hollow, the girths of the saddle gave way, and he felt it slipping from under him. He seized it by the pommel and endeavored to hold it firm, but in vain, and had just time to save himself by clasping old Gunpowder round the neck, when the saddle fell to the earth, and he heard it trampled under foot by his pursuer. For a moment the terror of Hans Van Ripper's wrath passed across his mind, for it was his Sunday saddle; but this was no time for petty fears; the goblin was hard on his haunches, and—unskillful rider that he was—he had much ado to maintain his seat, sometimes slipping on one side, sometimes on another, and sometimes jolted on the high ridge of his horse's backbone with a violence that he verily feared would cleave him asunder.

An opening in the trees now cheered him with the hopes that the church bridge was at hand. The wavering reflection of a silver star in the bosom of the brook told him that he was not mistaken. He saw the walls of the church dimly glaring under the trees beyond. He recollected the place where Brom Bones' ghostly competitor had disappeared. "If I can but reach the bridge," thought Ichabod, "I am safe." Just then he heard the black steed panting and blowing close behind him; he even fancied that he felt his hot breath.

Another convulsive kick in the ribs, and old Gunpowder sprang upon the bridge, he thundered over the resounding planks, he gained the opposite side; and now Ichabod cast a look behind to see if his pursuer should vanish, according to rule, in a flash of fire and brimstone. Just then he saw the goblin rising in his stirrups, and in the very act of hurling his head at him. Ichabod endeavored to dodge the horrible missile, but too late. It encountered his cranium with a tremendous crash; he was tumbled headlong into the dust, and Gunpowder, the black steed, and the goblin rider passed by like a whirlwind.

VII. *What Became of Ichabod Crane?*

The next morning the old horse was found without his saddle, and with bridle under his feet, soberly cropping the grass at his master's gate. Ichabod did not make his appearance at breakfast; dinner hour came, but no Ichabod. The boys assembled at the schoolhouse and strolled idly about the banks of the brook, but no schoolmaster. Hans Van Ripper now began to feel some uneasiness about the fate of poor Ichabod and his saddle. An inquiry was set on foot, and after diligent investigation they came upon his traces. In one part of the road leading to the church was found the saddle trampled in the dirt. The tracks of horses' hoofs deeply dented in the road, and evidently at a furious speed, were traced to the bridge, beyond which, on the bank of a broad part of the brook where the water ran deep and black, was found the hat of the unfortunate Ichabod, and close beside it a shattered pumpkin.

The brook was searched, but the body of the schoolmaster was not to be discovered. Hans Van Ripper, as executor of his estate, examined the bundle which contained all his worldly effects. They consisted of two shirts and a half, two stocks for the neck, a pair or two of worsted stockings, an old pair of corduroy smallclothes, a rusty razor, a book of psalm tunes full of dog's ears, and a broken pitch pipe. As to the books and furniture of the schoolhouse, they belonged to the community, excepting Cotton Mather's *History of Witchcraft*, a *New England Almanac*, and a book of dreams and fortune telling; in which last was a sheet of foolscap much scribbled and blotted in several fruitless attempts to make a copy of verses in honor of the heiress of Van Tassel. These magic books and the poetic scrawl were forthwith consigned to the flames by Hans Van Ripper, who from that time forward determined to send his children no more to school, observing that he never knew any good come of this same reading and writing. Whatever money the schoolmaster possessed, and he had received his quarter's pay but a day or two before, he must have had about his person at the time of his disappearance.

The mysterious event caused much speculation at the church on the following Sunday. Knots of gazers and gossips were collected in the churchyard, at the bridge, and at the spot where the hat and pumpkin had been found. The stories of Brouwer, the Bones, and a whole budget of others were called to mind; and when they had diligently considered them all and compared them with the symptoms of the present case, they shook their heads and came to the conclusion that Ichabod had been carried off by the Galloping Hessian. As he was a bachelor and in nobody's debt, nobody troubled his head any more about him. The school was removed to a different quarter of the Hollow, and another pedagogue reigned in his stead.

It is true, an old farmer who had been down to New York on a visit several years after, and from whom this account of the ghostly adventure was received, brought home the intelligence that Ichabod Crane was still alive, that he had left the neighborhood partly through fear of the goblin and Hans Van Ripper and partly because he had realized at the Van Tassel party that he was being dismissed by the heiress, that he had changed his quarters to a distant part of the country, had kept school and studied law at the same time, had been admitted to the bar, turned politician, electioneered, written for the newspapers, and finally had been made a justice of the Ten Pound Court.[24] Brom Bones, too, who shortly after his rival's disappearance conducted the blooming Katrina in triumph to the altar, was observed to look exceedingly knowing whenever the story of Ichabod was related, and always burst into a hearty laugh at the mention of the pumpkin; which led some to suspect that he knew more about the matter than he chose to tell.

The old country wives, however, who are the best judges of these matters, maintain to this day that Ichabod was spirited away by supernatural means; and it is a favorite story often told about the neighborhood round the winter evening fire. The bridge became more than ever an object of superstitious awe, and that may be the reason why the road

24. *Ten Pound Court:* an early civil, not criminal, court, where the issue involved could not exceed fifty dollars, or ten pounds.

has been altered of late years so as to approach the church by the border of the millpond. The schoolhouse being deserted soon fell to decay, and was reported to be haunted by the ghost of the unfortunate pedagogue; and the plowboy loitering homeward of a still summer evening has often fancied a voice at a distance, chanting a melancholy psalm tune among the tranquil solitudes of Sleepy Hollow.

Abridged

THINGS TO DO

1. Reread Washington Irving's "Rip Van Winkle" in *A Book of Fortitude* and compare it with "The Legend of Sleepy Hollow" as to setting, characters, and old legends retold. What period is represented in the stories?

2. Choose one character in "The Legend of Sleepy Hollow." Read aloud a paragraph describing that character. Then add details of appearance or manner from your own imagination.

3. Arrange a dramatization of the selection. Include such scenes as the schoolroom, the singing school, the party, and the midnight encounter. If possible, give the dramatization as a Halloween play for another grade.

I Know a Bank

WILLIAM SHAKESPEARE

I know a bank where the wild thyme blows,
Where oxlips and the nodding violet grows;
Quite over-canopied with luscious woodbine,
With sweet musk-roses, and with eglantine.
There sleeps Titania sometime of the night,
Lull'd in these flowers with dances and delight;
And there the snake throws her enamell'd skin,
Weed wide enough to wrap a fairy in.

PICTURING LIFE ON THE HIGHWAYS

Poets and artists love the highways of the world not for the wide road alone, but for the beauties of nature and the wealth of life they see along the way. There are many famous pictures painted by great and discerning artists. Some of these are *Spring*, by COROT; *The Peasant*, by VAN GOGH; *Cornfields in Provence*, by VAN GOGH; *The Stonebreakers*, by COURBET; *Stone City*, by WOOD; and that masterpiece by RUBENS, *Return from Egypt*.

The Bugle Song

ALFRED, LORD TENNYSON

[Choir to be arranged in three voices: high, medium, and low.]

Medium — The splendor falls on castle walls
And snowy summits old in story:
High — The long light shakes across the lakes,
Low — And the wild cataract leaps in glory.
High — Blow, bugle, blow, [Low] set the wild echoes flying,
High (Imitate bugle call) — Blow, bugle; [Low and medium] answer, echoes, dying, dying,
dying.

High — O hark, O hear! how thin and clear,
And thinner, clearer, farther going!
Medium — O sweet and far from cliff and scar
The horns of Elfland faintly blowing!
High — Blow, let us hear the purple glens replying,
High (Imitate bugle call) — Blow, bugle; [Low and medium] answer, echoes, dying, dying,
dying.

Medium — O love, they die in yon rich sky,
High — They faint on hill or field or river;
Low — Our echoes roll from soul to soul,
And grow for ever and for ever.
High (Imitate bugle call) — Blow, bugle, blow, [Low and medium] set the wild echoes
flying,
And answer, echoes, answer, dying, dying, dying.

Tavern

EDNA ST. VINCENT MILLAY

I'll keep a little tavern
  Below the high hill's crest,
Wherein all grey-eyed people
  May set them down and rest.

There shall be plates a-plenty,
  And mugs to melt the chill
Of all the grey-eyed people
  Who happen up the hill.

There sound will sleep the traveller,
  And dream his journey's end,
But I will rouse at midnight
  The falling fire to tend.

Aye, 'tis a curious fancy—
  But all the good I know
Was taught me out of two grey eyes
  A long time ago.

Daisies

BLISS CARMAN

Over the shoulders and slopes of the dune
I saw the white daisies go down to the sea,
A host in the sunshine, an army in June,
The people God sends us to set our hearts free.

The bobolinks rallied them up from the dell,
The orioles whistled them out of the wood;
And all of their singing was, "Earth, it is well!"
And all of their dancing was, "Life, thou art good!"

The Highwayman

ALFRED NOYES

Part I

The wind was a torrent of darkness among the gusty trees,
The moon was a ghostly galleon tossed upon cloudy seas,
The road was a ribbon of moonlight over the purple moor,
And the highwayman came riding—
  Riding—riding—
The highwayman came riding, up to the old inn-door.

He'd a French cocked-hat on his forehead, a bunch of lace at his chin,
A coat of the claret velvet, and breeches of brown doe-skin;
They fitted with never a wrinkle: his boots were up to the thigh!
And he rode with a jeweled twinkle,
  His pistol butts a-twinkle,
His rapier hilt a-twinkle, under the jeweled sky.

Over the cobbles he clattered and clashed in the dark inn-yard,
And he tapped with his whip on the shutters, but all was locked and barred;
He whistled a tune to the window, and who should be waiting there
But the landlord's black-eyed daughter,
  Bess, the landlord's daughter,
Plaiting a dark red love-knot into her long black hair.

And dark in the dark old inn-yard a stable-wicket creaked
Where Tim the ostler listened; his face was white and peaked;
His eyes were hollows of madness, his hair like mouldy hay,
But he loved the landlord's daughter,
  The landlord's red-lipped daughter,
Dumb as a dog he listened, and he heard the robber say—

"One kiss, my bonny sweetheart, I'm after a prize tonight,
But I shall be back with the yellow gold before the morning
light;
Yet, if they press me sharply, and harry me through the day,
Then look for me by moonlight,
Watch for me by moonlight,
I'll come to thee by moonlight, though hell should bar the
way."

He rose upright in the stirrups; he scarce could reach her
hand,
But she loosened her hair i' the casement! His face burnt like
a brand
As the black cascade of perfume came tumbling over his
breast;
And he kissed its waves in the moonlight,
(Oh, sweet black waves in the moonlight!)
Then he tugged at his rein in the moonlight, and galloped
away to the West.

Part II

He did not come in the dawning; he did not come at noon;
And out o' the tawny sunset, before the rise o' the moon,
When the road was a gypsy's ribbon, looping the purple moor,
A red-coat troop came marching—
  Marching—marching—
King George's men came marching, up to the old inn-door.

They said no word to the landlord, they drank his ale instead,
But they gagged his daughter and bound her to the foot of her narrow bed;
Two of them knelt at her casement, with muskets at their side!
There was death at every window;
  And hell at one dark window;
For Bess could see, through her casement, the road that *he* would ride.

They had tied her up to attention, with many a sniggering jest;
They had bound a musket beside her, with the barrel beneath her breast!
"Now keep good watch!" and they kissed her.
She heard the dead man say—
Look for me by moonlight;
  Watch for me by moonlight;
I'll come to thee by moonlight, though hell should bar the way!

She twisted her hands behind her; but all the knots held good!
She writhed her hands till her fingers were wet with sweat or blood!
They stretched and strained in the darkness, and the hours crawled by like years,
Till, now, on the stroke of midnight,
  Cold, on the stroke of midnight,
The tip of one finger touched it! The trigger at least was hers!

The tip of one finger touched it; she strove no more for the rest!
Up, she stood up to attention, with the barrel beneath her breast,
She would not risk their hearing; she would not strive again;
For the road lay bare in the moonlight;
  Blank and bare in the moonlight;
And the blood of her veins in the moonlight throbbed to her love's refrain.

  Tlot-tlot; *tlot-tlot*! Had they heard it? The horse-hoofs ringing clear;
Tlot-tlot, *tlot-tlot*, in the distance! Were they deaf that they did not hear?
Down the ribbon of moonlight, over the brow of the hill,
The highwayman came riding,
  Riding, riding!
The red-coats looked to their priming! She stood up, straight and still!

Tlot-tlot, in the frosty silence! *tlot-tlot*, in the echoing night!
Nearer he came and nearer! Her face was like a light!
Her eyes were wide for a moment; she drew one last deep breath,
Then her finger moved in the moonlight,
  Her musket shattered the moonlight,
Shattered her breast in the moonlight and warned him —with her death.

He turned; he spurred to the West; he did not know who stood
Bowed, with her head o'er the musket, drenched with her own red blood!
Not till the dawn he heard it, his face grew gray to hear
How Bess, the landlord's daughter,
  The landlord's black-eyed daughter,
Had watched for her love in the moonlight, and died in the darkness there.

Back, he spurred like a madman, shrieking a curse to the sky,
With the white road smoking behind him and his rapier brandished high!
Blood-red were his spurs i' the golden noon; wine-red was his velvet coat,
When they shot him down on the highway,
Down like a dog on the highway,
And he lay in his blood on the highway, with a bunch of lace at his throat.

And still of a winter's night, they say, when the wind is in the trees,
When the moon is a ghostly galleon tossed upon cloudy seas,
When the road is a ribbon of moonlight over the purple moor,
A highwayman comes riding—
Riding—riding—
A highwayman comes riding, up to the old inn-door.

Over the cobbles he clatters and clangs in the dark inn-yard;
And he taps with his whip on the shutters, but all is locked and barred;
He whistles a tune to the window, and who should be waiting there
But the landlord's black-eyed daughter,
Bess, the landlord's daughter,
Plaiting a dark red love-knot into her long black hair.

HELPS FOR DISCUSSION

1. What is the story told in this ballad? Who betrayed the lovers? How does the tragedy grow into a legend?

2. Read aloud lines or stanzas that create pictures for the reader. Describe what the poet causes you to see. Then read lines that express sounds. What do you seem to hear as you say the lines? What special words has the poet used to make the sounds vivid?

3. Reread the italicized lines on pages 167 and 169. Why are these lines printed in a different kind of type? In what tone of voice should they be read? Why?

4. Volunteer to read Scott's "Lochinvar." You will find it in *A Book of Fortitude* (Faith and Freedom Literary Readers). Compare the two ballads.

A distinguished American editor, Dr. Charles Eastman, described his own boyhood on the Sioux Reservation when he wrote

An Indian Boy's Training

CHARLES EASTMAN

My uncle, who educated me up to the age of fifteen years, was a good teacher. When I left the tepee in the morning, he would say, "Hakadah, look closely to everything you see"; and at evening, on my return, he used often to catechize me for an hour or so.

"On which side of the trees is the lighter-colored bark? On which side do they have most regular branches?"

It was his custom to let me name all the new birds that I had seen during the day. I would name them according to the color or the shape of the bill or their song or the appearance and locality of the nest—in fact, anything about the bird that impressed me as characteristic. I made many ridiculous errors, I must admit. He then usually informed me of the correct name. Occasionally I made a hit and this he would warmly commend.

He went much deeper into this science when I was a little older; that is, about the age of eight or nine years. He would say, for instance: "How do you know that there are fish in yonder lake?"

"Because they jump out of the water for flies at midday."

He would smile at my prompt but superficial reply.

"What do you think of the little pebbles grouped together under the shallow water? And what made the pretty curved marks in the sandy bottom and the little sandbanks? Where do you find the fish-eating birds? Have the inlet and the outlet of a lake anything to do with the question?"

He did not expect a correct reply at once to all the questions that he put to me on these occasions, but he meant to make me observant and a good student of nature.

"Hakadah," he would say to me, "you ought to follow the example of the shunktokecha (wolf). Even when he is surprised and runs for his life, he will pause to take one more look at you before he enters his final retreat. So you must take a second look at everything you see.

"It is better to view animals unobserved. I have been a witness to their courtships and their quarrels and have learned many of their secrets in this way. I was once the unseen spectator of a thrilling battle between a pair of grizzly bears and three buffaloes—a rash act for the bears; for it was in the moon of strawberries, when the buffaloes sharpen and polish their horns for bloody contests among themselves.

"I advise you, my boy, never to approach a grizzly's den from the front, but to steal up behind and throw your blanket or a stone in front of the hole. He does not usually rush for it, but first puts his head out and listens and then comes out very indifferently and sits on his haunches on the mound in front of the hole before he makes any attack. While he is exposing himself in this fashion, aim at his heart. Always be as cool as the animal himself." Thus he armed me against the cunning of savage beasts by teaching me how to outwit them.

"In hunting," he would resume, "you will be guided by the habits of the animal you seek. Remember that a moose stays in swampy or low land, or between high mountains near a spring or lake, for thirty to sixty days at a time. Most large game moves about continually, except the doe in the spring; it is then a very easy matter to find her with

the fawn. Conceal yourself in a convenient place as soon as you observe any signs of the presence of either, and then call with your birchen doe caller.

"Whichever one hears you first will soon appear in your neighborhood. But you must be very watchful, or you may be made a fawn of by a large wildcat. They understand the characteristic call of the doe perfectly well.

"When you have any difficulty with a bear or a wildcat—that is, if the creature shows signs of attacking you—you must make him fully understand that you have seen him and are aware of his intentions. If you are not well equipped for a pitched battle, the only way to make him retreat is to take a long sharp-pointed pole for a spear and rush toward him. No wild beast will face this unless he is cornered and already wounded. These fierce beasts are generally afraid of the common weapon of the larger animals—the horns; and if these are very long and sharp, they dare not risk an open fight.

"There is one exception to this rule—the gray wolf will attack fiercely when very hungry. But their courage depends upon their numbers; in this they are like white men. One wolf or two will never attack a man. They will stampede a herd of buffaloes in order to get at the calves; they will rush upon a herd of antelopes, for these are helpless; but they are always careful about attacking man."

Of this nature were the instructions of my uncle, who was widely known at that time as among the greatest hunters of his tribe.

All boys were expected to endure hardship without complaint. In savage warfare, a young man must, of course, be an athlete and used to undergoing all sorts of privations. He must be able to go without food and water for two or three days without displaying any weakness, or to run for a day and a night without any rest. He must be able to traverse a pathless and wild country without losing his way either in the day or nighttime. He cannot refuse to do any of these things if he aspires to be a warrior.

Sometimes my uncle would waken me very early in the

morning and challenge me to fast with him all day. I had to accept the challenge. We blackened our faces with charcoal, so that every boy in the village would know that I was fasting for the day. Then the little tempters would make my life a misery until the merciful sun hid behind the western hills.

I can scarcely recall the time when my stern teacher began to give sudden war whoops over my head in the morning while I was sound asleep. He expected me to leap up with perfect presence of mind, always ready to grasp a weapon of some sort and to give a shrill whoop in reply. If I was sleepy or startled and hardly knew what I was about, he would ridicule me and say that I need never expect to sell my scalp dear. Often he would vary these tactics by shooting off his gun just outside of the lodge while I was yet asleep, at the same time giving bloodcurdling yells. After a time I became used to this.

When Indians went upon the warpath, it was their custom to try the new warriors thoroughly before coming to an engagement. For instance, when they were near a hostile camp, they would select the novices to go after the water and make them do all sorts of things to prove their courage. In accordance with this idea, my uncle used to send me off after water when we camped after dark in a strange place. Perhaps the country was full of wild beasts, and, for aught I knew, there might be scouts from hostile bands of Indians lurking in that very neighborhood.

Yet I never objected, for that would show cowardice. I picked my way through the woods, dipped my pail in the water, and hurried back, always careful to make as little noise as a cat. Being only a boy, my heart would leap at every crackling of a dry twig or distant hooting of an owl until, at last, I reached our tepee. Then my uncle would perhaps say, "Ah, Hakadah, you are a thorough warrior," empty out the precious contents of the pail, and order me to go a second time. Imagine how I felt! But I wished to be a brave man. Silently I would take the pail and endeavor to retrace my footsteps in the dark.

With all this, our manners and morals were not neglected. I was made to respect the adults and especially the aged. I was not allowed to join in their discussions, nor even to speak in their presence, unless requested to do so. Indian etiquette was very strict, and among the requirements was that of avoiding the direct address. A term of relationship or some title of courtesy was commonly used instead of the personal name by those who wished to show respect. We were taught generosity to the poor and reverence for the "Great Mystery." Religion was the basis of our training.

I recall to the present day some of the kind warnings and reproofs that my good grandmother was wont to give me. "Be strong of heart—be patient!" she used to say. She told me of a young chief who was noted for his uncontrollable temper. While in one of his rages he attempted to kill a woman, for which he was slain by his own band and left unburied as a mark of disgrace—his body was simply covered with green grass. If I ever lost my temper, she would say: "Hakadah, control yourself; or you will be like that young man I told you of, and lie under a *green blanket*!"

In the old days, no young man was allowed to use tobacco in any form until he had become an acknowledged warrior and had achieved a record. If a youth should seek a wife before he had reached the age of twenty-two or twenty-three, and been recognized as a brave man, he was sneered at and considered an ill-bred Indian. He must also be a skillful hunter. An Indian cannot be a good husband unless he brings home plenty of game.

These precepts were in the line of our training for the wild life.

THINGS TO DO

1. Make a large chart outlining the items of an Indian boy's training. Use as headings *Hunting*, *Readiness and Courage*, *Manners and Morals*. Illustrate your chart with thumbnail sketches or mounted pictures.

2. Consult reference books for information on the author's tribe, the Sioux. Show on a map the region inhabited. Describe homes and clothing.

Home Thoughts

ODELL SHEPARD

October in New England,
  And I not there to see
The glamour of the goldenrod,
  The flame of the maple tree!

October in my own land—
  I know what glory fills
The mountains of New Hampshire
  And Massachusetts hills.

I know what hues of opal
  Rhode Island breezes fan,
And how Connecticut puts on
  Colors of Hindustan.

Vermont, in robes of splendor,
  Sings with the woods of Maine
Alternate hallelujahs
  Of gold and crimson stain.

The armies of the asters,
  Frail hosts in blue and gray,
Invade the hills of home—and I
  Three thousand miles away!

I shall take down the calendar,
  And from the rounded year
Blot out one name, October,
  The loveliest and most dear.

For I would not remember,
  While she is marching by,
The pomp of her stately passing,
  The magic of her cry.

Lilacs

AMY LOWELL

Lilacs,
False blue,
White,
Purple,
Color of lilac,
Your great puffs of flowers
Are everywhere in this my New England.
Among your heart-shaped leaves
Orange orioles hop like music-box birds and sing
Their little weak soft songs;
In the crooks of your branches
The bright eyes of song sparrows sitting on spotted eggs
Peer restlessly through the light and shadow
Of all Springs.
Lilacs in dooryards
Holding quiet conversations with an early moon;
Lilacs watching a deserted house
Settling sideways into the grass of an old road;
Lilacs, wind-beaten, staggering under a lopsided shock of bloom
Above a cellar dug into a hill.
You are everywhere.
You were everywhere.
You tapped the window when the preacher preached his sermon,
And ran along the road beside the boy going to school.
You stood by pasture-bars to give the cows good milking,
You persuaded the housewife that her dishpan was of silver
And her husband an image of pure gold.
You flaunted the fragrance of your blossoms
Through the wide doors of customhouses—
You, and sandalwood, and tea,
Charging the noses of quill-driving clerks
When a ship was in from China.

You called to them: "Goose-quill men, goose-quill men,
May is a month for flitting,"
Until they writhed on their high stools
And wrote poetry on their letter-sheets behind the propped-up ledgers.
The dead fed you
Amid the slant stones of graveyards.
Pale ghosts who planted you
Came in the night time
And let their thin hair blow through your clustered stems.
You are of the green sea,
And of the stone hills which reach a long distance.
You are of elm-shaded streets with little shops where they sell kites and marbles,
You are of great parks where everyone walks and nobody is at home.
You cover the blind sides of greenhouses
And lean over the top to say a hurry-word through the glass
To your friends, the grapes, inside.

Maine knows you,
Has for years and years;
New Hampshire knows you,
And Massachusetts
And Vermont.
Cape Cod starts you along the beaches to Rhode Island;
Connecticut takes you from a river to the sea.
You are brighter than apples,
Sweeter than tulips,
You are the great flood of our souls
Bursting above the leaf-shapes of our hearts,
You are the smell of all summers,
The love of wives and children,
The recollection of the gardens of little children,
You are State Houses and Charters
And the familiar treading of the foot to and fro on a road it knows.
May is lilac here in New England,

May is thrush singing "Sun up!" on a tip-top ash-tree,
May is white clouds behind pine trees
Puffed out and marching upon a blue sky.
May is green as no other,
May is much sun through small leaves,
May is soft earth,
And apple blossoms,
And windows open to a south wind.
May is a full light wind of lilac
From Canada to Narragansett Bay.

Lilacs,
False blue,
White,

Purple,
Color of lilac.
Heart-leaves of lilac all over New England,
Roots of lilac under all the soil of New England,
Lilac in me because I am New England,
Because my roots are in it,
Because my leaves are of it,
Because my flowers are for it,
Because it is my country
And I speak to it of itself
And sing of it with my own voice
Since certainly it is mine.

The man who wrote *A Kentucky Cardinal* enjoyed his neighbors. Once in a while he derived a kindly amusement from them as he did when he set

The Scarecrow in the Cherry Tree

JAMES LANE ALLEN

It is unwise to do everything that you can for people at once; for when you can do nothing more, they will say you are no longer like yourself, and turn against you. So I have meant to go slowly with the Cobbs in my wish to be neighborly, and do not think that they could reasonably be spoiled on one dish of strawberries in three weeks. But the other evening Mrs. Cobb sent over a plate of golden sally-lunn[1] on a silver waiter,[2] covered with a snow-white napkin; and acting on this provocation, I thought they could be trusted with a basket of cherries.

So next morning, in order to save the ripening fruit on a rather small tree of choice variety, I thought I should put up a scarecrow, and to this end rummaged a closet for some last winter's old clothes. These I crammed with straw, and I fastened the resulting figure in the crotch of the tree, tying the arms to the adjoining limbs, and giving it the dreadful appearance of shouting, "Keep out of here, you rascals, or

1. *sally-lunn:* a slightly sweetened cake, named for the woman who first made and sold it in the streets of Bath, England. 2. *waiter:* tray.

you'll get hurt!" And, in truth, it did look so like me that I felt a little uncanny about it myself.

Returning home late, I went at once to the tree, where I found not a quart of cherries, and the servants told of an astonishing thing: that no sooner had the birds discovered who was standing in the tree, wearing the clothes in which he used to feed them during the winter, than the news spread like wildfire to the effect that he had climbed up there and was calling out: "Here is the best tree, fellows! Pitch in and help yourselves!" So that the like of the chattering and fetching away was never seen before.

Anxious to save another tree, and afraid to use more of my own clothes, I went over to Mrs. Walters, and got from her an old bonnet and veil, a dress and cape, and a pair of her cast-off yellow gaiters.[3] These garments I strung together and prepared to look lifelike, as nearly as a stuffing of hay would meet the inner requirements of the case. I then seated the dread apparition[4] in the fork of a limb, and awaited results. The first thief was an old jay, who flew towards the tree with his head turned to one side to see whether anyone was overtaking him. But scarcely had he alighted when he uttered a scream of horror that was sickening to hear, and dropped on the grass beneath, after which he took himself off with a silence and speed that would have done credit to a passenger pigeon. That tree was rather avoided for some days, or it may have been let alone merely because others were ripening; so that Mrs. Cobb got her cherries, and I sent Mrs. Walters some also for the excellent loan of her veil and gaiters.

THINGS TO DO

1. From the actions of the birds, make character sketches of the author and of Mrs. Walters.

2. Write a description of someone in your neighborhood who has a quality of friendliness like Mrs. Cobb.

3. *gaiters:* a covering for ankles or instep.

4. *apparition* (ăp ȧ rĭsh'ŭn): something unusual that comes into sight.

Sun-Browned with Toil

EDWARD F. GARESCHE, S.J.

Sun-browned and worn with toil, he leaned awhile
On his bright spade, and looked into the West.
His eyes were soft with thought. Saint Francis came,
Noiseless, and stood beside, then gently said:
"Brother, what seest thou?" Deep he drew breath
Of long contentment. "When yon evening light
Touches my cottage rooftree—lo, see there
How flames the thatch beneath the glowing rays—
I love to look across the reddened world
And thank my God, who keeps me; love to muse
And through the circling hours and changing years,
As days tread slow on days, He works for me.
I see yon shaggy hillside, grown with vines;
His own all-sedulous[1] Hand doth mold each bud
And twine each tendril round its destined stay.
How soft the pastures roll! He greens them o'er
With countless grass tips, each His utter care,
As are the swinging stars. The chestnuts spread
Wide-armed and dark—He builds their buttressed[2] limbs
Against the storm, and when they groan and sway
They call to Him for succor. And the birds!
How far and free they ride the weightless air,
And fall and soar and circle—ah, they feel
In swiftest onrush of their dizzy flight
His Hand beneath them. And yon waving wheat
That ripples all its shining blades with joy
Beneath the summer's winds—He bids it grow,
It, and the clustered vines, to furnish forth
His Holy Table! So mine evening thoughts
Run on and on, thus mingled; all the world
Speaking of God, my Lord, and when the West
Flames like a chalice, and its flooding rays
Frame the fair sun, poised ere he veils his light,

1. *sedulous* (sĕd′ū lŭs): diligent in application or pursuit. 2. *buttressed:* supported firmly.

Methinks the whole vast world is figured there.
God is its Sun! and it but gleams to show
In myriad forms, the One Eternal Fair
That bade it be." He paused, and could no more.
Then Francis prayed, his eyes besieging heaven.
"O God, My Father, I do give Thee praise,
That Thou hast spoken to these simple hearts,
What pride and troubled learning faint to know.
They search the spheres for light: this man of toil
Sees Thee, O Light, in all Thy common world!
And where Thy love hath placed him, finds his peace."

THINGS TO DO

Arrange a bulletin board showing Saint Francis surrounded by many kinds of birds. Make it more attractive by adding other creatures loved by the saint. Include a neat copy of the poem on page 184.

Mending Wall

ROBERT FROST

Something there is that doesn't love a wall,[1]
That sends the frozen-ground-swell under it,
And spills the upper boulders in the sun;
And makes gaps even two can pass abreast.
The work of hunters is another thing:
I have come after them and made repair
Where they have left not one stone on a stone,
But they would have the rabbit out of hiding,
To please the yelping dogs. The gaps I mean,
No one has seen them made or heard them made,
But at spring mending-time we find them there.
I let my neighbor know beyond the hill;
And on a day we meet to walk the line[2]
And set the wall between us once again.
We keep the wall between us as we go.
To each the boulders that have fallen to each.

1. *wall:* the poet is speaking here of the walls made of loose stones picked up from the fields which serve as fences in New England. 2. *line:* the boundary line.

And some are loaves and some so nearly balls
We have to use a spell to make them balance:
"Stay where you are until our backs are turned!"
We wear our fingers rough with handling them.
Oh, just another kind of outdoor game,
One on a side. It comes to little more:
There where it is we do not need the wall:
He is all pine and I am apple-orchard.
My apple trees will never get across
And eat the cones under his pines, I tell him.
He only says, "Good fences make good neighbors."
Spring is the mischief in me, and I wonder
If I could put a notion in his head:
"*Why* do they make good neighbors? Isn't it
Where there are cows? But here there are no cows.
Before I built a wall I'd ask to know
What I was walling in or walling out,
And to whom I was like to give offense.

Something there is that doesn't love a wall,
That wants it down." I could say "Elves" to him,
But it's not elves exactly, and I'd rather
He said it for himself. I see him there,
Bringing a stone grasped firmly by the top
In each hand, like an old-stone savage armed.
He moves in darkness, as it seems to me,
Not of woods only and the shade of trees.
He will not go behind his father's saying,
And he likes having thought of it so well
He says again, "Good fences make good neighbors."

HELPS FOR DISCUSSION

Does the poet agree with his neighbor who says, "Good fences make good neighbors"? Quote lines from the poem to show the poet's point of view.

Saint Francis to the Birds

KATHARINE TYNAN HINKSON

Little sisters, the birds,
  We must praise God, you and I—
  You, with songs that fill the sky;
I, with halting words.

All things tell His praise,
  Woods and waters thereof sing,
  Summer, Winter, Autumn, Spring,
And the nights and days.

And the winds of heaven,
  And the solemn hills of blue,
  And the brown earth and the dew,
And the thunder even,

Sometimes when ye sing,
  Name my name, that He may take
  Pity for the dear song's sake
On my shortcoming.

Loveliest of Trees

A. E. HOUSMAN

Loveliest of trees, the cherry now
Is hung with bloom along the bough,
And stands about the woodland ride
Wearing white for Eastertide.

Now, of my threescore years and ten,
Twenty will not come again,
And take from seventy springs a score,
It only leaves me fifty more.

And since to look at things in bloom
Fifty springs are little room,
About the woodlands I will go
To see the cherry hung with snow.

HELPS FOR DISCUSSION

How many years are left to the poet to see cherry blossoms? Why does he consider the time short?

Roadways

JOHN MASEFIELD

One road leads to London,
  One road runs to Wales,
My road leads me seawards
  To the white dipping sails.

One road leads to the river,
  As it goes singing slow;
My road leads to shipping,
  Where the bronzed sailors go.

Leads me, lures me, calls me
  To salt green tossing sea;
A road without earth's road-dust
  Is the right road for me.

A wet road heaving, shining,
  And wild with seagulls' cries,
A mad salt sea-wind blowing
  The salt spray in my eyes.

My road calls me, lures me
  West, east, south, and north;
Most roads lead men homewards,
  My road leads me forth

To add more miles to the tally
  Of gray miles left behind,
In quest of that one beauty
  God put me here to find.

The House by the Side of the Road

SAM WALTER FOSS

There are hermit souls that live withdrawn
  In the place of their self-content;
There are souls like stars, that dwell apart,
  In a fellowless firmament;
There are pioneer souls that blaze their paths
  Where highways never ran—
But let me live by the side of the road
  And be a friend to man.

Let me live in a house by the side of the road
  Where the race of men go by—
The men who are good and the men who are bad,
  As good and as bad as I.
I would not sit in the scorner's seat
  Or hurl the cynic's ban—
Let me live in a house by the side of the road
  And be a friend to man.

I see from my house by the side of the road,
  By the side of the highway of life,
The men who press with the ardor of hope,
  The men who are faint with strife,
But I turn not away from their smiles nor their tears,

Both parts of an infinite plan—
Let me live in a house by the side of the road
And be a friend to man.

I know there are brook-gladdened meadows ahead,
And mountains of wearisome height;
That the road passes on through the long afternoon
And stretches away to the night.
And still I rejoice when the travelers rejoice
And weep with the strangers that moan,
Nor live in my house by the side of the road
Like a man who dwells alone.

Let me live in my house by the side of the road,
Where the race of men go by—
They are good, they are bad, they are weak, they are strong,
Wise, foolish—so am I.
Then why should I sit in the scorner's seat
Or hurl the cynic's ban?
Let me live in my house by the side of the road
And be a friend to man.

A Song of Thanks

EDWARD SMYTH JONES

For the sun that shone at the dawn of spring,
For the flowers which bloom and the birds that sing,
For the verdant robe of the gray old earth,
For her coffers filled with their countless worth,
For the flocks which feed on a thousand hills,
For the rippling streams which turn the mills,
For the lowing herds in the lovely vale,
For the songs of gladness on the gale,—
From the Gulf and the Lakes to the Oceans' banks,—
Lord God of Hosts, we give Thee thanks!

For the farmer reaping his whitened fields,
For the bounty which the rich soil yields,
For the cooling dews and refreshing rains,
For the sun which ripens the golden grains,

For the bearded wheat and the fattened swine,
For the stallèd ox and the fruitful vine,
For the tubers large and cotton white,
For the kid and the lambkin frisk and blithe,
For the swan which floats near the river-banks,—
Lord God of Hosts, we give Thee thanks!

For the pumpkin sweet and the yellow yam,
For the corn and beans and the sugared ham,
For the plum and the peach and the apple red,
For the dear old press where the wine is tread,
For the cock which crows at the breaking dawn,
And the proud old "turk" of the farmer's barn,
For the fish which swim in the babbling brooks,
For the game which hide in the shady nooks,—
From the Gulf and the Lakes to the Oceans' banks—
Lord God of Hosts, we give Thee thanks!

For the sturdy oaks and the stately pines,
For the lead and the coal from the deep, dark mines,
For the silver ores of a thousand fold,
For the diamond bright and the yellow gold,
For the river boat and the flying train,
For the fleecy sail of the rolling main,
For the velvet sponge and the glossy pearl,
For the flag of peace which we now unfurl,—
From the Gulf and the Lakes to the Oceans' banks,—
Lord God of Hosts, we give Thee thanks!

For the lowly cot and the mansion fair,
For the peace and plenty together share,
For the Hand which guides us from above,
For Thy tender mercies, abiding love,
For the blessed home with its children gay,
For returnings of Thanksgiving Day,
For the bearing toils and the sharing cares,
We lift up our hearts in our songs and our prayers,—
From the Gulf and the Lakes to the Oceans' banks,—
Lord God of Hosts, we give Thee thanks!

RALPH I SHEPHERD

IV

At Christmastide

Once, at least, in every year the spirit of Christ is born again in the hearts of men. Throughout a great part of the world men and women, boys and girls greet one another with words of joy. For a little while the cares and troubles of their everyday lives are forgotten as they celebrate the birthday of the Child who was born in a stable of Bethlehem. For a little while the love of one another, which He preached to His followers, glows again in the souls of mankind.

Through the long history of Christianity writers have used their finest art to set down something of this warm spirit of friendliness. Nearly every nation has thus expressed its Christmas joy. For centuries the Polish people have sung the splendid "Kolendy for Christmas." From the hearts of people in Italy, Spain, Portugal, Germany, France, England, and Ireland, as well as in scores of other nations, have risen beautiful carols to celebrate the birth of Christ. A German organist wrote the hymn "Silent Night," which is now sung all over the world at Christmastide.

The celebration of Christmas varies in the many lands. "Antu Christmas" pictures a type of civilization most unlike that presented in Dickens's London of *A Christmas Carol.* Joyce Kilmer's "Kings" is far different in style from Sister Violante do Ceo's "While to Bethlehem We Are Going." The Neapolitan "When Christ Was Born" expresses the Christmas message in a form unlike "Noel" or the Irish "Feast o' Saint Stephen." But neither time nor distance changes the essential observance of Christmas. Naples and Paris, Lisbon and New York, Killarney and Chicago, rural England and Manchuria have at Christmastide the common bond of people who love one another because they love the Christ Child Who came, long years ago, to save the whole wide world.

Luke ii, 8–20

And there were shepherds in the same district living in the fields and keeping watch over their flock by night. And behold, an angel of the Lord stood by them and the glory of God shone round about them, and they feared exceedingly.

And the angel said to them, "Do not be afraid, for behold, I bring you good news of great joy which shall be to all the people; for there has been born to you today in the town of David a Savior, who is Christ the Lord. And this shall be a sign to you: you will find an infant wrapped in swaddling clothes and lying in a manger." And suddenly there was with the angel a multitude of the heavenly host praising God and saying,

Glory to God in the highest, and peace on earth among men of good will.

And it came to pass, when the angels had departed from them into heaven, that the shepherds were saying to one another, "Let us go over to Bethlehem and see this thing that has come to pass, which the Lord has made known to us."

So they went with haste, and they found Mary and Joseph, and the babe lying in the manger. And when they had seen, they understood what had been told them concerning this child. And all who heard marvelled at the things told them by the shepherds. But Mary kept in mind all these words, pondering them in her heart. And the shepherds returned, glorifying and praising God for all that they had heard and seen, even as it was spoken to them.

By every art, through the ages since the birth of Christ, mankind has celebrated the following of

The Star of Bethlehem

ALICE CORBIN HENDERSON

"*And thou, Bethlehem—though thou art little among the thousands of Judah, yet out of thee shall he come forth that is to be the ruler of Israel; whose goings forth have been from of old, from everlasting.*"

SCENE: About midnight, in the stable of the Inn at Bethlehem.

[*Before the curtain an* ANGEL, dressed in conventional *symbolic costume and carrying a thin silver trumpet, makes announcement: He lifts the horn to his lips and blows one long, clear note; then addresses the people.*]

THE ANGEL WITH THE SILVER TRUMPET: Now for one day, from sun to sun,

The Lord of Love love's course will run:
Meekly He cometh as a child,
With Mary, Mother, Virgin mild,
Bending above Him, while the Dove
Shines, silver-crowned, from clouds above.

Now once again, with gold and myrrh
And frankincense, come unto her
The Wise Men, following the Star;
Shepherds, asleep in fields afar,
Waken again to see the Light,—
And hear a Voice sing in the night:

[*A voice sings from behind the curtain.*]

Behold, a Child is born today
Whom shepherds love and kings obey!
Behold, behold, a little Child
Is born to Mary, Virgin mild,—
A little Child of joy and love
Born to the kingdom of the Dove!

ANGEL [*stepping forward and becoming more conversational*]: Pay close attention, ye that bide on earth,
Pay close attention, ye that bide on earth,
And hear the story of our Master's birth.
How Wise Men, journeying from the east afar,
And Shepherds, waking, following the Star,
Sought to find Jesus: how, with lights like rain
They found the Inn o'erflowing, all in vain—
Until, outside, like any common stranger,
They found our Savior lying in a manger!

[*Exit.*]

[*The curtain goes up and discloses the interior of a rude stable lighted only by rushlights or lanterns. It is about midnight. There is a big door on the left near the front of the stage. At the back of the room,* MARY *is lying on a low cot. The* INNKEEPER, *his* WIFE, *and* CHILD *are toward the front.*]

INNKEEPER: Now all is well. The mother sleeps at last.
WIFE: And with the child all's well.—
Poor soul! Her pain,
As ever, is rewarded with the bliss
And endless pain of motherhood.

[*She busies herself about the place. The* INNKEEPER *takes up his lantern and goes out.*]

CHILD: I am afraid!
WIFE: What ails thee?
CHILD: The child there in the manger
Cried out my name,—
But when I went to look at it, it was asleep.
WIFE: Must not tell lies!
CHILD: Mother, I told no lie! And see how bright,
How very bright the light is over there!
WIFE: Heaven have mercy that we turned them out
To lie with cattle! I had better given
The bare board I call mine, and lain on earth
Than cause this anguish starting at my heart!

CHILD: The light—is brighter now—
And someone's there!

[*Knocking is heard at the door, drawing* WIFE'S *attention.*]

WIFE: Who's there?

CHILD: Not there, not there, but over by the manger.

[*An* ANGEL *appears by the manger. The knocking ceases a moment.*]

ANGEL: Peace on earth, good will to men,
For unto you this day is born, a Savior!
And this shall be a sign:
Within the little town of Bethlehem,
You'll find the Savior lying in a manger!

[*Disappears.*]

[*The* WIFE *has dropped on her knees and is still stupefied. The knocking at the door continues and the* CHILD *runs to the door, tiptoes, and lifts up the heavy latch. Enter the* INNKEEPER *and* JOSEPH.]

INNKEEPER: Up, woman, up! for there are strangers asking
If this is where the King is, he who is
The King of all Judea! It may be
That we here entertain him unaware!
The strangers bear rich presents and are seeking
The King, to greet him—
WIFE: He, indeed, *is* here!
INNKEEPER: And you have kept it from me? He has had
The light, the fare, the ordinary room
We give to any stranger?
WIFE: He has had
No light, no fare, not even any room,
Nor warmth save that of cattle,—there He lies,
The King of Kings, asleep in yonder manger!
INNKEEPER: You are crazy!
JOSEPH: No, she has seen a vision!
[*Knocking at the door again.*]
VOICES [*outside*]: Open, for here is born the King of Kings,
And here the Lord of Lords is born today!

[*Enter the* SHEPHERDS.]

FIRST SHEPHERD: We saw the Heavens open, and a Voice
Declaring "Peace on earth, good will to men!—
Go find the Savior, for the Lamb of God
Is born today and lieth in a manger."
SECOND SHEPHERD: And through this little town of Bethlehem,
We have come hurrying.—All the lights were low,
And people sleeping, and no one to ask
The way of,—still the spirit led us,
And over stone and pebble we have come,
And rested not until we reached this stable.

INNKEEPER: Where *is* the King?
THIRD SHEPHERD: Why, He is here. He lieth
Beside His Mother, sleeping in the manger.
INNKEEPER: Can I be crazy?—
But no, there were three kings that came to ask—
To ask if I could tell them of the King!—

[*Knocking at the door again. The* INNKEEPER *opens the door. The* THREE KINGS *enter.*]

FIRST KING: Where is the King?
SECOND KING: For we have seen—
THIRD KING: His star in the east, and are come to worship Him!
WIFE: The King is lying sleeping in the manger!
[MARY *is now sitting up, and the* WIFE *places the* BABY *in her arms. The* SHEPHERDS *kneel down on the right of the* VIRGIN, *and the* KINGS *move forward and kneel on the left.*]
FIRST KING: I bring you gold—
SECOND KING: I frankincense—
THIRD KING: I myrrh.
FIRST KING: Purity absolute—
SECOND KING: Fragrance of suffering—
THIRD KING: Bitter-sweet;
ALL KINGS: Glory above all men.
FIRST SHEPHERD: The Virgin Mother weeps.
SECOND SHEPHERD: Yea, sorrow above all sorrow
Touches the Virgin's eyes!
INNKEEPER: In all the time that I've been keeping inn,
I never have seen anything like this!
WIFE: The Child sits up as though He were a year!
[*There is a pause during which the music of the opening song is played, and the picture held. The* ANGEL *appears again beside the manger, back of the group, and stands there until the music ceases. With cessation of the music there is a stir among the people, indicating the return of the more normal tone of every day.*]

FIRST KING [*rises and speaks to* MARY]: All lore is written in the book of stars;
If we could read the stars, we could read all.
Alone upon the desert man sees more
Than from the crowded housetops, but a veil
Darkly obscureth more than wisest sage
Can ever in a thousand years discern.—
One moment only in a thousand years,
The veil is lifted, then the darkness settles,—
But we who watch forget the thousand years!

FIRST SHEPHERD: The sheep will wander far this moonlight night.

SECOND SHEPHERD: 'Tis late, and the bellwether will be strayed.

FIRST KING [*to* MARY]: You, Virgin Mother, hold the mystic keys
Of life and death, all mystery, from today.
Alone upon the desert we but keep
The lonely watch of wisdom with the stars.

[*The* KINGS *turn and start to go out.*]

THIRD SHEPHERD: We shall not soon forget this night of moonlight.

[*The* KINGS *and* SHEPHERDS *go out slowly.*]

CHILD: Sleep, little Babe, sleep, nor be dismayed
By cockcrow, or dog bark; I will tie
The dog up that he shall not bay the moon! [*Runs out.*]

[MARY *is now lying down again, with her head bent over the* BABE *as if asleep. The* KINGS *and the* SHEPHERDS *have gone out, and following them the* INNKEEPER, *the* CHILD, *and the* INNKEEPER'S WIFE. *The big door remains open, and the cool blue light of night comes into the room, making the lantern light pale.*]

JOSEPH [*standing by the door*]: How peaceful night lies over Bethlehem!

How solemnly and still the moon looks down
Out of a mist of cloud, and not a leaf
On any tree stirs with the faintest sound.
Glory to God in the highest! On earth,
Peace, and good will toward men.
It soon will be cockcrow. Mary sleeps.
And I will put this light out and lie down.

[*He extinguishes the light and the stage is in darkness.*]

[*Curtain falls.*]

THINGS TO DO

To stage this play, form committees to choose players, select costumes, provide properties, conduct rehearsals, and arrange for presentation.

ART OF CHRISTMASTIDE

What artist could resist the divine urge to paint the greatest story ever told? With skill and sympathy and reverence the truly great artists have set down on lasting canvas the eternal beauty of the first Christmas. There are so many great pictures of Christmas and of the Holy Family that we can list but a few: *Holy Night*, by CORREGGIO; *Journey of the Magi*, by SASSETTA; *Madonna of the Chair*, by RAPHAEL, and *Madonna (the Small Cowper)*, by RAPHAEL; *Holy Family of the Beardless Joseph*, by RAPHAEL; *Saint John the Baptist*, by DEL SARTO; *Virgin and Child*, by MORETTO; *Holy Family*, by BARTOLOMMEO; *Annunciation*, by FRA FILIPPO LIPPI; *Virgin Annunciate*, by MASOLINO DA PANICALE; *Madonna and Child*, by GIOTTO; *Madonna*, by MURILLO; *Annunciation, Birth of Our Lord* and *Adoration of the Shepherds*, by TISSOT.

From Germany, from France, and from Poland have come these three world-famous Christmas songs:

Silent Night

JOSEPH MOHR

Silent Night, Holy Night!
All is calm, all is bright,
'Round yon Virgin Mother and Child!
Holy Infant, so tender and mild,
Sleep in heavenly peace.

Silent Night, Holy Night!
Shepherds quake at the sight!
Glories stream from heaven afar,
Heav'nly hosts sing Alleluia;
Christ, the Saviour is born.

Silent Night, Holy Night!
Son of God, love's pure light,
Radiant beams from Thy holy face,
With the dawn of redeeming grace,
Jesus, Lord, at Thy birth.

Silent Night, Holy Night!
Guiding star, lend thy light,
See the eastern wise men bring,
Gifts and homage to our King,
Jesus, the Saviour is born.

Noel

HILAIRE BELLOC

On a winter's night long time ago
  (The bells ring loud and the bells ring low),
When high howled wind, and down fell snow
  (Carillon, Carilla).
Saint Joseph he and Notre Dame,
Riding on an ass, full weary came
From Nazareth into Bethlehem.
  And the small child Jesus smile on you.

And Bethlehem inn they stood before
  (The bells ring less and the bells ring more),
The landlord bade them begone from his door
  (Carillon, Carilla).
"Poor folk" (says he), "must lie where they may,
For the Duke of Jewry comes this way,
With all his train on a Christmas Day."
  And the small child Jesus smile on you.

Poor folk that may carol hear
  (The bells ring single and the bells ring clear)
See! God's one child had hardest cheer!
  (Carillon, Carilla).
Men grown hard on a Christmas morn;
The dumb beast by and a babe forlorn.
It was very, very cold when our Lord was born.
  And the small child Jesus smile on you.

THINGS TO DO

Prepare a program for the class, using this and similar Christmas hymns and carols in this unit. Preface each selection with a brief historical account of its origin.

Kolendy[1] for Christmas

From the Polish by Irena Dalgiewicz

Lullaby, little Jesus, my little pearl,
Lullaby, beloved, my little treasure,
Lullaby, little Jesus, lullaby, lullaby,
And Thou, His Mother, His weeping calm.

Close Thy little lids, a-blinking with tears,
Close Thy little lips, quivering with sobbing,
Lullaby, little Jesus, lullaby, lullaby,
And Thou, His Mother, His weeping calm.

I will give to Jesus sweet berries,
I will go with Him into the garden of His Mother's heart;
Lullaby, little Jesus, etc.

I will give to Jesus butter with bread,
I will place a loaf in His crib;
Lullaby, little Jesus, etc.

Lullaby, beautiful, my little angel,
Lullaby, gracious flower of the world;
Lullaby, little Jesus, etc.

I will give Thee, Jesus, candies sweet,
Raisins and almonds from my store;
Lullaby, little Jesus, etc.

I will give to the little One a beautiful apple,
I will give Him the heart of His beloved Mother;
Lullaby, little Jesus, etc.

Hush, hush, hush! may the little Child slumber,
Look, how He sleeps, the Infant;
Lullaby, little Jesus, etc.

Hush, hush, hush! slumber ye all,
Do not waken my little Child;
Lullaby, little Jesus, etc.

1. *Kolendy* (kŏ lĕn′dē): Polish Christmas carols.

One of the great stories of Christmastide was written by Charles Dickens. Who does not know old Scrooge, and Bob Cratchit, and especially Tiny Tim? Here is an opportunity to meet these famous people as they are described in

A Christmas Carol (*In Prose*)

Being a Ghost Story of Christmas

CHARLES DICKENS

Stave[1] *One · Marley's Ghost*

Marley was dead, to begin with. There is no doubt whatever about that. The register of his burial was signed by the clergyman, the clerk, the undertaker, and the chief mourner. Scrooge signed it; and Scrooge's name was good upon 'Change[2] for anything he chose to put his hand to. Old Marley was as dead as a doornail.

Scrooge knew he was dead? Of course he did. How could it be otherwise? Scrooge and he were partners for I don't know how many years. Scrooge was his sole friend and sole mourner. And even Scrooge was not so dreadfully cut up by the sad event, but that he was an excellent man of business on the very day of the funeral.

The mention of Marley's funeral brings me back to the point I started from. There is no doubt that Marley was dead. This must be distinctly understood, or nothing wonderful can come of the story I am going to relate.

Oh, but he was a tight-fisted hand at the grindstone, Scrooge! a squeezing, wrenching, grasping, scraping, clutching, covetous old sinner! Hard and sharp as flint, from which no steel had ever struck out generous fire; secret, and self-contained, and solitary as an oyster. The cold within him froze his old features, nipped his pointed nose, shriveled his cheek, stiffened his gait; made his eyes red, his thin lips blue; and spoke out shrewdly in his grating voice.

Nobody ever stopped him in the street to say, with gladsome looks, "My dear Scrooge, how are you? When will you

1. *stave:* a stanza, or division, of a song. Since Dickens called his story a carol he has named the divisions staves. 2. *'Change:* Exchange, the place where merchants and others meet to do business.

come to see me?" No beggars implored him to bestow a trifle, no children asked him what it was o'clock, no man or woman ever once in all his life inquired the way to such and such a place, of Scrooge. Even the blind men's dogs appeared to know him; and when they saw him coming on, would tug their owners into doorways and up courts; and then would wag their tails as though they said, "No eye at all is better than an evil eye, dark master!" But what did Scrooge care? It was the very thing he liked.

Once upon a time—of all the good days in the year, on Christmas Eve—old Scrooge sat busy in his countinghouse. It was cold, bleak, biting weather; foggy withal; and he could hear the people in the court outside go wheezing up and down, beating their hands upon their breasts, and stamping their feet upon the pavement stones to warm them. The City clocks had only just gone three, but it was quite dark already—it had not been light all day—and candles were flaring in the windows of the neighboring offices, like ruddy smears upon the palpable brown air. The fog came pouring in at every chink and keyhole, and was so dense without, that although the court was of the narrowest, the houses opposite were mere phantoms.

The door of Scrooge's countinghouse was open that he might keep his eye upon his clerk, who in a dismal little cell beyond, a sort of tank, was copying letters. Scrooge had a very small fire, but the clerk's fire was so very much smaller that it looked like one coal. But he couldn't replenish it, for Scrooge kept the coal box in his own room; and so surely as the clerk came in with the shovel, the master predicted that it would be necessary for them to part. Wherefore the clerk put on his white comforter, and tried to warm himself at the candle; in which effort, not being a man of a strong imagination, he failed.

"A merry Christmas, uncle! God save you!" cried a cheerful voice. It was the voice of Scrooge's nephew, who had so heated himself with rapid walking in the fog and frost, that he was all in a glow; his face was ruddy and handsome; his eyes sparkled, and his breath smoked.

"Bah!" said Scrooge. "Humbug!"

"Christmas a humbug, uncle!" said Scrooge's nephew. "You don't mean that, I am sure."

"I do," said Scrooge. "Merry Christmas! What right have you to be merry? You're poor enough."

"Come, then," returned the nephew gayly. "What right have you to be dismal? You're rich enough."

Scrooge, having no better answer ready on the spur of the moment, said, "Bah!" again; and followed it up with "Humbug!"

"Don't be cross, uncle," said the nephew.

"What else can I be," returned the uncle, "when I live in such a world of fools as this? Merry Christmas! Out upon merry Christmas! What's Christmas time to you but a time for paying bills without money; a time for finding yourself a year older, but not an hour richer? If I could work my will," said Scrooge, indignantly, "every idiot who goes about with 'Merry Christmas' on his lips, should be boiled with his own pudding, and buried with a stake of holly through his heart. He should!"

"Uncle!" pleaded the nephew.

"Nephew!" returned the uncle, sternly, "keep Christmas in your own way, and let me keep it in mine."

"Keep it!" repeated Scrooge's nephew. "But you don't keep it."

"Let me leave it alone, then," said Scrooge. "Much good may it do you! Much good it has ever done you!"

"There are many things from which I might have derived good, by which I have not profited, I dare say," returned the nephew; "Christmas among the rest. But I am sure I have always thought of Christmas time as a good time; a kind, forgiving, charitable, pleasant time; the only time I know of when men and women seem by one consent to open their shut-up hearts freely. And therefore, uncle, though it has never put a scrap of gold or silver in my pocket, I believe that it *has* done me good, and *will* do me good; and I say, God bless it!"

The clerk in the Tank involuntarily applauded.

"Let me hear another sound from *you*," said Scrooge, "and you'll keep your Christmas by losing your situation. You're quite a powerful speaker, sir," he added, turning to his nephew. "I wonder you don't go into Parliament."

"Don't be angry, uncle. Come! Dine with us tomorrow."

"Good afternoon," said Scrooge.

"I am sorry, with all my heart, to find you so resolute. But I have made the trial in homage to Christmas, and I'll keep my Christmas humor to the last. So A Merry Christmas, uncle!"

"Good afternoon!" said Scrooge.

"And A Happy New Year!"

"Good afternoon!" said Scrooge.

His nephew left the room without an angry word, notwithstanding. He stopped at the outer door to bestow the greetings of the season on the clerk, who, cold as he was, was warmer than Scrooge; for he returned them cordially.

"There's another fellow," muttered Scrooge, who overheard him; "my clerk, with fifteen shillings a week, and a wife and family, talking about a merry Christmas."

Meanwhile the fog and darkness thickened. The ancient tower of a church, whose gruff old bell was always peeping slyly down at Scrooge, became invisible, and struck the hours and quarters in the clouds, with tremulous vibrations afterwards as if its teeth were chattering in its frozen head up there. The cold became intense.

At length the hour of shutting up the countinghouse arrived. With an ill will Scrooge dismounted from his stool, and tacitly admitted the fact to the expectant clerk in the Tank, who instantly snuffed his candle out, and put on his hat.

"You'll want all day tomorrow, I suppose?" said Scrooge.

"If quite convenient, sir."

"It's not convenient," said Scrooge, "and it's not fair. If I was to stop half a crown for it, you'd think yourself ill-used, I'll be bound?"

The clerk smiled faintly.

"And yet," said Scrooge, "you don't think *me* ill-used, when I pay a day's wages for no work."

The clerk observed that it was only once a year.

"A poor excuse for picking a man's pocket every twenty-fifth of December!" said Scrooge, buttoning his greatcoat to the chin. "But I suppose you must have the whole day. Be here all the earlier next morning!"

The clerk promised that he would; and Scrooge walked out with a growl. The office was closed in a twinkling, and the clerk, with the long ends of his white comforter dangling below his waist (for he boasted no greatcoat), went down a slide on Cornhill,[3] at the end of a lane of boys, twenty times, in honor of its being Christmas Eve, and then ran home to Camden Town[4] as hard as he could pelt, to play at blindman's buff.

Scrooge took his melancholy dinner in his usual melancholy tavern; and having read all the newspapers, and beguiled the rest of the evening with his banker's book, went home to bed. He lived in chambers which had once belonged to his deceased partner. They were a gloomy suite of rooms, for nobody lived

3. *Cornhill:* an important street in London. 4. *Camden Town:* a suburb of London.

in the building but Scrooge, the other rooms being all let out as offices. The yard was so dark that even Scrooge, who knew its every stone, was fain to grope with his hands.

Now, it is a fact that there was nothing at all particular about the knocker on the door, except that it was very large. It is also a fact that Scrooge had seen it, night and morning, during his whole residence in that place; also that Scrooge had as little of what is called fancy about him as any man in the City of London. Let it also be borne in mind that Scrooge had not bestowed one thought on Marley. And then let any man explain to me, if he can, how it happened that Scrooge, having his key in the lock of the door, saw in the knocker, not a knocker, but Marley's face.

Marley's face. It was not in impenetrable shadow as the other objects in the yard were, but had a dismal light about it, like a bad lobster in a dark cellar. It was not angry or ferocious, but looked at Scrooge as Marley used to look, with ghostly spectacles turned up on its ghostly forehead. The hair was curiously stirred, as if by breath or hot air; and, though the eyes were wide open, they were perfectly motionless. That, and its livid color, made it horrible.

As Scrooge looked fixedly at this phenomenon, it was a knocker again. To say that he was not startled would be untrue. But he put his hand upon the key he had relinquished, turned it sturdily, walked in, and lighted his candle.

He *did* pause before he shut the door; and he *did* look cautiously behind it first, as if he half expected to be terrified with the sight of Marley's pigtail sticking out into the hall. But there was nothing on the back of the door, except the screws and nuts that held the knocker on; so he said "Pooh, pooh!" and closed it with a bang.

The sound resounded through the house like thunder. Every room above, and every cask in the wine merchant's cellars below, appeared to have a separate peal of echoes of its own. Scrooge was not a man to be frightened by echoes. He fastened the door, and walked across the hall, and up the stairs—slowly too,—trimming his candle as he went.

Up Scrooge went, not caring a button for the darkness;

darkness is cheap, and Scrooge liked it. But before he shut his heavy door, he walked through his rooms to see that all was right. He had just enough recollection of the face to desire to do that.

Quite satisfied, he closed his door, and locked himself in; double-locked himself in, which was not his custom. Thus secured against surprise, he took off his cravat; put on his dressing gown and slippers, and his nightcap; and sat down before the fire to take his gruel.

It was a very low fire indeed; nothing on such a bitter night. He was obliged to sit close to it, and brood over it, before he could extract the least sensation of warmth from such a handful of fuel. The fireplace was an old one, built by some Dutch merchant long ago, and paved all round with quaint Dutch tiles, designed to illustrate the Scriptures. If each smooth tile had been a blank at first, with power to shape some picture on its surface from the disjointed fragments of his thoughts, there would have been a copy of old Marley's head on every one.

"Humbug!" said Scrooge; and walked across the room.

After several turns, he sat down again. As he threw his head back in the chair, his glance happened to rest upon a bell, a disused bell, that hung in the room. It was with great astonishment, and with a strange, inexplicable dread, that as he looked, he saw this bell begin to swing. It swung so softly that it scarcely made a sound; but soon it rang out loudly, and so did every bell in the house.

This might have lasted half a minute, or a minute, but it seemed an hour. The bells ceased as they had begun, together. They were succeeded by a clanking noise, deep down below; as if some person were dragging a heavy chain over the casks in the wine merchant's cellar. Scrooge then remembered to have heard that ghosts in haunted houses were described as dragging chains.

The cellar door flew open with a booming sound, and then he heard the noise much louder, on the floors below; then coming up the stairs; then coming straight towards his door.

"It's humbug still!" said Scrooge. "I won't believe it."

His color changed though, when, without a pause, it came on through the heavy door, and passed into the room before his eyes. Upon its coming in, the dying flame leaped up, as though it cried, "I know him! Marley's Ghost!" and fell again.

The same face—the very same. Marley in his pigtail, usual waistcoat, tights, and boots. The chain he drew was clasped about his middle. It was long, and wound about him like a tail; and it was made (for Scrooge observed it closely) of cash boxes, keys, padlocks, ledgers, deeds, and heavy purses wrought in steel. His body was transparent; so that Scrooge, observing him, and looking through his waistcoat, could see the two buttons on his coat behind.

Though he looked the phantom through and through, and saw it standing before him; though he felt the chilling influence of its death-cold eyes, and marked the very texture of the folded kerchief bound about its head and chin, he was still incredulous, and fought against his senses.

"How now!" said Scrooge, caustic and cold as ever. "What do you want with me?"

"Much!"—Marley's voice, no doubt about it.

"Who are you?"

"Ask me who I *was*."

"Who *were* you then?" said Scrooge, raising his voice.

"In life I was your partner, Jacob Marley."

"Can you—can you sit down?" asked Scrooge, looking doubtfully at him.

"I can."

"Do it then."

The Ghost sat down on the opposite side of the fireplace, as if he were quite used to it.

"You don't believe in me," observed the Ghost.

"I don't," said Scrooge. "There's more of gravy than of grave about you, whatever you are! Humbug, I tell you—humbug!"

At this the spirit raised a frightful cry, and shook its chain with such a dismal and appalling noise, that Scrooge held on tight to his chair, to save himself from falling in a swoon. But how much greater was his horror, when the phantom taking off the bandage round its head, as if it were too warm to wear indoors, its lower jaw dropped down upon its breast! Scrooge fell upon his knees, and clasped his hands.

"Mercy!" he said. "Dreadful apparition, why do you trouble me?"

"Man of the worldly mind!" replied the Ghost, "do you believe in me or not?"

"I do," said Scrooge. "I must. But why do spirits walk the earth, and why do they come to me?"

"It is required of every man," the Ghost returned, "that the spirit within him should walk abroad among his fellow men, and travel far and wide; and if that spirit goes not forth in life, it is condemned to do so after death. It is doomed to wander through the world—oh, woe is me!—and witness what it cannot share, but might have shared on earth, and turned to happiness!"

Again the specter raised a cry, and shook its chain, and wrung its shadowy hands.

"You are fettered," said Scrooge, trembling. "Tell me why?"

"I wear the chain I forged in life," replied the Ghost. "I made it link by link, and yard by yard; I girded it on of my own free will, and of my own free will I wore it. Is its pattern strange to *you*?"

Scrooge trembled more and more.

"Or would you know," pursued the Ghost, "the weight and length of the strong coil you bear yourself? It was full as heavy and as long as this, seven Christmas Eves ago. You have labored on it since. It is a ponderous chain!"

Scrooge glanced about him on the floor, in the expectation of finding himself surrounded by some fifty or sixty fathoms of iron cable; but he could see nothing.

"Jacob," he said imploringly. "Old Jacob Marley, tell me more. Speak comfort to me, Jacob."

"I have none to give," the Ghost replied. "It comes from other regions, Ebenezer Scrooge, and is conveyed by other ministers,[5] to other kinds of men. Nor can I tell you what I would. A very little more, is all permitted to me. I cannot rest, I cannot stay, I cannot linger anywhere. My spirit never walked beyond our countinghouse, and weary journeys lie before me!"

Scrooge was very much dismayed to hear the specter going on at this rate, and began to quake exceedingly.

"Hear me!" cried the Ghost. "My time is nearly gone."

"I will," said Scrooge. "But don't be hard upon me! Don't be flowery, Jacob!"

"You will be haunted," resumed the Ghost, "by Three Spirits."

Scrooge's countenance fell almost as low as the Ghost's had done. "I—I think I'd rather not," he said.

"Without their visits," said the Ghost, "you cannot hope to shun the path I tread. Expect the first tomorrow, when the bell tolls one. Expect the second on the next night at the same hour. The third upon the next night when the last stroke of twelve has ceased to vibrate. Look to see me no more; and look that, for your own sake, you remember what has passed between us!"

When it had said these words, the specter took its wrapper from the table, and bound it round its head, as before. Scrooge ventured to raise his eyes again, and found his supernatural visitor confronting him in an erect attitude, with its chain wound over and about its arm.

5. *ministers:* messengers.

The apparition walked backward from him; and at every step it took, the window raised itself a little, so that when the specter reached it, it was wide open. It beckoned Scrooge to approach, which he did. When they were within two paces of each other, Marley's Ghost held up its hand, warning him to come no nearer. Scrooge stopped.

He became sensible of confused noises in the air; incoherent sounds of lamentation and regret; wailings inexpressibly sorrowful and self-accusatory. The specter, after listening for a moment, joined in the mournful dirge, and floated out upon the bleak, dark night.

Scrooge followed to the window, desperate in his curiosity. He looked out.

The air was filled with phantoms, wandering hither and thither in restless haste, and moaning as they went. Every one of them wore chains like Marley's Ghost; none were free.

Scrooge closed the window, and examined the door by which the Ghost had entered. It was double-locked, as he had locked it with his own hands, and the bolts were undisturbed. He tried to say "Humbug!" but stopped at the first syllable. And being, from the emotion he had undergone, or his glimpse of the Invisible World, or the lateness of the hour, much in need of repose, went straight to bed, without undressing, and fell asleep upon the instant.

Stave Two · The First of the Three Spirits

[As Marley's Ghost had predicted, the first spirit, the Ghost of Christmas Past, appeared before Scrooge when the bell tolled one. By its magical powers the Ghost transported Scrooge to his boyhood days. He saw himself as a child, lonely, neglected, in boarding school. He saw himself as a young man, an apprentice to jolly old Fezziwig, and re-lived again the happy days when his good-hearted master held a dance for all his apprentices to celebrate the merry Christmas season. He saw again his parting from the lovely girl whom he had once loved, but whom he pushed aside in his search for worldly goods.

"Spirit!" cried Scrooge, "remove me from this place!"

"I told you that these were shadows of the things that have been," said the Ghost. "That they are what they are, do not blame me!"

The Spirit departed and Scrooge sank into a heavy sleep.]

Stave Three · The Second of the Three Spirits

Awaking in the middle of a prodigiously tough snore, and sitting up in bed to get his thoughts together, Scrooge had no occasion to be told that the bell was again upon the stroke of one. Now, being prepared for almost anything, he was not by any means prepared for nothing; and, consequently, when the bell struck one, and no shape appeared, he was taken with a violent fit of trembling. Five minutes, ten minutes, a quarter of an hour went by, yet nothing came. All this time, he lay upon his bed, the very core and center of a blaze of ruddy light, which streamed upon it when the clock proclaimed the hour; and which, being only light, was more alarming than a dozen ghosts. At last, he began to think that the source and secret of this ghostly light might be in the adjoining room, from whence, on further tracing it, it seemed to shine. This idea taking full possession of his mind, he got up softly and shuffled in his slippers to the door.

The moment Scrooge's hand was on the lock, a strange voice called him by his name, and bade him enter. He obeyed.

It was his own room. There was no doubt about that. But it had undergone a surprising transformation. The walls and ceiling were so hung with living green that it looked a perfect grove, from every part of which bright gleaming berries glistened. The crisp leaves of holly, mistletoe, and ivy reflected back the light, as if so many little mirrors had been scattered there; and such a mighty blaze went roaring up the chimney, as that dull hearth had never known in Scrooge's time, or Marley's, or for many and many a winter season gone. Heaped up on the floor, to form a kind of throne, were turkeys, geese, game, roast boar, great joints of meat, sucking pigs, long wreaths of sausages, mince pies, plum puddings, barrels of oysters, red-hot chestnuts, cherry-cheeked apples, juicy oranges, luscious pears, immense cakes, and seething bowls of punch that made the chamber dim with their delicious steam. In easy state upon this couch, there sat a jolly Giant, glorious to see; who bore a glowing torch, in shape not unlike Plenty's horn, and held it up, high up, to shed its light on Scrooge, as he came peeping round the door.

"Come in!" exclaimed the Ghost. "Come in! and know me better, man!"

Scrooge entered timidly, and hung his head before this Spirit. He was not the dogged Scrooge he had been; and though the Spirit's eyes were clear and kind, he did not like to meet them.

"I am the Ghost of Christmas Present," said the Spirit. "Look upon me!"

Scrooge reverently did so. It was clothed in one simple deep green robe, or mantle, bordered with white fur. Its feet, observable beneath the ample folds of the garment, were also bare; and on its head it wore no other covering than a holly wreath set here and there with shining icicles. Its dark brown curls were long and free,—free as its genial face, its sparkling eye, its open hand, its cheery voice, and its joyful air. Girded round its middle was an antique scabbard; but no sword was in it, and the ancient sheath was eaten up with rust.

The Ghost of Christmas Present rose.

"Spirit," said Scrooge submissively, "conduct me where you will. I went forth last night on compulsion, and I learnt a lesson which is working now. Tonight, if you have aught to teach me, let me profit by it."

"Touch my robe!"

Scrooge did as he was told, and held it fast.

Holly, mistletoe, red berries, ivy, turkeys, geese, game, roast boar, meat, pigs, sausages, oysters, pies, puddings, fruit, and punch, all vanished instantly. So did the room, the fire, the ruddy glow, the hour of night, and they stood in the city streets on Christmas morning, where (for the weather was severe) the people made a rough, but brisk and not unpleasant kind of music, in scraping the snow from the pavement in front of their dwellings, and from the tops of their houses, whence it was mad delight to the boys to see it come plumping down into the road below, and splitting into artificial little snowstorms.

For the people who were shoveling away on the housetops were jovial and full of glee, calling out to one another and now and then exchanging a facetious snowball—better-natured missile far than many a wordy jest—laughing heartily if it went right and not less heartily if it went wrong. The poulterers' shops were still half open, and the fruiterers' were radiant in their glory. There were great, round, pot-bellied baskets of chestnuts, shaped like the waistcoats of jolly old gentlemen, lolling at the doors, and tumbling out into the street in their apoplectic opulence. There were ruddy, brown-faced broad-girthed Spanish Onions. There were pears and apples, clustered high in blooming pyramids; there were bunches of grapes, made to dangle from conspicuous hooks, that people's mouths might water gratis[6] as they passed; there were piles of filberts, mossy and brown, recalling, in their fragrance, ancient walks among the woods, and pleasant shufflings ankle deep through withered leaves; there were Norfolk Biffins,[7] setting off the yellow of the oranges and lemons, and urgently entreating and beseeching to be carried home in paper bags and eaten after dinner.

The Grocers'! oh the Grocers'! nearly closed, with perhaps two shutters down, or one; but through those gaps such glimpses! It was not alone that the scales descending on the counter made a merry sound, or that the twine and roller parted company so briskly, or that the canisters were rattled

6. *gratis* (grā'tĭs): for nothing, free. 7. *Norfolk Biffins:* an English variety of apple.

up and down like juggling tricks, or even that the blended scents of tea and coffee were so grateful to the nose, or even that the raisins were so plentiful and rare, the almonds so extremely white, the sticks of cinnamon so long and straight, the other spices so delicious, the candied fruits so caked and spotted with molten sugar as to make the coldest lookers-on feel faint and subsequently bilious. Nor was it that the figs were moist and pulpy, or that the French plums blushed in modest tartness from their highly decorated boxes, or that everything was good to eat and in its Christmas dress; but the customers were all so hurried and so eager in the hopeful promise of the day, that they tumbled up against each other at the door, clashing their wicker baskets wildly, and left their purchases upon the counter, and came running back to fetch them, and committed hundreds of the like mistakes in the best humor possible.

It was a remarkable quality of the Ghost, that notwithstanding his gigantic size, he could accommodate himself to any place with ease; and that he stood beneath a low roof quite as gracefully as he could have done in any lofty hall.

And perhaps it was the pleasure the good Spirit had in showing off this power of his, or else it was his own kind, generous, hearty nature, and his sympathy with all poor men, that led him straight to Scrooge's clerk's; for there he went, and took Scrooge with him, holding to his robe; and on the threshold of the door the Spirit smiled, and stopped to bless Bob Cratchit's dwelling with the sprinklings of his torch. Think of that! Bob had but fifteen "bob"[8] a week himself; he pocketed on Saturdays but fifteen copies of his Christian name; and yet the Ghost of Christmas Present blessed his four-roomed house!

Then up rose Mrs. Cratchit, Cratchit's wife, dressed out but poorly in a twice-turned gown, but brave in ribbons, which are cheap and make a goodly show for sixpence; and she laid the cloth, assisted by Belinda Cratchit, second of her daughters, also brave in ribbons; while Master Peter Cratchit plunged a fork into the saucepan of potatoes, and getting the

8. ***"bob":*** English slang for a small coin, usually a shilling, the equivalent of a quarter.

corners of his monstrous shirt collar (Bob's private property, conferred upon his son and heir in honor of the day) into his mouth, rejoiced to find himself so gallantly attired, and yearned to show his linen in the fashionable Parks. And now two smaller Cratchits, boy and girl, came tearing in, screaming that outside the baker's they had smelt the goose, and known it for their own; and basking in luxurious thoughts of sage and onion, these young Cratchits danced about the table, and exalted Master Peter Cratchit to the skies, while he (not proud, although his collars nearly choked him) blew the fire, until the slow potatoes bubbling up, knocked loudly at the saucepan lid to be let out and peeled.

"What has ever got your precious father then?" said Mrs. Cratchit. "And your brother, Tiny Tim! And Martha warn't as late last Christmas Day by half an hour!"

"Here's Martha, mother!" said a girl, appearing as she spoke.

"Here's Martha, mother!" cried the two young Cratchits. "Hurrah! There's *such* a goose, Martha!"

"Why, bless your heart alive, my dear, how late you are!" said Mrs. Cratchit, kissing her a dozen times, and taking off her shawl and bonnet for her with officious zeal.

"We'd a deal of work to finish up last night," replied the girl, "and had to clear away this morning, mother!"

"Well! Never mind so long as you are come," said Mrs. Cratchit. "Sit ye down before the fire, my dear, and have a warm, Lord bless ye!"

"No, no! There's father coming," cried the two young Cratchits, who were everywhere at once. "Hide, Martha, hide!"

So Martha hid herself, and in came little Bob, the father, with at least three feet of comforter, exclusive of the fringe, hanging down before him; and his threadbare clothes darned up and brushed, to look seasonable; and Tiny Tim upon his shoulder. Alas for Tiny Tim, he bore a little crutch, and had his limbs supported by an iron frame!

"Why, where's our Martha?" cried Bob Cratchit, looking round.

"Not coming," said Mrs. Cratchit.

"Not coming!" said Bob, with a sudden declension in his high spirits; for he had been Tim's blood horse all the way from church, and had come home rampant. "Not coming upon Christmas Day!"

Martha didn't like to see him disappointed, if it were only in joke; so she came out prematurely from behind the closet door, and ran into his arms, while the two young Cratchits hustled Tiny Tim, and bore him off into the washhouse, that he might hear the pudding singing in the copper.

"And how did little Tim behave?" asked Mrs. Cratchit, when she had rallied Bob on his credulity, and Bob had hugged his daughter to his heart's content.

"As good as gold," said Bob, "and better. Somehow he gets thoughtful, sitting by himself so much, and thinks the strangest things you ever heard. He told me, coming home, that he hoped the people saw him in the church, because he was a cripple, and it might be pleasant to them to remember, upon Christmas Day, who made lame beggars walk and blind men see."

Bob's voice was tremulous when he told them this, and trembled more when he said that Tiny Tim was growing strong and hearty.

His active little crutch was heard upon the floor, and back came Tiny Tim before another word was spoken, escorted by his brother and sister to his stool before the fire; and while Bob, turning up his cuffs,—as if, poor fellow, they were capable of being made more shabby,—compounded some hot mixture in a jug with gin and lemons, and stirred it round and round and put it on the hob to simmer, Master Peter and the two ubiquitous young Cratchits went to fetch the goose, with which they soon returned in high procession.

Such a bustle ensued that you might have thought a goose the rarest of all birds; a feathered phenomenon, to which a black swan was a matter of course—and in truth it was something very like it in that house. Mrs. Cratchit made the gravy (ready beforehand in a little saucepan) hissing hot; Master Peter mashed the potatoes with incredible vigor; Miss Belinda sweetened up the apple sauce; Martha dusted the hot plates; Bob took Tiny Tim beside him in a tiny corner at the table; the two young Cratchits set chairs for everybody, not forgetting themselves, and mounting guard upon their posts, crammed spoons into their mouths, lest they should shriek for goose before their turn came to be helped. At last the dishes were set on, and grace was said. It was succeeded by a breathless pause, as Mrs. Cratchit, looking slowly all along the carving knife, prepared to plunge it in the breast; but when she did, and when the long expected gush of stuffing issued forth, one murmur of delight arose all round the board, and even Tiny Tim, excited by the two young Cratchits, beat on the table with the handle of his knife, and feebly cried Hurrah!

There never was such a goose. Bob said he didn't believe there ever was such a goose cooked. Its tenderness and flavor, size and cheapness, were the themes of universal admiration. Eked out by the apple sauce and mashed potatoes, it was a sufficient dinner for the whole family; indeed, as Mrs. Cratchit said with great delight (surveying one small atom of a bone upon the dish), they hadn't ate it all at last! Yet every one had had enough, and the youngest Cratchits in particular were steeped in sage and onion to the eyebrows! But now, the plates being changed by Miss Belinda, Mrs. Cratchit left the room alone—too nervous to bear witness—to take the pudding up and bring it in.

Suppose it should not be done enough! Suppose it should break in turning out! Suppose somebody should have got over the wall of the back yard, and stolen it, while they were merry with the goose—a supposition at which the two young Cratchits became livid! All sorts of horrors were supposed.

Hallo! A great deal of steam! The pudding was out of the copper. A smell like a washing day! That was the cloth. A smell like an eating house and a pastry cook's next door to each other, with a laundress's next door to that! That was the pudding! In half a minute Mrs. Cratchit entered—flushed, but smiling proudly—with the pudding, like a speckled cannonball, so hard and firm, blazing in half of half a quartern of ignited brandy, and bedight[9] with Christmas holly stuck into the top.

Oh, a wonderful pudding! Bob Cratchit said, and calmly too, that he regarded it as the greatest success achieved by Mrs. Cratchit since their marriage. Mrs. Cratchit said that now the weight was off her mind, she would confess she had had her doubts about the quantity of flour. Everybody had something to say about it, but nobody said or thought it was at all a small pudding for a large family. Any Cratchit would have blushed to hint at such a thing.

At last the dinner was all done, the cloth was cleared, the hearth swept, and the fire made up. The compound in the jug being tasted, and considered perfect, apples and oranges were put upon the table, and a shovelful of chestnuts on the fire. Then all the Cratchit family drew round the hearth, in what Bob Cratchit called a circle, meaning half a one; and at Bob Cratchit's elbow stood the family display of glass. Two tumblers, and a custard cup without a handle.

These held the hot stuff from the jug, however, as well as golden goblets would have done; and Bob served it out with beaming looks, while the chestnuts on the fire sputtered and cracked noisily. Then Bob proposed:—

"A Merry Christmas to us all, my dears. God bless us!"

Which all the family reëchoed.

"God bless us every one!" said Tiny Tim, the last of all.

He sat very close to his father's side upon his little stool. Bob held his withered little hand in his, as if he loved the child, and wished to keep him by his side, and dreaded that he might be taken from him.

"Spirit," said Scrooge, with an interest he had never felt before, "tell me if Tiny Tim will live."

"I see a vacant seat," replied the Ghost, "in the poor chimney corner, and a crutch without an owner, carefully preserved. If these shadows remain unaltered by the Future, the child will die."

"No, no," said Scrooge. "Oh, no, kind Spirit! say he will be spared."

9. *bedight* (bē dīt′): adorned, decorated.

"If these shadows remain unaltered by the Future, none other of my race," returned the Ghost, "will find him here."

Scrooge trembled and cast his eyes upon the ground. But he raised them speedily on hearing his own name.

"Mr. Scrooge!" said Bob; "I'll give you Mr. Scrooge, the Founder of the Feast!"

"The Founder of the Feast indeed!" cried Mrs. Cratchit, reddening. "I wish I had him here. I'd give him a piece of my mind to feast upon, and I hope he'd have a good appetite for it."

"My dear," said Bob, "the children! Christmas Day."

"It should be Christmas Day, I am sure," said she, "on which one drinks the health of such an odious, stingy, hard, unfeeling man as Mr. Scrooge. You know he is, Robert! Nobody knows it better than you do, poor fellow!"

"My dear," was Bob's mild answer, "Christmas Day."

"I'll drink his health for your sake and the Day's," said Mrs. Cratchit, "not for his. Long life to him! A Merry Christmas and a Happy New Year! He'll be very merry and very happy, I have no doubt!"

The children drank the toast after her. It was the first of their proceedings which had no heartiness in it. Tiny Tim drank it last of all, but he didn't care twopence for it. Scrooge was the Ogre of the family. The mention of his name cast a dark shadow on the party, which was not dispelled for full five minutes.

After it had passed away, they were ten times merrier than before, from the mere relief of Scrooge the Baleful being done with. Bob Cratchit told them how he had a situation in his eye for Master Peter, which would bring in, if obtained, full five-and-sixpence weekly. The two young Cratchits laughed tremendously at the idea of Peter's being a man of business; and Peter himself looked thoughtfully at the fire from between his collars, as if he were deliberating what particular investments he should favor when he came into the receipt of that bewildering income. Martha, who was a poor apprentice at a milliner's, then told them what kind of work she had to do, and how many hours she worked at a stretch, and how she meant to lie abed tomorrow morning for a good long rest; tomorrow being a holiday she passed at home. All this time the chestnuts and the jug went round and round; and by and by they had a song, about a lost child traveling in the snow, from Tiny Tim, who had a plaintive little voice, and sang it very well indeed.

There was nothing of high mark in this. They were not a handsome family; they were not well dressed; their shoes were far from being waterproof; their clothes were scanty; and Peter might have known, and very likely did, the inside of a pawnbroker's. But they were happy, grateful, pleased with one another, and contented with the time; and when they faded, and looked happier yet in the bright sprinklings of the Spirit's torch at parting, Scrooge had his eye upon them, and especially on Tiny Tim, until the last.

Stave Four · The Last of the Spirits

[The Ghost of Christmas Present had vanished, and the Ghost of Christmas Yet to Come appeared before Scrooge. He gave Scrooge a glimpse into the future. Scrooge saw himself dead, unmourned and unloved. He glimpsed the sorrow in the humble Cratchit home at the death of Tiny Tim. And last the Ghost showed him a neglected grave with the name Ebenezer Scrooge upon the stone.

Shaken and remorseful Scrooge begged the Spirit to tell him if the vision that he had seen was of things that will be or of things that may be. The Spirit replied only with a trembling of his hand as he pointed at the headstone, and Scrooge promised, "I will honor Christmas in my heart, and try to keep it all the year. I will live in the Past, the Present, and the Future. The Spirits of all Three shall strive within me. I will not shut out the lessons that they teach."]

Stave Five · The End of It

Yes! and the bedpost was his own. The bed was his own, the room was his own. Best and happiest of all, the Time before him was his own, to make amends in!

"I will live in the Past, the Present, and the Future!" Scrooge repeated, as he scrambled out of bed. "The Spirits of all Three shall strive within me. Oh, Jacob Marley! Heaven, and the Christmas Time be praised for this! I say it on my knees, old Jacob, on my knees!"

He was so fluttered and so glowing with his good intentions, that his broken voice would scarcely answer to his call. "I am here; the shadows of the things that would have been, may be dispelled. They will be. I know they will!"

His hands were busy with his garments all this time, turning them inside out, putting them on upside down, tearing them, mislaying them.

"I don't know what to do!" cried Scrooge, laughing and crying in the same breath. "I am as light as a feather, I am as happy as an angel, I am as merry as a schoolboy. A Merry Christmas to everybody! A Happy New Year to all the world! Hallo here! Whoop! Hallo!"

He had frisked into the sitting room, and was now standing there, perfectly winded.

"There's the saucepan that the gruel was in!" cried Scrooge, starting off again, and frisking round the fireplace. "There's the door, by which the Ghost of Jacob Marley entered! There's the corner where the Ghost of Christmas Present sat! There's the window where I saw the wandering Spirits! It's all right, it's all true, it all happened. Ha, ha, ha!"

Really, for a man who had been out of practice for so many years, it was a splendid laugh, a most illustrious laugh. The father of a long, long line of brilliant laughs!

"I don't know what day of the month it is!" said Scrooge. "I don't know how long I've been among the Spirits. I don't know anything. I'm quite a baby. Never mind. I don't care. I'd rather be a baby. Hallo! Whoop! Hallo here!"

He was checked in his transports by the churches ringing out the lustiest peals he had ever heard. Clash, clang, hammer, ding, dong, bell! Bell, dong, ding, hammer, clang, clash! Oh, glorious, glorious!

Running to the window, he opened it, and put out his head. No fog, no mist; clear, bright, jovial, stirring, cold; cold, piping for the blood to dance to; golden sunlight; heavenly sky; sweet fresh air; merry bells. Oh, glorious, glorious!

"What's today?" cried Scrooge, calling downward to a boy in Sunday clothes, who perhaps had loitered in to look about him.

"Eh?" returned the boy, with all his might of wonder.

"What's today, my fine fellow?" said Scrooge.

"Today!" replied the boy. "Why, Christmas Day."

"It's Christmas Day!" said Scrooge to himself. "I haven't missed it. The Spirits have done it all in one night. They can do anything they like. Of course they can. Of course they can. Hallo, my fine fellow!"

"Hallo!" returned the boy.

"Do you know the Poulterer's, in the next street but one, at the corner?" Scrooge inquired.

"I should hope I did," replied the lad.

"An intelligent boy!" said Scrooge. "A remarkable boy!

Do you know whether they've sold the prize Turkey that was hanging up there? Not the little prize Turkey,—the big one?"

"What, the one as big as me?" returned the boy.

"What a delightful boy!" said Scrooge. "It's a pleasure to talk to him. Yes, my buck!"

"It's hanging there now," replied the boy.

"Is it?" said Scrooge. "Go and buy it, and tell 'em to bring it here, that I may give them the direction where to take it. Come back with the man, and I'll give you a shilling. Come back with him in less than five minutes, and I'll give you half a crown!"

The boy was off like a shot.

"I'll send it to Bob Cratchit's!" whispered Scrooge, rubbing his hands, and splitting with a laugh. "He shan't know who sends it. It's twice the size of Tiny Tim."

The hand in which he wrote the address was not a steady one, but write it he did, somehow, and went downstairs to open the street door, ready for the coming of the poulterer's man. As he stood there, waiting his arrival, the knocker caught his eye.

"I shall love it as long as I live!" cried Scrooge, patting it with his hand. "I scarcely ever looked at it before. What an honest expression it has in its face! It's a wonderful knocker! —Here's the Turkey. Hallo! Whoop! How are you! Merry Christmas!"

It *was* a Turkey! He could never have stood upon his legs, that bird. He would have snapped 'em short off in a minute, like sticks of sealing wax.

"Why, it's impossible to carry that to Camden Town," said Scrooge. "You must have a cab."

The chuckle with which he said this, and the chuckle with which he paid for the turkey, and the chuckle with which he paid for the cab, and the chuckle with which he recompensed the boy, were only to be exceeded by the chuckle with which he sat down breathless in his chair again, and chuckled till he cried.

He dressed himself "all in his best," and at last got out into the streets. The people were by this time pouring forth, as he had seen them with the Ghost of Christmas Present; and walking with his hands behind him, Scrooge regarded every one with a delighted smile. He looked so irresistibly pleasant, in a word, that three or four good-humored fellows said, "Good morning, sir! A Merry Christmas to you!" And Scrooge said often afterwards, that of all the blithe sounds he had ever heard, those were the blithest in his ears.

He went to church, and walked about the streets, and watched the people hurrying to and fro, and patted children on the head, and questioned beggars, and looked down into the kitchens of houses, and up to the windows; and found that everything could yield him pleasure. He had never dreamed that any walk—that anything—could give him so much happiness. In the afternoon, he turned his steps towards his nephew's house.

He passed the door a dozen times before he had the courage to go up and knock. But he made a dash, and did it.

"Is your master at home, my dear?" said Scrooge to the girl. Nice girl! Very.

"Yes, sir."

"Where is he, my love?" said Scrooge.

"He's in the dining room, sir, along with mistress. I'll show you upstairs, if you please."

"Thank'ee. He knows me," said Scrooge, with his hand already on the dining room lock. "I'll go in here, my dear."

He turned it gently, and sidled his face in, round the door. They were looking at the table (which was spread out in great array); for these young housekeepers are always nervous on such points, and like to see that everything is right.

"Fred!" said Scrooge.

"Why, bless my soul!" cried Fred, "who's that?"

"It's I. Your uncle Scrooge. I have come to dinner. Will you let me in, Fred?"

Let him in! It is a mercy he didn't shake his arm off. He was at home in five minutes. Nothing could be heartier. Wonderful party, wonderful games, wonderful unanimity, won-der-ful happiness!

But he was early at the office next morning. Oh, he was early there. If he could only be there first, and catch Bob Cratchit coming late! That was the thing he had set his heart upon.

And he did it; yes he did! The clock struck nine. No Bob. A quarter past. No Bob. He was full eighteen minutes and a half behind his time. Scrooge sat with his door wide open, that he might see him come into the Tank.

His hat was off, before he opened the door; his comforter too. He was on his stool in a jiffy; driving away with his pen, as if he were trying to overtake nine o'clock.

"Hallo!" growled Scrooge, in his accustomed voice as near as he could feign it. "What do you mean by coming here at this time of day?"

"I am very sorry, sir," said Bob. "I *am* behind my time."

"You are?" repeated Scrooge. "Yes. I think you are. Step this way, sir, if you please."

"It's only once a year, sir," pleaded Bob, appearing from the Tank. "It shall not be repeated. I was making rather merry yesterday, sir."

"Now, I'll tell you what, my friend," said Scrooge, "I am not going to stand this sort of thing any longer. And therefore," he continued, leaping from his stool, and giving Bob such a dig in the waistcoat that he staggered back into the Tank again, "and therefore I am about to raise your salary!"

Bob trembled, and got a little nearer to the ruler. He had a momentary idea of knocking Scrooge down with it, holding him, and calling to the people in the court for help and a strait-waistcoat.

"A Merry Christmas, Bob!" said Scrooge, with an earnestness that could not be mistaken, as he clapped him on the back. "A merrier Christmas, Bob, my good fellow, than I have given you for many a year! I'll raise your salary, and endeavor to assist your struggling family, and we will discuss your affairs this very afternoon, over a Christmas bowl of smoking bishop, Bob! Make up the fires, and buy another coal scuttle before you dot another *i*, Bob Cratchit!"

Scrooge was better than his word. He did it all, and infinitely more; and to Tiny Tim, who did NOT die, he was a second father. He became as good a friend, as good a master, and as good a man, as the good old city knew, or any other good old city, town, or borough, in the good old world. Some people laughed to see the alteration in him, but he let them laugh, and little heeded them; for he was wise enough to know that such as these would be blind anyway, and he thought it quite as well that they should wrinkle up their eyes in grins, as have the malady in less attractive forms. His own heart laughed, and that was quite enough for him.

He had no further intercourse with Spirits; and it was always said of him, that he knew how to keep Christmas well, if any man alive possessed the knowledge. May that be truly said of us, and all of us! And so, as Tiny Tim observed, God Bless Us, Every One!

Abridged

HELPS FOR DISCUSSION

1. What incidents show that Scrooge is well described on page 203? What did he plan to gain by unfriendliness? What was lost?

2. What did each of the four ghosts do to soften Scrooge's spirit? What evidence did he give of a change of heart?

3. What virtues did the Cratchits practice as a family which enabled them to rise gallantly above their poverty? Give illustrations.

4. In your opinion which character is the gayest? the most lovable? the most patient? Explain your choices.

Christmas in the Olden Time

SIR WALTER SCOTT

Heap on more wood!—the wind is chill;
But let it whistle as it will,
We'll keep our Christmas merry still.
Each age has deemed the new-born year
The fittest time for festal cheer:
Even, heathen yet, the savage Dane
At Iol[1] more deep the mead[2] did drain;
High on the beach his galleys drew,
And feasted all his pirate crew;
Then in his low and pine-built hall,
Where shields and axes decked the wall,
They gorged upon the half-dressed steer;
Caroused in seas of sable beer;
While round, in brutal jest, were thrown
The half-gnawed rib and marrow-bone;
Or listened all, in grim delight,
While Scalds[3] yelled out the joys of fight.
Then forth in frenzy would they hie,
While wildly-loose their red locks fly;
And, dancing round the blazing pile,
They make such barbarous mirth the while,
As best might to the mind recall
The boisterous joys of Odin's[4] hall.
  And well our Christian sires of old
Loved when the year its course had rolled
And brought blithe Christmas back again
With all its hospitable train.
Domestic and religious rite
Gave honor to the holy night:
On Christmas eve the bells were rung;
On Christmas eve the Mass was sung;
That only night, in all the year,

1. *Iol* (ī'ōl): a meeting-place of the Danes in early times. 2. *mead:* a winelike drink. 3. *scalds:* minstrels or poets. 4. *Odin:* in Norse mythology, the supreme deity of wisdom, poetry, and war.

Saw the stoled priest the chalice rear.
The damsel donned her kirtle sheen;
The hall was dressed with holly green;
Forth to the wood did merry-men go,
To gather in the mistletoe.
Then opened wide the baron's hall
To vassal, tenant, serf, and all;
Power laid his rod of rule aside;
And Ceremony doffed her pride.
The heir, with roses in his shoes,
That night might village partner choose;
The lord, underogating,[5] share
The vulgar game of "post and pair."[6]
All hailed, with uncontrolled delight,
And general voice, the happy night
That to the cottage, as the crown,
Brought tiding of salvation down.
  The fire, with well-dried logs supplied,
Went roaring up the chimney wide;
The huge hall-table's oaken face,
Scrubbed till it shone, the day to grace,
Bore then upon its massive board
No mark to part the squire and lord.
Then was brought in the lusty brawn,

5. *underogating:* weaving in and out in a country dance. 6. *post and pair:* a game of forfeits. 7. *brawn:* roast boar.

By old blue-coated serving-man;
Then the grim boar's-head frowned on high
Crested with bays and rosemary.[8]
Well can the green-garbed ranger tell
How, when, and where the monster fell;
What dogs before his death he tore,
And all the baiting of the boar.
The wassail[9] round, in good brown bowls,
Garnished with ribbons, blithely trowls.[10]
There the huge sirloin reeked; hard by
Plum-porridge stood, and Christmas pie;
Nor failed old Scotland to produce,
At such high-tide, her savory goose.
Then came the merry maskers in,
And carols roared with blithesome din;
If unmelodious was the song,
It was a hearty note, and strong.
Who lists may in their mumming[11] see
Traces of ancient mystery;
White skirts supplied the masquerade,
And smutted cheeks the visors made:
But, O! what maskers richly dight[12]
Can boast of bosoms half so light!
England was merry England, when
Old Christmas brought his sports again.
'Twas Christmas broached the mightiest ale;
'Twas Christmas told the merriest tale;
A Christmas gambol oft could cheer
The poor man's heart through half the year.

HELPS FOR DISCUSSION

Contrast the heathen celebration (stanza 1) with old-time Christmas festivities. How did feasts and amusements change? Show from the poem that Christianity brought culture and refinement to the people.

8. *bays and rosemary:* herbs used for seasoning. 9. *wassail* (wŏs''l): a holiday beverage of wine, spices, sugar, roasted apples. It was drunk as an expression of good wishes at Christmas in Old England. 10. *trowls:* moves around. 11. *mumming:* going about at Christmas time in disguise making merry. 12. *dight:* covered.

Nowhere is Christmas celebrated with greater reverence than in Ireland, the land of the Gael; and an Irish writer has pictured the beauty of that time in

Christmas and the Gael

BRIAN O'HIGGINS

At Christmas, Christmas in Ireland, long ago,
Without the wind might bluster and without the wind might blow;
Within was peace among us and the kind word to and fro—
At Christmas, Christmas in Ireland, long ago.

So sang a poet of our own day, recalling to our minds the kindliness and peace associated with the season of Christmas in the Ireland of our fathers. It is a true picture. No matter how bitter the feuds between families or clans, no matter how long people had passed each other by without speaking, the coming of Christmas wiped out the darkness, and shed again the light of love and friendship on heart and tongue and mind. No other season of the year held such charm and delight for the Gael[1] as Christmas; and pity 'tis that its real significance should wane in our day, and that our idea of Christmas joy should tend towards vulgarity and gluttony.

The Gaels of old held Christmas in such high esteem that they named December the month of Mary; and the highest honor they could pay to their own Saint Brigid was to call her the Foster-Mother of Christ, and name her the Mary of the Gael.

Perhaps no country had more beautiful customs connected with Christmas than Ireland; and every effort should be made to keep them alive, and to revive them where, like many other priceless possessions, they have been thrown away. One of the loveliest was the custom of placing a lighted candle in an unshuttered window at the front of each house on Christmas Eve, in memory and in honor of the first Christmas Night, and of the holy Wayfarers who made their way over rough roads through darkness.

Our ancestors vowed in their hearts that never in this land of hospitality should there be a wanderer, no matter how

1. *Gael* (gāl): a person of a race belonging to the Gaelic branch of the Celts. The Irish and Scottish are Gaels.

poor or lowly, abroad at the holy season without food or warmth or shelter; and so they placed the candle in the window, and left the door open till midnight, and any who came that way were sure of food and rest. It was believed, too, that at midnight, the Mother of God and her little Babe came into each house in which peace and good will dwelt, and left blessing forevermore.

When I was a boy there was, in our part of the country, a custom which I have not been able to find anywhere else, and which has now died out. For three weeks before Christmas we young fellows went out night after night on the hills and kept blowing horns for over an hour. The group of horn blowers in our townland was answered by another group a mile away; and so it went on all over the countryside every night, and finished on Christmas Eve. The old people told us it was done as long as they and their parents before them

could remember; and the object of it was to keep the wolves away from the Lamb of God.

Another belief was that on Christmas Eve, at midnight, the beasts in every stable went down on their knees in honor and in memory of the stable at Bethlehem; and it was said that any person who remained awake and went to the byre[2] of the cattle at that hour would obtain from the Infant Savior any special grace or favor asked for. In all customs of Christmas there was evidence of that great, childlike faith of the Gaelic race, which traducers[3] like to call superstition, but which was an unseen bond to keep our people very near to God during the ages of sorrow and persecution and defeat.

There are scores of legends connected with the Christmas of the Gael; and one of the most touching concerns the little outcast of the bird kingdom, the wren, which tells us why it is he is hunted from hedge to hedge on Christmas Day until he is finally killed, to be carried from door to door next day by the "wren boys," who solicit subscriptions from the woman of the house for his funeral.

The old story is that when the Blessed Virgin and Saint Joseph were fleeing into Egypt with the Infant Jesus to save Him from Herod's soldiers, they passed by a field where a party of workingmen were sowing wheat. Our Holy Mother and the Divine Infant were seated on the back of an ass, whose steps Saint Joseph directed over the rough, stony ground, while the blood from his own poor, travel-bruised feet stained with red spots the way he walked. He told the men if strangers came inquiring whether such travelers had passed that way, to say: "Yes, when we were sowing the corn." The soldiers of Herod appeared next day, pursuing the Holy Family, but the men in the field said in reply to their questions: "No such persons have passed here since the day we were sowing corn"; and they pointed to the grain which had grown to full ripeness during the night. And here is where the wren—sometimes called a chafer—comes into the story.

He was seated on a branch close by, the story says, and

2. *byre* (bīr): a stable for cattle. 3. *traducers:* slanderers.

when he heard the reply of the reapers, he squeaked out: "*Indé, indé*" ("yesterday, yesterday") but the soldiers did not understand, and they gave up the chase. The blood was still fresh on the ground where Saint Joseph had paused to speak to the workers, and by this the soldiers might have tracked the Holy Family had not a little robin, all the time they were questioning the reapers, busied himself covering over the blood stains with leaves, so that they were hidden from the gaze of the soldiers. That, they say, is how the robin got a red breast, and why he is called "Mary's little one," and is loved by the Irish people; while the wren is hunted by them because of his treachery to the Babe of Bethlehem.

It is a nice story, but the hunting and killing of the wren is not in keeping with the spirit of Christmas, and should be discontinued. Our Lord forgave the penitent thief on the Cross; He forgives us our most grievous sins, and I am sure He has long since forgiven the poor little wren which was, after all, more loose-tongued than vindictive.[4] It is a cowardly thing for men and boys to hunt to death the poor little bird that cannot utter a word of protest or offer resistance to their blows.

Let us hope that this custom will die out, and that all the old beautiful ones will be revived; that the time may soon come when we can throw wide our doors at the festive season, and welcome to our firesides all those wanderers of the night to whom the lighted candle in the unshuttered window sends forth a welcoming glow, telling them that Christmas in Ireland is a time of hospitality, of kindliness, of peace and of love.

THINGS TO DO

Use the selection as a radio script. Choose an announcer to introduce the program. A unison reading of the stanza may begin and end the broadcast. A narrator should read paragraphs 1, 7, 10–11. Five readers may present: December's name; candle and open door; protection of the Lamb; beasts at midnight; wren and robin. Construct a microphone and follow broadcasting conditions.

4. *vindictive:* revengeful.

Feast o' Saint Stephen

RUTH SAWYER

Listen all ye, 'tis the Feast o' Saint Stephen,
Mind that ye keep it, this holy even.
Open your door and greet ye the stranger,
For ye mind that the wee Lord had naught but manger.

Feed ye the hungry and rest ye the weary,
This ye must do for the sake of Our Mary.
'Tis well that ye mind—ye who sit by the fire—
That the Lord He was born in a dark and cold byre.

The best work of all is done by the worker who does his work for the love of Christ, and the love of Christ may be best shown in the love of neighbor which inspired a humble wood carver to make

The Third Lamb

ANNE D. KYLE

The people of Fals have always been wood carvers; but it used to be, a long time ago, that they made nothing except saints and madonnas. In those days Dritte was the best wood carver in the town. Folks came many days' journey to order from him statues of the saints.

Now, though Dritte was the best of all, the other wood carvers had no equals either, outside of their own town, and what church Dritte could not supply with saints, they did; and so, in time, since there are but so many churches in the world and each church can hold but so many saints, the demand for them grew less and less and finally stopped altogether.

At that the wood carvers of Fals were in a terrible case, as you can well imagine. Not one of them but had a store of saints in his workroom getting dusty and no one came to buy them. And if no one bought, how were they to feed their children? Starvation, that miserable beggar who lurks always around the next corner awaiting his opportunity, now stepped boldly out and thrust his skinny hands before their faces. Yet, for all that, it never occurred to one of them to try anything else. It would be sacrilege, they thought, to use the skill which enabled them to carve from a stupid block of wood the sweet face of the Mother of God! Nevertheless, for all their piety, their stomachs grew lanker and lanker, and their children cried for food.

Now Dritte was in the same way as all of them, except that he had no little child to whose wailing he must listen.

"It is as well our prayers were never answered," he said one evening to his wife Beata. "At least we have no son's cries to wring our hearts as starvation wrings our stomachs!" And he shook his head as there came the sound of weeping from the house next door.

"Oh, Dritte!"—Beata's eyes filled with tears—"do you think it could be really so wicked to make other things than saints for a little while? Surely God, Who loves the little children, would forgive—"

"Beata! You do not know what you say!" But though his voice was stern he put his arms about his wife. "God Himself taught us to use our knives for His glory. How therefore should we dare to change? Besides, He is doubtless even now providing for us. They say there are many churches in the flat country to the south. Who knows? Perhaps an angel has whispered to them of the wood carvers of Fals, and they have already dispatched a messenger to us with many fine orders! In fact, I am almost sure of it!"

Beata, however, only looked skeptical as she dried her eyes. Being more practical of mind than was her husband she did not believe for a moment that any messenger was on the way to Fals. She only patted his hand reassuringly and said: "Yes, yes, of course; now go and have a little more soup, Dritte."

"I have had all I wish," Dritte assured her. "And now I think I shall go back to the workshop and finish the little angel I am working on, so that if anyone should come—" And taking up a candle he left the room.

As he neared the door of his workshop, however, he paused surprised, for he thought he saw a light within. But when he entered, the little room lay still and dark as usual. It must have been the dazzle of his own candle in his eyes. He went

at once to his worktable and had begun to polish off the wings of the pretty little angel, when something moved over in the far corner of the room.

Dritte rose and, holding the candle high, looked about him. Could it be that a thief was here? But what thief was so badly off that he would steal a saint? And with that he saw in the dusty shadows of a far corner a boy who sat on the floor in front of a group of the Nativity, playing with the animals that knelt around the Manger to worship their little Lord within! He had made a procession of them. First came the ox with its spreading horns, and then the ass with its long ears, and then the goat with its pointed beard; and, even as Dritte stood there staring in dumbfounded horror, the boy reached out and picked up the goose—for what stable, even the holy one in Bethlehem, is without its goose?—and added it to the line. Then he sat back to enjoy the effect and Dritte heard him laugh very softly to himself.

Who was this blasphemous child anyway? wondered Dritte, more horror-stricken than ever. He knew every boy by sight in the little village, and this was surely none of them. But Nicholas's wife had a widowed sister from another village who was coming to live with them. Perhaps it was her son. A beautiful boy, too, with his delicate features and hair as softly glowing as the gold upon an altar when the candles are lighted. But what sort of upbringing had he had, if he knew no better than to play with the holy ox and ass of Bethlehem?

Just then the boy reached out again and took up the white lamb which leaned against the Virgin Mary's knees. Dritte could contain himself no longer.

"Boy! Boy! Don't you know those are no ordinary animals? They worship the Babe in the Manger! You must not touch them!"

The boy cuddled the little lamb—of such fair wood had Dritte carved it that it shone as soft and white as wool itself—and raised his calm eyes to Dritte's.

"The Babe does not mind," he said. "See how He laughs!" And he nodded toward the Infant, on Whose face was indeed the vague sweet smile that Dritte with great care had carved there.

The boy got to his feet. Dritte saw that they were bare and stained with much traveling. He wore only a straight homespun shift . . . so he, too, was poor like all the rest! He still held the lamb in his cupped hands.

"I wish to take this one with me," he announced. "With all the others you have made for Him, surely the Babe will not mind! And—I have no toys to play with when it is cold on the mountains."

At that Dritte, for all his horror, felt his heart grow soft with pity for the lonely child. So he said more gently:

"Put back the little lamb at the Virgin's knees, boy, for she might miss it if it were gone too long; and I will make you another one all for yourself—one that nods its head when you touch it."

"Will you?" The boy knelt at once, obediently, and put the lamb back by the Virgin's knees. "How soon will it be done?"

"Tomorrow," promised Dritte, seeing that he could not draw back now, and he argued with himself: "There is no hurry with that angel's wings; I cannot sell it anyway, and surely to please a little lad—" He remembered what Beata had said at supper. Aloud he added: "Yes, tomorrow you may come for it—but not too early; I might not have it done. Where do you live, boy?"

"Out there," waving his hand vaguely upward. "My mother and I together."

He was Nicholas's wife's sister's son, then, without a doubt. Dritte, left alone, returned to his worktable, shoved aside the angel, and selecting a fresh block of wood began to carve a lamb from it.

"Since it is for a gift and not for sale, it cannot matter much," he told his uneasy conscience. "Besides, he looked so disappointed when I refused him that lamb at the Virgin's knees; I had to do something!" Before he knew it he was whistling away to himself as beneath his skillful fingers the lamb began to take shape.

So industriously did Dritte work that before noon next day the lamb was done. He set it down on the table and stood off to admire it. In all his life, he knew he had made nothing better than this lamb. He reached out and touched its head gently, and at once it began to nod up and down. Dritte held his sides and laughed.

All at once from the tail of his eye he noticed a shadow fall across the doorway. "Come in!" he called gayly. "See what I have made for you."

A timid shuffle of feet, and there entered a ragged gypsy child with matted hair and black eyes set in deep brown hollows. On one hip she supported a baby, who, seeing the lamb upon the table, its head still nodding as if in welcome, shrieked with delight and stretched out dirty hands for it.

"What do you wish?" demanded Dritte, trying to keep his voice stern, but not succeeding very well, for children could melt his heart as easily as fire melts tallow.

"Scraps," said the child, and Dritte noticed the basket on her back. "Only there are none in the village nowadays, because everyone eats them themselves. And when I get back my father will beat me again because my basket is empty."

Her casual voice stung Dritte to the quick. "But it is not your fault that we have to eat even the crumbs now!"

"Bub—bub—bub—" crowed the baby, and managed to get a finger on the lamb's ear.

Dritte moved the lamb out of harm's way, but at once there was such a howl that to quiet it he cried, "Look!" and set the head to nodding up and down harder than ever. The roars, however, did not subside.

"He wants it," said the little gypsy girl, "and because he can't have it he will cry until father throws things at him to make him stop."

"Throws things at a little child!" cried Dritte in horror. "Here!" Impulsively he thrust the lamb into the baby's hands. "He shall not throw things at you this time!"

The gypsy girl stared at him for a moment; then she turned, hugging the gurgling baby and the lamb to her thin breast, and darted out of the shop, lest Dritte should change his mind.

Slowly he sat down and reached for another block of wood. What had come over him anyway—feeling sorry for a miserable gypsy, who doubtless had never been baptized? Dritte sighed.

Late that afternoon—for he had worked hard—he was putting the finishing touches on the second lamb when outside he heard boys' voices from which hunger had not wholly taken the merriment.

"God greet you, Dritte!" they cried to him, and then, growing bolder, trooped within. "What is that you make? A lamb! Look, it nods its head!"

"It is not for you." Dritte held it high. "It is for someone else." He smiled at the cloud of disappointment that fell across their eager faces, yet for all that he hated to refuse them. After all, he thought, mightn't it be a kind thing to do—to take their minds for a little while from their empty stomachs? Suddenly resolved, he held up his hand in silence. "Very well! I will tell you what I will do if you like. I will make you each what you wish. Now, speak in turn, what will you have?"

"A lamb, Dritte, just like this one!"

"A donkey that will shake its ears!"

"A cock that will flap its wings—"

"That is a rather large order, but I will try. And what do you want?" This to a little fellow who had stood silently all this time, his elbows on the table, his shining eyes fixed upon the lamb. He was little Drino, whose father and mother had been lately killed by an avalanche on the mountains. "You may have anything, you know!"

But Drino shook his head. "There is nothing I want, if I can't have this, Dritte, because tomorrow the priest is going to send me far away to an orphans' home, and there is no time to wait for another. If only I might have this one!" And he put his palms together, as if he prayed.

"I would gladly give it to you, Drino," said Dritte in great distress, "if I hadn't promised it." He looked over the heads of the eager throng, but he did not see the strange fair boy anywhere. Doubtless, thought Dritte, some errand for his mother had detained him. He looked down at little Drino again, and little Drino looked back at him. "Here, take it along!" said Dritte abruptly. "I cannot help it if that other is disappointed. Besides, I can have another lamb for him by tomorrow."

That night he told Beata all about it. "And of course it isn't as if I were cheating God," he hastened to defend himself; "I have already enough statues down there to stock a whole church—and if I do not do something while I wait for someone to buy them, I may lose my skill."

Beata said nothing, but she smiled a wise and tender smile.

"I wonder if this boy is really Nicholas's wife's sister's child," she said presently. "Yesterday I met Nicholas's wife at the fountain, and she said nothing about it. Surely she would have done so if her sister were already here, for she is a great gossip."

"Then who could it be?"

But Beata only shook her head. "How should I know, Dritte? Now hurry and make the third lamb at once—and call me when he comes for it. I would see this fair boy, too."

But though Dritte looked up from his work next day at every step that passed, and Beata lingered within reach of his call, night came and the boy had not returned. Nor the next day, nor the next. The third lamb, finer even than the other two, stood ready and waiting on the shelf by Dritte's workroom window, and presently there were other animals to keep it company—a donkey, and a rooster, and a pair of oxen with a yoke. One by one the boys came in and claimed their toys, but always it seemed there were broken ones to be replaced or other children to be supplied with new ones, and Dritte's shelf was never empty. But still the third lamb stood there unclaimed. The boy did not return.

One chill autumn day Dritte looked up and saw a stranger staring in through the window. His heart leaped. Could it be the messenger from the south? Trembling, he wiped his hands on his apron and rose as a knock sounded on his door.

"God greet you!" said the stranger without. Oh, he was clothed in velvet and furs! He would buy many saints, and tonight Dritte and Beata would have a feast of dumplings and lentils!

"God greet you, master, and come in!

"I saw your work through the window," said the stranger.

"Thank you!" Dritte clasped his hands. "Will you please to look around at your leisure? In that corner are the Saint Florians, and in that, the Saint Christophers, and yonder is a Nativity—"

But the stranger stopped him with an impatient gesture. "When I wish to see saints I go to church. It's the toys I am interested in." And before Dritte could recover from his astonishment he strode over and picked up the third lamb.

"How much will you take for these, my man?" He pointed at the shelf full of toys. And when Dritte would have protested, he added quickly: "Look you, I am a great merchant from the south. I will pay you well for them and leave a goodly order—"

"No!" cried Dritte violently, and he took the lamb from the man's hands and set it back upon the shelf. "I am sorry, my lord, but these are not for sale. Saints I will gladly make you, but toys I cannot." And to all the other's arguments he only shook a stubborn head until at last the stranger gave it up.

"I shall be at the village inn until after the noon hour," said the merchant as he turned to go. "If you wish to change your mind you will find me there."

'I cannot change my mind, my lord, even if I starve—unless, indeed, God should give me a sign."

"What is it, Dritte? What did he want?" Dritte roused himself and saw his wife, Beata, beside him. "Was it really the messenger come at last?"

"Messenger!" echoed Dritte bitterly, and told her all.

When he had finished she ventured: "But, Dritte, since you have done your best to serve Him up till now, perhaps—"

"Beata! You, too!" Dritte stared at her in agony.

She laid her head against his arm with a little sigh. "I used up the last of the flour today, Dritte, and Nanni, the goat, had barely a cup of milk to give this morning—"

With a groan he wrenched away from her and went rushing blindly out of the house. He cared not where his feet took him, until presently he ran full into the village priest making his way downhill toward the church.

"Aye, Dritte," said that good man, puffing. "God gave you the gift of eyesight to use, my son."

"I am sorry, *Padre*," replied Dritte humbly; "but I was so full of my own troubles—"

"Yes," said the priest, shaking his wise old head. "We are all that, I fancy. Now I will tell you something of someone else's trouble, for to my mind there's no better cure than that for one's own."

And he went on to say how he had just been far up on the mountainside to visit the small town of Ober-Fals. And there he had seen little Marte, Halli's only child, who had fallen from a precipice a month ago while hunting the last gentians.

"All day she lies flat upon her back," said the good priest. "She who could never be still a moment! Poor Halli is near to distraction over it. He, the richest man in our parish and nothing he can buy to cure, or even to make her lot a little easier. Yesterday, he told me, a gypsy band stopped at Ober-Fals, and one of the children came to his door offering to tell fortunes. Thinking it might amuse Marte, he had her in, and while she told the poor child's fortune, her baby brother played about the floor. He had a toy, a lamb carved out of wood, that nodded its head."

"Why!" cried Dritte, starting. "That must be the one I made and—"

"You?" The *padre* stopped. "Then you are the very one I want, Dritte! Marte, it seems, was more interested in the lamb than in her fortune. But when Halli tried to buy it, those stubborn gypsies would not give it up, though he offered them many times its value! Will you make her another one? Halli will pay you well, besides—"

"I want no pay," declared Dritte warmly. "And, *Padre*, it so happens that I have a lamb on hand now. I—I made it to amuse myself in my spare time, now that I have so few orders for saints. I will take it to her this very afternoon."

"You are a good man, Dritte," said the priest, and blessed him.

The clouds had come down quite low when Dritte started for Ober-Fals, the third lamb beneath his arm. After all, why should he not give it to Marte? The boy would surely never return now. He had not gone halfway before he felt the first keen sting of snow against his face. But he kept on steadily. Presently, as he climbed, he had the strangest feeling that he did not go alone. Once from the corner of his eye he thought he caught a fleeting shadow like the flutter of a skirt. Dritte quickened his pace. Surely it could be nothing human that went thus so silently!

It was with relief that he finally saw Halli's house ahead and he stepped inside, shaking the snow from his shoulders.

"See," he said, bringing out the third lamb shyly. "This is for Marte."

Some time later he started home again. Halli had pressed on him such food and drink as his stomach had not held for weeks, and would have kept him for the night, but Dritte refused. Beata would be looking for him. He would be grateful, though, if Halli would lend him a lantern. But he would take no pay for the lamb.

A gray twilight had set in as Dritte stumbled down the road again. The wind tore past him, the snow buffeted his face so that he had to keep his head down as he walked. For that reason he did not see that someone waited for him in the snow until he was full upon him. It was the fair boy himself who stood before him!

As Dritte stared, the boy smiled, and it seemed to the other as if a peculiar radiance surrounded them which came not so much from the lantern as from some light within the boy himself. "Where is my lamb, Dritte?" asked the boy.

"I—I kept it until today, but you never came," Dritte stammered, "and so—I gave it to Halli's daughter, Marte, who lies flat on her back in pain. But I will gladly make you another one, a fourth, if you will truly come for it."

But the boy shook his head. "I do not need a fourth," he said, and his voice was clear and sweet above the stormy wind. "The ones you gave to the gypsy child, to Drino, and to Marte, you gave also to me, you know."

"I—I do not understand," faltered Dritte. "You did not come—"

"Oh, Dritte, are you still so blind?" cried the boy, and with a gesture half tender, half reproachful, he flung his arms wide until, in the soft mysterious light about him, Dritte saw the shadow of a Cross upon the snow. Then at last he understood. Dropping on his knees he hid his face before the brightness of the Vision.

"Are you still so blind, Dritte," said the Boy's voice above

his bowed head, "that you cannot yet understand that to make toys may serve God's glory better than to carve the fairest saint? For the laughter of one happy child is sweeter in His ears than the praises of all the saints in Heaven!"

The Voice stopped; and when Dritte dared to raise his eyes, the Boy was gone. There was no light but the flickering radiance of his own lantern. He picked it up and stumbled on. Presently, however, shouts and hails through the storm checked him. Turning aside, he discovered a little group of horsemen huddled in the scant protection of a rock.

"Peasant, I will give you a purse of gold if you will lead us back to Fals."

"I am on my way there now. You have but to follow me."

"Now God be thanked!" cried a relieved voice, and Dritte recognized it as that of the merchant who had called on him that morning. "We had started for the pass, but the storm caught us."

When they were safely at the inn again, the merchant pressed a fat purse into Dritte's hand. "Nay, but you must take it! You have saved our lives. By my troth," as the light from the inn door fell on Dritte's face, "I believe it is the wood carver I talked with this morning!"

"Yes, my lord," said Dritte, "and if you still wish, I can start upon those toys you spoke of, tomorrow morning."

"So," nodded the other with a shrewd smile, "you have changed your mind."

"No," Dritte lifted his shining eyes, "but I have had a Sign."

THINGS TO DO

1. After try-outs, choose classmates to tell "The Third Lamb" to the primary grades at Christmas. Expressive voice tones, appropriate facial expression, and natural gestures are necessary in good story-telling.

2. Arrange an exhibit of pictures and models of wood carvings. Show how the church has utilized the art of wood carving.

3. After consulting reference books, give a class report on the art of wood carving, its history, tools, and processes.

4. Find and read aloud Sister M. Madeleva's poem, "The Shopper," in which she mentions a small wood carving from Jerusalem.

When Christ Was Born

Translated from the Neapolitan

When Christ was born in Bethlehem,
'Twas night but seemed the noon of day:
  The star whose light
  Was pure and bright,
Shone with unwav'ring ray;
  But one bright star,
  One glorious star
Guided the Eastern Magi from afar.

Then peace was spread throughout the land;
The lion fed beside the lamb;
  And with the kid,
  To pastures led,
The spotted leopard fed
  In peace, in peace
  The calf and bear,
The wolf and lamb reposed together there.

As shepherds watched their flocks by night,
An angel brighter than the sun
  Appeared in air,
  And gently said,
"Fear not, be not afraid,
  Behold, behold,
  Beneath your eyes,
Earth has become a smiling Paradise."

While to Bethlehem We Are Going

SISTER VIOLANTE DO CEO

From the Portuguese by John Bowring

While to Bethlehem we are going,
Tell me, Blas, to cheer the road,
Tell me why this lovely Infant
Quitted His divine abode?—
"From that world to bring to this
Peace, which, of all earthly blisses,
Is the brightest, purest bliss."

Wherefore from His throne exalted,
Came He on His earth to dwell—
All His pomp an humble manger,
All His court a narrow cell?—
"From that world to bring to this
Peace, which, of all earthly blisses,
Is the brightest, purest bliss."

Why did He, the Lord eternal,
Mortal pilgrim deign to be,
He who fashioned for His glory
Boundless immortality?—
"From that world to bring to this
Peace, which, of all earthly blisses,
Is the brightest, purest bliss."

Well then! let us haste to Bethlehem,
Thither let us haste and rest,
For of all heaven's gifts the sweetest
Sure is peace,—the sweetest, best.

HELPS FOR DISCUSSION

1. From what nations did the two preceding poems come? In each poem what is the supreme gift of the Christ Child?

2. Which poem is a dialogue between two travelers? Divide into two groups for concert reading of alternate questions and replies.

In the little town of Antu in faraway China two American missionary priests turned sadness into rejoicing when, after long hardships, they celebrated an

Antu Christmas

JAMES KELLER AND MEYER BERGER

The sun was gone and the air crackled and snapped with a cold far below zero when Antu[1] showed up in sight of the missionary priests. It was December 23, 1930. The two American missionaries had floundered and gasped their way all day through man-high drifts. Wind-blasted snow had picked their faces raw. They were on the verge of utter snowblindness as they crossed the upper Sungari River on solid ice and drove under Antu's West Gate. Antu is a walled town and lookouts are perched along the walls to sight possible enemies—local riots break out in this region occasionally when the lads get bored—but it seems there were no guards this night.

The West Gate was locked, but, scouting around the outer wall, the expedition found a crude inn still open. Their stomping entry, as they shook the snow from their furs, stopped local inn gossips mid-phrase. Here, as in earlier stops, the Americans' extraordinary height left the hometown talent agape. "It must have been the same when the Indians first saw Christopher Columbus," Father Sweeney is apt to say when he recounts it. When the inn's customers had looked awhile, they rushed into the open to spread the word about the gigantic freaks who had materialized out of the night. The inn owner suddenly found his place packed to the doors.

Those who couldn't squeeze into the inn did the next best thing. They punched through the inn's parchment windows and stared over the heads of their fellow-townsmen for a peek, shrilly calling the Antu term for "Holy Smoke!" From within the wall came a fussy little man, sharp-eyed and keen, and a bit on the pompous side. He was some kind of official.

1. *Antu* (ăn'tōō): a small settlement in China.

He shouldered his way through the excitedly chattering people and stared at the priests a long time. "Russians," he told the neighbors confidently. "Long noses from Siberia. I have seen others like these."

Father Bridge politely corrected him. "Americans," he told the fussy little man in Mandarin.[2] "We come from the Beautiful Land." The United States, it seems, is always the "Beautiful Land" to people on the steppes. The fact is, the name originated in the East through the accident that the Chinese character officially chosen to approximate the sound of its first syllable happens to mean "beautiful."

The fussy gentleman made a kind of stump speech about the Beautiful Land. "Americans," he said, in effect, "are a great people. No flies on Americans." This is not a true translation, Father Sweeney would hasten to explain, but it carries the germ of the speech. It was much longer and very flowery, but that's typical of Oriental speeches. You talk your way around a block to cross a conversational crack one foot away.

Next morning, after a night in the inn, the expedition entered the West Gate. The fussy little man, his confidence bolstered by further information from the Americans, proudly led them along narrow gutters through swarms of fellow citizens and shrieking children. These, he declaimed, were Catholic priests, representatives of the Catholic Church. This didn't seem to mean much, so he tried to get the idea over in a simple way. He said, "These foreigners walk the good road. Their church is the good road gate." The people nodded and crowded closer.

Father Sweeney and Father Bridge had been bearded when they reached the inn, but they had washed and shaved in the morning. They had been careful to scour the wooden wash basin with ashes and to use carbolic soap for lather as the basin was community property. Now, hemmed in by the hordes, the priests were clear-cheeked and ruddy. Antu, they noted, was a square city within square walls. It was protected by a medieval moat and its two main streets

2. *Mandarin:* the chief dialect of China.

crossed in the town's center, each street end stopping dead at a gate.

The missionaries recognized in drawn features and heavy-lidded eyes, all about them, the marks of opium smokers. They learned later that poppies are extensively cultivated outside Antu in the brief summer, and that the seeds are made into the sticky gum that is Asia's curse. The local chief of police was eager to help. He begged the visitors to have dinner in his humble home—a mud-walled, grass-thatched little place like most of the others in Antu—but they had to beg off. They explained they had come over difficult roads to celebrate an important holy day. He tried to be helpful anyway, but like the rest of the townsfolk, knew nothing of any Catholic immigrants from Shantung in Antu.

Father Sweeney looked at Father Bridge and Father Bridge looked back at Father Sweeney. It was heartbreaking, after the journey to bring Christmas to Antu, to find that the reports of forgotten Antu Christians were apparently myths, after all. They decided to celebrate the Mass alone. The inn was not a likely place for the celebration. There was no privacy. It was not a decent atmosphere for the Holy Sacrifice. At last, the priests found an old couple in a one-room mud hut near the inn who seemed willing to rent their place for the service. This couple, pagans, moved into the noisy inn.

The rented room was about ten feet wide and fifteen feet long. The thatch ceiling was low. In one corner stood a mud stove that was weak on heat but generous with smoke. In a farther corner were forty-gallon jugs of pickled Chinese cabbage, somewhat on the high side, and along one wall the traditional *k'ang*.[3] An old hen had the run of the place and kept getting underfoot, grumpily uttering a sort of running commentary on the poor pickings. There was an aged, long-haired tomcat, too, which slept most of the time on the *k'ang*. Oddly enough, it paid no heed to the grumpy hen.

Father Bridge set the rickety table in place as an altar with Father Sweeney's help. Still weary from their travels and

3. *k'ang* (kăng): a built-in bed.

not a little sore at heart over their failure to find the forgotten Christians to whom they had meant to bring Christmas, they finally dropped onto the *k'ang*. Father Sweeney was a long way from Clark Street in New Britain, Connecticut; Father Bridge was a far cry from the little mine shack in the Westmoreland Fields. Their surroundings were not the least like home on Christmas Eve, but they fell into deep sleep, just the same, with the decrepit tomcat purring a lullaby.

Father Bridge was the first up on Christmas morning. He awakened Father Sweeney with a deep-throated version of "Adeste Fideles." Then he sang "The Star-Spangled Banner," and Father Sweeney stood up and sleepily came to salute. When the anthem ended Father Sweeney said, "The same to you, sir, and many of them." The tomcat yawned. The gossipy old hen fluffed her feathers and started moving around.

Father Sweeney served the first Mass ever celebrated in far-off Antu. Before he had finished, Dr. Wong pushed open the creaky cottage door. Four Catholics who had lived a full decade in Antu—they were some of the sought-for immigrants from south of the Great Wall—stood behind him. Tears ran down their withered cheeks at sight of the little altar and the vested giant priests towering in the candlelight. During the second Mass another Chinese Christian slipped into the room. He had heard of the missioners from the Beautiful Land as he had passed the inn. The room glowed in the candles' weak beams. Father Bridge cupped his hands around the chalice to prevent the Sacred Host from freezing. When the Mass was ended he sang again, in sheer exultation: "O, Little Child of Bethlehem . . ."

The simple hymn faded and died in Antu's frozen air. Antu's little knot of Christians came to press the Shen Fu's[4] hands in gratitude. One old woman murmured, "Father, come back to us again. Do not discard our souls."

Father Bridge died in St. Mary's Hospital in San Francisco, three years later, in the month of April, when spring was at the windows. He was then thirty-eight. He had worked in

4. *Shen Fu's:* priest's.

the mines as a boy, in the Pittsburgh steel mills, with the American Expeditionary Forces in his youth, and had been ten years in the missions. He had never forgotten the first Christmas in frozen Antu. In brief respite from pain in the hospital he liked to tell about that far-off Christmas Day. He'd say: "I always thought the little room in Antu that morning was like the stable in Bethlehem, and that the worshippers were like the shepherds. I never knew a happier Christmas."

HELPS FOR DISCUSSION

1. Who was the original Catholic missionary to China?

2. By what means do you think the Chinese Catholics kept their faith alive while they had no priests?

3. Why did the Maryknoll Fathers travel so far and endure such hardships to reach Antu?

4. Describe the ceremony at Maryknoll when the missionaries depart for China and other foreign missions.

Kings

JOYCE KILMER

[Choir to be arranged in three voices: high, medium, and low.]

Low — The Kings of the earth are men of might,
And cities are burned for their delight,
Low, medium — And the skies rain death in the silent night,
All — And the hills belch death all day!

High — But the King of Heaven, who made them all,
Is fair and gentle, and very small;
High, medium — He lies in the straw, by the oxen's stall—
All — Let them think of Him to-day!

Gates and Doors

A Ballad of Christmas Eve

JOYCE KILMER

There was a gentle hostler
(And blessed be his name!)
He opened up the stable
The night Our Lady came.
Our Lady and Saint Joseph,
He gave them food and bed,
And Jesus Christ has given him
A glory round his head.

So let the gate swing open
However poor the yard,
Lest weary people visit you
And find their passage barred;
Unlatch the door at midnight
And let your lantern's glow
Shine out to guide the traveler's feet
To you across the snow.

There was a courteous hostler
  (He is in Heaven to-night)
He held Our Lady's bridle
  And helped her to alight;
He spread clean straw before her
  Whereon she might lie down,
And Jesus Christ has given him
  An everlasting crown.

Unlock the door this evening
  And let your gate swing wide,
Let all who ask for shelter
  Come speedily inside.
What if your yard be narrow?
  What if your house be small?
There is a Guest is coming
  Will glorify it all.

There was a joyous hostler
  Who knelt on Christmas morn
Beside the radiant manger
  Wherein his Lord was born.
His heart was full of laughter,
  His soul was full of bliss
When Jesus, on His Mother's lap,
  Gave him His hand to kiss.

Unbar your heart this evening
  And keep no stranger out,
Take from your soul's great portal
  The barrier of doubt.
To humble folk and weary
  Give hearty welcoming,
Your breast shall be to-morrow
  The cradle of a King.

RALPH I. SHEPHERD

V

In Their Own Lands

A good patriot is a good man. If he is true to God, he is true to his fellow men. If he does not love God, he does not love his country.

The love of truth and justice and righteousness is patriotism.

Every Catholic is a soldier—the soldier of Christ. Even the poorest of us is a crusader, just as were the knights of old who marched out to fight the infidel.

There have been many writers who measured love of country by this yardstick. They wrote of old frontiers and of new where spiritual war was waged, where men went out to battle not only for love of their fellow men but for the greater love of God.

Some of the most lasting literature has been concerned with men who suffered death rather than betray this high ideal of patriotism. These are stories of men beside campfires, on poppy-covered battlefields, on stormy seas, in victory and in defeat, but always of men who looked upward above national boundaries to glimpse the eternal stars of faith and friendliness.

The Papal Benediction

O almighty and merciful God, do Thou help us from on high, graciously attending to the prayers of this people, which humbly asks pardon for its sins and awaits Thy grace and benediction: extend Thy right hand over it with favor and pour forth the riches of divine blessing, that filled with every good thing, this people may know eternal blessedness and life. Through Christ our Lord. Amen.

Luke xix, 41-44

And when He drew near and saw the city, He wept over it, saying, "If thou hadst known, in this thy day, even thou, the things that are for thy peace! But now they are hidden from thy eyes. For days will come upon thee when thy enemies will throw up a rampart about thee, and surround thee and shut thee in on every side, and will dash thee to the ground and thy children within thee, and will not leave in thee one stone upon another, because thou hast not known the time of thy visitation."

One colony of the original thirteen which founded our nation began with the ideal of religious liberty for all who came to live within it. That colony was Catholic

Maryland

KATHERINE RANKIN

TIME: The twenty-first of April, 1649.
PLACE: The City of Saint Mary's, Maryland.

THE CAST

NARRATOR
MISTRESS BATTEN
MISTRESS WYATT
MACKENZIE, *the Presbyterian*
SAINT FOYE, *the Huguenot*
Men of Saint Mary's
A Rider
A Herald
PRESTON, *the Puritan*
Women of Saint Mary's
Sailors off the *Golden Fortune*
VOICES

Members of the Assembly:

GOVERNOR STONE
PHILIP CONNER
JOHN PILLE
JOHN INCE
THOMAS HATTON
WILLIAM BRETTON
WALTER PAKES
RICHARD BROWNE
THOMAS GREENE
JOHN MAUNSELL
ROBERT CLARKE
GEORGE MANNERS
CUTHBERT FENWICK
THOMAS THORNBOROUGH
ROBERT VAUGHAN
RICHARD BANKES

MUSIC: [*Roll of drums, built up to orchestra or organ playing triumphantly* "Maryland, My Maryland." *At end of one chorus music fades into soft background as tolling bell is softly heard.*]

NARRATOR: Today our nation, the United States of America, is the greatest democracy the world has ever known. Three hundred years ago it was a vast wilderness with only a few scattered settlements along its eastern seaboard. One of these settlements was Saint Mary's, the capital of the Catholic Province of Maryland. To it had come from the Old World men and women who wanted freedom for themselves and freedom for those who would follow them.

FIRST VOICE: The right to worship God.

SECOND VOICE: The right to work

THIRD VOICE: The right to speak.

FOURTH VOICE: The right to meet in assembly.

NARRATOR: [*Repeats softly.*] "The right to meet in assembly." [*Louder*] In the Province of Maryland, in the City of Saint Mary's, on an April day, three hundred years ago, a general assembly came together to pass the first laws in the American Colonies which assured religious toleration to men of all Christian creeds. Under an April sky, down the roads of tidewater country[1] rode lords and ladies of the manors and gentlemen burgesses[2] from the far-flung Hundreds.[3] With them rode freemen from the provincial plantations to voice in assembly their plea that they might live and let live. History has not forgotten them, those men who rode toward the assembly house on Mattapany[4] Street so that all people who had sought and found religious sanctuary in Maryland might remain free. On that April day they set their seal upon an immortal document of liberty—the Act of Religious Tolerance—whose spirit still lives in America though the men who signed it are long since deep in their cross-covered graves in old Catholic churchyards of the Maryland they founded.

MUSIC: [*Orchestra or organ not too loud,* "Maryland, My Maryland." *After a moment fades, but tolling bell grows louder.*]

NARRATOR: As they near the City of Saint Mary's they hear the long, slow tolling of the bell.

MUSIC: [*Strokes of bell are clearly heard.*]

NARRATOR: In front of the Assembly House stand the men and women of Maryland.

MISTRESS BATTEN: Do you know why the bell is tolling, Mistress Wyatt?

1. *tidewater country:* the land along the seacoast. 2. *burgesses:* representatives in the lower houses of the old Virginia and Maryland legislatures. 3. *Hundreds:* a term used in England for a small division of a county. The English settlers used the same term in colonial days. 4. *Mattapany* (măt à pȧ nī′).

Mistress Wyatt: I do not, Mistress Batten. We have ridden all the way from Resurrection Manor, and I have heard no word but that the ship *Golden Fortune*, three months out from Bristol, has come into port.

Mistress Batten: Then there'll be news from England. What have you heard, Mr. Mackenzie?

Mackenzie: [*Scottish voice*] I know nothing yet, Mistress Batten.

Mistress Batten: No word of the King?

Mackenzie: [*Confidentially*] When last I heard, King Charles was still prisoner of Oliver Cromwell and his Roundhead Parliament.[5]

Mistress Batten: [*Bitterly*] The Parliament in which you once sat as a member, Mr. Mackenzie.

Mackenzie: [*Sorrowfully*] Aye, the Parliament in which I once sat, the Parliament from which we Presbyterians were

5. *Oliver . . . Parliament:* Cromwell was the leader of the group that opposed the King of England during the Civil War in the seventeenth century. The followers of Cromwell were called "Roundheads" because they cut their hair short in contrast to the long hair and wigs then in fashion.

purged by Oliver Cromwell because we sought reconciliation with the King. Colonel Pryde stood at the door of the House of Commons and ordered us out because we opposed Cromwell's rule. We did not know where to flee for safety, with Cromwell's army at our heels. Some of us died at the Caledonian Road. Some of us came here to Maryland because Lord Baltimore, the Catholic, offered us haven. The Huguenots,[6] too, have reason to be grateful to the Calverts. Haven't you, Saint Foye?

SAINT FOYE: I have come today, Monsieur Mackenzie, to thank the Governor of the Province of Maryland for the kindness that has been shown to my people. The Huguenots had been driven from place to place. I had not expected such kindness and justice from the Catholics of Maryland, had you, Monsieur Preston?

MACKENZIE: [*Chuckling a little*] I wonder what the Puritan Preston will say, Mistress Batten? He has no affection for the Catholics.

MISTRESS BATTEN: [*Softly*] The Crown Colony of Virginia flung him out, Mr. Mackenzie. Preston should be grateful to Maryland. What *do* you say, Mr. Preston?

SAINT FOYE: What *do* you say, Monsieur Preston?

PRESTON: [*Dourly*] Maryland took me in, it is true, Mr. Saint Foye, but if I do not go back to Virginia I shall one day have power here.

MACKENZIE: That would not be fair, man.

PRESTON: The wheel turns. Anything's fair. Why do you think this chapel bell has been tolling?

MACKENZIE: We'll soon know. Here is a rider off the ship *Golden Fortune* now.

PRESTON: [*Sneering*] He's already brought his message to the palace of the Lord Proprietor. I was there and heard it.

[*Voices of men and women rising excitedly.*]

FIRST VOICE: Here is the rider now.

SECOND VOICE: Tell us what has happened in England.

THIRD VOICE: Why has the bell been tolling?

6. *Huguenots:* French Protestants.

RIDER: [*In voice of proclamation*] The King is dead! King Charles of England is dead!

[*Voices of men and women.*]

FIRST VOICE: The King!

SECOND VOICE: He says that Charles is dead.

THIRD VOICE: May he rest in peace!

FOURTH VOICE: Where is the Prince of Wales? Is he on the throne?

FIFTH VOICE: What does Cromwell say?

SIXTH VOICE: [*Deeper*] How did the King die?

RIDER: King Charles was executed by order of the High Court of Justice on the thirtieth day of January. He was beheaded—as all London watched—at Charing Cross.

[*Voices rising.*]

FIRST VOICE: Beheaded?

SECOND VOICE: The King beheaded?

THIRD VOICE: God have mercy on him! Who is to rule us?

FOURTH VOICE: What's to become of Maryland?

RIDER: The Prince of Wales has fled in terror to The Hague.

MACKENZIE: Cromwell has won again. 'Tis not the end, though. Young Charles will return. The Highlanders will rally under the banner of the Stuarts.[7] [*Voices and shouts of crowd rising.*] Up with Prince Charles! Down with the Roundheads!

CRIES OF PROTEST: [*Few and feeble*] No, no, up with Cromwell! Long live the Commonwealth!

VOICE: [*With Irish accent*] What news from Ireland, Rider?

RIDER: There's no news, sir, since the victory of Owen Roe O'Neill at the Blackwater.[8]

IRISH VOICE: Has Owen Roe retreated, Rider?

RIDER: I do not know. Cromwell has landed in Ireland and is marching toward Drogheda.[9]

IRISH VOICE: God help us all!

SAINT FOYE: Rider, tell me of my beloved France.

7. *The Stuarts:* the name of the English royal family to which Charles I, who had just been beheaded, and his son belonged. 8. *Blackwater:* a river in County Cork in Ireland. 9. *Drogheda* (drŏ'hē dȧ): a seaport in Ireland.

RIDER: King Louis the Fourteenth has left his palace after the Peace of Westphalia and another war has begun.

[*Voices of men and women.*]

FIRST VOICE: War, more war!

SECOND VOICE: Bloody executions!

THIRD VOICE: Charing Cross!

FOURTH VOICE: The King is dead!

FIFTH VOICE: Cromwell's up!

SIXTH VOICE: What will Lord Baltimore do?

SEVENTH VOICE: What will happen to us?

MISTRESS BATTEN: I must talk with Thomas Greene. Surely as Deputy Governor of Maryland he will know if we are safe here or if we, too, are to be persecuted for our Catholic faith by Oliver Cromwell.

MISTRESS WYATT: There is Thomas Greene now, talking with Thomas Hatton. He sees you. He is waiting for you, Mistress Batten.

MISTRESS BATTEN: Mr. Greene, we are uneasy. We fear Oliver Cromwell.

THOMAS GREENE: Who does not fear Cromwell, Mistress Batten? Cromwell despises Catholics. Hasn't he said that he "would look into no man's thoughts, but that if liberty of conscience meant liberty to exercise the Mass in public, that would never be granted by England"?

MISTRESS BATTEN: But the Roundheads are up! What's to become of us?

THOMAS GREENE: Mistress Batten, we Marylanders must be of stout heart. Lord Baltimore wants none of this bloody business. For a long time—while he has watched the clouds of intolerance rising over England—he has feared that this day of grave portent to Maryland would come. He has planned our safekeeping. Better than anyone else, Thomas Hatton here can tell you of Baltimore's hopes and plans for Maryland. Hatton is the man who has just brought from Lord Baltimore the draft of an act concerning religion. We'll pass it in the assembly today, will we not, Hatton?

HATTON: We will, indeed. Our religious liberty which has

always existed here in Maryland must be preserved. At this assembly we will see to it that Maryland shall be forever known as haven and refuge for all oppressed Christian people. There is room enough here for all.

MISTRESS BATTEN: But if Cromwell declares England a Commonwealth? What if he comes into full power, Mr. Hatton?

HATTON: Maryland is now a Crown Colony. Lord Baltimore, by token of his grant from King Charles, has the right to suggest the laws of Maryland; and the free men of Maryland have the power to enact those laws. We'll do it, won't we, Greene?

GREENE: Today the wisest law of all will be written in letters of gold in the records of Maryland.

[*Voices of sailors off the* Golden Fortune, *singing,* "Who'll be King but Charlie?"]

GREENE: [*As song fades*] What is the song the sailors off the *Golden Fortune* sing, Hatton?

HATTON: It is a ballad of the Scottish Stuarts, a song of the rebels. Oliver Cromwell would order them killed for the singing of it.

GREENE: Then I must learn the words.

[*Voices of men and women.*]

FIRST VOICE: Cavaliers up! We want no part of religious intolerance here.

SECOND VOICE: Marylanders want freedom!

THIRD VOICE: Give us laws to protect us.

[*Low excited murmur of crowd.*]

MISTRESS BATTEN: Never have I seen such crowds before the House of Assembly. They overflow the Square, all the way from the great white mulberry tree, past the Jesuit Chapel. See them, Mistress Wyatt!

MISTRESS WYATT: They're even crowding the steps of the houses from the tavern to Courtney's Fancy. Now the herald is mounting the Assembly steps. Listen, Mistress Batten!

HERALD: [*In loud proclamation*] Hear ye, hear ye! The Assembly of the Province of Maryland, having been convened by his Excellency, the Governor, is about to meet in this city of Saint Mary's. Hear ye, hear ye!

THOMAS GREENE: I have not been so stirred in my soul since that day sixteen years ago when I first saw the green hills of Maryland from the deck of the *Ark*. I would that Leonard Calvert had lived to behold this triumph of freedom.

HATTON: Right you are, Thomas Greene. Governor Stone is coming now with a parchment in his hand. It is the Act concerning Religion.

GREENE: But, look, Hatton. Back of the Governor is Preston, the Puritan. He is the Virginian, you know, with letters from Oliver Cromwell. Preston will want no part of this law of tolerance.

HATTON: But Saint Foye, the Huguenot, is pushing his way in between them. He is speaking with Governor Stone.

HERALD: Hear ye, hear ye, the Assembly of the Province of Maryland . . .

[*Voice fades as music comes up and out*, "Maryland, My Maryland." *Few bars and roll of drums.*]

SAINT FOYE: Your Excellency, I must have speech with you.

GOVERNOR STONE: I have no time just now, Mr. Saint Foye, but later—

SAINT FOYE: [*Confidentially but imperatively*] It must be now, Your Excellency. Over here, where we can be alone. Do you know that Preston plans to misuse your kindness to us? That if you grant, by act of Assembly, this religious toleration, he will use it to plot against you and Lord Baltimore's people? God knows that I, a Huguenot, need such an act; but I cannot take it by treachery.

GOVERNOR STONE: Sir, I appreciate your honesty in coming to me, but I cannot let treachery stand in the way of justice. Maryland was founded by Cecilius Calvert, Lord Baltimore, as sanctuary for Catholics oppressed in England. These Catholics opened the door to all oppressed peoples, and

Maryland shall remain sanctuary for all, even for Cromwell's Puritan friend Preston. The Catholics of Maryland wish it that way.

SAINT FOYE: But Preston plans to petition Cromwell to remove the capital from Catholic Saint Mary's to the town of Providence. There he—Preston—may be the governor.

GOVERNOR STONE: There will be bloodshed along the Severn River before that can happen, Saint Foye.

SAINT FOYE: He says his Roundheads will defeat the Maryland Cavaliers.

GOVERNOR STONE: That may come; but today, even though Charles the King is dead at Charing Cross, we shall act in Assembly to insure liberty to all.

HERALD: Oyez,[10] Oyez, the Governor of the Province of Maryland!

MEN'S VOICES: Hail to the Governor!

[*Voices of men and women.*]

FIRST VOICE: Give us laws to protect us, Your Excellency!

SECOND VOICE: May God and His saints guide you!

GOVERNOR STONE: [*Lifting voice*] The King is dead. England is in turmoil. The Rump Parliament[11] sits at Westminster; but here, in this province of Maryland, I promise you that men shall remain free.

VOICES: Hear, hear!

GOVERNOR STONE: Maryland was founded for freedom. By proclamation and oath Lord Baltimore has established and maintained this policy of religious liberty. Today his creed of tolerance, which we have practiced here since our coming, shall become a law of this new land. Today this Assembly of the Province will vote upon an Act concerning Religion. This is the Act:

"Forasmuch as in a well-governed and Christian commonwealth matters concerning Religion and the honor of God ought in the first place to be taken into serious considera-

10. *oyez* (ō′yĕs): a cry, meaning "Listen," used by criers of courts to secure silence.
11. *Rump Parliament:* Cromwell had expelled from the English Parliament all members who were opposed to his policies, leaving only a small group which is called the "Rump" Parliament.

tion and endeavored to be settled; be it therefore ordered and enacted by the right Honorable Cecilius Lord Baron of Baltimore, Lord and Proprietor of this Province, with the advice and consent of the General Assembly; that whatsoever person or persons within this Province and the Islands thereunto belonging, shall from henceforth, upon any occasion of offense or otherwise, in a reproachful manner or way, declare, call, or denominate any person or persons within this Province or within any of the ports by any name in a reproachful manner relating to matters of Religion shall for every offense forfeit by penalty of fine, public whipping, imprisonment or banishment."

VOICES: Hear, hear!

GOVERNOR STONE: I shall now read the most important clause of this Act of Tolerance. [*Solemnly*] "Whereas the enforcing of the conscience in matters of religion hath frequently fallen out to be a dangerous consequence in those commonwealths where it has been practised, and for the more quiet and peaceable government of this Province and the better to preserve mutual love and amity among the inhabitants thereof: Be it therefore also by the Lord Proprietary with the advice and consent of this assembly ordained and enacted that no person or persons within this Province professing to believe in Jesus Christ, shall from henceforth be anyways troubled, molested, or discountenanced for or in respect of his or her religion nor in the free exercise thereof, nor in anyways compelled to the belief or exercise of any other religion against his or her consent, so as they be not unfaithful to the Lord Proprietor, or molest or conspire against the civil government established or to be established in this Province."

VOICES: Hear, hear!

GOVERNOR STONE: Members of the Maryland Assembly, will you sign this act?

MEN'S VOICES: [*Enthusiastically*] Yes, yes, we will sign.

OTHER VOICES: Such a guaranty of tolerance was never written in the world before. Hurrah for Maryland!

GOVERNOR STONE: Gentlemen, say your names as you pass.

GREENE: Thomas Greene.

GOVERNOR STONE: I might have known, Thomas, that you would be the first signer. I knew that you would show no hard feeling because I supplanted you as governor of Maryland.

THOMAS GREENE: The cause of religious liberty transcends all petty personal dissensions, Governor Stone; but here is Cuthbert Fenwick behind me.

GOVERNOR STONE: The lord of Fenwick Manor, member of the first Maryland Assembly of Freemen that met here at Saint Mary's more than ten years ago.

FENWICK: I sign my name, Cuthbert Fenwick, because I believe that all men in Maryland should be as free as I, a Roman Catholic.

VAUGHAN: And I sign my name, Robert Vaughan.

PILLE: And I sign mine, John Pille.

BROWNE: And I, Richard Browne.

GOVERNOR STONE: The same Richard who came out to Maryland on the long voyage with Captain Wintour.

BANKES: And I'm another Richard, Richard Bankes.

GOVERNOR STONE: [*Affectionately*] My friend Richard Bankes. Sign here, Richard. You will be long remembered.

BANKES: And so will you, Governor Stone. There's a man with me here who has come all the way across the Chesapeake from Saint Michael's Hundred.

GOVERNOR STONE: Welcome, George Manners of Saint Michael's. We are come together today from all Maryland to declare to the world that we believe in God and intend to worship Him according to the dictates of our consciences. We are free men.

MANNERS: As a free man I write my name, George Manners, upon this document which shall be immortal.

THORNE: And I write mine, William Thorne from Somerset.

PAKES: I am Walter Pakes.

CONNER: Philip Conner.

BRETTON: William Bretton.

GOVERNOR STONE: It is an imposing list.

INCE: John Ince.

THORNBOROUGH: Thomas Thornborough of Neale's Plantation.

CLARKE: Robert Clarke, Your Excellency.

GOVERNOR STONE: Robert Clarke, Maryland's first deputy governor, and behind you is Thomas Hatton. What do you say, Thomas?

HATTON: I would die for religious freedom, Your Excellency. I would that I might set my mark in letters that would never fade.

GOVERNOR STONE: Time will do that for you, Thomas Hatton. In the centuries to come men in this land of freedom will remember that you were the same Thomas Hatton who carried this document of liberty from the bloodstained shores of England to the brighter, braver, freer soil of our own America. History will not forget you.

HATTON: History will soon forget me; but history will never forget what sixteen free men of Maryland have done this day.

MUSIC: [*Roll of drums built up to orchestra or organ playing triumphantly,* "Maryland, My Maryland."]

NARRATOR: The Act of Religious Tolerance was signed that day. The Assembly of the Province of Maryland ended its executive session, but the example it set for the new land of America led other men to other laws for religious freedom. In the colony of New York, thirty-four years later, another Catholic—the Irish-born Governor Thomas Dongan—summoned its first free assembly and won in it the passage of the Charter of Liberties.

Through another century the cause of religious freedom marched on. Finally—after the Thirteen Colonies had become the United States—the Congress of the nation gave to the States the first ten amendments to the Constitution, the Bill of Rights, with its guaranty to every citizen of the five fundamental rights of free men:

Freedom of speech;

Freedom of the press;

Freedom of the people peaceably to assemble;

Freedom to petition the government for redress of grievance; and, foremost, the right of freedom of religion. The free men of Maryland had not written their names in vain.

MUSIC: [*Organ and orchestra triumphantly in* "Maryland, My Maryland."]

My People Came to This Country

STRUTHERS BURT

My people came to this country
—And the seas were a green great space—
Because the trees were kind and tall
And the fields a pleasant place,
And brave men worshiped as they would
And thought with an open face.

My people came to this country
With dreams too quick for hate,

A neighbor was a light in the dark
Or a hand upon a gate,
And whence he came was no news at all
In the building of a state.

Now God bless every stick of it
And every path and post;
The broad slow rivers of the south,
The quick bright streams of the frost,
And the mountains like a mighty oath
That does not count the cost.

And God bless all the dipping fields
From the mountains to the sea,
And grant that I walk like a fearless man
For the blood that runs in me.

American Names

STEPHEN VINCENT BENÉT

I have fallen in love with American names,
The sharp names that never get fat,
The snakeskin-titles of mining-claims,
The plumed war-bonnet of Medicine Hat,
Tucson and Deadwood and Lost Mule Flat.

Seine[1] and Piave[2] are silver spoons,
But the spoonbowl-metal is thin and worn,
There are English counties like hunting-tunes
Played on the keys of a postboy's horn,
But I will remember where I was born.

I will remember Carquinez Straits,[3]
Little French Lick and Lundy's Lane,
The Yankee ships and the Yankee dates
And the bullet-towns of Calamity Jane.[4]
I will remember Skunktown Plain.

Rue des Martyrs[5] and Bleeding-Heart-Yard,
Senlis,[6] Pisa,[7] and Blindman's oast,
It is a magic ghost you guard
But I am sick for a newer ghost,
Harrisburg, Spartanburg, Painted Post.

I shall not rest quiet in Montparnasse.[8]
I shall not lie easy at Winchelsea.
You may bury my body in Sussex grass,
You may bury my tongue at Champmédy.[9]
I shall not be there. I shall rise and pass.
Bury my heart at Wounded Knee.

1. *Seine* (sān): a river in France. 2. *Piave* (pyä'vā): a river in Italy. 3. *Carquinez* (kär kē'nĕs) *Straits:* a body of water in California. 4. *Calamity Jane:* a frontier character of Deadwood, South Dakota. 5. *Rue des Martyrs* (rü dā mär'tēr): a street in Paris. 6. *Senlis* (säɴ lēs'): a department of France. 7. *Pisa* (pē'zȧ): a town in Italy. 8. *Montparnasse* (môɴ pär nȧs'): a district in Paris. 9. *Champmédy* (shäɴ mā dē'):

One of the finest tributes ever paid to an American Catholic bishop was spoken by his friend and neighbor, a Protestant minister, when he told of the work Bishop Cheverus had accomplished as

The Bishop of Boston

WILLIAM ELLERY CHANNING

The Catholic Church has produced some of the greatest and best men that ever lived, and that is proof enough of its possessing all the means of salvation. Who that hears the tone of contempt in which it is sometimes named, would suspect that Charlemagne, Alfred, Dante, Raphael, Michaelangelo, Tasso, Bossuet, Pascal, and Des Cartes were Catholics? Some of the greatest names in art and arms, on the throne and in the pulpit, were worn by Catholics. To come down to our time, has not the metropolis of New England witnessed a sublime example of Christian virtue in a Catholic bishop? Who, among our religious teachers, would solicit a comparison between himself and the devoted Cheverus? This good man, whose virtues and talents have now raised him to high dignities in Church and State, who now wears in his own country the joint honors of an archbishop and a peer, lived in the midst of us, devoting his days and nights and his whole heart to the service of a poor and uneducated congregation.

We saw him declining, in a great degree, the society of the cultured and refined, that he might be the friend of the ignorant and friendless; leaving the circles of polished life, which he would have graced, for the meanest hovels; bearing, with a father's sympathy, the burdens and sorrows of his large spiritual family; charging himself alike with their temporal and spiritual concerns; and never discovering, by the faintest indication, that he felt his fine mind degraded by his seemingly humble office. The good man, bent on his errands of mercy, was seen in our streets under the most burning sun of summer and the fiercest storms of winter, as if armed against the elements by the power of charity.

He enjoys among us what, to such a man, must be dearer than fame. His name is cherished where the great of this world are unknown. It is pronounced with blessing, with grateful tears, with sighs for his return, in many an abode of sorrow and want; and how can we shut our hearts against the proof of the power of the Catholic religion to form good and great men?

HELPS FOR DISCUSSION

1. Why did William Ellery Channing name the men mentioned in the first paragraph as outstanding Catholics?

2. What men might he have added to this list?

3. What virtues of Bishop Cheverus did William Ellery Channing emphasize?

Courtesy

HILAIRE BELLOC

Of courtesy, it is much less
Than Courage of Heart or Holiness,
Yet in my Walks it seems to me
That the Grace of God is in Courtesy.

On Monks I did in Storrington fall,
They took me straight into their Hall;
I saw Three Pictures on a wall,
And Courtesy was in them all.

The first the Annunciation;
The second the Visitation;
The third the Consolation,
Of God that was Our Lady's Son.

The first was of Saint Gabriel;
On Wings a-flame from Heaven he fell;
And as he went upon one knee
He shone with Heavenly Courtesy.

Our Lady out of Nazareth rode—
It was her month of heavy load;
Yet was Her face both great and kind,
For Courtesy was in Her Mind.

The third it was our Little Lord,
Whom all the Kings in arms adored;
He was so small you could not see
His large intent of Courtesy.

Our Lord, that was Our Lady's Son,
Go bless you, People, one by one;
My Rhyme is written, my work is done.

Nowhere is there greater need of Christian friendliness than in a wartime hospital for injured men of two hostile armies; and no one ever met that need with greater courage than did

Sister Josephine

MOTHER MARY ANGELA

In the summer of 1862 the Confederate Fort Charles, on the White River, was attacked on land by a force under the command of Colonel Fitch of Indiana, and from the water by gunboats commanded by Commodore Davis. In the midst of the battle the boilers of one of the gunboats exploded, frightfully scalding Captain Kelty, an officer in the Union Army, and some fifty others. The sufferers, in their agony, leaped into the river; and, as they did so, a broadside from Fort Charles poured bullets and grapeshot into their parboiled bodies.

The battle ended with the capture of the fort, and the wounded of both sides were taken to Mound City Hospital, a block of warehouses converted into a vast hospital, in which, after some of the great battles in the Mississippi Valley, as many as two thousand patients were treated by a staff of medical officers and nursed by twenty-eight Sisters—Sister Josephine being one of them. Colonel Fry, the Confederate commander of the fort, supposed to be dangerously wounded, and Captain Kelty were among the number brought to Mound City after the surrender of Fort Charles.

Captain Kelty was a general favorite among the men and officers of the Western flotilla. His sad state—the scalded flesh falling from the bones and pierced with bullets—excited his men almost to frenzy. He was tenderly placed in a little cottage away from the main building; and Colonel Fry, with a few other sufferers, was put in a front room on the second story of the hospital, under the immediate care of Sister Josephine.

The next day the report spread like wildfire through the hospital and among the one hundred Union soldiers detailed to guard it that Captain Kelty was dying. The wildest excitement prevailed; and in the frenzy of the moment Colonel Fry was denounced as Captain Kelty's murderer. It was declared that Colonel Fry had given the inhuman order to fire on the scalded men. Everyone firmly believed this. But it was not true; Colonel Fry was ignorant of the explosion on the gunboat when the order was given.

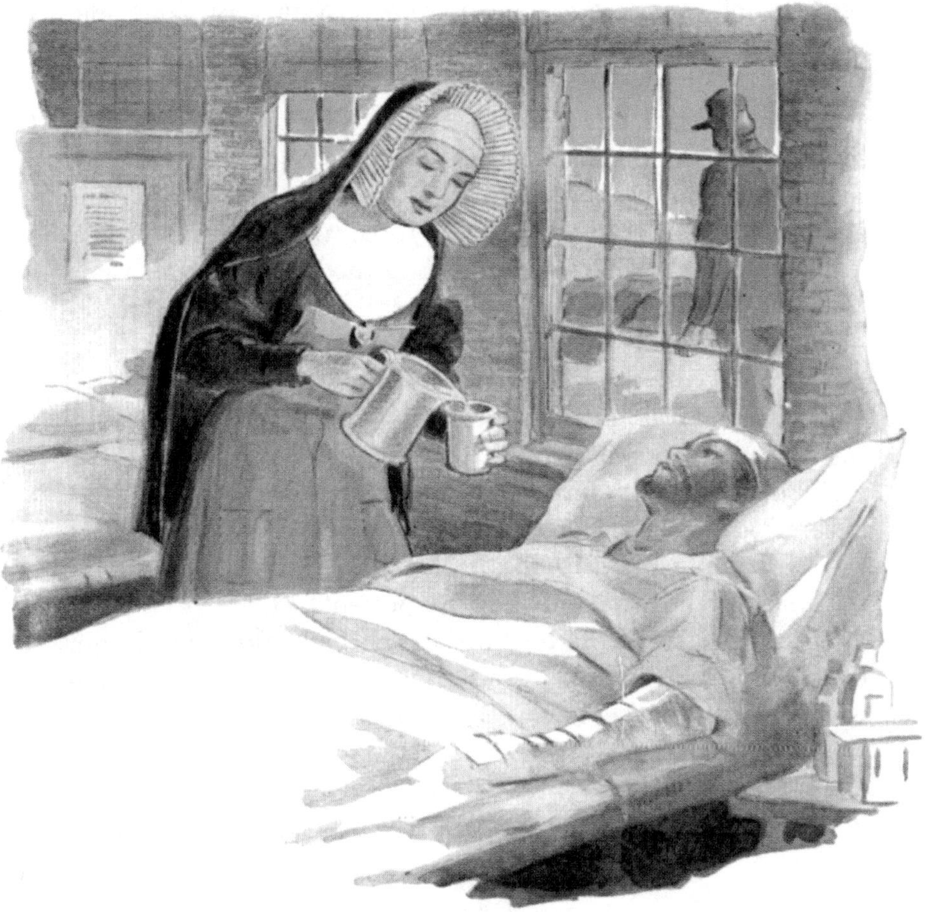

Sister Josephine, pale, yet wonderfully composed, went to the Sister in charge of the hospital to say that all the wounded, except Colonel Fry, had just been removed from the room under her care. The soldiers detailed to guard the hospital had built a rough scaffold in front of the two windows of the room and mounted it with loaded guns. They loudly declared that they would remain, and the instant they heard of Captain Kelty's death they would shoot Colonel Fry. Afterwards, Sister Josephine said, "The doctor made me leave the room, saying my life was in danger. He took the key from the door and gave it to 'Dutch Johnny,' telling him that he had entire charge of the man within."

Dutch Johnny was one of six brothers; five of whom had been killed at Belmont.[1] Johnny was so badly wounded and crippled in the same battle that he was useless for active service and was left to help in the hospital. But one idea possessed him—in revenge for his brothers' death he intended to kill five Confederates before he died.

In this fearful state of affairs the Sister in charge went to Doctor Franklin, Surgeon General of the staff, begging him to see that no murder be committed. Doctor Franklin answered that he was powerless to control events and that the captain of the company guarding the hospital was absent.

"Then," said the Sister, "I must call my twenty-seven Sisters from the sick; we will leave the hospital and walk down to Cairo." Cairo was three miles distant.

In vain did the doctor represent to her the sad state of all the patients she was leaving. She would not consent to remain in a house where murder might soon be committed, except on one condition: that the doctor would give her the key of Colonel Fry's room, and that the Sisters would have the care and entire control of the patient.

"But," protested the doctor, "it will be at the risk of your lives. If Captain Kelty dies—and I see no hope of his recovery—no power on earth can restrain those men from shooting Colonel Fry."

1. *Belmont:* an early battle in Grant's West Tennessee campaign in the Civil War.

"Oh, Doctor!" she said, "I have too much faith in the natural chivalry of every soldier—be he from North or South of the Mason and Dixon line—to fear he would shoot a poor wounded man while a Sister stood near him!"

Realizing that the Sisters would leave if their request were not granted, the doctor sent for Dutch Johnny, took the key from him, and gave it to the Sister in charge. The latter called for Sister Josephine, and both went in haste to the room of the wounded man.

As they turned the key and opened the door a fearful scene was before them. Colonel Fry lay on a cot, his arms, both broken, strapped up with cords fastened to the ceiling. One broken leg was strapped to the bed. Only his head seemed free. As he turned it and glared fiercely, as he thought, upon another foe, he seemed like some wild animal at bay and goaded to madness. Before Sister Josephine had been forced to leave the room, she had closed the windows, and lowered the blinds; but her successor, Dutch Johnny, had changed all this. He had rolled up the blinds and thrown up the lower sashes. And there, on the raised platform, not fifty feet from him, Colonel Fry could see the faces and hear the voices of the soldiers and gunboat men, shouting every few minutes for him to be ready to die, for they would shoot him as soon as they heard of Captain Kelty's death.

Very quietly and gently did Sister Josephine speak to the wounded man, moistening his parched lips with a cooling drink, giving what relief she could to his poor tortured body, and assuring him that she and the other Sister would not leave him. He need not fear that the soldiers would fire while they remained.

When the men outside saw the Sisters in the room they begged them to leave—even threatened—but to no purpose. Brave, noble Sister Josephine and her companion stood at their post all through that long afternoon and far into the night. They prayed perhaps more earnestly than they ever prayed before that Captain Kelty would not die; for, in spite of all their assuring words to Colonel Fry, they did not feel very certain that the life of the Confederate officer would be safe among frenzied men, bent on taking revenge into their own hands.

In the meantime it became known that Captain Kelty was a Catholic—a convert—though for many years he had neglected his religious duties. A messenger was sent to Cairo to bring Father Walsh to the dying man. When the priest came Captain Kelty was in delirium, and the Father could give him only Extreme Unction. Soon after, about nine o'clock, the captain sank into a quiet sleep. He awoke, perfectly conscious, near midnight, made his confession, received Holy Communion, and took some nourishment. The doctor said all danger was over, and a messenger ran in breathless haste to spread the glad tidings. The excited soldiers fired a few blank cartridges as a parting salvo,[2] jumped from the scaffold, and were seen no more. The rest of the night good Sister Josephine took care of her patient, undisturbed by any serious fear that they both might be sent into eternity before morning.

The naval officers came up the next day from Cairo. On the night before they had looked, as they feared, for the last time on the living face of Captain Kelty. Now they found him out of danger, and they laughed and cried with joy. In a whisper Captain Kelty asked them to be silent a moment. In a voice trembling with weakness he said, "While I thank these good doctors for all they have done, I must testify—and they will bear me out in what I say—that it was not their skill nor any earthly power that brought me back from the brink of the grave. It was the saving and life-giving Sacraments of the Catholic Church."

Colonel Fry and Captain Kelty had long known each other. Both had been naval officers but, at the beginning of the war, Captain Fry had left the service and had become Colonel Fry of the Confederate Army.

As soon as Captain Kelty was well enough to learn what had passed he declared Colonel Fry was guiltless of the barbarity of which he had been accused, and Sister Josephine was made the bearer to her patient of the delicacies sent to Captain Kelty, which he insisted on sharing with Colonel Fry.

2. *salvo:* a volley fired from guns.

As soon as Captain Kelty could travel he was taken to his home in Baltimore. For his bravery he was made Commodore and placed in command at Norfolk; but he was maimed for life. His right hand and arm, shriveled and wasted, hung lifeless by his side. Later, when he was able to take such a journey alone, he went back to Cairo to see again and thank those Sisters who, he said, under God, had saved his life in a double sense. He remained until his death a most fervent Catholic.

Colonel Fry, after many months of suffering, also recovered. He was paroled and returned to his home in New Orleans. There he became a Catholic, often declaring that good Sister Josephine's bravery and devotedness during that day and night of torture and agony were eloquent sermons that he could not resist.

A few years after the close of the war he was one of the leaders of that rash band of adventurers who invaded Cuba. His fate is well known. With those under his command he was captured and executed. But it is not so well known that he profited by the days spent in prison in instructing those with him; and many were converted to the holy Faith which first came to him through Sister Josephine.

Twenty-three years passed away when, quietly and calmly, as in the discharge of hospital duties, this good Sister, strengthened by the Sacraments of the Church, died at Saint Mary's.

Owing to the intense heat of the weather, it was deemed necessary to change the hour of burial from six o'clock in the morning to eight o'clock of the previous evening. Seldom was a procession more affecting: the Sisters—more than three hundred in number—all bearing lighted tapers; the reverend chaplains; and the venerable Father Sorin, Superior General of the Congregation of the Holy Cross, followed the remains of Sister Josephine through the beautiful grounds of Saint Mary's to the cemetery. The moon shone as brightly on her lifeless body as it had shone years ago through the open window on her brave, gentle form, when she saved from death the wounded prisoner in her charge.

THINGS TO DO

1. Work out a dramatization of scenes in the hospital room, using these characters: the two Sisters, Doctor Franklin, Colonel Fry, Dutch Johnny, and soldiers on the scaffold outside the window. As a final scene, bring in Captain Kelty for reconciliation with Colonel Fry. Emphasize the idea of Captain Kelty's return to the Church and Colonel Fry's conversion.

2. The following poem pictures a Civil War scene. Sketch, paint, or describe vividly what it helps you to see. What is the poet's spiritual message in the last line?

ART IN MANY LANDS

Every school child knows the GILBERT STUART portrait of *George Washington.* There are also many noted paintings of other characters of whom you have read in these stories, and there are pictures of places you know in stories. BASTIEN-LEPAGE painted a great picture of *Joan of Arc*, and you must see the pictures of *Abraham Lincoln*, by VOLK; of *The Fifer*, by MANET; *A View of Ghent*, by BAERTSOEN; *The Surrender of Breda*, by VELASQUEZ; *The Laughing Cavalier*, by HALS; *Washing the Feet of the Disciples*, by BROWN.

Bivouac on a Mountain Side

WALT WHITMAN

I see before me now a traveling army halting,
Below a fertile valley spread, with barns and the orchards
of summer,
Behind, the terraced sides of a mountain, abrupt, in places
rising high,
Broken, with rocks, with clinging cedars, with tall shapes
dingily seen,
The numerous camp-fires scattered near and far, some away
up on the mountain,
The shadowy forms of men and horses, looming, large-sized,
flickering,
And over all the sky—the sky! far, far out of reach, studded,
breaking out, the eternal stars.

Abraham Lincoln made many great speeches; but in no one of them did he show deeper feeling than he did when, from the platform of the railroad train that was taking him to Washington, he spoke his

Farewell Address to the People of Springfield

ABRAHAM LINCOLN

My Friends: No one, not in my situation, can appreciate my feeling of sadness at this parting. To this place, and the kindness of these people, I owe everything. Here I have lived a quarter of a century, and have passed from a young to an old man. Here my children have been born, and one is buried. I now leave, not knowing when or whether ever I may return, with a task before me greater than that which rested upon Washington. Without the assistance of that Divine Being who ever attended him, I cannot succeed. With that assistance, I cannot fail. Trusting in Him who can go with me, and remain with you, and be everywhere for good, let us confidently hope that all will yet be well. To His care commending you, as I hope in your prayers you will commend me, I bid you an affectionate farewell.

THINGS TO DO

Find selections in the writings of great men which show how they depended upon God and how they called upon Him in times of stress. Be ready to read these to the class.

Abraham Lincoln Walks at Midnight

VACHEL LINDSAY

It is portentous, and a thing of state
That here at midnight, in our little town
A mourning figure walks, and will not rest,
Near the old court-house pacing up and down.

Or by his homestead, or in shadowed yards
He lingers where his children used to play,
Or through the market, on the well-worn stones
He stalks until the dawn-stars burn away.

A bronzed, lank man! His suit of ancient black,
A famous high top-hat and plain worn shawl
Make him the quaint great figure that men love,
The prairie-lawyer, master of us all.

He cannot sleep upon his hillside now.
He is among us:—as in times before!
And we who toss and lie awake for long,
Breathe deep, and start, to see him pass the door.

His head is bowed. He thinks of men and kings.
Yea, when the sick world cries, how can he sleep?
Too many peasants fight, they know not why;
Too many homesteads in black terror weep.

The sins of all the war-lords burn his heart.
He sees the dreadnaughts scouring every main.
He carries on his shawl-wrapped shoulders now
The bitterness, the folly and the pain.

It breaks his heart that kings must murder still,
That all his hours of travail here for men
Seem yet in vain. And who will bring white peace
That he may sleep upon his hill again?

America

RABBI ABBA HILLEL SILVER

God built Him a continent of glory and filled it with treasures
untold:
He carpeted it within soft-rolling prairies and columned it
with thundering mountains;
He studded it with sweet-flowing fountains and traced it with
long-winding streams;
He planted it with deep-shadowed forests and filled them with
song.
Then He called unto a thousand peoples and summoned the
bravest among them.
They came from the ends of the earth, each bearing a gift
and a hope.
The flow of adventure was in their eyes and in their hearts
the glory of hope.
And out of the bounty of earth and the labor of men, out of
the longing of hearts and the prayer of souls, out of the
memory of ages and hopes of the world,
God fashioned a nation in love, blessed it with a purpose
sublime—and called it

AMERICA.

A kindly German farmer and his wife cared for and gave their name
to a little black boy who had been born in slavery in Missouri.
Their kindness and the help of a Swiss neighbor led the boy up to a great career.
Dr. George Washington Carver was the boy whom these people showed how
to help himself and the world in

Vineyards in the Sun

SHIRLEY GRAHAM AND GEORGE D. LIPSCOMB

Farmer Carver's spirit was that of the midwest pioneers. He would not be beaten by hardship. And now his farm began to prosper. He was far from rich, but again good crops were harvested, the barn was filled with golden corn and the huge smokehouse was full of meat.

Three years had passed since George had come to live and work on the farm. Boys born in slavery had no birthdays, but George must have been about ten on that early, crisp fall morning when he tumbled off his cot. No one had to call him. Long before the old speckled rooster crowed for day he was out in the barn, milking the cow, fixing the mush for the pigs, polishing the harness, and feeding the horse. He paused long enough to whisper in the mare's ear, "Eat well, so we can go fast—fast!" Then off to the chicken yard, passing as he went beneath the new grape arbors. There was a pleasant snap in the air, and his handful of grapes was nicely chilled. Um-um, they were good! He sniffed the air, wrinkling his nose like a bunny. So many good smells—new-mown hay, ripe apples, corn shucks, heavy leaves, and now these luscious grapes!

The arbor was thick and the grapes plentiful. Farmer Carver had been dubious at first. Experiments could be expensive, but it had been hard to withstand the enthusiasm of the Swiss farmer, Hermann Jaegar, who had come from the next county and ridden up and down the countryside encouraging the farmers to raise grapes. He had said the soil and climate were just right for them and he had given them slips to start their vines. In George he had found an ardent disciple. It had been George who had carried out the instructions, George who had trained the vines along the frames, George who had kept them trimmed and who had watched carefully for hungry bugs. Now, Farmer Carver was very glad he had decided to grow grapes. Because of them special honor had come to this section of Missouri. The French government had bought cuttings from the grapevines of Hermann Jaegar. Learning that the French vineyards were being destroyed, this exile from his home vineyards had suggested to the French that they use cuttings and seeds from the wild grapes of the Ozarks as new roots for their vines. The suggestion was accepted. Now, Hermann Jaegar was told he was a patriot, and France would use all the cuttings he could spare. And so the Ozark hills were transmitting their fresh, young sap to the worn-out vineyards of France where vines were taking on new life and vigor.

It was to Farmer Jaegar's place many miles away that George was going this morning. Since Farmer Carver had to go to the county seat, Neosho, he had decided to drive on over to visit the Swiss' fifty acres of vineyard. The idea of raising more grapes had occurred to him and so he decided to take George along to learn what he could.

"That boy picks ideas out of the air when it comes to growing things," he had confided to his wife.

"He certainly asks enough questions!"

Farmer Carver groaned. "Almost I wish he was not yet able to talk. This afternoon while helping me in the barn he asked, 'Why is grass green? What makes grasshoppers jump? Why do morning glories fold up in the afternoon?' And, 'How long does it take to make a rainbow?' "

Frau Carver laughed. "So that's why you sent him in to me! Well, I'm glad. With his help I finished my preserving at least an hour earlier."

"He's lots handier around a cook stove than he is with a plow," the farmer commented dryly.

"His growth is slow, but he's a smart boy." Then Frau Carver added thoughtfully, "He's nine or ten years old now and ought to be going to school."

Farmer Carver frowned. "There's no place for a colored child to go to school around here. What would he do with book learning?"

"He should know how to read and write."

The matter of George's schooling was dropped for the time being. But after supper Farmer Carver said, "George, we're getting up extra early in the morning. I'm driving over to Newton County, and you can go with me to Hermann Jaegar's place."

"Oh! the grape man?" chirped George in his high, little voice.

Farmer Carver laughed. "Yes, that one."

The boy's eyes shone with excitement. He was silent a moment. Then, "Why are grapes purple?"

"I don't know," answered the farmer, while his wife looked on, smiling over her mending. "All grapes are not purple, but nobody knows why some are purple and some—not." He turned away decisively

George thought a moment and then asked, "Does God know?"

"Of course he does, answered the farmer devoutly.

"Then I'll ask Him," and George slipped quickly out of the room.

The farmer's face turned red. He opened his mouth to call, but Frau Carver laid her hand on his arm and spoke gently, "No, my husband! Let him go!"

"But—but—" protested the man, "it is not—right! He should not talk like that. Why, he sounded as if he were going to meet God out there—around the house!"

"Maybe he will," answered his wife quietly.

"Susan!"

Farmer Carver was lost in deep thought for a few minutes, then said, "You are right. He must learn to read. We cannot have a heathen growing up in our house. He must learn to read the Bible!"

"Mrs. Mueller gave him an old speller. He takes it with him every time he goes over there to work in her yard. She says he is learning every word in it."

"He must learn to read the Bible," repeated the stern old farmer, who had been reared in the strict German Lutheran church. "He must learn to know God!"

George was a very happy boy when several hours later that morning he and Mr. Carver rolled along the dirt road approaching Neosho. George sat in the back of the cart, his bare feet hanging over the side. No one was concerned about George's appearance. He was just the Carvers' "boy" and, as such, anything with which he covered his body was accepted as sufficient. The pants he wore had once belonged to Farmer Carver. Simply by cutting off the worn legs and pulling a string about the upper part they were fitted to his slight frame. Mrs. Mueller had given him his coat. It had been left at her house by a visiting nephew, considerably larger than George. If the small boy made a grotesque figure no one cared, least of all he himself. As from a mighty chariot of state, he viewed the passing world and found it good.

Dog fennel, pennyroyal and goldenrod flamed in the fields. Trees touched with the breath of autumn wore their last party dress of gold and red. Purple hills rose in the distance, and the sky was very blue. They passed apple orchards sweet with ripe apples and hay all stacked and ready for the barns. Negroes digging potatoes stopped to wave, and once a flock of geese waddled by. Many of the freed slaves had gone away, but here and there those remaining could be seen—"squatting" on a piece of poor land or living in bare cabins nearer the town, from which they went out to do odd jobs. The boy's

vivid imagination pictured the interiors of those cabins from the one he knew—his mother's. He was keenly interested in the people living in them. He wondered why somebody didn't dig up the beautiful goldenrod growing along the side of the road and replant it in the cabin yards.

"Well, here we are in Neosho," called the farmer, looking back over his shoulder. "Better come up here on the seat with me."

George quickly climbed over the sacks of wheat piled in the cart and scrambled up to the narrow seat. He was glad, because the many wagons, buggies, and people passing along the streets frightened him, and he felt more secure close to the big farmer. Without realizing why, he shrank from the crude ugliness through which they were now passing.

Neosho had been a mining "boomtown" in the early days, serving the three lead mines in the vicinity. During the War between the States, it had been the center of bitter fighting. In October, 1863, General Joseph Shelby had attacked the Federal troops garrisoned within the courthouse, driven them out, and burned the courthouse to the ground. For a long time rebellious guerrilla soldiers had terrorized the neighborhood until, in 1866, order was established. But only one of the mines resumed work, sections of the town were abandoned, and the shacks fell in ruins. Recently a large flour mill had been opened, and the town was beginning to take on renewed activity.

Their first stop was at the mill. The farmer went inside, and George struggled with the heavy sacks of wheat until one of the mill hands, giving him a playful shove, sent the small boy sprawling in the gutter.

"Out of our way, beetle," said the man, laughing. "If one of these sacks fell on you, you'd be part of the flour!"

"And the flour would be *brown*!" called out another. At this they all laughed.

George picked himself up. His thoughts were confused. He realized the men did not want to hurt him—but how he wished he could carry the sacks easily! He wondered if small, weak black boys ever grew big and strong and whether or not they changed color so that they no longer differed from all the other people who were doing things. From the way the men laughed it would seem that *brown* flour would be very bad indeed. George wondered why.

Soon the cart was emptied, and they were off again. The streets were wider now and lined with big trees. Behind neat lawns sat painted houses. In the very center of the town a little park surrounded a large spring, after whose clear, cool water the Indians had named the early settlement. Here George climbed down to water the horse and, after a moment, Farmer Carver, taking his pipe from his mouth, remarked, "This is a good place to eat our lunch, eh, George?"

Without waiting for a reply, he reached under the seat and took out the parcel Frau Carver had carefully placed there. Seating himself on the ground under a tree, he divided the contents and held out to George his portion. Frau Carver had known they would be hungry and the thick pieces of cornbread and boiled fat bacon were generous. The fact that an ear of corn was cold did not rob it of its good rich flavor, and as he ate George thought this was all very nice indeed. Village folk passing through the square observed the big white farmer and the very small dark boy sitting under the tree silently eating. When he had finished, Farmer Carver, still saying nothing, leaned against the tree trunk and looked up thoughtfully into its leaf-trimmed branches. George did not at all mind the farmer's long silences. Big people's talk to him usually consisted of orders which disturbed his observations. He was happier when they were silent.

An hour later they were crossing the White River. Never had he seen so much water, and he leaned so far out trying to see everything that the farmer said sharply, "Careful there!"

George drew back into his seat, but he thought how wonderful it would be to sink down under that shining expanse. The thought of drowning did not occur to him.

The first sight of Hermann Jaegar's vineyards impressed even the stolid German farmer. And George held his breath. Row after row of vines on the hillside, and in the midst of lovely gardens, the great white house. Behind that house was something which caused George to stare—a glass house in which he could see green, growing things! Here they found Monsieur Jaegar, as he was called.

While the two men exchanged greetings, George slipped by and, fascinated, walked slowly between the benches. He had heard of Heaven. This, he thought, must be it! Timidly he extended his hand and touched delicate leaves. He caressed them with his fingers. He stopped before one box and began carefully to examine the earth, the tiny frames, the stems. Softly he spoke to them, saying how lovely they were and asking what they were. He did not know that he was singing. But Monsieur Jaegar had turned and, motioning Farmer Carver to silence, was listening.

"The little black boy," he whispered, "look!"

Farmer Carver did not understand his exact words, but he did recognize his friend's amazement.

"Yes," he answered, "he likes plants. He takes care of my grape arbors."

At this the Swiss farmer came up behind George and said softly, "My child, you—" he stopped and then with some effort, "you—you love—plants?"

George looked up at him. Instantly there was a flash of understanding between them. Certainly he could not have told how he knew, but he was certain that beyond all doubt here was a man who saw as he did.

"Yes—yes," he stretched his arms wide, "everything!"

"That is good!" The Swiss nodded his head. He took the little brown hands in his, flexing the fingers. "The hand of a gardener—his touch brings life." Patting the hand gently and letting it go he turned to Farmer Carver.

"*He* tended your grapes? But he is too small!"

In low tones the farmer then told George's simple story—how his mother had been stolen and how Frau Carver had cared for the sickly babe.

"He will never be strong. What will he do? Negroes can only work—and here he is now, freed, and unable to take care of himself." Farmer Carver shook his head sadly.

But Monsieur Jaegar again approached the boy, still busy examining the boxes. "Come," he said, smiling, "I will show you something about grapes."

Going to one of the boxes he explained, "Here are vines of wild grapes—I gathered them from the side of the hill and brought them here. The grapes are rather sour and small."

"But," interrupted George eagerly, "they are good. I found some growing beside my creek." Then he added shyly, "Me and the rabbits like them very much."

The Swiss smiled, "Ah, yes, little one, you and the little creatures of the woods. God puts them there for you."

George gazed at him with wide eyes.

"And now," continued Monsieur Jaegar, pointing to another box, "here are grapes raised in Virginia. They are very sweet, but the vines are frail. They rot quickly and the grapes are pithy. Now, look carefully."

He broke a piece from each of the two vines, fastened them together and stuck the two slips into a third box which contained similar small double plants.

"Here I bring the two together. The two produce one vine. I, Jaegar, work with God making better grapes. The wild vines are sturdy and strong; blended with the vines from Virginia they give—" he went to the door and with a sweeping gesture indicated the thick, green arbors, "grapes which we can ship to all the world!"

George's eyes were very round. This must be God, he was thinking, this kind man with his long black hair and swarthy face. The man was still speaking.

"You see the hills and all the fields and all the hills and fields beyond—they belong to the good God—all the earth belongs to God! And," now he was looking closely into the little boy's rapt face, "This God—this great God—is *your* Father."

"My—my—" the boy stammered.

"Yes, you are one of his little creatures—like all small ones of the woods—you have no one else. But, see," he took the boy's hand again, "He has given you the grower's hand. You too must work with God, as I do!"

He turned away and after a moment George looked down at his hands, spreading the fingers and observing them closely for the first time. The "grower's hand" this wonderful man had said! Reaching into the box he let the loose dirt play through his fingers. And God was *his* father! But God had everything. He remembered Farmer Carver reading from the great Book. "The earth is the Lord's." He remembered the words well.

They turned their faces toward home late in the afternoon. Silently they watched the sun set behind the distant hills and saw the purple shadows fill the valley. Farmer Carver was thinking over this visit. New things had been shown him, things about cultivation of soil and planned crops. Much of the advice had come too late for his poor farm to benefit. He was growing old. Help was hard to get. He had no sons. He wished George were big enough to take over. But, with all his genius for growing things, George could not even plow.

George might have been asleep, he sat so still. But inside that tiny frame deep fires were kindling. Without being able to put it into words, he knew something very wonderful had happened to him that day.

After George had eaten such a meal as he did not dream could be, Monsieur Jaegar had come to him with an open book in his hand. Tears filled George's eyes as he shook his head. He recognized some of the words from his speller, but he could make no sense. The Swiss had only said, "Take it. Already you know much other people do not know—for you see more. But someday you will be able to read this book. You must read all the books. Then your Father will teach you many things."

Now the book was hugged close inside George's ragged shirt. He had hardly dared glance at it.

As they returned through Neosho, Farmer Carver made one comment. "Hermann Jaegar says there is a school here for colored children. You could go there."

George said nothing. Words were not necessary. The Carver farm no longer claimed him. From now on the earth was his—and, quickly, he must be about his Father's business.

HELPS FOR DISCUSSION

1. What special interest of the boy George Washington Carver led him to his first opportunity in the kind of work he wished to do?

2. How did George take the first steps in reading? Why was he not in school? What special education did Farmer Carver insist that George must have? Where was a school found?

3. When did George come into realization that he had a responsibility to work for God?

THINGS TO DO

1. Read a life of George Washington Carver. Report upon his tragic start, his education, his scientific work, and his unselfish character.

2. In his laboratory, this world-famous scientist made hundreds of products from peanuts and from sweet potatoes. List some of these. Explain their importance to Southern farmers.

Rhapsody

WILLIAM STANLEY BRAITHWAITE

I am glad daylong
For the gift of song,
For time and change and sorrow;
For the sunset wings
And the world-end things
Which hang on the edge of tomorrow.
I am glad for my heart
Whose gates apart
Are the entrance-place of wonders,
Where dreams come in
From the rush and din
Like sheep from the rains and thunders.

Opportunity

EDWARD ROWLAND SILL

This I beheld, or dreamed it in a dream:
There spread a cloud of dust along a plain;
And underneath the cloud, or in it, raged
A furious battle, and men yelled, and swords
Shocked upon swords and shields. A prince's banner
Wavered, then staggered backward, hemmed by foes.
A craven[1] hung along the battle's edge,
And thought, "Had I a sword of keener steel—
The blue blade that the king's son bears,—but this
Blunt thing—!" he snapped and flung it from his hand,
And lowering crept away and left the field.
Then came the king's son, wounded, sore bestead,[2]
And weaponless, and saw the broken sword,
Hilt-buried in the dry and trodden sand,
And ran and snatched it, and with battle shout
Lifted afresh he hewed his enemy down,
And saved a great cause that heroic day.

1. *craven:* coward. 2. *sore bestead:* hard pressed.

Hundreds of thousands of young men died for their countries in the time of two world wars. Among them were two who had already written poems of the soldier's sacrifice—Alan Seeger and Joyce Kilmer. Their verses and the verses of others convey the spirit of the soldier in time of war.

I Have a Rendezvous with Death

ALAN SEEGER

I have a rendezvous[1] with Death
At some disputed barricade,
When Spring comes round with rustling shade
And apple blossoms fill the air.
I have a rendezvous with Death
When Spring brings back blue days and fair.

It may be he shall take my hand
And lead me into his dark land
And close my eyes and quench my breath;
It may be I shall pass him still.
I have a rendezvous with Death
On some scarred slope of battered hill,
When Spring comes round again this year
And the first meadow flowers appear.

God knows 'twere better to be deep
Pillowed in silk and scented down,
Where love throbs out in blissful sleep,
Pulse nigh to pulse, and breath to breath,
Where hushed awakenings are dear.
But I've a rendezvous with Death
At midnight in some flaming town,
When Spring trips north again this year,
And I to my pledged word am true
I shall not fail that rendezvous.

HELPS FOR DISCUSSION

Discuss the meaning of the titles used in the three preceding poems. Explain how the thought of each poem is related to the title chosen by the poet.

1. *rendezvous* (rän'dĕ vo͞o): a meeting by appointment.

Rouge Bouquet

JOYCE KILMER

[Choir to be arranged in three voices: high, medium, and low.]

Medium In a wood they call the Rouge Bouquet[1]
There is a new-made grave today,
Low Built by never a spade nor pick
Yet covered with earth ten meters[2] thick.
Medium There lie many fighting men,
  Dead in their youthful prime,
High Never to laugh nor love again
  Nor taste the Summertime.
All For Death came flying through the air
And stopped his flight at the dugout stair,
Touched his prey and left them there,
  Clay to clay.
Medium He hid their bodies stealthily
In the soil of the land they fought to free
  And fled away.
Low Now over the grave abrupt and clear
  Three volleys ring;
And perhaps their brave young spirits hear
  The bugle sing:
High (Imitating bugle taps) "Go to sleep!
Go to sleep!
Medium Slumber well where the shell screamed and fell.
Let your rifles rest on the muddy floor,
You will not need them any more.
All Danger's past;
High (Imitating bugle taps as a background for last line) Now at last,
Go to sleep!"

Medium There is on earth no worthier grave
To hold the bodies of the brave
Than this place of pain and pride
Where they nobly fought and nobly died.

1. *Rouge Bouquet* (rōōzh bōō kā'): a French expression meaning "a bunch of red flowers." 2. *meters:* a measure of length. A meter is a little over 39 inches.

High, medium Never fear but in the skies
Saints and angels stand
Smiling with their holy eyes
On this new-come band.
All St. Michael's sword darts through the air
And touches the aureole on his hair
As he sees them stand saluting there,
His stalwart sons:
Medium And Patrick, Brigid, Columkill
Rejoice that in veins of warriors still
The Gael's blood runs.
High And up to Heaven's doorway floats,
From the wood called the Rouge Bouquet,
A delicate cloud of bugle notes
That softly say:
Low "Farewell!
Farewell!
Medium, high Comrades true, born anew, peace to you!
Your souls shall be where the heroes are
And your memory shine like the morning-star.
All Brave and dear,
High (Imitating bugle taps as background for the last line) Shield us here.
Farewell!"

The Battlefield

EMILY DICKINSON

They dropped like flakes, they dropped like stars,
Like petals from a rose,
When suddenly across the June
A wind with finger goes.

They perished in the seamless grass,—
No eye could find the place;
But God on his repealless list
Can summon every face.

When Monica, mother of Saint Augustine, lay dying in Italy, far from her African home, she said, "Bury me here, for nowhere is far from God. All that I ask is that, wherever you go to the altar of God, you will remember me." This, too, is the poet's thought in

Night in Romagne[1]

JOHN J. FINN

Last night I walked among the placid dead
Who stir not, neither sigh in their deep sleep
But rest content; while through their grassy spread
Soft breezes creep.

Caught in the torrid tumult war unfolds,
From out the carnage of the mad advance
They came into the soothing cool that holds
Fall nights in France.

A sacred guard, the ghostly crosses show
Above the clinging mist that shrouds their graves;
Faithful they stand, to tell in sun or snow,
Of Him Who saves.

And stars that once on Caesar's armies shone
Look down on new young bodies dead for Mars;
Then turn, at dawn, to where their souls live on
Beyond the stars.

1. *Romagne* (rô mȧn'y'): a large American cemetery in France in the Argonne. Here about twenty thousand American soldiers of World War I are buried.

The love of men for one another
has often led heroes to sacrifice their lives
that others might live.
In **World** War II one of the most famous
instances of this heroism came with the sinking
of the United States Army transport, ***Dorchester,***
carrying troops from the United States to Europe.
Four chaplains, a Catholic, two Protestants, and a Jew, gave up their life belts
to young sailors as the ship ***Dorchester*** went down.
Their glory lives in poems like this:

To Each of Four Lost with the *Dorchester*

ANNABELLE WAGNER BERGFELD

If he had lived, then he had gone his way
With only parish folk to name his name;
But he is dead and none can pass his church
Untouched or unreminded of the flame
Of love that burns so brightly it can give
A life as freely as another might
Offer a cigarette to passing friend
Or lean to give another man a light.

His church is here; its simple Gothic lines
Remind one with a stern simplicity
Of one who might be reading Sunday Mass
But for the blackness of a northern sea.
The night was dark, but all of life was his,
And, standing calm, serene above the strife,
He gave his belt to save a frightened boy
And by his act renounced his claim to life.

Now life is his and he's forever young
Who stood with others on the sagging deck
And watched the lifeboats vanish in the night—
Their frailness greater than the hulking wreck
That was the *Dorchester*. There stands his church—
Reminding one in stern simplicity
Of one who might be reading Sunday Mass
But for the bleakness of a northern sea.

Hero of two hundred battles, patriot, enemy of oppression, the great aim of Simón Bolívar[1] was to establish America as "a continent of brotherhood and justice." Here is the inspiring story of the struggle for democracy of

Bolívar, the Great Liberator

BRASSIL FITZGERALD

His school chair was a saddle. His schoolyard stretched for wind-swept miles to the far blue clouds that were mountains. He was the only student, a boy of fourteen with a wide-smiling mouth. He rode a high-stepping gray, and easily, his reins slack, his slimness loose and relaxed in the saddle. His black eyes studied the distance, where dust hung in the clear bright air. A faint bawling of cattle came from the dust, and around it black dots moved swiftly. Those dots were cowboys, the llaneros,[2] *his* llaneros.

His teacher rode with him, knee to knee; a middle-aged man and stout, both hands gripping his saddle horn, the while between jounces he lectured his student.

"Every caballero,[3] Simón, should know the history of the illustrious don George Washington. Are you listening?"

"Yes, señor, with deep interest," the boy answered politely, but his eyes were wistful, watching the cowboys.

"Mark me now," the teacher continued, "when he was a boy, George Washington was not at all like you, Simón. Not at all. *He* was serious. It is told that when a child, at the family hacienda[4] at Virginia, he cut down a fruit tree. When —" Teacher shouted, "You shameless rascal! Whoa! Come back here." School was out. Simón had spurred his gray, and was fast away. The rascal rode singing.

Behind in the dust teacher bounced, calling, "You'll come to no good end. Whoa, there! Wretch that I am! Wasting my life with this teaching!" He didn't mean that. He was just cross for the moment.

When George Washington died at Mount Vernon, Simón was a lad of sixteen, amusing himself, and not his elders, in

1. *Simón Bolívar* (sē mōn′ bō lē′vär). 2. *llaneros* (lyä nā′rōs): people who live on the plains of South America, hence, cowboys or herdsmen. 3. *caballero* (kä′bäl yā′rō): a Spanish gentleman. 4. *hacienda* (ä syĕn′dä): a large estate.

Caracas,[5] the principal city of Venezuela. Simón was an orphan, a very wealthy one. With his elder brother and his two sisters he was the heir to a splendid town house in Caracas, to great plantations, to silver mines, and cattle ranches. A slim, handsome youth, with black curls, black eyes, and a big gay mouth, he could do as he pleased, and did. He sang ballads under the grilled windows of the girls of Caracas. He danced at the governor's palace in the splendid uniform of white and gold of a junior lieutenant in the local militia, the White Guard. "An impudent young idler," the Spanish governor thought him. But the governor's lady thought him charming. And the lady was right. In the years to come many would smile to Simón's smile: a queen of Spain, grave statesmen, and a girl of Madrid, like a small white flower.

Simón was sixteen. In the candlelit drawing-room of his home in Caracas, Simón was getting a scolding. His uncle and guardian, Don Carlos, was doing the scolding, saying now sternly, "His Excellency, the governor, is displeased with you, Simón. He complains that you are a disturbing influence among your brother officers of the White Guard."

Simón shrugged a velvet shoulder. "I'm sick of the White Guard, my uncle." His long upper lip curled with scorn. "Have you heard what the Spanish officers call us? The White Mice!"

Don Carlos lifted his hands helplessly. "You are stubborn, and willful! You have much to be thankful for."

"The poorest North American is more fortunate than I, being free," the boy answered.

"You think of but one freedom, my son—political freedom. But the one essential, the basic freedom, is freedom from evil. Under any system of government only the good are truly free. Those who serve evil are slaves," said his uncle.

But the boy said bitterly, "We must deliver ourselves from evil, as the North Americans did."

His uncle did not answer and the silence was troubled, for men of Caracas had died for such talk, in cages. Then Don

5. *Caracas* (kä rä'käs).

Carlos broke the long silence. "I want you to go abroad, Simón, to Europe."

Simón stood, smiling his wide, white smile. "It is my duty, my dear Uncle Carlos, to obey you in all things. When do I sail?" He sailed on January 17, 1799.

In Madrid, in an upper room of a great house Doña María Teresa del Toro sat, her big lovely eyes demure on her sewing, listening to Auntie, her duenna, her chaperon.

"I'm surprised at you," Auntie was saying. "You are no child, María. You're fifteen years old. You should know better. I tremble to think of what the good Sisters would say of such shameless conduct."

"But, Auntie, I didn't do anything."

"Don't be impertinent, miss. When that young man came into the garden you should have curtsied and retired at once."

"But he spoke to me, Auntie."

"Hm! The bold thing! What did he say to you?"

The girl's voice was meek. "Nothing, Auntie. Just 'What a lovely garden!' And I said, it seemed but polite, 'But do you not have gardens in Venezuela, sir?' And he said—he must be very interested in gardening, and surely, Auntie, that is not wicked,—for he said, 'But in no gardens at home have I seen such loveliness.' And I said, 'You mean our camellias, sir?' " The girl's voice was a half sigh. "Then you came." . . .

One year later, Simón and María were married in the great cathedral in Madrid; for better or worse, in sickness and health, until death should them part. Simón brought his child bride home to Venezuela, to the splendid house in Caracas, to his hacienda, to a storybook life of luxury and laughter.

Simón explained to María that all Spanish America was ruled by two viceroys,[6] responsible only to the king of Spain. From Mexico City a viceroy ruled Mexico and Central America. From Lima, in Peru, another ruled the Spanish colonies of South America. Under these viceroys were assistant tyrants, called captains general. There was one in Caracas. In all Venezuela his word was law. Simón's voice would quicken as he talked. "He could put me in chains, María, for buying a book or for owning a printing press. Were I to plant olive trees here, or wine grapes, he would send his soldiers to root them up. That's because Spain has olives and wine to sell us.

"Some day we shall find, María, a patriot leader like George Washington. Then we will break our chains. Then we will say to the king of Spain, to all Europe, what our brothers of the north have said." Simón's voice was fierce and proud. "Listen, María, for this is the answer to tyrants. This is democracy's credo. 'We hold these truths to be self-evident, that all men are created equal, that they are endowed by their Creator with certain inalienable rights, that among these are life, liberty, and the pursuit of happiness.' " Simón was smiling now in the dimness, a smile like a sword curve. " 'That whenever any form of government becomes destructive of these ends, it is the right of the people to alter or abolish it—' "

They were very happy for ten months. Then María fell sick of a tropical fever. She died in Simón's arms, and his youth died with her. . . .

Simón was in Europe, wandering from city to city, seeking escape from his grief. His old teacher, Rodríguez, called him a fool. With eyes like wet stones in a white, sick face, Simón looked at his friend and asked humbly, "Can you help me?"

6. *viceroys* (vīs'roiz): ruling representatives of a king.

Rodríguez could, and did. Together they walked the roads of France, eating in farm kitchens the coarse food of the peasants, sleeping in humble inns the dreamless sleep of peasants. Rodríguez was a wise teacher. He preached no long sermons. Trudging happily along in the roadside dust, he talked of the friends he visited in books.

One summer evening in 1805 the two travelers climbed the Holy Mount on the outskirts of Rome. They sat on the grass in companionable silence. The roofs of the city below them burned with the sunset-fires. Rodríguez started to speak, and then didn't, seeing Simón's face. There was a strangeness on it.

In the city below, the church bells rang, long golden notes in the hushed golden air. When the silence came back, Simón spoke, his voice but a murmur. "I swear by the God of my fathers, and by my native land, that my hands will never tire, nor my soul rest, until I have broken the chains that bind us to Spain." That whisper changed our world.

When Bolívar went home to Venezuela to begin his lifework, no crowd cheered, no bands played. His relatives were glad to see him, and the family friends; but they were not impressed with his vague talk of a mission, a great work to be done. To the old gentlemen of Caracas he was just that young Bolívar who talked too much. To the patriots meeting in secret to plan resistance to Spain he was just another recruit, and welcome more for his wealth than his talents.

Simón Bolívar took his last possession, his sword, to Cartagena, where the patriots of New Granada held a strip of the sea-coast. There he was given command of two hundred men, Negroes, Indians, and mestizos.[7] Bolívar smiled his big smile at his ragamuffins, told them he was proud to command them, that each of them was worth three Spaniards. They grinned back, shuffling their bare feet in the dust, believing. In six days, with these half-breeds who thought themselves heroes, Bolívar fought six battles and won six battles.

Yet Bolívar was often defeated. In 1814, after three years of struggle, he was an exile again. Secret agents of Spain had tracked him to his refuge on the British island of Jamaica.

7. *mestizos* (mĕs tē′zōs): persons of mixed blood.

But he escaped and, with two hundred borrowed dollars, sailed again for his native land.

Bolívar, in 1819, led his army across the continent and over the main range of the Andes. It was the rainy season, the beginning of winter. The lowland plains were flooded. Bolívar's three thousand men marched in water to their belts. And the rain fell. It melted to paste their corn-meal tortillas.[8] There were no roads, no bridges. They swam the swollen rivers, holding to their horses' tails. The things on the muddy banks that looked like logs were alligators. The deadly fish struck unseen. Swords and muskets rusted; shoes and blankets rotted. Feet and legs swelled from the bites of poisonous insects. Burning with fever and coughing, Bolívar led his men across the flooded plains. In the rain they heard him singing, grinned their wolf grins, and sang, too.

On the eighteenth day they saw the mountains, and the sun. It was good on their faces. For three days they ate and slept, and woke to eat again. Then they moved on, up the first slopes of the Andes. As they climbed, the trails grew steep. The air turned thin and cold. They began to suffer from headaches and nausea, the dread mountain sickness that turns swiftly to drowsiness; and those who sleep die. The well pricked the sick with their bayonets, and left those who could not rise to the chaplain, who bit his thumbs to stay awake himself. The snow fell, covering the dead. The living climbed on, crossing canyons on bridges of vines, following trails where a slip meant death. Many slipped.

On the sixth night, thirteen thousand feet high in the mountains, they camped on a rock-strewn plateau. They were out of food. There was no wood for fires. The wind was sleet. The living envied the dead that long night.

Wrapped in his horse blanket, Bolívar moved from group to group, sharing all that was left to him, his will to endure. What were his thoughts that long dreadful night? No one can know. But this we do know: on some such night, lifting his eyes and his thoughts from the unbearable present, Bolívar dreamed of a brotherhood of all the free nations of America.

8. *tortillas:* (tôr tē′yäz): thin, flat unleavened cakes, baked on a heated stone.

More than any statesman of his generation he foresaw the dangers and the destiny of America.

The morning came, and hope, for the rocky trail turned downward. They had done it, the impossible. They had crossed the main range of the Andes. Three thousand had marched the first day; on the last, twelve hundred marched.

The villagers of Socha saw them coming, skeletons and scarecrows led by a ghost. "El Libertador!" the natives cried. "El Libertador!" And the ghost smiled, that wide white smile. "The Liberator." Bolívar loved that title. There was but one he preferred to it. When the work was done, and the fighting, he wrote to the Congress that would honor him, "Change, I beg you, all my titles for that of Good Citizen."

The Good Citizen danced that night in Socha in borrowed finery, in the mayor's Sunday suit. At dawn he woke his long-suffering staff to search the country for men and horses. Three days later he met and defeated the army of Spain.

That was the turning point. From there he marched from victory to victory, until between the two oceans his people were free. He lives in their hearts. He should live in our hearts, George Washington's brother, and equal in glory.

Written as occasional verse at the time of the sinking in Havana Harbor of the United States battleship *Maine* in 1898, this poem found its way into critical as well as popular acclaim. For half a century America has loved

The Fighting Race

JOSEPH I. C. CLARKE

"Read out the names!" and Burke sat back,
  And Kelly drooped his head.
While Shea—they call him Scholar Jack—
  Went down the list of the dead.
Officers, seamen, gunners, marines,
  The crews of the gig and yawl,
The bearded man and the lad in his teens,
  Carpenters, coal passers—all.

Then, knocking the ashes from out his pipe,
  Said Burke in an offhand way:
"We're all in that dead man's list, by Cripe!
  Kelly and Burke and Shea."
"Well, here's to the *Maine*, and I'm sorry for Spain,"
  Said Kelly and Burke and Shea.

"Wherever there's Kellys there's trouble," said Burke.
  "Wherever fighting's the game,
Or a spice of danger in grown man's work,"
  Said Kelly, "you'll find my name."
"And do we fall short," said Burke, getting mad,
  "When it's touch and go for life?"
Said Shea, "It's thirty-odd years, bedad,
  Since I charged to drum and fife
Up Marye's Heights,[1] and my old canteen
  Stopped a rebel ball on its way.
There were blossoms of blood on our springs of green—
  Kelly and Burke and Shea—
And the dead didn't brag." "Well, here's to the flag!"
  Said Kelly and Burke and Shea.

"I wish't was in Ireland, for there's the place,"
  Said Burke, "that we'd die by right,
In the cradle of our soldier race,
  After one good stand-up fight.
My grandfather fell on Vinegar Hill,
  And fighting was not his trade;
But his rusty pike's in the cabin still,
  With Hessian[2] blood on the blade."
"Aye, aye," said Kelly, "the pikes were great
  When the word was 'clear the way!'
We were thick on the roll in ninety-eight—
  Kelly and Burke and Shea."
"Well, here's to the pike and the sword and the like!"
  Said Kelly and Burke and Shea.

1. *Marye's Heights:* battleground in the Civil War. 2. *Hessian:* mercenary soldier.

And Shea, the scholar, with rising joy,
  Said, "We were at Ramillies;
We left our bones at Fontenoy
  And up in the Pyrenees;
Before Dunkirk, on Landen's plain,
  Cremona, Lille, and Ghent,[3]
We're all over Austria, France, and Spain,
  Wherever they pitched a tent.
We've died for England from Waterloo
  To Egypt and Dargai;[4]
And still there's enough for a corps or crew,
  Kelly and Burke and Shea."
"Well, here is to good honest fighting blood!"
  Said Kelly and Burke and Shea.

"Oh, the fighting races don't die out,
  If they seldom die in bed,
For love is first in their hearts, no doubt,"
  Said Burke; then Kelly said:
"When Michael, the Irish Archangel, stands,
  The angel with the sword,
And the battle-dead from a hundred lands
  Are ranged in one big horde,
Our line, that for Gabriel's trumpet waits,
  Will stretch three deep that day,
From Jehoshaphat to the Golden Gates—
  Kelly and Burke and Shea."
"Well, here's thank God for the race and the sod!"
  Said Kelly and Burke and Shea.

THINGS TO DO

Boys may give a concert reading of "The Fighting Race," dividing at times into three groups for Kelly, Burke, and Shea. Girls may read "In Flanders Fields." One poem should be expressed in stirring martial tones; the other in quiet, solemn tones.

3. *Ramillies . . . Ghent:* famous battles in which Irish regiments fought.
4. *Waterloo . . . Dargai:* noted British campaigns.

The Canadian officer who wrote of the red poppies blooming in the fields of Flanders expressed the ideal of millions of people in World War I, just as two other poets expressed the spirit of their native England in two poems which have become world-famous.

In Flanders Fields

JOHN McCRAE

In Flanders fields the poppies blow
Between the crosses, row on row,
That mark our place; and in the sky
The larks, still bravely singing, fly
Scarce heard amid the guns below.

We are the Dead. Short days ago
We lived, felt dawn, saw sunset glow,
Loved and were loved, and now we lie
In Flanders fields.

Take up our quarrel with the foe:
To you from failing hands we throw
The torch; be yours to hold it high.
If ye break faith with us who die
We shall not sleep, though poppies grow
In Flanders fields.

The Soldier

RUPERT BROOKE

If I should die, think only this of me:
  That there's some corner of a foreign field
That is forever England. There shall be
  In that rich earth a richer dust concealed;
A dust whom England bore, shaped, made aware,
  Gave, once, her flowers to love, her ways to roam,
A body of England's, breathing English air,
  Washed by the rivers, blest by suns of home.

And think, this heart, all evil shed away,
  A pulse in the eternal mind, no less
    Gives somewhere back the thoughts by England given;
Her sights and sounds; dreams happy as her day;
And laughter, learnt of friends; and gentleness,
    In hearts at peace, under an English heaven.

The Spires of Oxford

(As Seen from the Train)

WINIFRED M. LETTS

I saw the spires of Oxford
  As I was passing by,
The gray spires of Oxford
  Against a pearl-gray sky.
My heart was with the Oxford men
  Who went abroad to die.

The years go fast in Oxford,
  The golden years and gay,
The hoary Colleges look down
  On careless boys at play.
But when the bugles sounded war
  They put their games away.

They left the peaceful river,
  The cricket-field, the quad,
The shaven lawns of Oxford,
  To seek a bloody sod—
They gave their merry youth away
  For country and for God.

God rest you, happy gentlemen,
  Who laid your good lives down,
Who took the khaki and the gun
  Instead of cap and gown.
God bring you to a fairer place
  Than even Oxford town.

Love of country is set deep within the heart of man. Poets have sung of it in verses like these:

My Native Land

SIR WALTER SCOTT

Breathes there the man with soul so dead
Who never to himself hath said,
  This is my own, my native land!
Whose heart hath ne'er within him burned,
As home his footsteps he hath turned
  From wandering on a foreign strand?
If such there breathe, go, mark him well;
For him no minstrel raptures swell;
High though his titles, proud his name,
Boundless his wealth as wish can claim,
Despite those titles, power, and pelf,
The wretch, concentrated all in self,
Living, shall forfeit fair renown,
And, doubly dying, shall go down
To the vile dust from whence he sprung,
Unwept, unhonored, and unsung.

Scotia

ROBERT BURNS

O Scotia! my dear, my native soil!
  For whom my warmest wish to Heaven is sent,
Long may thy hardy sons of rustic toil
  Be blest with health, and peace, and sweet content!
  And O! may Heaven their simple lives prevent
From luxury's contagion, weak and vile!
  Then, howe'er crowns and coronets be rent,
A virtuous populace may rise the while,
And stand a wall of fire around their much-lov'd Isle.

The peace treaty at the end of the Franco-Prussian War gave Alsace to Germany. The schools became German schools. The boy who tells the story was a student in one of them in which the schoolmaster taught him

The Last Lesson

ALPHONSE DAUDET

That morning it was quite late before I started for school, and I was terribly afraid I should be scolded, for Monsieur Hamel had told us that he would question us upon participles, and I did not know the first thing about them. For a moment I thought of escaping from school and roving through the fields.

The day was so warm, so clear! The blackbirds were whistling on the outskirts of the woods. In Rippert Meadow, behind the sawmill, the Prussians were drilling. All these things were far more attractive to me than the rule for the use of participles. But I mustered up strength to resist temptation and hurried on to school.

As I reached the town hall, I saw a group of people; they loitered before the little grating, reading the placards posted upon it. For two years every bit of bad news had been announced to us from that grating. There we read what battles had been lost, what requisitions made; there we learned what orders had issued from headquarters. And though I did not pause with the rest, I wondered to myself, "What can be the matter now?"

As I ran across the square, Wachter, the blacksmith, who, in company with his apprentice, was absorbed in reading the notice, exclaimed, "Not so fast, child! You will reach your school soon enough!"

I believed he was making game of me, and I was quite out of breath when I entered Monsieur Hamel's small domain.

Now, at the beginning of the session there was usually such an uproar that it could be heard as far as the street. Desks were opened and shut, lessons recited at the top of our voices, all shouting together, each of us stopping his ears that he might hear better. Then the master's big ruler would descend upon his desk, and he would say, "Silence!"

I counted upon making my entrance in the midst of the usual babel and reaching my seat unobserved, but upon this particular morning all was hushed. Sabbath stillness reigned. Through the open window I could see that my comrades had already taken their seats; I could see Monsieur Hamel himself, passing back and forth, his formidable iron ruler under his arm.

I must open that door. I must enter in the midst of that deep silence. I need not tell you that I grew red in the face, and terror seized me.

But, strangely enough, as Monsieur Hamel scrutinized me there was no anger in his gaze. He said very gently, "Take your seat quickly, my little Franz. We were going to begin without you."

I climbed over the bench and seated myself. But when I had recovered a little from my fright, I noticed that our master had donned his beautiful green frock coat, his finest silk calotte,[1] which he wore only on inspection days, or upon those occasions when prizes were distributed. Moreover, an extraordinary solemnity had taken possession of my classmates. But the greatest surprise of all came when my eye fell upon the benches at the farther end of the room. Usually they were empty, but upon this morning the villagers were

1. *calotte* (kȧ lŏt′): a close cap without a brim.

seated there, solemn as ourselves. There sat old Hauser, with his three-cornered hat, there sat the venerable mayor, the aged carrier, and other personages of importance. All of our visitors seemed sad, and Hauser had brought with him an old primer, chewed at the edges. It lay wide open upon his knees, his big spectacles reposing upon the page.

While I was wondering at all these things, Monsieur Hamel had taken his seat, and in the same grave and gentle tone in which he had greeted me, he said to us, "My children, this is the last day I shall teach you. The order has come from Berlin that henceforth in the schools of Alsace and Lorraine[2] all instruction shall be given in the German tongue only.

2. *Alsace* (ăl'săs) *and Lorraine:* French territory then occupied by Germany.

Your new master will arrive tomorrow. Today you hear the last lesson you will receive in French, and I beg you will be most attentive."

My "last" French lesson! And I scarcely knew how to write! Now I should never learn. My education must be cut short. How I grudged at that moment every minute I had lost, every lesson I had missed for the sake of hunting birds' nests. And those books which a moment before were so dry and dull, so heavy to carry—my grammar, my Bible history—seemed now to wear the faces of old friends whom I could not bear to bid farewell. It was with them, as with Monsieur Hamel, the thought that he was about to leave, that I should see him no more, made me forget all the blows of his ruler, and the many punishments I had received.

Poor man! It was in honor of that last session that he was arrayed in his finest Sunday garb, and now I began to understand why the villagers had gathered at the back of the classroom. Their presence at such a moment seemed to express a regret that they had not visited that schoolroom oftener; it was their way of telling our master they thanked him for his forty years of faithful service and desired to pay their respects to the land whose empire was departing.

I was busied with these reflections when I heard my name called. It was now my turn to recite. Ah! what would I not have given then, had I been able to repeat from beginning to end that famous rule for the use of participles loudly, distinctly, and without a single mistake; but I became entangled in the first few words and remained standing at my seat, swinging from side to side, my heart swelling. I dared not raise my head. Monsieur Hamel was addressing me.

"I shall not chide thee, my little Franz; thy punishment will be great enough. So it is! We say to ourselves each day, 'Bah! I have time enough. I will learn tomorrow.' And now see what results. Ah, it has ever been the greatest misfortune of our Alsace that she was willing to put off learning till tomorrow! And now these foreigners can say to us, and justly, 'What! you profess to be Frenchmen, and can neither speak nor write your own language?' And in all this, my poor Franz, you are not the chief culprit. Each of us has something with which to reproach himself.

"Your parents have not shown enough anxiety about having you educated. They preferred to see you spinning, or tilling the soil, since that brought them in a few more sous.[3] And have I nothing with which to reproach myself? Did I not often send you to water my garden when you should have been at your tasks? And if I wished to go trout fishing, was my conscience in the least disturbed when I gave you a holiday?"

One topic leading to another, Monsieur Hamel began to speak of the French language, saying it was the strongest, clearest, most beautiful language in the world, which we must keep as our heritage, never allowing it to be forgotten, telling us that when a nation has become enslaved, she holds the key which shall unlock her prison as long as she preserves her native tongue.

Then he took a grammar and read our lesson to us, and I was amazed to see how well I understood. Everything he said seemed so very simple, so easy! I had never, I believe, listened to anyone as I listened to him at that moment, and never before had he shown so much patience in his explanations. It really seemed as if the poor man, anxious to impart everything he knew before he took leave of us, desired to strike a single blow that might drive all his knowledge into our heads at once.

The lesson was followed by writing. For this occasion Monsieur Hamel had prepared some copies that were entirely new, and upon these were written in a beautiful round hand, "*France, Alsace! France, Alsace!*"

These words were as inspiring as the sight of the tiny flags attached to the rods of our desks. It was good to see how each one applied himself, and how silent it was! Not a sound save the scratching of pens as they touched our papers. Once, indeed, some beetles entered the room, but no one paid the least attention to them, not even the tiniest pupil; for the youngest were absorbed in tracing their straight strokes as

3. *sous* (so͞o): bronze French coins worth about one cent.

earnestly and conscientiously as if these, too, were written in French! On the roof of the schoolhouse the pigeons were cooing softly, and I thought to myself as I listened, "And must they also be compelled to sing in German?"

From time to time, looking up from my page, I saw Monsieur Hamel, motionless in his chair, his eyes riveted upon each object about him, as if he desired to fix in his mind, and forever, every detail of his little school.

Remember that for forty years he had been constantly at his post, in that very schoolroom, facing the same playground. Little had changed. The desks and benches were polished and worn, through long use; the walnut trees in the playground had grown taller; and the hop-vine he himself had planted curled its tendrils about the windows, running even to the roof. What anguish must have filled the poor man's heart, as he thought of leaving all these things, and heard his sister moving to and fro in the room overhead, busied in fastening their trunks! For on the morrow they were to leave the country, never to return. Nevertheless his courage did not falter; not a single lesson was omitted. After writing came history. The little ones sang their "*Ba, Be, Bi, Bo, Bu,*" together. Old Hauser, at the back of the room, had put on his spectacles and, holding his worn primer in both hands, was spelling out the letters with the little ones.

He, too, was absorbed in his task; his voice trembled with emotion, and it was so comical to hear him that we all wanted to laugh and to cry at the same moment. Ah! never shall I forget that last lesson!

Suddenly the church clock struck twelve and then the Angelus was heard.

At the same moment, a trumpet-blast under our window announced that the Prussians were returning from drill. Monsieur Hamel rose in his chair. He was very pale, but never before had he seemed to me so tall as at that moment.

"My friends—" he said, "my friends—I—I—"

But something choked him. He could not finish his sentence.

Then he took a piece of chalk, and grasping it with all his strength, wrote in his largest hand,—

VIVE LA FRANCE![4]

He remained standing at the blackboard, his head resting against the wall. He did not speak again, but a motion of his hand said to us, "That is all. You are dismissed."

HELPS FOR DISCUSSION

1. When and where did the events of the story take place? Why was the further teaching of French children in the French language by French teachers forbidden in this province? What happened to the district in succeeding wars?

2. Why was the schoolroom so quiet as Franz entered? How did Monsieur Hamel look and act? Why were villagers present?

3. Explain Monsieur Hamel's talk beginning, "I shall not chide thee . . ." and ending, "as long as she preserves her native tongue."

4. What dramatic sounds ended the lesson? What was the significance of Monsieur Hamel's final message on the blackboard?

4. *Vive la France*! (vēv lä fräns): Long live France!

Belgian Towns

FREDERICK WILLIAM FABER

Was it in many hearts at once, or one—
What was the land, the place, the cause, the hour,
When it first dawned in men, that there is power
In numbers, that the healthy streams which run
In poor men's veins are red like other blood?
O blissful dawn! the thoughtful and the good
Do thee glad homage in these antique haunts,
Where from ten thousand wills a Popular State
Sprang like an arrow from a bow, elate
Beneath the pressure of degrading wants.
Here, in this street of Ghent, where evening smiles,
The Church and Freedom seem but one great name,
And surely they so deemed who reared these piles,
As knowing whence and how their freedom came.

Totalitarian State

MARGARET MÜNSTERBERG

Patriot, we want you whole:
Your fighting body, your fervent soul!
All for the sovereign nation's sake.
"My life, oh master, you may take,"
The youth replies, "my blood and bone.
But my fervent soul is not my own—
Not mine to yield at threat of sword:
My soul belongs to Christ, my Lord!"

THINGS TO DO

1. From the book *These are Our Freedoms*, committees may read aloud "We Guard Our Liberties" (page 106) and "We Worship God" (page 158). How do these selections answer the demand in "Totalitarian State"?

2. Write a paragraph telling why you are glad that you live in a land of religious liberty.

These poems, written by an English poet before the Russian people were forbidden by government the public exercise of their religion, portray the spirit of a God-loving people.

Harvest in Russia

MAURICE BARING

The breeze has come at last. The day was long;
The bats are flitting in the airy dome;
And hark! the reapers are returning home,
I hear the burden of their quiet song.
A voice intones; the chorus make reply,
Take up the burden and the chant prolong;
The music swells and soars into the sky
And dies away intense, and clear, and strong.

Now through the trees the stately shapes I see
Of women with their instruments of toil,
Calm in their sacerdotal majesty;
And backward, through the drifting mists of years,
I see the Sacraments that blessed the soil,
As old as the first drop of mortal tears.

A June Night in Russia

MAURICE BARING

Tonight there is a concert. First the chime
Of sheep-bells plays the overture; the dogs
Blend their harsh music with the croaking frogs,
The watchman's rattle punctuates the time.
Like water bubbling in a crystal jar
The nightingale begins a liquid trill,
Another answers; and the world's so still
You'd think that you could hear that falling star.

I scarcely see for light the stars that swim
High in the heaven which is not dark, but dim.
The women's voices echo far away;
And on the road two lovers sing a song;
They sing the joy that only lasts a day,
They sing the pain that lasts a whole life long.

How They Brought the Good News from Ghent to Aix[1]

ROBERT BROWNING

I sprang to the stirrup, and Joris, and he;
I galloped, Dirck galloped, we galloped all three;
"Good speed!" cried the watch as the gate bolts undrew;
"Speed!" echoed the wall to us galloping through.
Behind shut the postern,[2] the lights sank to rest,
And into the midnight we galloped abreast.

Not a word to each other; we kept the great pace,
Neck by neck, stride by stride, never changing our place.
I turned in my saddle and made its girths tight,
Then shortened each stirrup, and set the pique[3] right,
Rebuckled the cheek-strap, chained slacker the bit,
Nor galloped less steadily Roland a whit.

'Twas moonset at starting; but while we drew near
Lokeren,[4] the cocks crew, and twilight dawned clear;
At Boom[5] a great yellow star came out to see;
At Düffeld[6] 'twas morning as plain as could be;
And from Mecheln[7] church steeple we heard the half-chime,—
So Joris broke silence with "Yet there is time!"

At Aerschot[8] up leaped of a sudden the sun,
And against him the cattle stood black every one,
To stare through the mist at us galloping past;
And I saw my stout galloper Roland at last,
With resolute shoulders, each butting away
The haze, as some bluff river headland its spray;

And his low head and crest, just one sharp ear bent back
For my voice, and the other pricked out on his track;

1. *Aix* (ĕks): a town in France. 2. *postern:* a door or gate. 3. *pique* (pēk): the point of a saddle; the pommel. 4. *Lokeren* (lōk'ẽr ĕn): a Belgian town. 5. *Boom* (bo͞om): a Belgian town. 6. *Düffeld* (dü fĕlt'): a Belgian town. 7. *Mecheln* (mĕk'ĕln): a Belgian city. 8. *Aerschot* (är'skŏt): a Belgian town.

And one eye's black intelligence,—ever that glance
O'er its white edge at me, his own master, askance;
And the thick, heavy spume-flakes[9] which aye and anon
His fierce lips shook upwards in galloping on.

By Hasselt,[10] Dirck groaned; and cried Joris, "Stay spur!
Your Roos[11] galloped bravely,—the fault's not in her;
We'll remember at Aix"—for one heard the quick wheeze
Of her chest, saw the stretched neck, and staggering knees,
And sunk tail, and horrible heave of the flank,
As down on her haunches she shuddered and sank.

So we were left galloping, Joris and I,
Past Looz[12] and past Tongres,[13] no cloud in the sky;

9. *spume-flakes:* froth. 10. *Hasselt* (häs'ĕlt): a Belgian village. 11. *Roos* (rōs): the name of Dirck's horse. 12. *Looz* (lô'ŏz): a town in northern France. 13. *Tongres* (tôn'gr'): a town in Belgium.

The broad sun above laughed a pitiless laugh;
'Neath our feet broke the brittle, bright stubble like chaff;
Till over by Dalhem[14] a dome-spire sprang white,
And "Gallop," gasped Joris, "for Aix is in sight!"

"How they'll greet us!"—and all in a moment his roan
Rolled neck and croup[15] over, lay dead as a stone;
And there was my Roland to bear the whole weight
Of the news which alone could save Aix from her fate,
With his nostrils like pits full of blood to the brim,
And with circles of red for his eye-sockets' rim.

Then I cast loose my buff-coat, each holster let fall,
Shook off both my jack-boots,[16] let go belt and all,
Stood up in the stirrup, leaned, patted his ear,
Called my Roland his pet name, my horse without peer,—
Clapped my hands, laughed and sung, any noise, bad or good,
Till at length into Aix Roland galloped and stood.

And all I remember is, friends flocking round
As I sat with his head 'twixt my knees on the ground;
And no voice but was praising this Roland of mine,
As I poured down his throat our last measure of wine,
Which (the burgesses voted by common consent)
Was no more than his due who brought good news from
Ghent.

HELPS FOR DISCUSSION

1. Why did three horsemen start? How many finished? Browning dated the poem in the 1600's. What might have been the nature of the good news? How would such important news be sent today?

2. What other poem in this book gives the impression of a horseman's urgent haste? Find in both poems expressions of speed.

3. Notice that the rhythm of the poem is the rhythm of galloping. Read lines and stanzas that illustrate this effect.

4. Review Longfellow's "Paul Revere's Ride" in *A Book of Fortitude.* Compare the two poems as to story, ways of telling route and time, rhythm, and expression.

14. *Dalhem* (däl'ĕm): a Belgian town. 15. *croup:* back. 16. *jack-boots:* heavy riding boots.

Two Countries

SIR CECIL SPRING-RICE

"I vow to thee, my country—all earthly things above—
Entire and whole and perfect, the service of my love.
The love that asks no questions; the love that stands the test,
That lays upon the altar the dearest and the best;
The love that never falters, the love that pays the price,
The love that makes undaunted the final sacrifice.

"And there's another country, I've heard of long ago—
Most dear to them that love her, most great to them that know—
We may not count her armies, we may not see her king;
Her fortress is a faithful heart, her pride is suffering—
And soul by soul and silently her shining bounds increase,
And her ways are ways of gentleness, and her paths are peace."

In a time when the danger of state domination threatened the world
Pope Pius XI wrote one of his most famous letters. These brief paragraphs highlighted
the inspiring letter which was addressed

To Youth

PIUS XI

Today, as We see you threatened with new dangers and new molestations,[1] We say to you: if anyone should preach to you a Gospel other than the one you received on the knees of a pious mother, from the lips of a believing father, or through teaching faithful to God and His Church, "let him be anathema."[2]

That is why We tell the young: Sing your hymns of freedom, but do not forget the freedom of the children of God.

1. *molestations:* acts of being disturbed. 2. *anathema* (*ȧ* năth'ē m*ȧ*): any person or thing cursed or denounced.

A Hymn

G. K. CHESTERTON

O God of earth and altar,
  Bow down and hear our cry,
Our earthly rulers falter,
  Our people drift and die;
The walls of gold entomb us,
  The swords of scorn divide,
Take not thy thunder from us,
  But take away our pride.

From all that terror teaches,
  From lies of tongue and pen,
From all the easy speeches
  That comfort cruel men,
From sale and profanation
  Of honor and the sword,
From sleep and from damnation,
  Deliver us, good Lord.

Tie in a living tether
  The prince and priest and thrall,[1]
Bind all our lives together,
  Smite us and save us all;
In ire and exultation
  Aflame with faith, and free,
Lift up a living nation,
  A single sword to thee.

THINGS TO DO

Notice again the title of Unit V and read aloud page 259. Then review the unit, explaining how each selection emphasizes the thought of title and introduction. Close by reading reverently in unison G. K. Chesterton's "A Hymn."

1. *thrall:* a slave.

VI

On the Sea and in the Sky

One of the laws of the sea is the law of friendliness. When a ship in distress sends out an SOS signal any other ship within range of its call answers the summons. Although the radio call is modern, the custom of aid-giving is ancient. Perhaps that is why the pirate and the buccaneer, sea bandits who break this law of aid to others, have earned a particularly evil reputation. Certainly they are the arch-villains of literature. Real, traditional, or fictional, they stand out as striking examples of wrongdoing with Captain Kidd and Long John Silver heading the list.

There are, however, pleasanter tales of ships and sailormen. The high adventure of sailing ships is well told by writers of England and the United States, probably because both English and Americans are sea-going people. No one can know literature who does not know the great sea poems and sea stories of these two countries.

What the sea has meant to fishermen, to sailors, and to those who live upon its shores has been for centuries the subject of great literature. In our own day the airman and those who ride the skies with him into the vast world of clouds and mist have found new beauty and adventure there. They have opened another realm for writing, which has hardly been explored. It is a realm in which the youthful and courageous fliers, soaring in high flight above the wall of Nanking and over the airfields of Africa, make real for us. It is a glimpse of the littleness of man and the immensity of God.

Blessing for a New Ship

Show favor, Lord, to our entreaties, and bless with Thy right hand of holiness this ship and all who shall be borne in it, as Thou didst deign to bless the ark of Noah which spanned the flood: stretch forth Thy hand, O Lord, as Thou didst hold it forth to blessed Peter walking on the waters; send down from heaven Thy holy angel to guide and guard it always, with all who shall be in it, from every danger: and mayest Thou see Thy servants, their difficulties set at naught, ever in peaceful harbor or on tranquil course; and when their business has been brought to good conclusion, grant Thou to them once more a joyful recall to all that they hold dear. Who livest and reignest, God, world without end. Amen.

Mark iv, 35-40

And he said to them on that day, when evening had come, "Let us cross over to the other side." And sending away the crowd, they took him just as he was, in the boat; and there were other boats with him. And there arose a great squall, and the waves were beating into the boat, so that the boat was now filling. And he himself was in the stern of the boat, on the cushion, asleep. And they woke him and said to him, "Master, does it not concern thee that we are perishing?" Then rising up, he rebuked the wind, and said to the sea, "Peace, be still!" And the wind fell and there came a great calm. And he said to them, "Why are you fearful? Are you still without faith?" And they feared exceedingly and said to one another, "Who then is this, that even the wind and the sea obey him?"

How many boys—and girls, too—have thrilled to the story of ***Treasure Island***!
The adventure of the seven seas opens before you as you meet

The Old Sea Dog at the "Admiral Benbow"

ROBERT LOUIS STEVENSON

Squire Trelawney, Dr. Livesey, and the rest of these gentlemen having asked me to write down the whole particulars about Treasure Island, from the beginning to the end, keeping nothing back but the bearings of the island, and that only because there is still treasure not yet lifted, I take up my pen in the year of grace 17—, and go back to the time when my father kept the "Admiral Benbow" inn, and the brown old seaman first took up his lodging under our roof.

I remember him as if it were yesterday, as he came plodding to the inn door, his sea-chest following behind him in a hand-barrow; a tall, strong, heavy, nut-brown man; his tarry pigtail[1] falling over the shoulders of his soiled blue coat; his hands ragged and scarred, with black, broken nails; and a sabre[2] cut across one cheek, a dirty, livid white. I remember him looking round the cove and whistling to himself as he did so, and then breaking out in that old sea-song that he sang so often afterwards:—

"Fifteen men on the dead man's chest—
Yo-ho-ho, and a bottle of rum!"

in the high, old tottering voice that seemed to have been tuned and broken at the capstan[3] bars. Then he rapped on the door with a bit of stick like a handspike that he carried, and when my father appeared, called roughly for a glass of rum. This, when it was brought to him, he drank slowly, like a connoisseur,[4] lingering on the taste, and still looking about him at the cliffs and up at our signboard.

"This is a handy cove," says he, at length; "and a pleasant sittyated grog-shop.[5] Much company, mate?"

1. *tarry pigtail:* a colloquialism meaning a queue of hair, formerly worn by sailors, and coated with tar. 2. *sabre* (sā′bẽr): a sword with a curved blade. 3. *capstan:* a drum or cylinder used on shipboard for lifting heavy weights. 4. *connoisseur* (kŏn′ĭ-sûr′): one well versed in any subject. 5. *grog-shop:* an inn or tavern that sells liquors.

My father told him no, very little company, the more was the pity.

"Well, then," said he, "this is the berth for me. Here you, matey," he cried to the man who trundled the barrow; "bring up alongside and help up my chest. I'll stay here a bit," he continued. "I'm a plain man; rum and bacon and eggs is what I want, and that head[6] up there for to watch ships off. What you mought call me? You mought call me captain. Oh, I see what you're at—there"; and he threw down three or four gold pieces on the threshold. "You can tell me when I've worked through that," says he, looking as fierce as a commander.

And, indeed, bad as his clothes were, and coarsely as he spoke, he had none of the appearance of a man who sailed before the mast; but seemed like a mate or skipper, accustomed to be obeyed or to strike. The man who came with the barrow told us the mail had set him down the morning before at the "Royal George"; that he had inquired what inns there were along the coast, and hearing ours well spoken of, I suppose, and described as lonely, had chosen it from the others for his place of residence. And that was all we could learn of our guest.

He was a very silent man by custom. All day he hung round the cove, or upon the cliffs, with a brass telescope; all

6. *head:* a headland or high point of land overlooking the sea.

evening he sat in a corner of the parlour next the fire, and drank rum and water very strong. Mostly he would not speak when spoken to; only look up sudden and fierce, and blow through his nose like a fog-horn; and we and the people who came about our house soon learned to let him be. Every day, when he came back from his stroll, he would ask if any seafaring men had gone by along the road. At first we thought it was the want of company of his own kind that made him ask this question; but at last we began to see he was desirous to avoid them. When a seaman put up at the "Admiral Benbow" (as now and then some did, making by the coast road for Bristol), he would look in at him through the curtained door before he entered the parlour; and he was always sure to be as silent as a mouse when any such was present. For me, at least, there was no secret about the matter; for I was, in a way, a sharer in his alarms. He had taken me aside one day, and promised me a silver fourpenny on the first of every month if I would only keep my "weather-eye open for a seafaring man with one leg," and let him know the moment he appeared. Often enough, when the first of the month came round, and I applied to him for my wage, he would only blow through his nose at me, and stare me down; but before the week was out he was sure to think better of it, bring me my fourpenny piece, and repeat his orders to look out for "the seafaring man with one leg."

How that personage haunted my dreams, I need scarcely tell you. On stormy nights, when the wind shook the four corners of the house, and the surf roared along the cove and up the cliffs, I would see him in a thousand forms, and with a thousand diabolical[7] expressions. Now the leg would be cut off at the knee, now at the hip; now he was a monstrous kind of a creature who had never had but the one leg, and that in the middle of his body. To see him leap and run and pursue me over hedge and ditch was the worst of nightmares. And altogether I paid pretty dear for my monthly fourpenny piece, in the shape of these abominable[8] fancies.

But though I was so terrified by the idea of the seafaring

7. *diabolical* (dī ȧ bŏl′ĭ kăl): devilish. 8. *abominable* (ȧ bŏm′ĭ nȧ b'l): hateful.

man with one leg, I was far less afraid of the captain himself than anybody else who knew him. There were nights when he took a deal more rum and water than his head would carry; and then he would sometimes sit and sing his wicked, old, wild sea-songs, minding nobody; but sometimes he would call for glasses round, and force all the trembling company to listen to his stories or bear a chorus to his singing. Often I have heard the house shaking with "Yo-ho-ho, and a bottle of rum"; all the neighbours joining in for dear life, with the fear of death upon them, and each singing louder than the other, to avoid remark. For in these fits he was the most overriding companion ever known; he would slap his hand on the table for silence all round; he would fly up in a passion of anger at a question, or sometimes because none was put, and so he judged the company was not following his story. Nor would he allow anyone to leave the inn until he had drunk himself sleepy and reeled off to bed.

His stories were what frightened people worst of all. Dreadful stories they were; about hanging, and walking the plank, and storms at sea, and the Dry Tortugas,[9] and wild deeds and places on the Spanish Main.[10] By his own account he must have lived his life among some of the wickedest men that God ever allowed upon the sea; and the language in which he told these stories shocked our plain country people almost as much as the crimes that he described. My father was always saying the inn would be ruined, for people would soon cease coming there to be tyrannised over and put down, and sent shivering to their bed; but I really believe his presence did us good. People were frightened at the time, but on looking back they rather liked it; it was a fine excitement in a quiet country life; and there was even a party of the younger men who pretended to admire him, calling him a "true sea-dog," and a "real old salt," and such like names, and saying there was the sort of man that made England terrible at sea.

In one way, indeed, he bade fair to ruin us; for he kept on staying week after week, and at last month after month,

9. *Dry Tortugas* (tôr tōō′gäz): the Spanish name for ten islands off the coast of Florida.
10. *Spanish Main:* the area around the Caribbean Sea, once the scene of great piratical activity.

so that all the money had been long exhausted, and still my father never plucked up the heart to insist on having more. If ever he mentioned it, the captain blew through his nose so loudly, that you might say he roared, and stared my poor father out of the room. I have seen him wringing his hands after such a rebuff, and I am sure the annoyance and the terror he lived in must have greatly hastened his early and unhappy death.

All the time he lived with us the captain made no change whatever in his dress but to buy some stockings from a hawker.[11] One of the cocks[12] of his hat having fallen down, he let it hang from that day forth, though it was a great annoyance when it blew. I remember the appearance of his coat, which he patched himself up-stairs in his room, and which, before the end, was nothing but patches. He never wrote or received a letter, and he never spoke with any but the neighbours, and with these, for the most part, only when drunk on rum. The great sea-chest none of us had ever seen open.

He was only once crossed, and that was towards the end, when my poor father was far gone in a decline that took him off. Dr. Livesey came late one afternoon to see the patient, took a bit of dinner from my mother, and went into the parlour to smoke a pipe until his horse should come down from the hamlet, for we had no stabling at the old "Benbow." I followed him in, and I remember observing the contrast the neat, bright doctor, with his powder[13] as white as snow, and his bright, black eyes and pleasant manners, made with the coltish country folk, and above all, with that filthy, heavy, bleared scarecrow of a pirate of ours, sitting far gone in rum, with his arms on the table. Suddenly he—the captain, that is—began to pipe up his eternal song:—

Fifteen men on the dead man's chest—
  Yo-ho-ho, and a bottle of rum!
Drink and the devil had done for the rest—
  Yo-ho-ho, and a bottle of rum!

11. *hawker:* peddler. 12. *cocks:* the large, stiff flaps of a hat. 13. *powder:* powdered wig.

At first I had supposed "the dead man's chest" to be that identical big box of his up-stairs in the front room, and the thought had been mingled in my nightmares with that of the one-legged seafaring man. But by this time we had all ceased to pay any particular notice to the song; it was new, that night, to nobody but Dr. Livesey, and on him I observed it did not produce an agreeable effect, for he looked up for a moment quite angrily before he went on with his talk to old Taylor, the gardener, on a new cure for the rheumatics. In the meantime, the captain gradually brightened up at his own music, and at last flapped his hand upon the table before him in a way we all knew to mean—silence. The voices stopped at once, all but Dr. Livesey's; he went on as before, speaking clear and kind, and drawing briskly at his pipe between every word or two. The captain glared at him for a while, flapped his hand again, glared still harder, and at last broke out with a villainous, low oath: "Silence there, between decks!"

"Were you addressing me, sir?" says the doctor; and when the ruffian had told him, with another oath, that this was so, "I have only one thing to say to you, sir," replies the doctor, "that if you keep on drinking rum, the world will soon be quit of a very dirty scoundrel!"

The old fellow's fury was awful. He sprang to his feet, drew and opened a sailor's clasp-knife, and, balancing it open on the palm of his hand, threatened to pin the doctor to the wall.

The doctor never so much as moved. He spoke to him, as before, over his shoulder, and in the same tone of voice; rather high, so that all in the room might hear, but perfectly calm and steady:

"If you do not put that knife this instant in your pocket, I promise, upon my honour, you shall hang at next assizes."[14]

Then followed a battle of looks between them; but the captain soon knuckled under, put up his weapon, and resumed his seat, grumbling like a beaten dog.

"And now, sir," continued the doctor, "since I now know there's such a fellow in my district, you may count I'll have

14. *assizes* (ă sīz'ĕz): the meeting of the judges of the county court.

an eye upon you day and night. I'm not a doctor only; I'm a magistrate; and if I catch a breath of complaint against you, if it's only for a piece of incivility like to-night's, I'll take effectual means to have you hunted down and routed out of this. Let that suffice."

Soon after Dr. Livesey's horse came to the door, and he rode away; but the captain held his peace that evening, and for many evenings to come.

THINGS TO DO

1. Draw a strip cartoon of the Admiral Benbow Inn and the four persons in the selection. What should be shown in drawing the captain, the father, the boy, and Doctor Livesey?

2. Make a blackboard list of words and expressions that give the selection a sea flavor and hint at a pirate tale.

3. The selection is the opening chapter of Stevenson's *Treasure Island.* Cite sayings and incidents that are first clues to a plot.

4. Read the book *Treasure Island.* Join with classmates to give a report of the story.

Ever since Homer sang
on the shores of the Aegean,
poets have told their love of the sea.

Sea Memories

HENRY WADSWORTH LONGFELLOW

Often I think of the beautiful town[1]
  That is seated by the sea;
Often in thought go up and down
The pleasant streets of that dear old town,
  And my youth comes back to me.
    And a verse of a Lapland song
    Is haunting my memory still:
    "A boy's will is the wind's will,
And the thoughts of youth are long, long thoughts."

I can see the shadowy lines of its trees,
  And catch, in sudden gleams,
The sheen of the far-surrounding seas,
And islands that were the Hesperides[2]
  Of all my boyish dreams.
    And the burden of that old song,
    It murmurs and whispers still:
    "A boy's will is the wind's will,
And the thoughts of youth are long, long thoughts."

I remember the black wharves and the slips,
  And the sea-tides tossing free;
And the Spanish sailors with bearded lips,
And the beauty and mystery of the ships,
  And the magic of the sea.
    And the voice of that wayward song
    Is singing and saying still:
    "A boy's will is the wind's will,
And the thoughts of youth are long, long thoughts."

1. *town:* Portland, Maine, the boyhood home of the poet. 2. *Hesperides* (hĕs-pĕr′ĭ dēz): in Greek mythology a garden in the far west, hence in Africa, where grew the golden apples sought by Hercules.

Sea Fever

JOHN MASEFIELD

I must go down to the seas again, to the lonely sea and the sky,
And all I ask is a tall ship and a star to steer her by,
And the wheel's kick and the wind's song and the white sail's
shaking,
And a gray mist on the sea's face, and a gray dawn breaking.

I must go down to the seas again, for the call of the running
tide
Is a wild call and a clear call that may not be denied;
And all I ask is a windy day with the white clouds flying,
And the flung spray and the blown spume, and the sea-gulls
crying.

I must go down to the seas again, to the vagrant gypsy life,
To the gull's way and the whale's way where the wind's like
a whetted knife;
And all I ask is a merry yarn from a laughing fellow-rover,
And quiet sleep and a sweet dream when the long trick's over.

The Sea Gypsy

RICHARD HOVEY

I am fevered with the sunset,
I am fretful with the bay,
For the wander-thirst is on me
And my soul is in Cathay.

There's a schooner in the offing,
With her topsails shot with fire,
And my heart has gone aboard her
For the Islands of Desire.

I must forth again tomorrow!
With the sunset I must be
Hull down on the hill of rapture
In the wonder of the sea.

Saint Brendan, who is said to have discovered America long before Columbus, is rightly called the Saint of Navigators, for the Irish have ever been at home upon the sea. It is natural that a tale of the sea shows

How Dark Patrick Saved the Bank of Ireland

SEUMAS MACMANUS

Ye see it was this way. The Bank of Ireland was at that time owned by a man of the O'Neills, a mean fellow who didn't take after his ancestors, had little of their spunk, and less of their pride—but a heart set on money-making. The low fellow sold out the ancestral estates and bought the Bank of Ireland. Then, the devil tempting him to make a pile at one haul, he engaged a sea captain—the best to be got on the coasts of Ireland—fitted him with a ship, with meat and drink to last him three years, and sent him voyaging the known world—to find where and how the most money was to be made on a speculation of any shape.

This fella sailed for three years and three days, and returned at the end of it to tell his master that in the South Seas the savages would give their one eye, if they had only one, for scalpeens[1] and that there was lashin's and lavin's[2] of money to be made by sending there a venture of that commodity. He guaranteed O'Neill that for every pound's[3] worth of scalpeens he'd send to the South Seas he'd bring home ten pounds of money.

O'Neill, he jumped with joy when he heard this. He not only gathered every penny he owned himself, and likewise every penny that was in the Bank but, moreover, sent messengers east and west, for to notify every man who had a shilling[4] of money put by to fetch it in and lend it to him for a year and a day, and at the end of that time draw it back doubled or throubled.[5]

This was a grand offer, entirely and, without looking into it, or considering it, the greed of gain made many a poor man,

1. *scalpeens:* from the Gaelic *scailpin,* a salted mackerel. 2. *lashin's and lavin's:* great quantities. 3. *pound:* a unit of English money, normally equal to $4.86 in United States money. 4. *shilling:* an English silver coin, about the value of a quarter in the United States. 5. *throubled:* trebled.

who could ill afford it, rush his money to Dublin as fast as his heels could help him, and give it straight into the Bank for a year and a day's loan.

The money O'Neill took in, in three weeks' time, was miraculous. The Bank had to rent seven houses, and clear them out from cellar to garret, to hold all the gold and silver that was peltin' them.

O'Neill next sent word round the coasts of Ireland, England, and Scotland to notify all people who had a store of scalpeens for to bring them without delay to Dublin and get for them a bigger price than was ever paid in these kingdoms afore. So, in the course of another three weeks, if a scalpeen could save your life you couldn't get one for love, money, or tibaccy. O'Neill then engaged every ship and boat that carried a rag of canvas on any of the four seas, and loaded them to the water's edge with scalpeens. And, under his old sea captain, he sent off the fleet to sail to the South Sea Islands. And the

captain had guaranteed that he would be back, himself and the whole fleet and a cargo of money, well within the year and a day. And it's tol' that, in them days when O'Neill was loadin' the scalpeens, a man might hop on the tops of masts from Dublin to Scotland.

Well, that fared well, and it didn't fare ill—as they say in the old stories—and the year and a day wore round; and then every man, woman, and child in Ireland who had a penny invested in the Bank of Ireland tramped to Dublin in droves for to draw their money and their int'rest. But lo and behold ye, the captain and his fleet hadn't returned! And the people, they got into a mortal bad way, though O'Neill tried to mollify them as best he could with the news he had from a sea captain, just landed in Dublin, who said he had fallen in with the fleet on the shores of South America, and they loaded to the lip with money; but they were so battered by a terrific whirlwind which had chanced on them that they couldn't reach Ireland till after their due. And O'Neill asked of the people to give him just ten days till his fleet would be here, and he'd be needin' all their help to carry the creels[6] of money out of the ship's holds.

The people gave him this. But at the ten days' end there was still no word. Then the people, after persuasion, granted him ten days more. At the end of this ten days, there was still neither sight nor sign of the ships; only O'Neill informed them that a lugger, come in from Timbuctoo with a cargo of thimbles, had sighted his ships anigh the Sahara, only sailing dead slow by reason of the terrible load of money they were weighted with. And he begged and prayed again for more time.

It was by the greatest of trouble, and the greatest of influence, that O'Neill now coaxed them not to wreck the Bank and hang himself from a rafter. After a deal of arguing, they granted him still another ten days' grace—but they swore by all the Bibles in Dublin that if their money wasn't forthcoming again at the end of that time they wouldn't leave

6. *creels:* large wicker baskets, commonly used for carrying fish.

two sticks of his Bank together, nor two bones of his body unbroken.

And well he knew, to his black sorrow, that they were, this time, determined to do for him. His heart was sitting on his soles, for he was sore afeard that the fleet wouldn't be in within the time. Private messengers, then, he sent throughout the land, gathering to Dublin every great man that could be found, and gathering them into the biggest room in the Bank of Ireland, where he made offer of his weight in gold, when the boats came in, to any man could invent some plan of saving himself and his Bank till the arrival.

This collection of Ireland's cleverest men sat for three days and three nights, hardly eatin' and never risin'—debatin' and arguin' plans. Every man had a plan of his own, and each man knew his plan was superior to his neighbor's and swore by it. But all of the plans put together, if they were tried, couldn't save two slates[7] on the Bank of Ireland.

Now, far off, in the far parts of Donegal,[8] Dark Patrick, looking around and witnessing the woe and lamentation that was over the country, and the ruin going to be wrought on it if the Bank of Ireland failed, saw it his duty to step in. He gathered together his little bundle and, mounting it on his blackthorn stick on his shoulder, faced for Dublin.

It was on the very last and final day of the Bank of Ireland's grace that Dark Patrick arrived in Dublin. Without looking for lodgings or getting a bit to eat, he inquired his way to the Bank and to the Council Chamber of it—where all the clever men of Ireland were met—and there he knocked at the door and, with his little bundle, walked into their midst. All the great men turned in their seats to gaze at the funny picture, and though he'd disturbed their council they couldn't help but smile. But Patrick, no feature of him changing, inquired which was the Bank's owner. And O'Neill, at the council table's head, himself says, "I'm him. What is your wish with me, or what can I do for you, good man?"

"I don't know," says Dark Patrick, says he, "that you can

7. *slate:* material used for roofing. 8. *Donegal* (dŏn′ĕ gôl): a county in northern Ireland.

do anything for me. But I've come to see if I can be of any service to you, sir."

"Oh," says O'Neill, says he, "is that the way? I think, then," says he, "you might see my head servant, and talk to him. He'll know if there's anything you can do in the kitchen or around the stables."

"Beggin' your pardon," says Dark Patrick, says he, back to him, "but it's yourself I'm come to see. It's in regards to the Bank of Ireland," says he, "that I've come—in hopes I might be of service to it."

Says O'Neill, says he, "Oh, the Bank itself? I see. Whether is it a plasterer you are, a glazier, or a slater?"

"Neither the one nor the other," says Dark Patrick.

"Then," says O'Neill, says he, "what in the name of wonder do you do, or what sort of job are you looking for?"

Says Dark Patrick, says he, "I have traveled here all the way from Donegal, in hopes that I might be of service to you in saving the Bank, and saving the country and all my poor fellow countrymen the terrible ruin that's staring them."

At this, there wasn't a great gentleman of all the great gentlemen in the room but lay back in his chair, opened his throat, and roared till 'twas wonder Patrick's neighbors didn't hear their enjoyment back in Donegal.

"My good man," says O'Neill, says he, when he was able to speak for the laughin', "I'm sure I must be very thankful, and forever obliged to ye. Still," says he, "I think you may return back to your mountains again; for, if these grand-dressed gentlemen that you see around this table aren't able to invent some way of saving my Bank, I'm afeared you'll hardly do it." He was trying hard to speak kind to Patrick, for he wasn't bad-hearted at all.

Dark Patrick, he took no notice whatsomever of the gentlemen's guffawing, but modestly tried to persuade O'Neill that 'twould be no harm to let him have a chance anyhow.

But O'Neill, whose nerves were in disorder, now got cantankerous and ordered him to clear out or he'd call in the soldiers to have him removed as a nuisance.

Patrick bowed his head, and wished them all good day, and

good luck with their consitherations—and not only left the room, and the Bank, but set out for home again. And that night he slept at a poor inn, where he got a bed for fourpence,[9] ten miles north of Dublin.

Lo and behold ye! At an early hour the next morning he was awakened by a shout through the house to know if there was sleeping here a little dark-whiskered man from Donegal. And when Patrick made answer, and said that he was him, and inquired what was wanted of him, he learned there was a messenger arrived on a galloping horse from Dublin, to say that the owner of the Bank of Ireland had found all the clever men to fail him, with his fate staring him in the face at twelve this day; and that, as he walked up and down the room all night, he had considered maybe, after all, he did wrong to turn Patrick away; and that he had sent the trustiest messenger, and the fastest horse in his stables, posthaste on the north road, to over-take and ask him to come back and give his advice for whatsomever it might be worth, anyhow. If it failed, sure it would still be no worse than the best.

9. *fourpence:* about eight cents.

Dark Patrick consithered within him for a few minutes; and he then told the messenger he was ready to return with him, mounted the horse provided, and galloped back to Dublin. And when he got there—which was at a late breakfast time—he found the city in uproar, for there was yet neither tale nor tidings of the fleet, and every poor man who thought he had lost money in the venture was demanding the hanging of O'Neill; and it was certain sure that, at twelve o'clock, if their money wasn't paid them, the Bank of Ireland would be pulled down, and O'Neill himself taken apart limb from limb.

Dark Patrick, he neither halted nor delayed, but rode straight to the Bank, where O'Neill was waiting him—this day, all alone, for all the grand-dressed gentlemen, unable at last to do anything for him, had made off and left him to his fate. He welcomed Dark Patrick and said that, as all others had failed him, and the worst had come to the worst, it was no harm for him to have his try. If he didn't do any good, sure he couldn't do any harm.

Dark Patrick bowed for the honor, and then questioned O'Neill till he satisfied himself that the fleet was, sure enough, safe on its way, and couldn't now be far from the coast of Ireland, and that it carried loads and lashin's of money to pay, and double pay, all claims. When he'd contented himself on this point, he inquired what was the most money, in gold and silver, O'Neill could beg, borrow, or in anyways come honestly by.

O'Neill said that, as he had borrowed five hundred thousand pounds, the most money he could now obtain, beg or borrow, to pay off the debt, would be one thousand. "So," says he to Dark Patrick, "if it's your plan to pacify these howlin' savages by offering them one pound against every five hundred that I owe them, you might better have stayed where you were."

"By your leave," Dark Patrick replied, "if you expect me, for my part, to save your Bank, I'll be expectin' you, for your part, to keep all impolite obsarvations to yourself, for the present. Go," says he, "at once, and get me this thousand pound, in gold and silver."

O'Neill, abashed in the face, went off without other pro or con,[10] and in a jiffy had back with him a string of bags containing gold and silver to the amount of a thousand pounds.

"So far so good," says Dark Patrick. "Now we've got to make haste. What," says he, proceeding to the window, and looking at the houses opposite, "what is that establishment that I see fornenst me?"

"That establishment fornenst you," says O'Neill, says he, "is a manufactory of horny buttons."

"Well and good," says Dark Patrick. "I now want you to do three things."

"Name them," says O'Neill.

Says Dark Patrick, "In the first place, you'll hire—at any cost—for this day, that manufactory opposite, and have it completely cleared out instantaneously. The next thing, you'll get me sixty trusty men, with picks and shovels, whom you can rely your life on. And, in the third place, get me a score o' herring barrels."

Says O'Neill, says he, shaking his head, "I see neither rhyme nor reason in your requests."

Says Dark Patrick, "I don't suppose you do. If you did, you'd ha' had no cause of sending a messenger after me last night to bring me here this morning. Are you prepared to do as I direct, or are you not? Say it, and be quick."

O'Neill consithered with himself for a minute and then he says, desperately, "I'm prepared to do any thing you direct—no matter how blatherskite[11] it is."

"Then," says Dark Patrick, says he, "have them three things done immediate, if not sooner."

In short time O'Neill had engaged the manufactory opposite and turned it inside out. He brought Dark Patrick sixty men with picks and shovels, and twenty herring barrels. And he stood by to see what in the name o' wonder the next crazy move was going to be.

"Now," says Dark Patrick, says he, "I want you to start twenty of these men in the cellar of the Bank, and twenty more in the cellar of the manufactory opposite, working for

10. *pro or con:* argument. 11. *blatherskite:* silly.

life and death, cutting a passage from one cellar to the other under the street. Then they'll fill the barrels to the lip with the clay they take out. The thousand pounds in gold and silver, and the other twenty men," says he, "is to come with me."

Across the street he started with his twenty men, with the bags of money, and whilst the men in the two cellars were working like fury, cutting their way under the street, Dark Patrick had his men start the fires in the factory. He got twenty frying pans and put them on the fires, and got hammers and anvils, which he set on a bench by the windows that looked into the street. Onto the frying pans he spilled the bags of gold and silver, and made the men blow the bellows like murder till the coins were red hot. Then he set the men carrying the frying pans to the window bench, where he started them beating the coins on the anvils—at the same time opening the windows so the noise would get properly into the street, and to the crazed crowds gathered in front of the Bank beyond. And he instructed the beaters to make clatter and clang like the end of the worl' was on its way.

The passage underneath the street being now completed, the herring barrels, clay-filled, were fetched in and covered, atop the clay, each with a couple of layers of hot coins—some with gold coins and others of them with silver—and whilst ten men went on frying the money, and ten more beating it out on the anvils at the window, the remainder were started carrying the high-heaped barrels across the street to the Bank—and, as fast as they got there, carrying them back to the manufactory again by the tunnel.

When the street crowds beheld the sight of a line of barrels filled to the lip with gold coins and silver, all smoking hot, come streaming over the street, there was a tremendous hubbub raised. A hundred greedy ones made grab for handfuls of coins off the barrel tops—but dropped them with a yell and a screech the same instant, and flew frantic up and down the street, their hands burned off them.

So fast did the carriers do their duty that when the last barrel was going in the Bank the first was coming out again

of the door of the factory. And through the windows of the manufactory the astounded people could see, with their own eyes, ten men, as busy as nailers, hammering out on the anvils heaps and piles more of steaming silver and gold coins. And the word soon went round that the Gover'ment had come to the aid of O'Neill, and started minting money for him as fast as men could cast and trim it, and trundle it to the Bank. And round Dublin ran the greatest sensation known to that city since the creation of cats.

O'Neill, then, appeared on the front steps of his Bank and, by Patrick's directions, gave out to the crowd that all who now wanted their money were to enter, one by one, put in their claims, and carry away with them all the gold and silver, together with compound interest, that they had so kindly loaned him. Only, he remarked, as the money was still smoking hot, coming from the coinery, they should fetch plates with them to receive their allotments, and save the hands from being burned off them. But, he added, them who preferred waiting till the money cooled would there-by be drawin' extra compound interest on it.

When the people heard this their amazement was a sight to behold. They picked a dozen of themselves, and sent them in with plates to draw their money and report upon what they observed. When these came back, their plates piled with smoking money, they told how that they saw the barrels o' money going down to the cellars in a string for storage and, by this time, there must be a thousand barrels o' money in the cellar, if there was one. Their money, they said, had been served across the counter to them in great iron scoops, for no man, to be sure, could handle it while it was boiling.

Now, not only did the crowds not want to draw their own money, being greedy to get the big interest, but them that had just drawn it hurried back with their plates again, for to redeposit it. Moreover, every man who could rap or run another pound made haste to put it into the Bank, also. And the tremendous crowd waned like a waft of smoke—went away secure, and happy-hearted, to their homes in Ireland's four corners.

O'Neill was a glad-hearted man that day and, for the first time in three weeks, closed his eyes in sound sleep that night. Dark Patrick, at his special entreaty, stayed with him for three days longer, till his mackerel fleet came safely in, crowding the sea 'twixt Ireland, England, and Scotland, so that no other ship could pass up or down between those countries for a fortnight.

And 'tis told that it took three hundred men three days and three nights carrying from the fleet to the Bank the bags of gold that they had brought back with them in exchange for the scalpeens, so that O'Neill was able to pay off, with double and treble compound interest, every creditor he had in Ireland, and still have for himself an independent fortune.

It was him was the elated man. He near threw himself at the feet of Dark Patrick, as he asked him to name his reward and, if it was anything not exceeding all he possessed, it would be granted.

Dark Patrick said, "Good man, it wasn't for you, nor for your sake, I did the little sarvice; but such as it is, I did it for the sake of my poor fellow countrymen, whom you had nigh ruined. Nevertheless," says he, "as you have benefited from it, I'll claim from you my reward. I'll ask two things," he says. "The first is that you'll never again in like manner risk the poor people's money—and the second is that you'll not again presume that a man mayn't have wisdom because he wears a frieze suit,[12] has no castor hat[13] on his head nor gold watch in his pocket."

O'Neill was full of apologies and promises, but begged that Dark Patrick would name a money reward likewise.

Dark Patrick said that he owned, in Donegal, a little farm which, by industry, gave him enough to live on and make him content. "Over and above that," says he, "gold is a burden, instead of a boon, and 'twill be a happy day for you the day you realize that same." He refused to touch or handle a penny from him; but, tying up again his little bundle, slung it on the stick over his shoulder, and trudged out of Dublin with his face to the North.

HELPS FOR DISCUSSION

1. What do you know about Saint Brendan the Navigator? When did he live? What did he have in common with Leif Ericsson? What part does he play in the selection?

2. Suggest some of the plans that you think might have been proposed by the "collection of Ireland's cleverest men." What was Dark Patrick's plan? What was accomplished by heating the money?

3. This tale is a legend told of a popular and saintly hero in the early days of Ireland's history. How has Seumas MacManus made the story amusing? What deep wisdom is found in the words of Dark Patrick on this page?

4. In a dramatic reading of the story, which parts should you arrange to have given in dialogue, which read by a narrator, and which omitted? Join with others to present the reading.

12. *frieze* (frēz) *suit:* a suit made of coarse woolen cloth. 13. *castor hat:* a hat made of beaver, worn only by the wealthy at that time.

The Waves of Breffny

EVA GORE-BOOTH

The grand road from the mountain goes shining to the sea,
And there is traffic on it and many a horse and cart;
But the little roads of Cloonagh are dearer far to me
And the little roads of Cloonagh go rambling through my
heart.

A great storm from the ocean goes shouting o'er the hill,
And there is glory in it, and terror on the wind;
But the haunted air of twilight is very strange and still,
And the little winds of twilight are dearer to my mind.

The great waves of the Atlantic sweep storming on their way,
Shining green and silver with the hidden herring shoal;
But the little waves of Breffny have drenched my heart in
spray,
And the little waves of Breffny go stumbling through my soul.

The Three Fishers

CHARLES KINGSLEY

Three fishers went sailing away to the West,
  Away to the West as the sun went down;
Each thought on the woman who loved him the best,
  And the children stood watching them out of the town;
For men must work, and women must weep,
And there's little to earn, and many to keep,
  Though the harbor bar be moaning.

Three wives sat up in the lighthouse tower,
  And they trimmed the lamps as the sun went down;
They looked at the squall, and they looked at the shower,
  And the night-rack came rolling up ragged and brown.
But men must work, and women must weep,
Though storms be sudden, and waters deep,
  And the harbor bar be moaning.

Three corpses lay out on the shining sands
  In the morning gleam as the tide went down,
And the women are weeping and wringing their hands
  For those who will never come home to the town;
For men must work, and women must weep,
And the sooner it's over, the sooner to sleep;
  And good-by to the bar and its moaning.

GREAT ART THAT PICTURES SEA AND SKY

How many pictures can you mention that portray sea and sky? Here are some famous ones: *Christ on the Sea of Galilee*, by DELACROIX; *Fishing Boats at Arles*, by VAN GOGH; *Fishermen*, by MONET; *Harbor Scene*, by LORAIN; *Return of the Fishermen*, by SOROLLA; *Madonna of the Harpies*, by DEL SARTO; *Mary, Patroness of China*, by WANG SU-TA; *Approach to Venice*, by TURNER; *Windmill*, by VAN RUYSDAEL; *Cockle Gatherers*, by A E (GEORGE RUSSELL); *Moonlight, Wood's Island Light*, and *Fog Warning*, by WINSLOW HOMER; *Children of the Sea*, by JOSEF ISRAELS.

"Break, Break, Break"

ALFRED, LORD TENNYSON

[Choir to be arranged in three voices: high, medium, and low.]

Low — Break, break, break,
  On thy cold gray stones, O Sea!
And I would that my tongue could utter
  The thoughts that arise in me.

Medium — O well for the fisherman's boy,
  That he shouts with his sister at play!
High — O well for the sailor lad,
  That he sings in his boat on the bay!

Medium — And the stately ships go on
  To their haven under the hill;
Low — But O for the touch of a vanished hand,
  And the sound of a voice that is still!

Medium — Break, break, break,
  At the foot of thy crags, O Sea!
All — But the tender grace of a day that is dead
  Will never come back to me.

Sea-Birds

FRAY ANGELICO CHAVEZ

In days when Albion's[1] seamen knew
Why they salute the quarter-deck
  (It held a shrine to Mary),
They named the hungry fowl that flew
About the galley at their beck,
  "Chickens Matris Carae."[2]

Dear Mother, with your apron blue
Shoo your chicks off reef and wreck
  (Gregory's angels,[3] marry![4])

1. *Albion's:* England's. 2. *Matris Carae* (mắt rĭs kā′rĭ): the Latin name for a kind of sea bird, often called stormy petrels. The translation of the phrase, *matris carae,* ("mother of chickens") has given to them the name of "Mother Carey's chickens." 3. *Gregory's angels:* Pope Gregory called the Angles of England "angels." Thus the reference means Englishmen. 4. *marry:* an Anglo-Saxon phrase meaning "by Mary."

Back to Peter's ship and crew—
And you upon the quarter-deck
To feed them, Mother Carey.

HELPS FOR DISCUSSION

1. The first stanza of this poem tells of a time when all England was Catholic, and ships that sailed the seas had shrines to the Virgin. Where was this shrine usually set? What did seamen do?

2. Where are the quarter-deck and the galley on a sailing ship? Why did stormy petrels fly above the galley?

3. The second stanza of the poem is a prayer that England may be brought back to the Church. What does the poet mean by "reef and wreck"? by "Peter's ship and crew"?

The Coasters

THOMAS FLEMING DAY

Overloaded, undermanned,
Trusting to a lee,
Playing I-spy with the land,
Jockeying the sea—
That's the way the Coaster goes,
Through calm and hurricane:
Everywhere the tide flows,
Everywhere the wind blows,
From Mexico to Maine.

O East and West! O North and South!
We ply along the shore,
From famous Fundy's[1] foggy mouth,
From floes of Labrador;
Through pass and strait, on sound and sea,
From port to port we stand—
The rocks of Race[2] fade on our lee,
We hail the Rio Grande.

Fundy: The Bay of Fundy, an inlet of the Atlantic Ocean separating Nova Scotia from New Brunswick. High tides make it very dangerous for sailors. 2. *Race:* Cape Race, the southeast point of Newfoundland.

Our sails are never lost to sight;
On every gulf and bay
They gleam, in winter wind-cloud white,
In summer rain-cloud gray.

We hold the coast with slippery grip;
We dare from cape to cape:
Our leaden fingers feel the dip
And trace the channel's shape.
We sail or bide as serves the tide;
Inshore we cheat its flow,
And side by side at anchor ride
When stormy head-winds blow.
We are the offspring of the shoal,
The hucksters of the sea;
From customs theft and pilot toll
Thank God that we are free.

Legging on and off the beach,
Drifting up the strait,
Fluking down the river reach,
Towing through the gate—
That's the way the Coaster goes,
Flirting with the gale:
Everywhere the tide flows,
Everywhere the wind blows,
From York to Beavertail.[3]

Here and there to get a load,
Freighting anything;
Running off with spanker stowed,
Loafing wing-and-wing—
That's the way the Coaster goes,
Chumming with the land:
Everywhere the tide flows,
Everywhere the wind blows,
From Ray to Rio Grande.[4]

We split the swell where rings the bell
On many a shallow's edge,
We take our flight past many a light
That guards the deadly ledge;
We greet Montauk[5] across the foam,
We work the Vineyard[6] Sound,
The Diamond[7] sees us running home,
The Georges[8] outward bound;
Absecon[9] hears our canvas beat
When tacked off Brigantine[10];
We raise the Gulls[11] with lifted sheet,
Pass wing-and-wing between.

3. *York to Beavertail:* New York to a tiny island off Rhode Island. 4. *Ray to Rio Grande:* from the southwest point of Newfoundland to the Mexican river. 5. *Montauk* (mŏn tôk′): a point on the eastern end of Long Island, New York. 6. *Vineyard:* Martha's Vineyard, an island off the coast of Massachusetts. 7. *Diamond:* a cape in the St. Lawrence River. The citadel of Quebec is located on it. 8. *The Georges:* a cape on northeast Nova Scotia. 9. *Absecon* (ăb sē′kŏn): an island off New Jersey, on which Atlantic City is located. 10. *Brigantine:* an island near Atlantic City, New Jersey. 11. *the Gulls:* a fixed light on an island at the end of Long Island Sound.

Off Monomoy[12] we fight the gale,
We drift off Sandy Key[13];
The watch of Fenwick[14] sees our sail
Scud for Henlopen's[15] lee.
With decks awash and canvas torn
We wallow up the Stream[16];
We drag dismasted, cargo borne,
And fright the ships of steam.
Death grips us with his frosty hands
In calm and hurricane;
We spill our bones on fifty sands
From Mexico to Maine.

Cargo reef in main and fore,
Manned by half a crew,
Romping up the weather shore,
Edging down the Blue—
That's the way the Coaster goes,
Scouting with the lead:
Everywhere the tide flows,
Everywhere the wind blows,
From Cruz to Quoddy Head.[17]

Roll Down to Rio

RUDYARD KIPLING

I've never sailed the Amazon,
I've never reached Brazil;
But the *Don* and *Magdalena*,
They can go there when they will!
Yes, weekly from Southampton,
Great steamers, white and gold,
Go rolling down to Rio

12. *Monomoy:* Monomoy Island and Monomoy Point are off the southeast extremity of Cape Cod. 13. *Sandy Key:* near St. Petersburg, Florida. 14. *Fenwick:* a lighthouse located on a barrier beach, hardly large enough to be called an island, on the border of Maryland and Delaware. 15. *Henlopen:* a lighthouse on the Delaware coast. 16. *Stream:* the Gulf Stream. 17. *Cruz to Quoddy Head:* Vera Cruz, a seaport town in Mexico, to Passamaquoddy Bay, an inlet in the Bay of Fundy, between Maine and New Brunswick.

Roll down—roll down to Rio!
And I'd like to roll to Rio
Some day before I'm old!

I've never seen a jaguar,[1]
Nor yet an armadill[2]—
O dilloing in his armor,
And I s'pose I never will,
Unless I go to Rio
These wonders to behold—
Roll down—roll down to Rio—
Roll really down to Rio!
Oh, I'd love to roll to Rio
Some day before I'm old!

Who Pilots Ships

DANIEL WHITEHEAD HICKY

Who pilots ships knows all a heart can know
Of beauty, and his eyes may close in death
And be content. There is no wind to blow
Whiter than foam-white wind and no wind's breath
Sweeter than tropic wind. There is no star
That throbs with cold white fire as North stars do,
No golden moon-path lovelier than the far
Path burning on the sea when dusk is blue.
There is no rain so swift as rain that flies
In bright battalions with a storm begun,
No song that shakes the heart like amber cries
Of gulls with wings turned yellow in the sun.
Who pilots ships, when life's last heartbeats stop,
Has drained the cup of beauty drop by drop.

1. *jaguar* (jăg'wär): a large catlike animal marked with black spots. 2. *armadill* (är mȧ dĭl'): for *armadillo*, an animal found in tropical America whose body is encased in an armor of small bony plates.

An American woman, wife of the first man to make the eastward flight from the United States to France, saw more than the physical aspects of countries when she flew ***North to the Orient.*** That is why there is literary value in her chapter on

The Wall of Nanking

ANNE MORROW LINDBERGH

The wall of Nanking is such a dominating feature of the city that it seems almost a geographical one. Fliers are apt to picture places in purely geographical terms. And as I remember our fleeting visit to Nanking, I see first a river,[1] a mountain, and a wall.

The river takes precedence in my mind, for we followed its broad course for miles, ponderous, inevitable, ahead of us, our road to Nanking. It was also the road of innumerable other travelers below: big river boats chugging up the current; top-heavy junks with their square parchment-colored sails, webbed like a bat's wing; heavily loaded rafts, and even thin slivers of sampans[2]—all marking a way to the crowded docks of Nanking.

The mountain rising east of Nanking I remember because it is typical of a new country that we approached after leaving the coastal plains of China. Those endless stretches of small fields disappear as one travels up the Yangtze and low hills climb from the horizon. "Purple Mountain," also, because of its height and sharpened peak, forms a landmark, visible to a flier long before the smoke of a city or the outline of a wall. As we came nearer, its gentle slopes seemed to be encroaching on the city, as the river encroached on the opposite side. One physical feature faces the other, vying in strength.

And between them stands the wall of Nanking, throwing its gray rope around hills and fields, railroads and canals, mud huts and tiled roofs, pointed eaves and towers, crowded streets and shaded gardens, drawing them all together into what is now the capital of China. A walled city has an unmistakable quality of majesty. It stands isolated as an island, self-sufficient as a ship, unassailable as a mountain.

1. *river:* the Yangtze (yäng'tsĕ'), a very long river, one of the most important in China. 2. *sampans:* small boats used in the harbors of China.

It seems to have all the attributes of a monarch. And looked at from the air, the city of Nanking does wear its wall like a crown.

From the ground one is still more conscious of its majesty, looking up at the crenelated[3] outline, or passing under the massive gates. For the traffic of Nanking, jostling down the narrow streets, still threads through needle-eye gates. A bustling line of rickshaws,[4] the ragged blue coats of the runners flapping in the breeze; long-gowned men and women; venders, balancing from their shoulder poles the weight of stove and food basket; workmen, in harsh blue coats, and trousers rolled halfway up their bare legs, carrying three or four bags of flour on their shoulders; small high Cinderella-pumpkin coaches; squeaking wheelbarrows; a boy trying to sell two small fish squeezed in his fist; a woman with a few branches of sweet-smelling wild olive—all making their way over the cobblestoned street to one of the peak-roofed gates of the Nanking wall.

3. *crenelated* (krĕn'ĕl āt ĕd): walls built for defense of a city had open spaces, or crenels, at the top. This gave a saw-toothed appearance. 4. *rickshaws* (rĭk'shôs): two-wheeled carriages of the Orient, drawn by one or more men.

It was the eastern gate we passed under on our way to the plane. We had landed on Lotus Lake, just outside the city. The flooded waters stretched to the foot of the wall, like a medieval moat. Willows stood knee-deep on the edges, trailing their branches in the water, and sampans pressed down the submerged grass. Here we anchored our plane and came each morning to begin our survey flights. Here we left it each night, its orange wings still catching the light from an evening sky.

In the morning the wall was gray and hard, every brick standing out in its hardness. But in the evening, shadows from the moss and vines growing in the cracks gave it a purplish bloom, as though it caught some reflection from the opposite mountain. Massive as a mountain, too, it stood there in the twilight. The plane in front of it, glistening and sleek, swayed gently in the wind. It seemed to me as I watched, one against the other, that there was an argument between the two. Not only the perpetual argument of youth against age, but machine-made against man-made; things fleeting against things lasting; motion against rest; ambition against acceptance. It was an argument without end. I do not know who won, but as we poled home in the shadows, I could imagine it echoing back and forth:

"I am a wall. Generations have passed under my gates; wars and destruction have broken over me like waves. I am still here—a wall."

"I am a plane. Power and speed. I traverse space and race with time. You are bound; but I can fly—I am a plane."

"I am a wall. You are a plane; you will be gone tomorrow. But I—I will be here forever—a wall."

"... a plane ..."

"... a wall ..."

HELPS FOR DISCUSSION

1. Contrast life in Nanking with life in some American city.

2. What was the argument between the plane and the wall? Can you add other points on both sides to continue this argument?

To an Aviator

DANIEL WHITEHEAD HICKY

You who have grown so intimate with stars
And know their silver dripping from your wings,
Swept with the breaking day across the sky,
Known kinship with each meteor that swings—

You who have touched the rainbow's fragile gold,
Carved lyric ways through dawn and dusk and rain
And soared to heights our hearts have only dreamed—
How can you walk earth's common ways again?

No one has ever expressed the glory of flight more splendidly than did Antoine de Saint-Exupéry, one of the world's great airmen. Here he sets down the responsibilities which are the lot of a

Night Warden

ANTOINE DE SAINT-EXUPÉRY

The clerks were drowsing in the Buenos Aires office when Rivière entered. He had kept his overcoat and hat on, like the incessant traveler he always seemed to be. His spare person took up so little room, his clothes and graying hair so aptly fitted into any scene, that when he went by hardly anyone noticed it. Yet, at his entry, a wave of energy traversed the office. The staff bustled, the head clerk hurriedly compiled the papers remaining on his desk, typewriters began to click.

The telephonist was busily slipping his plugs into the standard and noting the telegrams in a bulky register. Rivière sat down and read them.

All that he read, the Chile episode excepted, told of one of those favored days when things go right of themselves and each successive message from the airports is another bulletin of victory. The Patagonia mail, too, was making headway; all the planes were ahead of time, for fair winds were bearing them northward on a favoring tide.

"Give me the weather reports."

Each airport vaunted its fine weather, clear sky, and clement breeze. The mantle of a golden evening had fallen on South America. And Rivière welcomed this friendliness of things. True, one of the planes was battling somewhere with the perils of the night, but the odds were in its favor.

Rivière pushed the book aside.

"That will do."

Then, a night warden whose charge was half the world, he went out to inspect the men on night duty, and came back.

Later, standing at an open window, he took the measure of the darkness. It contained Buenos Aires yonder, but also, like the hull of some huge ship, America. He did not wonder at this feeling of immensity; the sky of Santiago de Chile might be a foreign sky, but once the air-mail was in flight toward Santiago you lived, from end to journey's end, under the same dark vault of heaven. Even now the Patagonian fishermen were gazing at the navigation lights of the plane whose messages were being awaited here. The vague unrest of an airplane in flight brooded not only on Rivière's heart but, with the droning of the engine, upon the capitals and little towns.

Glad of this night that promised so well, he recalled those other nights of chaos, when a plane had seemed hemmed in

with dangers, its rescue well-nigh a forlorn hope, and how to the Buenos Aires Radio Post its desperate calls came faltering through, fused with the atmospherics of the storm. Under the leaden weight of sky the golden music of the waves was tarnished. Lament in the minor of a plane sped arrowwise against the blinding barriers of darkness, no sadder sound than this!

An emergency landing-ground sent in a radio message.

Plane in sight. Plane signals: Engine Trouble; about to land.

That meant half an hour lost. Rivière felt that mood of irritation the traveler knows when his express is held up by a signal and the minutes no longer yield their toll of passing hedgerows. The large clock hand was turning now an empty hemicycle,[1] within whose compass so many things might have fitted in. To while away the interval Rivière went out and now the night seemed hollow as a stage without an actor. Wasted—a night like this! He nursed a grudge against that cloudless sky with its wealth of stars, the moon's celestial beacon, the squandered gold of such a night.

But, once the plane had taken off, the night once more grew full of beauty and enthralment; for now the night was carrying life, and over it Rivière kept his watch.

"What weather have you?"

He had the query transmitted to the crew. Ten seconds later the reply came in: "Very fine."

There followed a string of names, towns over which the plane had passed and, for Rivière's ears, these were so many names of cities falling one by one before a conqueror.

HELPS FOR DISCUSSION

Explain the phrases *whose charge was half the world, the moon's celestial beacon, the night was carrying life.* Find other poetic phrases from this gifted airman's pen. From his book *Wind, Sand and Stars* select another air incident to read aloud.

1. *hemicycle:* a half circle.

Strangely, nothing seems known about Francis E. Falkenbury except that he is said to have been a high-school student when he wrote this poem. It appeared in ***McClure's Magazine,*** where it won the praise of famous critics. The poet has apparently written no other verse. The critics know of him only that he wrote

South Street

FRANCIS E. FALKENBURY

As I came down to the long street by the water, the sea-ships
dropped their masts like ladies bowing,
Curtseying friendly in a manner olden,
Shrouds and sails in silken sunlight flowing,
Gleaming and shimmering from silvern into golden,
With the sea-winds through the sunlit spaces blowing.
As I came down to South Street by the glimmering, tossing
water, the sweet wind blew, oh, softly, sweetly blew
O'er the lean, black docks piled high with curious bales,
Odorous casks, and bundles of foreign goods,
And all the long ships with their fair, tall sails,
Lading the winey air with the spices of alien woods.

As I came down to South Street by the soft sea-water,
I saw long ships, their mast-heads ever bowing:
Sweet slender maids in clinging gowns of golden,
Curtseying stately in a fashion olden,
Bowing sweetly—each a king's fair daughter—
To me, their millionth, millionth lover,
I, the seventh son of the old sea-rover,
As I came down to South Street by the myriad moving water.

Lord of the Winds

MARY COLERIDGE

Lord of the winds, I cry to Thee,
  I that am dust,
And blown about by every gust
  I fly to Thee.

Lord of the waters, unto Thee I call.
  I that am weed upon the waters borne,
    And by the waters torn,
Tossed by the waters, at Thy feet I fall.

Travel Song

SISTER M. MADELEVA, S.S.C.

Know you the journey that I take?
Know you the voyage that I make?
The joy of it one's heart could break.

No jot of time have I to spare,
Nor will to loiter anywhere,
So eager am I to be there.

For that the way is hard and long,
For that gray fears upon it throng,
I set my journey to a song.

And it grows wondrous happy so.
Singing, I hurry on for oh!
It is to God, to God, I go.

HELPS FOR DISCUSSION

1. Review selections in this unit, recalling the friendliness theme. Why are sea and air stories included in *A Book of Friendliness*?

2. Which poems in the unit show the sea's beauty, adventure, or solemn grandeur? Read in concert the closing poem.

VIII

Among the Nations

Mutual understanding among the nations is not the only basis for peace; but it is one of the good firm bases. For mutual understanding builds friendliness, and friendliness among the nations is the keystone of the future peace of the world.

In no way can there be better understanding of nations than through knowledge of their literature. We read stories of America that we may better know our native land. We must cross our own borders to learn the ways of other people in other lands.

Men have blazed trails of friendliness to recite the praises of another people and to set down ways in which people of many races have helped one another.

Missionaries, the great apostles of good will between nations, have written or been written of in the world's great literature.

Poets have sung the unity of mankind under God.

Someone has said that, if one really knew his neighbor as he knew himself, he would surely follow Christ's commandment to love his neighbor as himself.

1 Corinthians, xii, 12-13

For as the body is one and has many members, and all the members of the body, many as they are, form one body, so also is it with Christ.

For in one Spirit we were all baptized into one body, whether Jews or Gentiles, whether slaves or free; and we were all given to drink of one Spirit.

Matthew viii, 1-4

Now when he had come down from the mountain, great crowds followed him. And behold, a leper came and worshipped him, saying, "Lord, if thou wilt, thou canst make me clean." And stretching forth his hand Jesus touched him, saying, "I will; be thou made clean." And immediately his leprosy was cleansed. And Jesus said to him, "See thou tell no one; but go, show thyself to the priest, and offer the gift that Moses commanded, for a witness to them."

Ephesians ii, 18-22

You are now no longer strangers and foreigners, but you are citizens with the saints and members of God's household: you are built upon the foundation of the apostles and prophets with Christ Jesus Himself as the chief corner stone. In Him the whole structure is closely fitted together and grows into a temple holy in the Lord; in Him you too are being built together into a dwelling place for God in the Spirit.

Welcome

RAUL OTERO REICHE OF BOLIVIA

O stupendous America,
that one day greeted the Spanish sails
with the white scarf of an Andean snowfall!

Song of the Americas

JULIA COOLEY ALTROCCHI

Our native land,
But not our native land alone
(Our narrow strip of sand and stone,
Our private fields, our little gear),
Not *our* America alone,
But every place of men from pole to pole
In this ancestral hemisphere,
The mighty whole
From Mexico to the Horn-swirled spray,
The Argentine to Hudson Bay,
Natal to Nome,
All, all our neighborhood, our home,
The widened acres of our soul!

Not this domain alone,
Our flowering bush and thorn,
Our village loyalties outworn,
But all America, North, Central, South,
One land at birth,
One mass flung from the flaming mouth
Of Cauldron earth,
One rock, one mountain chain, one clay,
Rich with the clambering seed
Of men and corn,
A thousand races but a single breed,
One dust, one destiny, one living need
From White Alaska to the whiter Horn!

No favored flag from one small mast unfurled,
But one immense desire,
One banner plumed with flameless fire,
One hope, one mighty scheme
Of winged freedom beating at earth's door,
One goal of peace for half the world,
One great Andean dream!
A single continental soul
From pole to snowy pole,
From shore to clasping shore,
All, all America, the mighty whole,
One rock, one mountain-chain, one clay,
One mortal dust, one common way!

Love of freedom is as deep in the hearts of our Latin American neighbors as it is in our own; and few men have expressed it more bravely than has Bishop de Andrea of Buenos Aires when he spoke of

Liberty

MIGUEL DE ANDREA

Sometimes I am asked why I defend liberty so much. It might as well be asked why I defend life. I defend liberty because I do not want to cease being man in the great, noble, and Christian sense of the word.

The liberty that God gives us is the great faculty of doing the good; it is the supreme faculty and should be as inviolable as life. There is more of duty in it than of right. It is the faculty of doing one's duty, always, in all circumstances.

On the crest of the mountains between Chile and Argentina stands that great symbol of neighborly peace, the huge statue of

The Christ of the Andes

ANNA P. HANNUM

Far, far away to the south of these United States, on the other side of the equator, at the farthest end of South America, are the countries of Chile and Argentina. While we are picking roses they are shivering in winter; they have their roses and warm weather at Christmas. In their winter the sun is away at the north making us warm, and they talk about the South Pole when they want to name the coldest place they can.

You might think that would be a very topsy-turvy place to be in, but you must not expect to hear that people walk on their heads or build their houses upside down, for they are not really very different, after all, from North Americans. They have their election days when they choose their presidents and congressmen (though they do not call them so) and then there are speeches, parades, brass bands and great excitement just as we have here. Although they have their flower time at Christmas, they do not love the Christ Child any less for that. In fact, if they had not loved the Christ Child very dearly, there would not have been any story to tell, but you see they did. This was the way it happened.

It was really the fault of the Andes Mountains. The Argentine Republic is on the Atlantic Ocean side of South America, and Chile on the Pacific side. The Andes Mountains rise between. These are very, very high mountains, so high that the snow never melts on their tops, but stays there both in summer and in winter, as on our Rockies. In fact, they are really the southern end of the Rockies, but have a different name.

Since the mountains are very high, and so snowy and rocky, and very steep, you can easily see that it would be hard work for surveyors to scramble up with their tripods to find out just where the boundary line between the two countries really ought to be. They did what they could, and the places that did not seem to matter much they took for granted.

Thus it happened that in some places nobody knew where the boundary line really was, but the rulers of both countries thought they knew; and you may be sure they thought it was just where it would give their own particular country the largest share of the land and the best right to the lakes and rivers. If they had been two naughty boys, one would have said, "I tell you the rights to these lakes and rivers are mine," and the other, "They're not; they're mine."

Then they would have begun to pound each other; this would not have decided at all which one really owned the lakes and rivers, but only which one had the stronger fists. Although not naughty boys, they behaved much like them, for they squabbled in long Spanish words, and then began to get ready to fight it out.

Each one tried to surpass the other in building big warships, making a great number of guns, and drilling large numbers of soldiers; and the poor people of both countries, who did not care at all where the boundary was, had to pay for it, even though they had not money left to buy shoes for their children.

This was the way things were going when the women and clergymen of the country made up their minds to try to put a stop to it.

The good Bishop Benavente,[1] of Argentina, went around the country pleading for peace and trying to make the people understand what a very foolish thing war is.

After they were done fighting, he said, they would not know any better than before to whom the land and the rights to the waterways really did belong. They would be merely causing suffering to their families and spending their money foolishly. He begged the people to remember Christ and to keep the peace.

Over in Chile, Bishop Java went among his people and talked to them in the same way. Before long the two bishops and their faithful priests made the people see how foolish it would be to hate and wound and kill one another, when they

1. *Benevente* (bā nā vĕn'tĕ).

might settle the question without hurting anyone and become better friends than before.

The two countries agreed to ask the King of England to be their judge. Like a wise judge he gave each a part of the country in dispute and settled the question of the rights of the waterways so that everyone was well satisfied and thankful to have the matter happily ended. In their friendly joy they made treaties of peace.

Now the question arose, what should be done with all the cannon and warships and forts, which would not be needed, if there was to be no war? It was finally agreed that the ships should be sold to merchants, to carry useful things—wool, wheat, metals—all over the world. The soldiers were to be sent home to work in the fields and mines, and the money formerly spent for ships and guns was to be used in making better roads and safer harbors.

At the time, a beautiful statue of Christ had been made by a young sculptor of Argentina, named Mateo Alonso,[2] from a bronze cannon which had been taken years before when Argentina was fighting against Spain for her independence. The cannon had been molded into a great figure of Christ more than twenty-five feet high, with one hand stretched out to bless the two peaceful countries, and the other holding a cross.

One hundred thousand dollars was raised, mostly by the women of both countries, to pay for this wonderful statue. The leading part in the work was taken by Angela de Oliveira Cezar de Costa.[3]

On May 28, 1903, the day the treaty of peace was signed, Señora de Costa invited the president of Argentina and General Montt, the representative of the President of Chile, to come to the yard of a large college in Argentina to inspect the great statue. While they were there, she asked permission to have it placed on the highest accessible pinnacle of the Andes, on the boundary line that had been the cause of dispute. This was granted and, after the winter had passed, the work of getting it up the mountains was begun.

2. *Mateo Alonso* (mȧ tā′ō *ȧ* lŏn′zō). 3. *Angela Oliveira Cezar de Costa* (ăn′jĕ l*ȧ* ŏ lĭ vē′rä sā zär dē kŏs′tä).

The statue was so large and heavy that this was very difficult to do. It was carried by rail to the base of the mountain. The rest of the way was so rough and steep that not even the biggest and strongest railroad engine could climb it; so the statue was placed on gun carriages, drawn by mules. Where the road was too bad for the mules to climb safely, the people took the ropes and helped for fear the precious statue might fall and break.

There was great joy on the day when the statue was finally ready and in its place. Hundreds of people toiled up the steep road the night before to be ready for the hymns and prayers when the statue should be unveiled. The Argentines camped on the Chilean side of the boundary, and Chileans on the Argentine side, to show their friendship and good will. When the statue was at last ready to be unveiled there was a great burst of music and firing of guns. The sound echoed far over the mountains and through the valleys, and everyone joined his voice to the chorus.

Then all waited in breathless silence while the veil was lifted, and the lovely face of Christ looked down upon them, seeming to say again, as of old, "Blessed are the peacemakers, for they shall be called the children of God." In the hearts of those hundreds of people the angels sang again their chorus of "Peace on earth, to men of good will."

There stands the statue now, strong and immovable as the Andes themselves, where Chile and Argentina may look and remember for ages to come. They have learned the lesson of peace, and these are the words that have been written on the granite at the base of the statue:

Sooner shall these mountains crumble to dust than Argentines and Chileans break the peace which at the feet of Christ, the Redeemer, they have sworn to maintain.

HELPS FOR DISCUSSION

1. What teachings of Christ did Bishop Benavente and Bishop Java impress upon the people of their countries? How could their example of peacemaking be followed in the world today?

2. How long has the Christ of the Andes stood on the boundary? Show that the pledge is kept in good faith.

The culture of Spain came with the Spanish ships to the Western World; and the Latin lands have long cherished such hymns as the one which sings the praises of the Virgin of the Spanish Guadalupe[1] from which the Mexican Guadalupe was named:

Song to the Virgin Mary

PERO LOPEZ DE AYALA

Translated from the Spanish by Thomas Walsh

Lady, as I know thy power,
I place my hopes in thee;
Thy shrine in Guadalupe's tower
My pilgrim steps shall see.

1. *Guadalupe* (gwä dä lo͞o′pā).

Thy welcome ever was most sweet
  To those who come in care;
When from this prison I retreat,
  I'll seek thine image there.

Lady, as I know thy power,
  I place my hopes in thee;
Thy shrine in Guadalupe's tower
  My pilgrim steps shall see.

In all my sorrows would I call
  On thee, Sweet Advocate;
My heart adores thee more than all,
  And so my sins seem great.

Lady, as I know thy power,
  I place my hopes in thee;
Thy shrine in Guadalupe's tower
  My pilgrim steps shall see.

Thou art the star that shows the way,
  The balm that heals my wrong;
In gentleness be mine today
  And lead to heaven along.

Lady, as I know thy power,
  I place my hopes in thee;
Thy shrine in Guadalupe's tower
  My pilgrim steps shall see.

HELPS FOR DISCUSSION

1. What vow does the poet make? Read stanzas repeating it.

2. Explain why there is a Guadalupe in Mexico. Read and report upon the Mexican story of Our Lady of Guadalupe. (See *These are Our Horizons*, pages 397-399.)

3. In religion, art, language, and science trace the evidences of early Spanish influence in the civilization of the Americas.

Times Were Hard in Pontiac

GILBERT PARKER

It was soon after the Rebellion, and there was little food to be had and less money, and winter was at hand. Pontiac,[1] ever most loyal to old France, though obedient to the English, had herself sent few recruits to be shot down by Colborne, but she had emptied her pockets in sending to the front the fullness of her barns and the best cattle of her fields. She gave her all; she was frank in giving, hid nothing; and when her own trouble came there was no voice calling on her behalf. And Pontiac would rather starve than beg. So, as the winter went on, she starved in silence, and no one had more than sour milk and bread and a potato now and then. The Curé,[2] the Avocat,[3] and the Little Chemist fared no better than the habitants,[4] for they gave all they had right and left, and themselves often went hungry to bed. And the truth is that few outside Pontiac knew of her suffering; she kept the secret of it close.

It seemed at last, however, to the Curé that he must, after all, write to the world outside for help. That was when he saw the faces of the children get pale and drawn. There never was a time when there were so few fish in the river and so little game in the woods. At last, from the altar steps one Sunday, the Curé, with a calm, sad voice, told the people that, for "the dear children's sake," they must sink their pride and ask help from without. He would write first to the Bishop of Quebec; "For," said he, "Mother Church will help us; she will give us food, and money to buy seed in the spring; and, please God, we will pay all back in a year or two!" He paused a minute, then continued: "Someone must go, to speak plainly and wisely of our trouble, that there be no mistake—we are not beggars, we are only borrowers. Who will go? I may not myself, for who would give the Blessed Sacrament, and speak to the sick, or say Mass and comfort you?"

1. *Pontiac:* a local unit in the Province of Quebec, Canada. 2. *Curé* (kü rā′): a parish priest. 3. *Avocat:* a lawyer. 4. *habitants* (hăb′ĭ tănts): colonial settlers of French Canada.

There was silence in the church for a moment, and many faces meanwhile turned instinctively to M.[5] Garon the Avocat, and some to the Little Chemist.

"Who will go?" asked the Curé again. "It is a bitter journey, but our pride must not be our shame in the end. Who will go?"

Everyone expected that the Avocat or the Little Chemist would rise; but while they looked at each other, waiting and sorrowful, and the Avocat's fingers fluttered to the seat in front of him, to draw himself up, a voice came from the corner opposite, saying: "M'sieu le Curé, I will go."

A strange, painful silence fell on the people for a moment, and then went round an almost incredulous whisper: "Parpon, the dwarf!"

Parpon's deep eyes were fixed on the Curé, his hunched body leaning on the railing in front of him, his long, strong arms stretched out as if he were begging for some good thing. The murmur among the people increased, but the Curé raised his hand to command silence, and his eyes gazed steadily at the dwarf. It might seem that he was noting the huge head, the shaggy hair, the overhanging brows, the weird face of this distortion of a thing made in God's own image. But he was thinking instead of how the angel and the devil may live side by side in a man and neither be entirely driven out—and the angel conquer in great times and seasons.

He beckoned to Parpon to come over, and the dwarf trotted with a sidelong motion to the chancel steps. Every face in the congregation was eager, and some were mystified, even anxious. They all knew the singular power of the little man—his knowledge, his deep wit, his judgment, his occasional fierceness, his infrequent malice; but he was kind to children and the sick, and the Curé and the Avocat and their little group respected him. Once everybody had admired him: that was when he had sung in the Mass, the day of the funeral of the wife of Farette the miller, for whom he worked. It had been rumored that in his hut by the Rock of Red Pigeons, up at Dalgrothe Mountain, a voice of most wonderful power and

5. *M.:* the abbreviation for *monsieur* (mẽ syû′), a French title of courtesy.

sweetness had been heard singing; but this was only rumor. Yet when the body of the miller's wife lay in the church, he had sung so that men and women wept and held each other's hands for joy. He had never sung since, however; his voice of silver was locked away in the cabinet of secret purposes which every man has somewhere in his own soul.

"What will you say to the Bishop, Parpon?" asked the Curé.

The congregation stirred in their seats, for they saw that the Curé intended Parpon to go.

Parpon went up two steps of the chancel quietly and caught the arm of the Curé, drawing him down to whisper in his ear.

A flush and then a peculiar soft light passed over the Curé's face, and he raised his hand over Parpon's head in benediction and said: "Go, my son, and the blessing of God and of His dear Son be with you."

Then suddenly he turned to the altar, and, raising his hands, he tried to speak, but only said: "O Lord, Thou knowest our pride and our vanity, hear us, and—"

Soon afterward, with tearful eyes, he preached from the text:

"*And the Light shineth in darkness, and the darkness comprehendeth it not.*"

Five days later a little, uncouth man took off his hat in the chief street of Quebec, and began to sing a song of Picardy[6] to

6. *Picardy* (pĭk'år dĭ): an old province in northern France.

an air which no man in French Canada had ever heard. Little farmers on their way to the market by the Place de Cathedral stopped, listening, though every moment's delay lessened their chances of getting a stand in the market-place. Butchers and milkmen loitered, regardless of waiting customers; a little company of soldiers caught up the chorus, and to avoid involuntary revolt, their sergeant halted them, that they might listen. Gentlemen strolling by—doctor, lawyer, officer, idler—paused and forgot the raw climate, for this marvelous voice in the unshapely body warmed them, and they pushed in among the fast-gathering crowd. Ladies hurrying by in their sleighs lost their hearts to the thrilling notes of:

"Little gray fisherman,
Where is your daughter?
Where is your daughter so sweet?
Little gray man who comes
Over the water,
I have knelt down at her feet,
Knelt at your Gabriell's feet—*ci ci!*"

Presently the wife of the governor stepped out from her sleigh, and, coming over, quickly took Parpon's cap from his hand and went round among the crowd with it, gathering money.

"He is hungry, he is poor," she said with tears in her eyes. She had known the song in her childhood, and he who used to sing it to her was in her sight no more. In vain the gentlemen would have taken the cap from her; she gathered the money herself, and others followed, and Parpon sang on.

A night later a crowd gathered in the great hall of the city, filling it to the doors, to hear the dwarf sing. He came on the platform dressed as he had entered the city, with heavy, homemade coat and trousers, and moccasins, and a red woolen comforter about his neck—but this comforter he took off when he began to sing. Old France and New France, and the loves and hates and joys and sorrows of all lands, met that night in the soul of this dwarf with the divine voice, who did not give them his name, so that they called him, for want of a better title, the Provençal.[7] And again two nights afterwards it was the same, and yet again a third night and a fourth, and the simple folk, and wise folk also, went mad after Parpon the dwarf.

Then, suddenly, he disappeared from Quebec City, and the next Sunday morning, while the Curé was saying the last words of the Mass, he entered the Church of St. Saviour at Pontiac. Going up to the chancel steps he waited. The murmuring of the people drew the Curé's attention, and then, seeing Parpon, he came forward.

Parpon drew from his breast a bag, and put it in his hands, and beckoning down the Curé's head, he whispered.

The Curé turned to the altar and raised the bag towards it in ascription and thanksgiving, then he turned to Parpon again, but the dwarf was trotting away down the aisle and from the church.

"Dear children," said the Curé, "we are saved, and we are not shamed." He held up the bag. "Parpon has brought us two thousand dollars; we shall have food to eat, and there shall be more money against seed-time. The giver of this good gift demands that his name be not known. Such is all true charity. Let us pray."

So hard times passed from Pontiac as the months went on, but none save the Curé and the Avocat knew who had helped her in her hour of need.

Triumphalis

BLISS CARMAN

Soul, art thou sad again,
With the old sadness?
Thou shalt be glad again
With a new gladness,
When April sun and rain
Mount to the teeming brain
With the earth-madness.

7. *Provencal* (prō vän säl′): a troubador, or singer. The natives of the romantic section of southeastern France that was called Provence were once famous for their skill as troubadors.

When from the mould again,
Spurning disaster,
Spring shoots unfold again,
Follow thou faster
Out of the drear domain
Of dark, defeat, and pain,
Praising the Master.

Light for thy guide again,
Ample and splendid;
Love at thy side again,
All doubting ended.
(Ah, by the dragon slain,
For nothing small or vain
Michael contended!)

Thou shalt take heart again,
No more despairing;
Play thy great part again,
Loving and caring.
Hark, how the gold refrain
Runs through the iron strain,
Splendidly daring!

Thou shalt grow strong again,
Confident, tender,—
Battle with wrong again,
Be truth's defender,—
Of the immortal train
Born to attempt, attain,
Never surrender!

HELPS FOR DISCUSSION

1. What does the title, "Triumphalis," suggest? What does spring, with returning life and light, summon the soul to do?

2. In what ways does the fourth stanza remind you of Parpon, the singing dwarf, of the preceding selection?

A northern missionary, who wrote *Flying Priest over the Arctic*, tells the story of his high adventure when he answered the call of

SOS—Arctic Bay

REVEREND PAUL SCHULTE, O.M.I.

At last there was my destination—Arctic Bay, five hundred miles north of the Arctic Circle and eleven hundred miles from the North Pole. It is the last trading post in the north and the northernmost mission in the world. Here mountains rise eighteen hundred feet into the icy Arctic sky.

There were Eskimo tents at the entrance of the Bay. Great was the commotion I caused. Mine was the first airplane ever seen thereabouts. The Eskimos waved their hands wildly above their heads to welcome the "Flying Priest." The dogs howled, looked up at me, and wagged their bushy tails. Directly ahead of me, at the end of the Bay, were the red and white buildings of the Hudson's Bay Company. Close to them was a little white tent with a small cross on top. "In this tent," I thought, "I shall find Father Cochard, dead or alive."

Everything moved too slowly for me. I flew the "courtesy circle" around the mission tent. Was it for one alive or dead? Was I too late or was I in time? After the plane had been taxied slowly to the shore, two white men came walking down from the Hudson's Bay Company building and smilingly extended their greetings, "How do you do?"

I answered with the same greeting: "How do *you* do?"

Then I handed the gentlemen their mail and asked eagerly, "How is Father Cochard?"

Even as I put the question, my eyes were searching their faces for the answer. "He is alive," they replied, both speaking at once, "but he is in great pain."

"Thank God!" broke from my lips. "I will fly him to Chesterfield, to the hospital, and the Grey Nuns will nurse him back to health."

Father Cochard was in the house of the Hudson's Bay Company. After lying ill in his tent without heat and with high fever, he had been found by Allen Scott, who had brought him into his house and taken care of him, as he would a dear friend. When Father Cochard saw me he could not speak for joy. He wept and pressed my hand. He could not believe that he was to be taken where he could get medical care. I had never seen this Father before, but in that moment we became friends for life.

After he had calmed down, I offered him an orange. How his eyes brightened up! For the four years that he had lived in the Arctic, he had not even seen an orange, much less eaten one. He now ate three of them with relish—and I was glad to watch him, for it increased my hopes for his recovery.

"Just wait, good friend, and you will see how quickly we shall get you back on your feet!" I told him. For the present, however, he was far from recovery.

While I was by his side, he whispered into my ear: "Father Schulte, when I offered my last Holy Mass and realized that I was too ill to attempt saying Mass again, I consecrated ten Sacred Hosts in order to be able to receive Holy Communion during my remaining days until the hour of death. Would you be so kind as to take these Sacred Hosts with you to Igloolik?"

No one could have been prouder than I was at that moment. I walked to the little tent, opened the Mass kit, and found the Sacred Hosts. I knelt down and adored Our Lord in the Blessed Sacrament. I whispered a prayer in this northernmost chapel of the world, and then I placed the linen cloth, with the Sacred Hosts folded within it, upon my heart. I became profoundly conscious of the special grace and distinction which was conferred on me. Unexpectedly I felt refreshed, calm, and convinced that my return flight to the hospital would succeed and that the suffering missionary would be cured of his illness.

Father Cochard was given a bowl of warm soup. Then he was dressed for his journey. The most difficult part of this operation was that of pulling his heavy reindeer coat over his head. I had heated the cabin of the plane, but I also wanted to prevent the patient from catching cold, and perhaps pneumonia, on his way to the ship. Father Cochard shook hands with all the Eskimos, Catholic and pagan alike, who came to bid him farewell.

The task of carrying him to the boat and rowing him to the plane was a sad and touching one. With the greatest possible care we lifted him finally into the plane, where I had spread out my sleeping bag and a couple of reindeer skins to form a soft resting place for him. His eyes showed extreme fatigue and exhaustion, but they brightened with a smile of contentment when I clasped his hand to congratulate him on his brave behavior while we carried him to the plane. I wanted also to give him courage for the flight.

The surrounding scene was not unlike what one might see in Norway—fiords, mountains, and glaciers. The fog huddled in the valleys, but the north wind stormed above the mountain tops. I wanted to take advantage of this wind, for it can drive the fog before it as a dog drives a flock of sheep. It was four o'clock when the plane rose from the waters of Arctic Bay. After I had said a prayer and made the Sign of the Cross, I dipped my wings over the Hudson's Bay building, thus waving my thanks and farewell to the brave men I was leaving. Soon we were swallowed up in the fog.

Climbing steadily to escape from it and to benefit by the north-northwest wind, we soon were five thousand feet above land and sea. A wondrous sensation of security and peace pervaded my body and soul. Ten minutes later we emerged into bright sunshine. Then I could have shouted for joy and delight. I was carrying a sick missionary from his bed of pain to recovery and new health. More thrilling by far, I was carrying the Sacred Hosts from a tent on Arctic Bay to the church of Igloolik—my airplane the Lord's chapel and my breast His resting place.

I could not burn any candles in my plane, but the sun, the glorious lamp of heaven, lit at the beginning of time by the Creator, shone brightly in the sky. I had no blessed altar stone, nor a gilded tabernacle whereon I could have rested my Saviour; but He, the Saviour, deigned to rest upon my heart. I had no choir to sing His praises, but the motor hummed its most magnificent melody, two hundred and forty-five horsepower strong, to praise the Creator of the world, while the tears of joy in the eyes of Father Cochard and in my own eyes were expressive of the fact that the two and a half hours which it took us to reach Igloolik, were for us a glorious and too short "Hour of Adoration" above the clouds. Never in my life have I meditated so lovingly upon the Canticle *Benedicite.* In these hours I not only prayed that glorious canticle, but I lived it.

All ye works of the Lord, bless the Lord—the Saviour was with me and near me—where the Saviour is, there His angels also are—I sensed this—angels were carrying a flying tabernacle through the air in silent holy adoration—*Bless the Lord, all ye heavens*—around me the fierce Arctic sky, cradle of storm, pouring forth its exultant gales as a hymn of praise—for the Creator Who was mysteriously carried in an airplane—*O all ye waters that are above the Heavens, bless the Lord*—waters of the Arctic Ocean, of the fiords and inlets of the Arctic—the waves below me were bending and rolling in the same direction in which I was flying, forming white combs as if to accompany and aid me—*O ye sun and moon, bless the Lord*—the sun was pointing me the way—standing to the southwest and moving toward the south, whither I was following, while the moon stood, as if in reserve, ready to move into position the moment the sun should fail—and all the stars hovering modestly in their distant places prepared to give their light at their Master's demand—*O ye ice and snow, bless the Lord*—mountains, glaciers, never-melting snow below me, in unsullied purity, without breaking their unfathomable silence, flashed a greeting as we went by—*O ye nights and days, bless the Lord*—the long Arctic night symbolically confessed creation's dependence on its Maker, while the sun betokened the perpetual light in store for God's children—*O ye clouds, bless the Lord*—tenderly and affectionately soft white vapors brushed against the airplane which hastened on, but distanced the clouds and left them to trail behind—*Ye whales and all that move in the waters, bless the Lord*—playing their part faithfully in God's plan they gave mute but eloquent testimony to His great power and unfailing providence—

It had taken me four and a half hours to fly from Igloolik to Arctic Bay. On the return flight the wind aided us. The surprised and terrified Eskimos below us, who had never seen a plane, gazed upward at the great and mysterious bird in the skies. My courageous patient had become very weak, although he had not been air sick. Many times I pressed his hand to encourage him. He smiled his thanks because he wanted to be kind to me. He had traveled the route from Arctic Bay to Igloolik by dog sled four times. It had always taken him from four to five weeks. We made the distance this day in two hours and a half. Often during the flight he looked down, and when he recognized some landmark he made a gesture suggesting travel by sledge and smiled his wonder.

We made good speed and at six-thirty in the evening we were able to land safely at Igloolik. Our Brothers at the mission had been waiting for us anxiously, and, as soon as they saw that Father Cochard was in the plane, a heavy weight rolled from their hearts. I did not, however, allow him to be lifted from the plane. We refreshed him and nursed him where he was, while the plane was being refueled. I carried the Blessed Sacrament into the chapel and gave thanks to Our Lord for the honor of having been allowed to carry Him in my plane.

At eight o'clock I started with Father Cochard and Brother Beaudoin, my mechanic who had been waiting for me at Igloolik, on what proved to be the most difficult flight so far in my career—back toward Repulse Bay on the Arctic Circle. Had there been a weather report covering this territory, I should not have started. It was my second night flight within two days. I felt myself obliged to fly the patient as swiftly as possible to Chesterfield Inlet, and since the weather was fair at Igloolik, I took off and soared away.

Soon the air became misty. No sun, no moon. The night began. The visibility was bad. I had to come down to an elevation of one thousand feet, and then still lower to one hundred feet—till at last I was flying not far above the ice. I shuddered at the thought of having to land on this endless expanse of pack ice. A forced landing in a spot like this would be a gruesome experience. Turning sharply to the west I began to battle head winds. My supply of gasoline would carry me through if only the fog did not get thicker. I prayed that the moon might be shining when we landed. In the meantime I steered toward a group of islands, which I seemed to recognize. Suddenly Beaudoin exclaimed: "Father, that other island over there is Southampton Island! I see it clearly. The islands toward which you are steering are shadows of the fog which hangs below the moon!"

"Nevertheless, Brother, I shall fly toward these shadows, because I must know what they are!" I told him.

A short time after this both of us felt relieved to see that the shadows really were the islands which we were seeking.

And it was only five minutes more before we were above the mission of "Our Lady of the Snows" at Repulse Bay. Now the thunderous roar of our engine was rousing the sleeping missionaries and Eskimos from their sleeping bags. The moon, good old lady, was smiling again. I felt sorry that because of the west winds I could not land facing the moon and the path of light that it shed on the water. In the darkness I picked out one of the two islands and, with the throttle left a little open, I landed. There was no other way. I had to make a smooth landing, as we could not strap down our patient.

With the greatest care we took Father Cochard to shore in a canoe. From there we carried him in a chair to the mission, where we prepared hot milk and toast for him. A soft bed was made of reindeer skins, but the poor man developed a fever and did not sleep all night from internal heat and pain. No wonder! The previous day had been too strenuous for him. It had been strenuous enough even for a healthy and robust person.

I slept in my sleeping bag, and in my dreams I continued to fly through the night, fog, and ice. In the morning I heard church hymns sung in the Eskimo language. Father Lacroix was saying Holy Mass and all the Eskimos were receiving Holy Communion. My Holy Mass followed this. After breakfast Father Cochard was transported back to the canoe and to the plane with the same loving care that he had received at Arctic Bay the day before. At ten-thirty we took off for Chesterfield Inlet on the last leg of our flight.

There was a little fog, but the whole day was before us. In a few minutes we had climbed out of the fog and were soaring above it. Now the visibility became good. The plane kept steadily to its course and within two and a half hours from the time of its take-off it was over Chesterfield Inlet. I flew the customary circle around the hospital to honor the doctor and the Sisters, and then landed in the harbor.

At the hearty welcome given to him by Bishop Clabaut, the Fathers, Sisters, and Eskimos, Father Cochard broke down and wept. It seemed unbelievable to him that he had actually reached safety.

Ode

ARTHUR O'SHAUGHNESSY

[Choir to be arranged in three parts, low, medium, and high.]

High We are the music makers,
Low And we are the dreamers of dreams,
High, low Wandering by lone sea-breakers,
And sitting by desolate streams;—
Medium World-losers and world-forsakers,
On whom the pale moon gleams:
All Yet we are the movers and shakers
Of the world forever, it seems.

Medium With wonderful deathless ditties
We build up the world's great cities,
Low And out of a fabulous story
We fashion an empire's glory:
High One man with a dream, at pleasure,
Shall go forth and conquer a crown;
All And three with a new song's measure
Can trample an empire down.

Low We, in the ages lying
In the buried past of the earth,
Built Nineveh[1] with our sighing,
And Babel[2] itself in our mirth;
Medium And o'erthrew them with prophesying
To the old of the new world's worth;
All For each age is a dream that is dying,
Or one that is coming to birth.

1. *Nineveh* (nĭn′ĕ vĕ): an ancient city of Assyria. 2. *Babel* (bā′bĕl): the city and tower in the ancient land of Babylon where the confusion of tongues brought about the interruption of its building.

Friendliness is not always a question of speaking the same language. The French explorer Paul du Chaillu made friends with African tribesmen who welcomed him joyously, calling him "Chally" when they met him again

On the African Coast

PAUL DU CHAILLU

On the fifth of August we sailed from London. The days passed pleasantly on board the *Mentor*. By the end of the month of August we were not far from the Tropic of Cancer. September glided away calmly, and on the seventh of October Captain Vardon said that the following day we should come in sight of land.

Accordingly, the next morning I heard from the maintop the cry of "Land! land!" Two hours afterward from the deck I could discern the low lands of the Commi country. Nearer and nearer the coast we came, until we could see the white surf breaking with terrific force on the shore, and hear the booming sound of the angry waves as they dashed against the breakers. The country was so monotonous in its outlines that we could not make out exactly where we were; we only knew that we were south of Cape Lopez, and not very far from it. I thought it strange that I could not recognize the mouth of the Fernand Vaz or Commi River.

No canoes could ride through the surf, so no natives could

come on board. In the evening we stood off the land and shortened sail, and afterward we cast anchor.

The next morning we sailed again in a southerly direction, and at last we saw a canoe pass through the breakers; it came alongside, and the Negroes in it shouted in English, "Put down the anchor! Plenty of ivory, plenty of everything; load the ship in a fortnight."

We had passed the Fernand Vaz, having sailed too far south. The mouth of the river itself is very difficult to discover. It was discernible only by the white surf combing over its bar, by large flocks of fish-eating birds hovering in the air above it, and by a long, white sandy point forming the extremity of the land on the left bank.

As we approached the river, two canoes left the shore and made for the vessel. In the first, as it neared us, I recognized my friend, a chief, whose villages occupied the mouth of the river. He climbed up the vessel's side, went to shake hands with the captain, and then advanced toward me to do the same.

I had not said a word, but upon my raising my hat which had been pulled down so as partly to conceal my face, and turning round upon him, he stepped back in astonishment, and, recognizing me at once, cried out in his own language, "Are you Chally, or his spirit? Have you come from the dead? For we have heard you were dead. Tell me quickly, for I do not know whether I am to believe my own eyes." And I said, "I am Chally, your friend!" The good fellow embraced me in a transport of joy, but he hugged me so tight and so long that I wished his friendship had been less enthusiastic. Four years had nearly gone by since I had left the Commi country.

As the second canoe came nearer, I ordered the chief not to say a word. My heart leaped for joy, for in it were my own people from the dear, good old African town of mine. Sholomba, the nephew of King Ranpano, was there, and my boy Macondai; all my former canoe men were in that canoe. I longed for them to come on board. I could hardly restrain myself; but I felt that I must appear as if I did not know them, and see whether they would recognize me.

In a moment they were on deck, and a wild shout of joy came from them, "Our white man has come back! Chally! Chally!" and they all rushed toward me. Good fellows! In their savage natures they loved me, and they remembered the friend who had never wronged them. I was seized and almost pulled to pieces, for they all wanted to hug me at the same time. Captain Vardon looked with perfect amazement at the scene of greeting. They seemed to be crazy with joy to see me again.

Then followed a long and confused account of what had taken place since my departure, all talking at the same time.

When we had come back to our senses, the next subject to be considered was how I was to get ashore. Of course I wished to go by the mouth of the river, but Sholomba assured me it could not be done. The mouth of the Fernand Vaz had changed much for the worse, and it would be less dangerous to run a canoe through the surf to the beach than to attempt to cross the bar of the river. It was now the beginning of the rainy season, when the winds are less violent than in the dry season, but the surf had not subsided from the agitation of the heavy south winds of the dry season.

The anchor was cast, and I left the *Mentor* for the chief's canoe, which was a better one than the other.

All was excitement in the canoe, and the men sang. The chief, looking more and more anxious as we approached the rollers, rested outside for a while, and then, at the proper moment, skillfully directed the frail canoe over the crest of a huge wave, which bore us with lightning speed to the beach, where I was caught up by the natives that were waiting for us, and carried safely to dry land. Tremendous huzzas were given.

Once more I stood on African soil.

HELPS FOR DISCUSSION

Who was "Chally"? What was his mission to Africa? Account for the friendliness of the African tribesmen toward the French explorer. How did he land again on African soil?

At the entrance to the Sahara Desert stands a large white statue of the great Cardinal Lavigerie, the Apostle to Africa, who dedicated his life to winning to Christ the land to whom he wrote the invocation

To Africa

CARDINAL LAVIGERIE

I come to thee, O my dear Africa. I had sacrificed all to thee when, urged on by an evident impulse from God, I relinquished all to devote myself to thy service. But what can one man's life avail in such an enterprise? Hardly have I sketched the work. I have only been a voice in the desert hailing to those who are to trace the way for the Gospel. I am dying, having only been able to suffer for thee and, by my sufferings, prepare thee apostles.

HELPS FOR DISCUSSION

1. What figure of speech is used by the Cardinal to express his devotion to the land he loved and helped? What forerunner of Christ spoke of his work in the same way (Matthew iii, 1–3)?

2. Read and report upon Cardinal Lavigerie's work for the establishment of African missions and for the prevention of slavery.

3. Contrast hardships of life in the Sahara with those encountered by Father Cochard. Why have so many members of Catholic orders sacrificed comfort for the perils of remote places?

ART AMONG THE NATIONS

No reading of the countries of the world can be called complete unless you come to know the best paintings and sculpture of some of these lands. As expressions of national pride there are the sculptured figures of the statue, *The Marseillaise*, by RUDE, on the Arch of Triumph in Paris. Some great pictures are *Riderless Races at Rome*, by GÉRICAULT, and *A Polish Nobleman*, by REMBRANDT. There are pictures, too, of deeper significance. Among them are *The Virgin of Seville*, by MURILLO; *Hagar and Ishmael*, by CAZIN; *Madonna of Peace*, by BEATO ANGELICO; *Madonna and Child in Glory*, by PERUGINO; *Self-Portrait*, by REMBRANDT; *Portrait of a Young Man*, by FRANS HALS; *The Inn*, by COROT; *The Holy Family*, by WANG SU-TA.

An American missionary, going through Palestine, saw this incident of friendliness which moved him to write

A Thank You to Abu and the Boys

JOHN J. CONSIDINE, M.M.

On my first morning in Jerusalem I was in the narrow streets before dawn to say Mass at the altar of the Holy Sepulcher. The city had its charm at this hour. All was hushed; there was an infrequent shaft of smudgy light as a householder stirred himself, a dimmed lantern moving along the street; there was a rare passer-by, his face swathed in rags against the cool air. At a corner a young man slept on a step, his hand holding the rope of his donkey, patient beside him. The basilica[1] was impressive in its stillness. Only birds chattering in the cupola of the chapel of Saint Helena broke the quiet, nature's sweetly jubilant accompaniment for the Mass which every day is the same here: "He is risen as He said. . . . Behold the place where they laid Him."

During the climb back up the long hill, in the crowded alley which serves as a street, I met Abu and the boys. Down the slope, feeling his way over the cobbles with his stick, came a blind young man, a Moslem.[2] As he neared me, two ragged urchins on a doorstep to my right, Moslems also, bounced up and ran toward him.

"Ay, Abu!" they cried.

"Ay!" he called back with a gentle, quiet smile.

All three squeezed each other's hands affectionately. Then one of the boys, who apparently had anticipated this moment,

1. *basilica* (bȧ sĭl′ĭ kȧ): a place of worship, usually oblong in shape. 2. *Moslem* (mŏz′lĕm): a believer in Mohammed.

thrust his hand vigorously into his pocket and drew out a large crust of bread which he pressed into the blind man's hand. The face with the sightless eyes shone radiantly. Arm in arm, the three brushed past me, the bringer of the bread fairly beside himself with joy. I had the sensation of being out of breath. I gazed with strange new interest at the stream of humans that poured by me.

That afternoon, while I was picking my way through the turmoil outside the Jaffa Gate, an Arab coolie,[3] struggling under the killing weight of a bale of goods, cried that his burden was slipping—would someone straighten it on his back? A spare, hard-bitten camel driver stopped his beast; drawing on hidden wells of strength, he threw the great bale into place again, then casually returned to his camel.

Next day I came upon a small boy huddled in a gutter, pouring his heart into the caresses he gave a puppy which he held in his lap while he wept over him most forlornly.

"What is the matter?" I asked a bystander.

"His dog has been hurt," replied the man, his eyes agleam with sympathy.

I rode to Beirut[4] and watched a Moslem father, a fellow passenger, lavish his love on his two children. In Bagdad, at the Royal Hospital, the Sisters of the Presentation receive thousands of the city's wretched every day. As the nuns bustled about, I watched old Moslem mothers paw the Sisters' veils in reverence and shout vigorous greetings.

"What are they saying?" I asked the Mother.

"They have a habit of calling after us," she explained, " 'May Allah bless you for your goodness!' "

On reflection I asked myself if it were not rather unreasonable to get excited over these simple evidences of feeling, of fellowship, of elementary gratitude, which after all should comprise the least common denominator of decency in all human beings. Balanced against them were the mountains of calloused chicanery[5] found everywhere in the Near East.

3. *coolie* (kōō'lĭ): an unskilled laborer. 4. *Beirut* (bā rōōt'): a city in Syria.
5 *chicanery* (shĭ kān'ĕr ĭ): trickery.

To complete my adventures with this train of incidents, I shall jump ahead some months in my story. I sat one morning with old Bishop Jarlin in Peking, China's one-time capital. "What caught your attention as you came into Asia from the West?" he asked.

"Why, I am almost ashamed to say," I told him, "that my strongest first impression was one of surprise to discover that non-Christians give play to their affections, show the warmth of friendship, practice a natural charity." And I rehearsed my experiences with Abu, the blind man, and the rest.

"Excellent!" he cried. "I had exactly the same experience. When I arrived here in Peking as a young priest, I took a walk the first morning. In a quiet alley I came upon a Chinese mother, her babe tucked inside her robe, pressing it fondly to her bosom and whispering to it little endearments. I was quite startled—'What! Have these pagans such love?' And then I was startled with myself that I could have been so stupid as to expect otherwise.

"A pity, isn't it, how easily we forget that everyone, whether born a king or a savage, has the gift of affection and a fund of natural goodness? The striking thing about men over the earth is not that they have differences which separate them, but that they have such remarkable likenesses in which they meet. Why do we put chasms[6] between peoples by insisting that they are inexorably[7] strange and strangers?"

"Thanks!" I whispered to Abu and to his ragamuffin friends as I left the Bishop's garden. "Thanks for touching off in me a very good thought. Thanks for reminding me that all men are one under the sun."

THINGS TO DO

1. Mention sights and sounds which the author uses in the first paragraph to present his word picture of Jerusalem.

2. Write or tell an incident in your daily life to illustrate the truth expressed in the last two paragraphs.

3. Read the book *Across a World*, from which this selection is taken. Relate another experience of Father Considine.

6. *chasms* (kăz'ms): deep openings. 7. *inexorably* (ĭn ĕk'sō rȧ blĭ): not to be persuaded or moved.

A Belgian priest, Joseph de Veuster, better known as Father Damien, exiled himself to care for the lepers on the Pacific Island of Molokai.[1] Years afterward, when he was ill, discouraged, and lonely there came

A Helper to Molokai

ANN ROOS

A tall man was climbing down the rope ladder slung from the rail of the steamer and lowering himself into one of the rowboats below. As the little craft approached, Damien watched it with keen interest. A visitor to Molokai was a rare event. Lepers seldom arrived singly, and even from a distance this man had none of the air of one banished to desolation and death. He sat erect, looking eagerly about him. His glance swept the great gray bulk of rock and seemed to rest, halfway up the cliff, upon the little plateau of the leper colony and on the figure of the priest who sat in his shabby carriage, watching.

The rowboat pitched and tossed in the churning sea and pulled up to the frail wharf with difficulty. The man climbed out, pulling his luggage after him. Damien watched him with growing surprise. Who was this man with his spare figure and brown beard? He had brought with him two heavy bags, unusual in the casual visitor who stayed just long enough to dispatch his business and then hurried away. Damien had been expecting no one, and the newly established resident physician at the little hospital had not mentioned the possible arrival of any one of the members of the medical staff of the Honolulu Board of Health who occasionally came for a few hours to make special examinations or tests.

The visitor turned in the direction of the road leading upward to Kalawao[2] and started to climb toward the spot where the priest sat. As he drew nearer, Damien was conscious of a lithe, rangy body, clad in light tropical clothing, and a casual, easy bearing. His face was rather thin, with an exceptionally broad forehead, from which the wavy brown hair receded slightly at the temples. The priest, his face immobile,[3]

1. *Molokai* (mō′lô kä′ē): an island of the Hawaiian group. 2. *Kalawao* (kä lä-wä′ô): a part of Molokai. 3. *immobile* (ĭ mō′bĭl): motionless.

glanced sharply at the man as he approached, but made no sign and gave no greeting.

The man did not seem to notice the priest's lack of cordiality. He walked toward the carriage, and spoke in a quiet voice. "I am Joseph Dutton."

Damien did not extend his hand or speak, but peered steadily at the man, his dark face expressionless. The stranger continued.

"I have come to stay here, if you will be so good as to permit it. I would like to be of service if I can."

Damien's parched lips opened to answer, but for a moment he could think of nothing to say. In the course of his service on Molokai he had received many offers of help, mostly in the form of letters. This had been especially true since the papers had got hold of the fact that he had contracted leprosy, and they had published the story far and wide. Many of these offers had been sincere, but from persons either too far away or too ill-equipped for the life they proposed to take on. And the high intentions of some died in the very writing, and Damien had never heard from them again.

But this was the first time that a layman with this intent had actually stepped upon the shores of Molokai. There was a quiet conviction about the man which was at once disconcerting and reassuring. But that he was both earnest and capable was hardly to be believed. Damien had been the victim of too many disillusionments[4] in the matter of co-operation to be elated even by the convincing manner of this stranger. At length he spoke, his voice rough with the growing hoarseness which his disease had brought upon him.

"Many people have said they wanted to help," he said, "but most of them have had in their minds the thought of being martyrs to the lepers. That is not enough to make a man of use in this place."

The stranger did not seem to feel the snub in the priest's voice and answered quietly. "I have no wish to find a romantic adventure. My life has had enough of those things. I am strong and well. I have long wanted to find the place where my strength could be useful to those who do not have it. When I heard of Molokai, I felt I had found this place. See—I can stand a great deal of labor." He drew his sinewy length erect, and the priest was struck again by the quiet power which seemed to be in the man.

"But your credentials," protested Damien, shifting the reins a little uneasily. This man was convincing. There was a curious serenity in his face which attracted the priest in a way which he could not explain.

The man drew a worn leather wallet from his pocket and extracted several letters. "I have already had several talks with Bishop Keockman," he said. "He knows all about me. He feels that you and I would work well together. Here is his letter to you and some of my own papers which you might like to examine."

Damien took the sheaf of papers without a word and sat for a long time carefully reading them. The Bishop's letter was direct and definite. He urged Damien to give this Joseph Dutton a trial. He seemed to feel no doubt of his suitability.

4. *disillusionments:* disappointments.

Still the priest hesitated. He had had helpers before, but always he had been glad when they had departed and he could work alone in the ways which seemed to him best. Some of the experiences with his assistants had been bitter ones and he had no wish to repeat them. Differences in temperament in one's helpers were difficult enough to handle, at best, but locked in the lonely isolation of this island, small irritations often became unbearable. He himself, he knew, was not an easy man to work with. He was impetuous,[5] irritable, authoritative,[6] often annoying to his co-workers in his persistent indifference to comfort and what they called the common decencies of life.

He had struggled against some of these traits and prayed earnestly that they might not blind him to the merits of his helpers so that the welfare of his beloved lepers might not suffer. Damien in his heart was a humble man.

But here was a man who gave him a strange sense of confidence. Could it be that God was sending him, in His own good time, the kind of helper of whom he had always dreamed, reliable and constant, without pride and without fear? So often disappointed, he dared not believe that this was so, yet hope rose within him.

"Are you willing to promise that you will stay upon Molokai for at least three years?" This, he knew, would be a test of the man's good faith.

"I wish to stay upon Molokai always," the man answered.

The priest gazed for a long moment into the serene depths of the stranger's eyes. Then he moved over and made room for him on the frayed leather seat of the wagon.

"Come," he said, lifting the reins and flicking the bony horse with a switch. "We will go to the hospital. You will be wanting to learn about the dressings."

Then, as an afterthought, he added, "I shall call you Brother Joseph."

And Joseph Dutton and Joseph de Veuster jogged along together up the rocky road to Kalawao.

5. *impetuous* (ĭm pĕt′ū ŭs): impulsive; acting or speaking quickly. 6. *authoritative* (ô thŏr′ĭ tā′ tĭv): demanding obedience from others.

THINGS TO DO

1. Read about Molokai and find it on the map. Report upon the state of the leper colony today.

2. Read *Man of Molokai* from which this selection was taken. Read also "The Fleet and Brother Joseph" in *These are Our Horizons*, pages 342–344. Tell incidents that interest you.

3. Present a character sketch of Father Damien.

Father Damien

JOHN BANISTER TABB

O God, the cleanest offering
Of tainted earth below,
Unblushing to Thy feet we bring—
"*A leper white as snow!*"

A Prophecy

ALFRED, LORD TENNYSON

For I dipt into the future, far as human eye could see,
Saw the vision of the world, and all the wonder that would be;

Saw the heavens fill with commerce, argosies of magic sails,
Pilots of the purple twilight, dropping down with costly bales;

Heard the heavens fill with shouting, and there rained a ghastly dew,
From the nations' airy navies grappling in the central blue;

Far along the world-wide whisper of the south wind rushing warm,
With the standards of the peoples plunging through the thunder-storm;

Till the war drum throbbed no longer, and the battle flags were furled
In the parliament of man, the federation of the world.

There the common sense of most shall hold a fretful realm in awe,
And the kindly earth shall slumber, lapt in universal law.

HELPS FOR DISCUSSION

1. In what century did Alfred, Lord Tennyson live? Was there any United Nations or similar organization in his time?

2. How much of Tennyson's prophecy has come true?

3. What is the universal law which will bring about universal peace? How can each of us help to advance peace?

In one of the teeming cities of the Orient some struggling Little Sisters of the Poor renewed their belief in

A Bountiful Providence

A. W. SMITH

I

It was no practical thought that led the Little Sisters of the Poor to own and use a shigram.[1] The workings of a bountiful Providence had provided it in the first instance, and it never occurred to the Little Sisters to question the wisdom of its provision.

Before even Sister Veronica came to Bombay, some forty years ago, that particular shigram had been the pride of the House of the Sisterhood in the slums off Grant Road. Then it was black and new and shiny. Now it was still moderately black, but no longer new or shiny, and the hair had long ago begun to come through the leather of the cushions. All the same, it was still known as the "new shigram," for in those dim and distant days when fodder was cheap and wages low and a horse could be kept for twenty rupees[2] a month or less, the Sisters had owned two shigrams and three horses.

Then it was that the new shigram was really new, and it remained the new shigram even after Banoo, a little drunk, though the Little Sisters did not realize it, had scraped a wheel off the old shigram on a gatepost at the City Hospital and finished it forever. By that time keeping a horse was more expensive. It now cost twenty-two rupees a month, and twenty-three if one was not very careful about the amount

1. *shigram* (shē′grăm): a kind of carriage used in Bombay. 2. *rupees* (rōō pēz′): East Indian silver coins worth about thirty-six cents each.

of "foot oil" the syce[3] included in his monthly bills. The trams,[4] too, had arrived, swaying and clanging all the way from one point of the city to another, so that there was really no point in keeping more than one horse and the new shigram.

It was a bitter blow to Aloysius Francis when the Little Sisters came to the point of keeping only the new shigram and one horse. He had been with the Little Sisters before even Sister Veronica came on the scene, and when Banoo had his accident with the old shigram he was in the position of head coachman, with two men under him and a commission on all the corn that was bought, and the right to put in the monthly bills for shoeing, grass, repairs to saddlery, and new brooms and baskets. His most guarded privilege was, of course, the item at the bottom for foot oil, a composition which syces consider indispensable for keeping the hoof of the horse in good condition. This always brought his bills to less than ten rupees. He had long ago discovered that this was about the limit of what the Little Sisters would pay without asking any questions.

It was never quite clear how Aloysius Francis got to the position of head syce. Providence again, presumably, but without doing any injustice to anyone, one would suspect that Providence was ably assisted by Aloysius Francis himself. To begin with, of course, he was not called Aloysius Francis. He was merely a low-caste Hindu lad of the syce class.

The Little Sisters offered an opportunity and he settled down to take it. Quite early in his career he became a Christian, was renamed Aloysius Francis and, not long after, became head syce. Every day he squared his lean shoulders and, setting himself on the box, handled whip and rein as if he were driving four-in-hand. There was certainly style about him, but the Little Sisters paid for it.

When Banoo scraped off the wheel Aloysius Francis was very angry indeed, but his anger was tempered by the knowledge that repair would mean more rupees slipping through his fingers, some of which would be bound to stick. When,

3. *syce* (sīs): a groom whose chief care is horses. 4. *trams:* streetcars.

however, he heard that there were to be no repairs, that the shigram had been sold where it lay, and that two of the three horses in the stable were to be sold, his anger knew no bounds. He kicked and cuffed poor Banoo, who never had been very bright, and finally threw him out of the compound.[5] He then set to work immediately to find another job. The glory and most of the profit of being head syce were gone.

He went to syces he knew all over Bombay, but in each case the answer was the same—that horses were few and becoming fewer, and there were not enough jobs to go around.

He made the best of his bad luck. He shrugged his shoulders and stayed to work at the House of the Little Sisters. The one horse that was kept after Banoo's adventure with the gatepost was reasonably young, a dark gray Australian, big-boned, with feet like soup plates, a Roman nose, and a large head set not quite badly enough for him to be called ewe-necked.[6] He had a long, raking, loose-actioned trot, a regular delivery-cart style, but little Aloysius Francis, perched high on the box, managed somehow to collect him into some kind of action.

For ten years Aloysius Francis drove the gray horse, harnessing him daily into the new shigram and driving him round from the stables at the back of the Sisterhood House. Daily on those patrols from the poverty-stricken house the Little Sisters rode, pair and pair, behind the gray with Aloysius Francis high on his box ever striving for style.

Whenever she could manage it, Sister Veronica came across the dusty compound to talk to the old horse in his stall. Aloysius Francis could generally be found on his string bed outside his quarters, and as she came he would arise and bring, wrapped in a dirty cloth, carrots, little pieces of sugar cane, or brown balls of the raw sugar.

The old gray could recognize Sister Veronica in her white habit almost before she had come round the corner of the veranda, and he would whinny in his stall until she came

5. *compound:* in the Orient, an area enclosed by four walls. In this case the House of the Sisters, servant quarters, and stables were all included in the compound. 6. *ewe-necked:* a thin, insufficiently arched neck, like that of a sheep.

across to talk to him. As she leaned over the bars of his stall and whispered to him of things she would never see again,—round green hills with firm galloping turf, stone walls, grass banks, and blackthorn hedges, racing skies and hounds streaming away on the far side of a valley in her far-off Ireland,—he would nuzzle and blow into her sleeve and pretend to try to eat the beads of her rosary.

II

The old gray began to get very old, but the Little Sisters still drove behind him. He was now nearly twenty-five and his Roman nose was more Roman than ever, the hollows above his eyes more pronounced. His back grew more and more dipped, and the withers[7] stood up high and bony. He had come to a stage when he could no longer take the new shigram with its blistered faded paint over even Camballa Hill and he now had to be driven round by the sea along Warden Road or else through the heavy traffic in the streets behind the Willingdon Club.

One day—one of those days in May when Bombay bakes in stillness under a low, heavy sky—Sister Veronica and Sister Barbara had to drive down to one of the poor quarters

7. *withers:* the ridge between the shoulder bones of a horse.

near the Sassoon Dock. As they drew closer to the waterfront they found a semblance of a breeze from the sea, and the heat became more bearable, but in the lanes between the high tenements in the city there was no breath to stir the heavy human smell.

No one who could avoid it was out in that heat. The policemen in blue cotton uniforms and primrose-colored turbans gasped in the shade at the corners. Office messengers and water sellers, the only other people who really had to be out, panted under umbrellas. The old gray trotted listlessly in front of the clanging bell. In the narrow lanes nothing stirred. In the little shops, mere holes in the walls where merchants sold onions, grains, mustard-seed oil, and the clear yellow butter of India that melted and dripped from the kerosene oil tins in which it was packed, the smell grew thicker and sweeter. There was only heat and smell, and high up in one of the tenements a baby cried a thin hopeless wail, and across the way a woman, her voice strident in anger, shrieked angrily.

Sister Veronica, old and bent in the service of the poor, leaned back in the shigram and wiped the sweat which dimmed the lenses of her steel-rimmed spectacles. With a thin hand she pushed the veil back a little from her forehead where the starched white linen stuck in the heat. She stole a look at Sister Barbara beside her. There were so many hot Bombay days to come for Little Sister Barbara. So many enterings of squalid rooms, so many monsoons,[8] so much of walking pair and pair, head bent, indistinguishable under the standardizing veil, in and out of the same crowded tenements. Sister Veronica had no illusions. Forty years had cured her belief in picturesque poverty.

She sighed and looked out of the window. They had turned away from the sea and into narrow streets between tall buildings. A solid wave of heat struck her face, bringing with it all the varied smells of the city. As she looked she felt the old horse stumble between the shafts. There was nothing new in that, for of late he had stumbled more than once. She felt

8. *monsoons:* winds which sweep across India just before the rainy season begins.

Aloysius Francis pull him to his feet again. She knew, although she could not see, that the little man had braced himself against his ledge and she heard the crack of the whip as the new shigram resumed its leisurely progress through the streets. Aloysius Francis clanged the bell twice to show what confidence he had.

There were a few more paces; the even clip-clop of the broad shallow feet faltered; another stumble, another recovery, and then the old gray horse went down for good.

By the time Sister Veronica had got out of the shigram Aloysius Francis was already at the horse's head, undoing the throat lash and slipping the cracked bridle over the ears. The old gray lay with head outstretched and legs crumpled loosely under him. He had broken his knees in his fall, and there was a tiny trickle of blood where the skin was cut.

Sister Veronica turned to Sister Barbara, who stood behind her. The child seemed to live in a gilded mystical world of her own.

"You go on, child," she said. "You know the way. I will see what can be done and follow as soon as I can."

There was nothing to be done, she knew, except to telephone to the municipality for a cart to take away the old gray and to tell Aloysius Francis to arrange for the new shigram to be taken back to the House off Grant Road. She had seen horses die in the street from heat stroke before, and the sight of the municipal cart with four stiff legs pointing to the sky was not unfamiliar. She suddenly felt old and defenseless. Aloysius Francis, standing waiting for orders, the bridle in his hands, watched her in silence.

A policeman in a dark-blue cotton uniform pushed through the crowd that had collected, the crowd which with empty brown faces pushed and surged in a ring, the crowd which became instantly greater. Here were doings indeed. A *mem-sahib*,[9] a dead horse, a shigram, and a policeman—enough to talk about for a week.

The policeman was friendly, but could offer little advice. He smiled amiably, but did nothing useful. He boxed the ears

9. *mem-sahib* (mĕm′sä′ĭb): a title used by Indians when addressing a European lady.

of a little boy who pushed too close and ordered off a woman who came to beg with skinny hand outstretched. No one paid any attention to him.

Sister Veronica took charge. The incident was over.

III

The House of the Little Sisters off Grant Road was in a district of Bombay known as Byculla. The city of Bombay is largely engaged in cotton milling, but Byculla for some reason is given up to horses. Possibly it is because it is near the race course, which would account for one or two training stables, but there must be other reasons, and one can only imagine that the horses are there for the best of reasons—that it has always been like that.

The presence of horses in Byculla, however, did not help the Little Sisters much now that they needed something to replace the gray. Sister Veronica, more from habit than anything else, walking round the corner of the veranda, suddenly realized that their horse was there no longer. The problem was how to replace him. In the past their horses had been given to them, but nowadays no one seemed to have any horses—at least not one to spare.

Aloysius Francis was the most concerned. He could see quite clearly that, having no horse, the Little Sisters would soon have no use for a head syce. His reasoning was sound. Standing before Sister Veronica on one brown skinny foot and scratching in the dust with the toe of the other, he gave it as his opinion that the best way to get another horse was to buy one.

And the cost might be what?

Aloysius Francis looked around him. He sought information from the sky, the trees, a kite[10] wheeling in the air, from the ground. He was wondering how much he dared say.

"Well, say two hundred rupees," he hazarded at last, "but of course that would not be a very good one."

"As good as the gray?"

10. *kite:* a hawklike bird.

"Yes, about as good as the gray," he supposed. Indeed, as luck would have it, he had a friend in the bazaar[11] who had just what the Little Sister *Mem-sahib* wanted, but this friend was asking three hundred rupees. However, leave it to him and he thought he could arrange it for two hundred.

Aloysius Francis thought lovingly of the fat silver rupees that would pass through his hands in the transaction and the ten per cent commission which was customary.

Armed with this information, Sister Veronica returned to the House.

The following morning as she was going out to take a tram for town she met Aloysius Francis in the compound.

"Are the Sister *Mem-sahibs* going to buy the new horse?" he asked.

"No," said Sister Veronica sadly, "the Sister *Mem-sahibs* have no money to buy a new one, but one will be provided. Let us ask and we shall receive, Aloysius Francis. We believe, and one will be provided," and she went on her way.

A week passed and nothing happened. Although the mat-

11. *bazaar* (ba zär′): in the Orient, a market place.

ter was not mentioned again, each of the Little Sisters knew that the question of the new horse was uppermost in the others' minds. Surely one must be provided. Not one of them admitted a doubt that some day they would drive out again in the city behind a new horse in the new shigram. How it would come about no one of them could tell, but they knew that it would come about.

After the week of waiting Aloysius Francis had doubts about the efficacy of the plan. He was old and in his experience of a hard world he knew that horses were bought and sold. Who had ever heard of one being "provided"?

The week flowed into a second week and Bombay became hotter and muggier. The skies were heavy and leaden colored and the wind seemed uncertain of the quarter from which it intended to blow. The harbor was empty of small craft. Everything waited for the first fury of the storm that would bring in the monsoon blowing steadily from the southwest.

Every evening Sister Veronica went out to the empty stables, just as she had done when there were horses there to feed with carrots. It was a habit of forty years, and she stood every night leaning over the bars looking at the stable clean-swept and bare.

Aloysius Francis watched her and wondered if anyone really could believe that a horse could be provided. If he expressed a doubt he would get the same answer, and even he would be convinced—for a moment.

IV

Then a night came when the sun sank white and silvery like a huge moon into a glassy, steely sea. That hot still evening was followed by a storm of wind and rain. Heavy drops lashed on to wet pavements, the palms bent double, and cars honking like frogs felt their way home through flooded streets. The temperature fell by tens of degrees, and Bombay woke to a new world, clean-washed and comparatively cool.

Sister Veronica, looking from the top veranda of the House in the clear light of early morning, was not surprised to see a horse, bright bay with a white sock on the near foreleg, grazing in the compound. The horse had been provided.

Even to her eye he was more of a horse than any she had seen before. His satiny skin shone, though a little draggled after the rain. The muscles rippled over his quarters as he moved.

She chirruped at him and he raised his small head and stood looking, ears cocked, the very picture of what a horse should be.

Sister Veronica went downstairs and, taking a piece of bread, she liberally salted it. She went out into the compound. The bright bay came willingly to her hand and felt with a soft muzzle for the salted bread. He licked up the last speck of salt.

She called for Aloysius Francis.

"The horse has come," she said. "Get the bridle and let us put him into the new shigram."

Aloysius Francis seemed a little doubtful when he came round the corner of the house, bridle in hand. He looked over the bay with an appraising eye.

"Is that the horse?" he asked.

"Yes, we have got our horse," Sister Veronica replied. "He has been provided. Put the bridle on him and get out the new shigram."

Aloysius Francis approached him rather gingerly. The throat lash and cheek pieces had to be let out a couple of holes, but the horse quietly let himself be bitted,[12] and Aloysius Francis felt his confidence returned. He backed him in between the shafts and hooked on the traces. Sister Veronica stood back to survey his work.

The bay seemed somewhat uncertain of what was expected of him, but he allowed himself to be led docilely enough. At first he started and laid his ears back at the rumble of wheels behind him, but at a word from Aloysius Francis his ears went forward. Aloysius Francis mounted the box.

"Wait here," said Sister Veronica; "I have to go to town." In a moment, she stepped into the shigram.

12. *bitted:* allowed the bit to be slipped into his mouth.

Aloysius Francis picked up the reins. The bay started to fidget, so he moved him quietly forward at a walk around the compound, the bay stepping daintily. Aloysius Francis felt a surge of pride. No other head syce in Bombay had such a horse. More from habit than anything else he took up the whip and lightly flicked the shining withers. Immediately he wished he hadn't.

The gate stood open, and fortunately at that early hour the road was clear of traffic. Aloysius Francis was powerless. All he could do was to watch those shoulders working like pistons[13] and hope for the best.

V

It was Crown Sergeant O'Neill of the Mounted Police who stopped them. Twenty-one years in the cavalry had taught him something of horses, and it took him a moment to recover his senses when he saw a thoroughbred in front of a carriage like that. He galvanized into action.

A moment later he stood dismounted at the head of the bay, his own horse standing obediently by the roadside. Aloysius Francis climbed stiffly down from the box.

"Here, where did you get this horse?" asked Crown Sergeant O'Neill suspiciously.

Aloysius Francis's teeth were chattering when he replied. "He was sent to us," he said. "We needed a horse for the *Mem-sahibs* and he came to us."

"Oh, he did, did he?" said the Crown Sergeant. "Where do you come from anyway?"

"I am the head syce and coachman to the Little Sisters *Mem-sahibs*," said Aloysius Francis proudly.

"Oh, the Little Sisters," said the Crown Sergeant, rubbing his chin thoughtfully. "Well, you'd better take that horse's head and lead him back where you got him, and I will come with you. Now, no monkey tricks," he went on warningly, "or you'll get something you won't like."

pistons: moving cylinders.

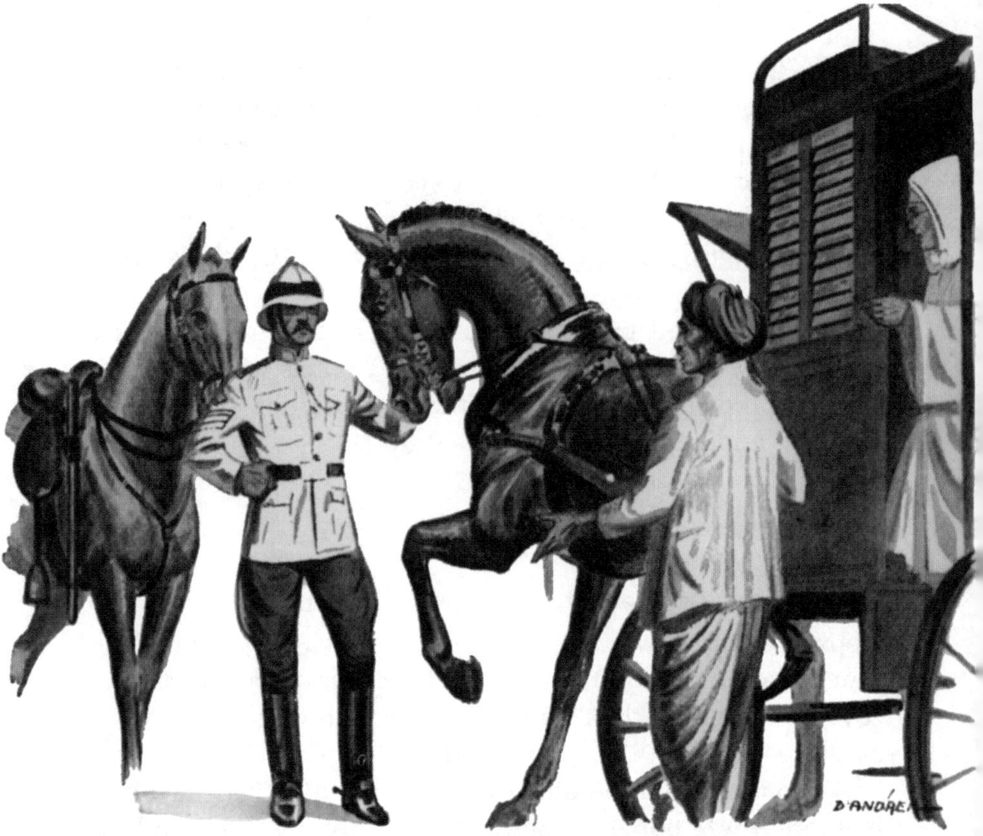

"But he was sent to us," said Sister Veronica. "We lost our horse from heat stroke and prayed for another, and here he is."

The Crown Sergeant tried to hide a smile under his mustache. "I am very sorry, Sister," he said. "Providence may provide, but it doesn't provide horses like that," and he looked at the bay with an admiring eye. "You had better let me have him to take him back where he belongs," he went on.

"Do you think you know where he belongs?" asked Sister Veronica disconsolately.

The Crown Sergeant thought a moment. "We-e-ell," he said slowly, "maybe I do and maybe I don't, but he looks to me very much like Friday's Child."

"Friday's Child? What's that?" said Sister Veronica inquiringly.

"Why, Friday's Child? Not know Mr. Gaunt's Friday's

Child, that won the Governor's Cup last December and then made the double with the Melbourne Stakes? Why, of course, he's Friday's Child!"

"But I don't understand," said Sister Veronica. "What are the Governor's Cup and the Melbourne Stakes?"

"Well, I suppose you wouldn't understand. They're races and this is a race horse, one of the finest ever imported from Australia. He must have got out last night in the storm. Well, I'll be taking him along now, Miss."

VI

Gaunt was glad to have his horse back. He ran his hands down the clean forelegs, and even he could find nothing amiss after the adventure.

He laughed a good deal when the Crown Sergeant told his story, and then he thoughtfully lit a strong cigar, pushed his thumbs into the armholes of his waistcoat, and walked down to the long line of stables where the thirty or forty horses under his care were being fed and watered.

He stopped when he came to the end stall. In it was a chestnut-colored horse, old and gone in the wind, but still good for light work. He took out a pencil and notebook and wrote:

Dear Madam:

I am sending another horse which I think will be more suitable for your work than the one provided this morning. Next time you want a horse, you come to me and I will see what I can do for you. Don't tempt Providence again.

HELPS FOR DISCUSSION

1. What is the principal work done by the Little Sisters of the Poor? How do they get the money to carry on this work? How do the people whom they serve in India differ from those whom they serve in other lands? How are they similar to other people?

2. Why did Sister Veronica think that the new horse was "a gift of Providence"?

Christ's Little Sister

JOHN BANISTER TABB

Little Sister of the Poor,
Asking alms from door to door,
  Ever on you go;
Clothed in the garb of meekness,
Finding strength in others' weakness,
  Soothing others' woe.

Little Sister of the Poor,
Rich in patience to endure
  Stern Redemption's load;
Cold and rain and parching heat
Hinder not heroic feet
  On the Royal Road.

Little Sister of the Poor,
When your weary day is o'er
  Rest there may not be;
For the aged, sick, and needy
Vigil claim and succor speedy,
  Turning unto thee.

Little Sister of the Poor,
Narrow is the way but sure,
  Heavenward leading on;
For the Master's word thou knowest,
"What unto the least thou doest
  Unto me is done."

HELPS FOR DISCUSSION

1. Read in the Catholic Encyclopedia the simple beginnings of the Little Sisters of the Poor when a French abbé asked three young workingwomen to care for an aged blind person. Then explain the expressions *asking alms, heroic feet, your weary day.* Read aloud two stanzas which describe the devoted work of the Sisters.

2. Explain the title and the last three lines of the poem.

The daughter of one of the greatest scientists of modern times tells how that scientist, her mother, lived as she worked for the good of all mankind upon her

Great Discovery

EVE CURIE

In spite of their prosaic character—or perhaps because of it—some notes written by Madame Curie in that memorable year 1898 seem to us worth quoting. Some are to be found in the margins of a book called *Family Cooking*, with respect to a recipe for gooseberry jelly: "I took eight pounds of fruit and the same weight in crystallized sugar. After an ebullition[1] of ten minutes, I passed the mixture through a rather fine sieve. I obtained fourteen pots of very good jelly, not transparent, which 'took' perfectly."

In a school notebook covered with gray linen, in which the young mother had written little Irène's weight day by day, her diet, and the appearance of her first teeth, we read under the date of July 20, 1898, some days after the publication of the discovery of polonium[2]:

"Irène says 'thanks' with her hand. She can walk very well now on all fours. She says, 'Gogli, gogli, go.' She stays in the garden all day on a carpet. She can roll, pick herself up, and sit down."

On August 15:

"Irène has cut her seventh tooth, on the lower left. She can stand for half a minute alone. For the past three days we have bathed her in the river. She cries, but today (fourth bath) she stopped crying and played with her hands in the water.

"She plays with the cat and chases him with war cries. She is not afraid of strangers any more. She sings a great deal. She gets up on the table when she is in her chair."

Three months later, on October 17, Marie noted with pride: "Irène can walk very well, and no longer goes on all fours."

On January 5, 1899: "Irène has fifteen teeth!"

Between these two notes—that of October 17, 1898, in

1. *ebullition* (ĕb'ŭ lĭsh'ŭn): boiling. 2. *polonium* (pō lō'nĭ ŭm): an important chemical substance.

which Irène no longer goes on all fours, and that of January 5, in which Irène has fifteen teeth—and a few months after the note on the gooseberry preserve, we find another note worthy of remark.

It was drawn up by Marie and Pierre Curie and a collaborator[3] called G. Bémont. Intended for the Academy of Science,[4] and published in the *Proceedings* of the session of December 26, 1898, it announced the existence of a second new chemical element in pitchblende.[5]

Some lines of this communication read as follows:

"The various reasons we have just enumerated lead us to believe that the new radioactive substance contains a new element to which we propose to give the name of RADIUM."

THINGS TO DO

1. Read about radium in the encyclopedia. Be able to tell of its discovery, source of production, and uses.

2. From the selection and from further reading, show that Madame Curie was both a good mother and a great scientist.

3. *collaborator:* co-worker. 4. *Academy of Science:* a society of learned Frenchmen united for the advancement of science. 5. *pitchblende:* a brown or black mineral which is a source of radium.

Poets often cross borders to sing the praises of the people and the places of other lands. In these three poems an Irish-American, a Spanish-American and a Frenchman sing of Poland and of Czechoslovakia.

To Ignace Paderewski

THOMAS AUGUSTINE DALY

Not yours? The softly spoken word
Whose simple native pathos stirred—
As surely as the melodies
You drew divinely from the keys—
The deeps of every soul that heard?
The faltering tongue, the practiced hand,
Whiche'er you use, great-hearted Pole!
You speak what all can understand—
The Language of the Soul.

Not ours? This land of which you tell,
Where Kosciusko[1] fought and fell,
And now a tortured nation stands,
With streaming eyes and empty hands,
Heroic in the face of hell?
Not yours alone this holy ground;
Of one great whole it is a part—
What hills, what sundering seas shall bound
The Country of the Heart?

1. *Thaddeus Kosciusko* (kŏs ĭ ŭs'kō) (*1746–1819*): a Polish patriot who volunteered to aid the colonies in the War of Independence in which he served as an engineer and was rewarded by Congress and given the rank of Brigadier-General, a large grant from public lands, and an annual pension. He returned to Poland to fight the Russians who were invading his native land. There, in action, he died.

Lady of Lidice[1]

FRAY ANGELICO CHAVEZ

From God's lofty City
My Lady looks down,
the remembered lover
of every small town,
looks down less with pity
than wistfulness over
the town that is not;
for gone are its people,
each household and cot,
the quaint Slavic steeple
that tendered them cover,
a smoldering plot.

From God's lofty City
My Lady looks down,
forever the lover
of every small town.

1. *Lidice* (lē'dē chĕ): a small town in Czechoslovakia which was completely wiped out, its inhabitants all killed, by the Germans in Second World War.

The Infant of Prague

PAUL CLAUDEL

Without—the great world dead, December snow,
But in the little room what cozy glow
Of firelight weaving shadows on the wall!
The kettle's song—peace brooding over all.
Above the beds, high on his sturdy shelf
Beneath a glass, the Blessed One Himself,
The little Christ of Prague, is looking down.
Dressed in His splendid robe, His halo-crown,
He holds the world safe in one hand and spreads
The other over sleepy little heads
That trust it so. The hearth illumines Him,
As shines the Host in sanctuary dim,
The Infant God, Who till the new day's start
Shall guard the little brothers of His heart.
Hushed as a breath exhaled, His presence fills

This simple room, the Eternal One who wills
To be the equal of the humblest here.
No hurt can come to us while He is near.
Jesus, Our Brother, watches while we rest,
Our own, as these are ours that we like best:
The lovely doll, the wooden horse, the sheep,
Safe in the corner, safe for us who sleep.
Beyond the curtained snugness of the room
Some kind of clock sounds through the snowy gloom.
The child in his warm bed, with happy sigh
That One he loves is hovering by
To fend away all danger and all harm,
Stirs drowsily, and stretches out his arm;
Makes vain attempt to rouse himself and then
Drifts back contented to his dreams again.

Man's admiration for courage may bring together nations that were once enemies. The Christian Poles and the Moslem Turks met in friendliness as they listened to a

Song at Samarcand

ERIC P. KELLY

The Polish spirit is the spirit of song, the song of sorrow, of courage, of an everlasting hope. And that song which most typifies the Polish spirit is the little hymn called the Heynal,[1] which is sounded hourly from the tower of the Church of the Trumpeter, in Krakow.[2] Its sweet notes rise from a trumpet whose brass bell is clearly discernible from the street many hundreds of feet below. And at the end of the little strain is a sudden breaking off of the melody, in what Poles call the Broken Note.

Now the story of this song and the Broken Note is known to many people throughout the world. It is the story of a youthful watchman who played a trumpet in this tower when on duty there while the Tartars[3] were besieging the city, far back in the year 1241. He did not leave when the city was taken and burned, for he had taken an oath to stay at his post

1. *Heynal* (hā'nähl). 2. *Krakow* (krä'ko͞of): a city in Poland. 3. *Tartars:* people of Tartary, of Mongol or Turkish origin.

of duty, and he was shot through the body by a Tartar arrow which sped from a hostile bow below him. He was playing at the time he was shot, and he tried to finish the Heynal as he had sworn, but as his life ebbed slowly away, he sounded a last note, which was broken off when death overtook him. Therefore, from that day to this, the Krakow trumpeters have finished the Heynal on the Broken Note.

This story had a marvelous—I might say a miraculous—sequel in the year 1943, exactly seven hundred and two years later. A Polish historian, whose word cannot be doubted, had been a prisoner in Russia, and was on his way with other soldiers to Palestine, when they happened to stop for the night in Samarcand.[4]

A priest from the Mosque[5] of Mahomet situated on the edge of the city approached them. He was greatly excited.

That which follows is quoted from a Polish newspaper published in London.

4. *Samarcand* (săm'ẽr kănd): an ancient city in central Asia, now in Soviet Russia.
5. *Mosque* (mŏsk): a place of public religious worship of the Mohammedans.

"Are you from Lechistan?" asked the holy man.

"We are."

"And are you soldiers, truly?"

"We are."

"And do you believe in God, your old God?"

"We do. We have priests; we carry the Cross."

"One more question. Have you trumpeters among you?"

"We have."

The priest grew more and more excited. Finally he cried out: "Then will you do us a great favor? Will you have your trumpeters come to our market place tomorrow evening and play in front of the Mosque, at the place where lies the tomb of the great Timur Khan?"[6]

"What shall they play?"

"The sacred hymn that is played from the balcony of the great church of your land every hour. I do not know its name—"

"Oh, that must be the Heynal," said one of the soldiers. "Yes, our trumpeters will gladly play it for you."

The priest burst into tears and hurried away. The next evening the square was crowded with the inhabitants, all of them descendants of Tartars. Excitement was visible everywhere. Young and old fell on their knees before the four Polish trumpeters sent by their commander, kissing their hands and their coats. The trumpeters did not understand what it was all about, but they advanced to the tomb of the great Tartar leader, and played the Heynal. After they played it once they were asked to play it again. They complied. Again. They played for the third time.

Then the scene became indescribable. The whole city went into a transport of joy. And the old priest, explaining, said to the Poles: "That removes the curse of our race. It happened seven hundred and two years ago that one of the warriors of the Tartars shot with a bow and killed a Polish trumpeter while he was playing a sacred song. After that a

6. *Timur Khan* (tĭ mo͞or′ kän): a great leader of the Tartars, who died in 1405, after conquering a large part of Asia.

curse fell upon our land. We were defeated in battle; we were enslaved. And an old prophet of that day said that the curse would never be taken away until soldiers from Poland, believing in the old God, and bearing trumpets, should play the same tune before the grave of Timur Khan. Thus is the prophecy fulfilled. Samarcand's dark days are over, and a new era comes when the Tartars will become a free people, and will live like brothers with all nations ever after."

Thus the Trumpeter of Krakow who died seven hundred years ago for his country and his faith is still helping to bring peace to a troubled world.

THINGS TO DO

1. Tell the story of the Trumpeter of Krakow and the Broken Note. Show that the battle of Krakow was one of the great battles between the Christian and the Moslem.

2. Explain why the Moslems at Samarcand wished reconciliation with the people they had once fought.

For Whom the Bell Tolls

JOHN DONNE

The Church is Catholic, universal,
and so are all her actions;
all that she does, belongs to all.
When she baptizes a child
that action concerns me,
and when she buries a man
that action concerns me.

No man is an island, entire of itself;
every man is a piece of the continent,
a part of the main.
Any man's death diminishes me
because I am involved in mankind.
Never send to know for whom the bell tolls:
it tolls for thee.

Radio links the nations of the world. One poet has carried the thought of linking still farther in her poem

Proof

ETHEL ROMIG FULLER

If radio's slim fingers
Can pluck a melody
From night and toss it over
A continent or sea;
If songs, like crimson roses,
Are culled from thin, blue air,
Why should mortals wonder
If God can hear their prayer?

The Ship Divine

WALT WHITMAN

One thought ever at the fore—
That in the Divine Ship, the World, breasting Time and Space,
All Peoples of the globe together sail, sail the same voyage,
    are bound to the same destination.
What whispers are these,
O lands, running ahead of you, passing under the seas?
Are all nations communing?
Is there going to be but one heart to the globe?

O my brave soul!
O farther, farther sail!
O daring joy, but safe! are they not all the seas of God?
O farther, farther, farther sail!

HELPS FOR DISCUSSION

1. From the three preceding poems, quote lines that help us to understand the unity of all people as children of God.

2. In the following selection, what principles of world peace are pointed out by Pope Pius XII?

From the watchtower of the Vatican the Vicar of Christ looks out over all the nations; and no one speaks better than does he for the unity of the nations in his plea for

Peace for the World

POPE PIUS XII

World peace will not by itself be born. It must be born of the Spirit. It must be rooted, nurtured, guarded, and preserved in the soul of man. Hatred and the lack of mutual understanding in peoples have formed a fog too dense for Reason's light yet to penetrate. But with wisdom will come crystal-clear the realization that there is only one way of escaping from the mesh in which war and hate have wrapped the world. That way is return to unity, a unity not restricted to any one people, but a universal solidarity established on the foundation of mutual interests and common destinies of all peoples.

Nations and their leaders must be governed and govern by God's laws if the world is to have peace, that peace which Saint Augustine describes as ordered harmony among men.

A peace worthy of the name can only be a peace built and consolidated in sincerity and loyalty, in justice and reality; a peace of resolute force to overcome or preclude those economic and social conditions which might, as they did in the past, lead to new conflicts; a peace that can be approved by all right-minded men of every people and every nation; a peace which future generations will gratefully regard as the happy outcome of a fearsome period; a peace that will restore human dignity and liberty.

A peace worthy of the name must be a peace with justice which, with impartial measure, gives to each what is his and exacts from each what he owes; a justice which does not give all things to all, but to all gives love and to no one does evil; a justice which is the child of truth and the mother of freedom and greatness; a peace that under the merciful guidance of God may let us so pass through temporal prosperity that we may not lose eternal happiness.

Stranger at the Peace Table

ESTHER BALDWIN YORK

There is a Stranger in the council hall
  Where nations meet to plan the peace again.
He sits unnoticed by the farther wall,
  His eyes upon the leaders among men.
His ears attend their clearly laid designs
  For living in tomorrow's homes and marts,
As though beneath their spoken words and lines
  He hears the inner voices of their hearts.

But when the delegates of all the world
  Have cried their million wants, and lists are long,
And after blueprints, charts, and plans are hurled
  In varied protest at the core of wrong,
He is our hope; He is the peace we seek.
O listen, world, and let the Stranger speak!

A Prayer for the Nations

FRAY ANGELICO CHAVEZ

O God of Life and Liberty
And the Pursuit of Happiness,
Of Faith and Hope and Charity,
By which You quicken, nurse, and bless,
Look down and in Your mercy quell
The rising storms—all is not well.

When *Faith* is failing, men deny
That Life is Yours and but a loan
For us to use and profit by;
But they now claim it as their own
To choke Life at its very source
Or stop it ere it runs its course.

When *Hope* of higher things is lost,
The make of baser ones their need
To have and hold at any cost;
And so they sacrifice to greed,
With ritual of a tyrant's nod,
The Freedom of the sons of God.

When *Love* is dead, they will pursue
Their Happiness in selfish gain,
While to their kind they prove untrue;
Yet all their running is in vain
When in this race they fail to find
That Happiness was left behind.

O God of Life in Faith, and of
The Liberty which Hope can know!
O God of Happiness through Love,
Have mercy on us here below!
Send down to earth again these three:
Firm Faith, strong Hope, sweet Charity!

RALPH I. SHEPHERD

VIII

In Christ Our Lord

From the beginning of Christianity men have heard with joy the words of Christ, "No longer do I call you servants, but I have called you friends."

The infinite God thus offers to mankind not only a divine friendliness, but a perfect friendship. In His Name men and women and children of all times and places have tried to build up His friendship and have gone out to share it with others. These are the saints, the friends most true to Christ and to their fellowmen.

Love of Jesus Christ for man and love of man for Him run like golden threads through the tapestry of Christian literature. Some of the world's greatest books, like the *Imitation of Christ*, have shown clearly how to weave these threads into the fabric of life, following the pattern of the Designer of the world.

The Bible is the world's greatest literature. Nothing that has ever been written can compete with its mighty stories of tribes and of nations; its text of godliness; its magnificent vista of the kingdom of heaven.

Our prayers are great literature as well as powerful invocation. *Our Father who art in Heaven* is an earnest poem repeated by the soul of man. Our *Hail Mary*, our Confession, our Act of Contrition, all the prayers we say at Mass and at Benediction are literary monuments to God.

For all literature stems from an impulse of the heart, but only the great literature stems from love of God and one's fellow men.

The Beatitudes

Matthew v, 3–16

Blessed are the poor in spirit,
for theirs is the kingdom of heaven.
Blessed are the meek,
for they shall possess the earth.
Blessed are they who mourn,
for they shall be comforted.
Blessed are they who hunger and thirst for justice,
for they shall be satisfied.
Blessed are the merciful,
for they shall obtain mercy.
Blessed are the pure of heart,
for they shall see God.
Blessed are the peacemakers,
for they shall be called children of God.
Blessed are they who suffer persecution for justice' sake,
for theirs is the kingdom of heaven.
Blessed are you when men reproach you, and persecute you, and, speaking falsely, say all manner of evil against you, for my sake.

Rejoice and exult, because your reward is great in heaven.

. . . .

You are the light of the world. A city set on a mountain cannot be hidden. Neither do men light a lamp and put it under the measure, but upon the lamp-stand, so as to give light to all in the house. Even so let your light shine before men, in order that they may see your good works and give glory to your Father in heaven.

Simon Peter was one of the first and most loving followers of Christ.
But even Simon Peter once wondered
how he might best serve the Lord as he set out

On the Appian Way

HENRYK SIENKIEWICZ

For thirty-three years after the death of his Master he knew no rest. Staff in hand, he had gone through the world and declared the "good tidings." His strength had been exhausted in journeys and toil, till at last, when in that city,[1] which was the head of the world, he had established the work of his Master, one bloody breath of wrath had burned it, and he saw that there was need to take up the struggle anew. And what a struggle! On one side Caesar, the Senate, the people, the legions holding the world with a circle of iron, countless cities, countless lands,—power such as the eye of man had not seen; on the other side he so bent with age and toil that his trembling hand was hardly able to carry his staff.

At times, therefore, he said to himself that it was not for him to measure with the Caesar of Rome,—that Christ alone could do that.

All these thoughts were passing through his care-filled head, when he heard the prayers of the last handful of the faithful. They, surrounding him in an ever-narrowing circle, repeated with voices of entreaty, "Hide thyself, Rabbi, and lead us away from the power of the 'Beast.' "[2]

Finally Linus also bowed his tortured head before him.

"O lord," said he, "the Redeemer commanded thee to feed His sheep, but they are here no longer, or tomorrow they will not be here; go, therefore, when thou mayst find them yet. The word of God is living still in Jerusalem, in Antioch, in Ephesus, and in other cities. What wilt thou do by remaining in Rome? If thou fall, thou wilt merely swell the triumph of the 'Beast.' The Lord has not designated the limit of John's life; Paul is a Roman citizen, they cannot condemn him without trial; but if the power of hell rise up against thee, O

1. *city:* Rome. 2. *the Beast:* Nero, the emperor of Rome, who persecuted the Christians.

teacher, those whose hearts are dejected will ask, 'Who is above Nero?' Thou art the rock on which the church of God is founded. Let us die, but permit not the victory of Antichrist over the vicegerent of God, and return not hither till the Lord has crushed him who shed innocent blood."

"Look at our tears!" repeated all who were present.

Tears flowed over Peter's face. After a while he rose, and, stretching his hands over the kneeling figures, said, "May the name of the Lord be magnified, and may His will be done!"

About dawn of the following day two dark figures were moving along the Appian Way toward the Campania.

One of them was Nazarius; the other the Apostle Peter, who was leaving Rome and his martyred co-religionists.

The sky in the east was assuming a light tinge of green, bordered gradually and more distinctly on the lower edge with saffron color. Silver-leafed trees, the white marble of villas, and the arches of aqueducts, stretching through the plain toward the city, were emerging from shade. The greenness of the sky was clearing gradually and becoming permeated with gold. Then the east began to grow rosy and illuminate the Alban Hills, which seemed marvelously beautiful, lily-colored, as if formed of rays of light alone.

The light was reflected in trembling leaves of trees, in the dewdrops. The haze grew thinner, opening wider and wider views on the plain, on the houses dotting it, on the cemeteries, on the towns, and on groups of trees, among which stood white columns of temples.

The road was empty. The villagers who took vegetables to the city had not succeeded yet, evidently, in harnessing beasts to their vehicles. From the stone blocks with which the road was paved as far as the mountains, there came a low sound from the bark shoes on the feet of the two travelers.

Then the sun appeared over the line of hills; but at once a wonderful vision struck the Apostle's eyes. It seemed to him that the golden circle, instead of rising in the sky, moved down from the heights and was advancing on the road. Peter stopped, and asked, "Seest thou that brightness approaching us?"

"I see nothing," replied Nazarius.

But Peter shaded his eyes with his hand, and said, after a while, "Some figure is coming in the gleam of the sun."

But not the slightest sound of steps reached their ears. It was perfectly still all around. Nazarius saw only that the trees were quivering in the distance, as if someone were shaking them, and the light was spreading more broadly over the plain. He looked with wonder at the Apostle.

"Rabbi! what ails thee?" cried he with alarm.

The pilgrim's staff fell from Peter's hands to the earth; his eyes were looking forward, motionless; his mouth was open; on his face were depicted astonishment, delight, rapture.

Then he threw himself on his knees, his arms stretched forward; and this cry left his lips, "O Christ! O Christ!"

He fell with his face to the earth, as if kissing someone's feet. The silence continued long; then were heard the words of the aged man, broken by sobs, "*Quo vadis, Domine?*"[3]

Nazarius did not hear the answer; but to Peter's ears came a sad and sweet voice, which said, "If thou desert my people, I am going to Rome to be crucified a second time."

The Apostle lay on the ground, his face in the dust, without motion or speech. It seemed to Nazarius that he had fainted or was dead; but he rose at last, seized the staff with trembling hands, and turned without a word toward the seven hills of the city.

3. *Quo vadis, Domine* (kwō vä′dĭs, dŏm′ĭ nē): Where are you going, Master?

The boy, seeing this, repeated as an echo, "*Quo vadis, Domine?*"

"To Rome," said the Apostle, in a low voice.

And he returned.

Paul, John, Linus, and all the faithful received him with amazement; and the alarm was the greater, since at daybreak, just after his departure, pretorians[4] had surrounded Miriam's house and searched it for the Apostle. But to every question he answered only with delight and peace, "I have seen the Lord!"

That same evening he went to the Ostian cemetery[5] to teach and baptize those who wished to bathe in the water of life.

And thenceforward he went there daily, and after him went increasing numbers. It seemed that out of every tear of a martyr new confessors were born, and that every groan on the arena found an echo in thousands of breasts. Caesar was swimming in blood, Rome and the whole pagan world was mad. But those who had enough of transgression and madness, those who were trampled upon, those whose lives were misery and oppression, all the weighed-down, all the sad, all the unfortunate, came to hear the wonderful tidings of God, Who out of love for men had given Himself to be crucified and redeem their sins.

When they found a God whom they could love, they had found that which the society of the time could not give anyone, happiness and love.

And Peter understood that neither Caesar nor all his legions could overcome the living truth,—that they could not overwhelm it with tears or blood, and that now its victory was beginning. He understood with equal force why the Lord had turned him back on the road. That city of pride, crime, wickedness, and power was beginning to be His city, and the double capital, from which would flow out upon the world government of souls and bodies.

4. *pretorians* (prē tō'rĭ ăns): picked troops from the Roman army whose chief duty was to act as bodyguard to the Roman emperor. 5. *Ostian* (ŏs'tĭ *a*n) *cemetery:* a secret meeting place, near the city of Rome, of the early Christians.

One of the most beautiful of the legends of King Arthur's Court has been retold in a great poem by an American poet. Some of the most familiar lines in American literature may be found in

The Vision of Sir Launfal

JAMES RUSSELL LOWELL

Prelude to Part First

Over his keys the musing organist,
Beginning doubtfully and far away,
First lets his fingers wander as they list,[1]
And builds a bridge from Dreamland for his lay[2]:
Then, as the touch of his loved instrument
Gives hope and fervor, nearer draws his theme,
First guessed by faint auroral flushes[3] sent
Along the wavering vista of his dream.

Not only around our infancy
Doth heaven with all its splendors lie;
Daily, with souls that cringe and plot,
We Sinais[4] climb and know it not.

Over our manhood bend the skies;
Against our fallen and traitor lives
The great winds utter prophecies;
With our faint hearts the mountain strives;
Its arms outstretched, the druid wood
Waits with its benedicite[5];
And to our age's drowsy blood
Still shouts the inspiring sea.

At the devil's booth are all things sold,
Each ounce of dross[6] costs its ounce of gold;
For a cap and bells our lives we pay,

1. *list:* please, wish. 2. *lay:* song, poem. 3. *auroral flushes:* the first rosy hints of dawn. 4. *Sinais* (sī'nīz): Mount Sinai was the Biblical mountain of the Prophet Moses. 5. *benedicite* (bĕn ē dĭs'ĭ tē): a blessing. 6. *dross:* something without worth or value.

Bubbles we buy with a whole soul's tasking:
'Tis Heaven alone that is given away,
'Tis only God may be had for the asking;
No price is set on the lavish summer;
June may be had by the poorest comer.

And what is so rare as a day in June?
Then, if ever, come perfect days;
Then Heaven tries earth if it be in tune,
And over it softly her warm ear lays;
Whether we look, or whether we listen,
We hear life murmur, or see it glisten;
Every clod feels a stir of might,
An instinct within it that reaches and towers,
And, groping blindly above it for light,
Climbs to a soul in grass and flowers;
The flush of life may well be seen
Thrilling back over hills and valleys;
The cowslip startles in meadows green,
The buttercup catches the sun in its chalice,
And there's never a leaf nor a blade too mean
To be some happy creature's palace;
The little bird sits at his door in the sun,
Atilt like a blossom among the leaves,
And lets his illumined being o'errun
With the deluge of summer it receives;
His mate feels the eggs beneath her wings,
And the heart in her dumb breast flutters and sings;
He sings to the wide world, and she to her nest,—
In the nice ear of Nature which song is the best?

Joy comes, grief goes, we know not how;
Everything is happy now,
Everything is upward striving;
'Tis as easy now for the heart to be true
As for grass to be green or skies to be blue,—
'Tis the natural way of living:
Who knows whither the clouds have fled?

In the unscarred heaven they leave no wake[7];
And the eyes forget the tears they have shed,
The heart forgets its sorrow and ache;
The soul partakes the season's youth,
And the sulphurous rifts of passion and woe
Lie deep 'neath a silence pure and smooth,
Like burnt-out craters healed with snow.
What wonder if Sir Launfal now
Remembered the keeping of his vow?

Part First

I

"My golden spurs now bring to me,
And bring to me my richest mail,
For tomorrow I go over land and sea
In search of the Holy Grail.[8]
Shall never a bed for me be spread,
Nor shall a pillow be under my head,

7. *wake:* trace or track.

8. *Holy Grail:* in English legends it was held to be the chalice used by Christ at the Last Supper with his disciples, from which it passed into the possession of Joseph of Arimathea, who later brought it to Britain. After the death of its keeper, the Grail vanished, and the great quest for it began.

Till I begin my vow to keep;
Here on the rushes[9] will I sleep,
And perchance there may come a vision true
Ere day create the world anew."
  Slowly Sir Launfal's eyes grew dim,
  Slumber fell like a cloud on him,
And into his soul the vision flew.

II

The crows flapped over by twos and threes;
In the pool drowsed the cattle up to their knees,
  The little birds sang as if it were
  The one day of summer in all the year,
And the very leaves seemed to sing on the trees:
The castle alone in the landscape lay
Like an outpost of winter, dull and gray:
'Twas the proudest hall in the North Countree,
And never its gates might opened be,
Save to lord or lady of high degree;
Summer besieged it on every side,
But the churlish stone her assaults defied;
She could not scale the chilly wall,
Though around it for leagues her pavilions tall
Stretched left and right,
Over the hills and out of sight;
  Green and broad was every tent,
  And out of each a murmur went
Till the breeze fell off at night.

III

The drawbridge dropped with a surly clang,
And through the dark arch a charger sprang,
Bearing Sir Launfal, the maiden knight.[10]
In his gilded mail, that flamed so bright

9. *rushes:* a floor covering used in medieval times. 10. *maiden knight:* untried, knight inexperienced in battle.

It seemed the dark castle had gathered all
Those shafts the fierce sun had shot over its wall
   In his siege of three hundred summers long,
And, binding them all in one blazing sheaf,
   Had cast them forth: so, young and strong,
And lightsome as a locust-leaf,
Sir Launfal flashed forth in his maiden mail,
To seek in all climes for the Holy Grail.

IV

It was morning on hill and stream and tree,
   And morning in the young knight's heart;
Only the castle moodily
Rebuffed the gifts of the sunshine free,
   And gloomed by itself apart;
The season brimmed all other things up
Full as the rain fills the pitcher-plant's[11] cup.

V

As Sir Launfal made morn through the darksome gate,
   He was 'ware of a leper, crouched by the same,
Who begged with his hand and moaned as he sate;
   And a loathing over Sir Launfal came;
The sunshine went out of his soul with a thrill,
   The flesh 'neath his armor 'gan shrink and crawl,
And midway its leap his heart stood still
   Like a frozen waterfall;
For this man, so foul and bent of stature,
Rasped harshly against his dainty nature,
And seemed the one blot on the summer morn,—
So he tossed him a piece of gold in scorn.

11. *pitcher-plant:* a swamp plant whose petals open and form a cup.

VI

The leper raised not the gold from the dust:
"Better to me the poor man's crust,
Better the blessing of the poor,
Though I turn me empty from his door;
That is no true alms which the hand can hold;
He gives nothing but worthless gold
  Who gives from a sense of duty;
But he who gives but a slender mite,
And gives to that which is out of sight,
  That thread of the all-sustaining Beauty
Which runs through all and doth all unite,—
The hand cannot clasp the whole of his alms,
The heart outstretches its eager palms,
For a god goes with it and makes it store
To the soul that was starving in darkness before."

Part Second

I

There was never a leaf on bush or tree,
The bare boughs rattle shudderingly;
The river was dumb and could not speak,
  For the weaver Winter its shroud had spun;
A single crow on the tree-top bleak
  From his shining feathers shed off the cold sun;
Again it was morning, but shrunk and cold,
As if her veins were sapless and old,
And she rose up decrepitly
For a last dim look at earth and sea.

II

Sir Launfal turned from his own hard gate,
For another heir in his earldom sate;
An old, bent man, worn out and frail,
He came back from seeking the Holy Grail;
Little he recked of his earldom's loss,

No more on his surcoat[12] was blazoned the cross.
But deep in his soul the sign he wore,
The badge of the suffering and the poor.

III

Sir Launfal's raiment thin and spare
Was idle mail 'gainst the barbèd air,
For it was just at the Christmas time;
So he mused, as he sat, of a sunnier clime,
And sought for a shelter from cold and snow
In the light and warmth of long ago;
He sees the snake-like caravan crawl
O'er the edge of the desert, black and small,
Then nearer and nearer, till, one by one,
He can count the camels in the sun,
As over the red-hot sands they pass
To where, in its slender necklace of grass,
The little spring laughed and leapt in the shade,
And with its own self like an infant played,
And waved its signal of palms.

12. *surcoat:* a coat worn over armor.

IV

"For Christ's sweet sake, I beg an alms";
The happy camels may reach the spring,
But Sir Launfal sees naught save the gruesome thing,
The leper, lank as the rain-blanched bone,
That cowers beside him, a thing as lone
And white as the ice-isles of Northern seas
In the desolate horror of his disease.

V

And Sir Launfal said, "I behold in thee
An image of Him who died on the tree;
Thou also hast had thy crown of thorns,
Thou also hast had the world's buffets and scorns,
And to thy life were not denied
The wounds in the hands and feet and side:
Mild Mary's Son, acknowledge me;
Behold, through him, I give to Thee!"

VI

Then the soul of the leper stood up in his eyes
   And looked at Sir Launfal, and straightway he
Remembered in what a haughtier guise
   He had flung an alms to leprosie,
When he girt his young life up in gilded mail
And set forth in search of the Holy Grail.
The heart within him was ashes and dust;
He parted in twain his single crust,
He broke the ice on the streamlet's brink,
And gave the leper to eat and drink,
'Twas a moldy crust of coarse brown bread,
   'Twas water out of a wooden bowl,—
Yet with fine wheaten bread was the leper fed,
   And 'twas red wine he drank with his thirsty soul.

VII

As Sir Launfal mused with a downcast face,
A light shone round about the place;
The leper no longer crouched at his side,
But stood before him glorified,
Shining and tall and fair and straight
As the pillar that stood by the Beautiful Gate,—
Himself the Gate whereby men can
Enter the temple of God in Man.

VIII

His words were shed softer than leaves from the pine,
And they fell on Sir Launfal as snows on the brine,
That mingle their softness and quiet in one
With the shaggy unrest they float down upon;
And the voice that was calmer than silence said,
"Lo, it is I, be not afraid!
In many climes, without avail,
Thou has spent thy life for the Holy Grail;
Behold it is here,—this cup which thou
Didst fill at the streamlet for Me but now;
This crust is my body broken for thee,
This water his blood that died on the tree;
The Holy Supper is kept, indeed,
In whatso we share with another's need;
Not what we give, but what we share,
For the gift without the giver is bare;
Who gives himself with his alms feeds three,
Himself, his hungering neighbor, and me."

IX

Sir Launfal awoke as from a swound[13]:
"The Grail in my castle here is found!
Hang my idle armor up on the wall,
Let it be the spider's banquet hall;
He must be fenced with stronger mail
Who would seek and find the Holy Grail."

13. *swound:* swoon.

X

The castle gate stands open now,
And the wanderer is welcome to the hall
As the hangbird[14] is to the elm-tree bough;
No longer scowl the turrets tall,
The Summer's long siege at last is o'er;
When the first poor outcast went in at the door,
She entered with him in disguise,
And mastered the fortress by surprise;
There is no spot she loves so well on ground,
She lingers and smiles there the whole year round;
The meanest serf on Sir Launfal's land
Has hall and bower at his command;
And there's no poor man in the North Countree
But is lord of the earldom as much as he.

HELPS FOR DISCUSSION

1. How does the poet think of himself in the Prelude? What thoughts does the music awaken? What is the theme of the Prelude?

2. Read aloud the lines in the Prelude that describe early summer. What sights and sounds rejoice mankind? What is the effect upon man's soul? Read stanzas III and IV in Part First and explain how the season is reflected in Sir Launfal's life?

3. Read the contrasting winter scene in Part Second. Find the lines that show its correspondence to the life of Sir Launfal.

4. What words of Sir Launfal express the deep meaning of the poem? How do these words embody the teaching of Jesus: "As long as you did it for one of these, the least of my brethren, you did it for me" (Matthew xxv, 40)?

5. What was the Vision that Sir Launfal saw in his dream? How did the Vision change the course of his life?

6. The poem is famed for its beauty of language, as well as of thought. What do such figures of speech as the following bring to your mind: *catches the sun in its chalice*; *deluge of summer*; *the weaver Winter*; *in its slender necklace of grass, the little spring laughed*? Find other expressions of poetic loveliness.

14. *hangbird:* a Baltimore oriole, called a hangbird because its nest is suspended.

The Fool's Prayer

EDWARD ROWLAND SILL

The royal feast was done; the King
Sought some new sport to banish care,
And to his jester cried: "Sir Fool,
Kneel now, and make for us a prayer!"

The jester doffed his cap and bells,
And stood the mocking court before;
They could not see the bitter smile
Behind the painted grin he wore.

He bowed his head, and bent his knee
Upon the Monarch's silken stool;
His pleading voice arose: "O Lord,
Be merciful to me, a fool!

"No pity, Lord, could change the heart
  From red with wrong to white as wool;
The rod must heal the sin: but Lord,
  Be merciful to me, a fool!

" 'Tis not by guilt the onward sweep
  Of truth and right, O Lord, we stay:
'Tis by our follies that so long
  We hold the earth from heaven away.

"These clumsy feet, still in the mire,
  Go crushing blossoms without end;
These hard, well-meaning hands we thrust
  Among the heart-strings of a friend.

"The ill-timed truth we might have kept—
  Who knows how sharp it pierced and stung?
The word we had not sense to say—
  Who knows how grandly it had rung?

"Our faults no tenderness should ask,
  The chastening stripes must cleanse them all;
But for our blunders—oh, in shame
  Before the eyes of heaven we fall.

"Earth bears no balsam for mistakes;
  Men crown the knave, and scourge the tool
That did his will; but Thou, O Lord,
  Be merciful to me, a fool!"

The room was hushed; in silence rose
  The King, and sought his gardens cool,
And walked apart, and murmured low,
  "Be merciful to me, a fool!"

The woman who had been queen of France and queen of Scotland
and the man who discovered America wrote memorable prayers. They are

Prayer before Execution

MARY STUART, QUEEN OF SCOTS

O merciful Father, my hope is in Thee!
O gracious Redeemer, deliver Thou me!
My bondage bemoaning, with sorrowful groaning,
I long to be free;
Lamenting, relenting, and humbly repenting,
O Jesu, my Saviour, I languish for Thee.

Version of John Fawcett, 1782

A Prayer of Action

CHRISTOPHER COLUMBUS

It is the Lord who hath inspired me with the right thought, and who will lend me His aid to bring the work to a happy conclusion. For I know, and it is my firm conviction—with which not even a breath of doubt is mingled—that His most High Majesty hath occasioned all that is good, further that no opinion over any matter is allowed without the agreement from Above. When Peter sprang into the lake, he walked upon the waters so long as his faith remained firm; the mountains will obey him that has faith, though it be not greater than a millet-seed; he who believes, let him ask; knock and it shall be opened unto you. Today also nobody need fear to enter with clean hands in the name of the Redeemer upon an undertaking which is just and fulfilled honourably in His service. Our Lord hath according to His pleasure assigned a purpose to each individual thing; He is the Patron of every potentiality of our human nature. O how overwhelmingly good is the Lord, Whose Will is that mankind should be active and also provides them with the means of being so. Day and night and every moment of our existence should we humbly give Him thanks.

Of Works Done Out of Charity

THOMAS À KEMPIS

No evil should be done either for any thing in the world, or for the love of any man; but for the profit of one that stands in need, a good work is sometimes freely to be given up for a while, or rather to be changed for a better.

For this is not the undoing of a good work, but the exchanging it for a better.

Without charity the outward work profits nothing; but whatever is done through charity, be it never so little and contemptible, all becomes fruitful.

For God weighs more with how much love a man works than how much he does.

He does much who loves much.

He does much who does well what he does.

He does well who serves rather the common weal than his own will.

That seems often to be charity which is rather yearning of the flesh; because natural inclination, our own self-will, hope of reward, love of our own ease, will seldom be wanting.

He that has true and perfect charity, seeks himself in nothing, but desires only the glory of God to be wrought in all things.

He envies no man, because he loves no private joy; nor does he desire to rejoice in himself; but above all good things to be made happy in God.

He attributes nothing of good to any man, but refers it wholly to God, from whom all things proceed as from their fount; in whom as their last end all the saints rest with joy.

Oh, he that had but one spark of true charity would doubtless perceive that all earthly things are full of vanity.

HELPS FOR DISCUSSION

1. From what book is this selection quoted (see page 435)?

2. How does Thomas à Kempis explain the difference between selfish charity and *true and perfect* charity? What sentences help you to understand the meaning of *friendliness*?

The Tumbler of Our Lady

POEM BY HENRY ADAMS

NARRATIVE BY WALTER CROARKIN

A tumbler, a street acrobat, was disgusted with the world and was fortunate enough to obtain admission into the famous monastery of Clairvaux,[1] where Saint Bernard once was blessed by the Virgin's presence. Ignorant at best, and especially ignorant of letters, music, and the offices of a religious society, he found himself unable to join in the services:

For he had learned no other thing
Than to tumble, dance, and spring;
Leaping and vaulting, that he knew,
But nothing better could he do.
He could not say his prayers by rote;
Not "Pater Noster"; not a note;
Not "Ave Mary" nor the Creed;
Nothing to help his soul in need.

1. *Clairvaux* (klĕr'vō'): a village in France, the cite of the Cistercian Abbey founded by Saint Bernard.

Tormented by the sense of his uselessness to the society whose bread he ate without giving a return in service, and afraid of being expelled as a useless member, one day while the bells were calling to Mass he hid in the crypt,[2] and in despair began to soliloquize[3] before the Virgin's altar, at the same spot, one hopes, where the Virgin might have shown herself, in her infinite bounty, to Saint Bernard a hundred years before.

"Ha!" said he, "how I am ashamed!
To sing his part goes now each priest,
And I stand here, a tethered beast,
Who nothing do but browse and feed,
And waste the food that others need.
Shall I say nothing, and stand still?
No! by God's Mother, but I will!
She shall not think me here for naught:
At least I'll do what I've been taught!
At least I'll serve in my own way
God's Mother in her church today.
The others serve to pray and sing;
I will serve to leap and spring."
Then he strips him of his gown,
Lays it on the altar down;
Not to show his body bare,
But keeps a jacket, soft and thin,
Almost a shirt to tumble in,
Clothed in this supple woof of maille[4]
His strength and health and form showed well,
And when his belt is buckled fast,
Toward the Virgin turns at last:
Very humbly makes his prayer:
"Lady!" says he, "to your care
I commit my soul and frame.
Gentle Virgin, gentle Dame,
Do not despise what I shall do,
For I ask only to please you,

2. *crypt* (krĭpt): a vault underground. 3. *soliloquize* (sō lĭl'ō kwīz): talk to oneself. 4. *woof of maille* (mail): a woven fabric of metal, known as a coat of mail.

To serve you like an honest man,
So help me, God, the best I can.
I cannot chant, nor can I read,
But I can show you here instead,
All my best tricks to make you laugh,
And so shall be as though a calf
Should leap and jump before its dam.
Lady, who never yet could blame
Those who serve you well and true,
All that I am, I am for you."

Then he begins to jump about,
High and low, and in and out,
Straining hard with might and main;
Then, falling on his knees again,
Before the image bows his face:
"By your pity! by your grace!"
Says he, "Ha! my gentle queen,
Do not despise my offering!"

In his earnestness he exerted himself until, at the end of his strength, he lay exhausted and unconscious on the altar steps. Pleased with his own exhibition, and satisfied the Virgin was equally pleased, he continued these devotions every day, until at last his constant and singular absence from the regular services attracted the curiosity of a monk, who kept watch on him and reported his eccentric exercise to the Abbot.

The medieval monasteries seem to have been gently administered. Indeed, this has been made the chief reproach of them, and the excuse for robbing them for the benefit of a more energetic crown and nobility who tolerated no beggars or idleness but their own; at least, it is safe to say that few well regulated and economically administered modern charities would have the patience of the Abbot of Clairvaux, who instead of calling up the weak-minded tumbler and sending him back to the world to earn a living by his profession, went with his informant to the crypt, to see for himself what the strange report meant. We have seen at Chartres[5] what a

5. *Chartres* (shär'tr'): a famous cathedral in the town of the same name in France.

crypt may be, and how easily one might hide in its shadows while Mass is said at the altars. The Abbot and his informant hid themselves behind a column in the shadow and watched the whole performance to its end when the exhausted tumbler dropped unconscious on the steps of the altar, with the words:

"Lady!" says he, "no more I can,
But truly I'll come back again!"

You can imagine the dim crypt; the tumbler lying unconscious beneath the image of the Virgin; the Abbot peering from the shadow of the column, and wondering what sort of discipline he could inflict for this unforeseen infraction of rule; when suddenly, before he could decide what next to do, the vault above the altar, of its own accord, opened:

The Abbot strains his eye to see,
And from the vaulting, suddenly,
A Lady steps,—so glorious,—
Beyond all thought so precious,—
Her robes so rich, so nobly worn,—
So rare the gems the robes adorn,—
As never yet so fair was born.
Along with her the angels were,
Archangels stood beside her there;
Round about the tumbler group
To give him solace, bring him hope;
And when round him in ranks they stood,
His whole heart felt its strength renewed.
So they haste to give him aid
Because their wills are only made
To serve the service of their Queen,
Most precious gem the earth has seen.
And the Lady, gentle, true,
Holds in her hand a towel new;
Fans him with her hand divine
While he lies before the shrine.
The kind Lady, full of grace,
Fans his neck, his throat, his face!

Fans him herself to give him air!
Labors, herself, to help him there!
The Lady gives herself to it;
The poor man takes no heed of it;
For he knows not and cannot see
That he has such fair company.

Beyond this we need not care to go. If you cannot feel the color and quality—the union of naïveté[6] and art, the refinement, the infinite delicacy, and tenderness—of this little poem, then nothing will matter much to you.

THINGS TO DO

1. The story of "The Tumbler of Our Lady" has been made into a drama and an opera. Describe what might be the acts and scenes of the drama. Discuss songs and musical accompaniments that might be arranged for the opera.

2. Plan and rehearse a dramatic reading of the selection. Choose one reader to present the prose sections and another to read the words spoken by the Tumbler. Arrange the rest of the poem as choral reading. Give your presentation for another class.

3. Consider in silence your own talents and how you would wish to use them for the honoring of God's Mother.

6. *naïveté* (nä ēv'tā'): the quality of being unaffectedly simple.

Lovely Things

SISTER M. NOEL

I shall remember lovely things:
The thrilling joy when a bluebird wings
Its way through the dusk of eventide
To a quiet tree on the mountain side;
The dainty flit of a butterfly;
The delicate blue of a drifting sky;
The silent call of the evening star;
The rose's perfume wafted far.
I shall remember lovely things:
A smile, a tear, a heart that sings.

Barter

SARA TEASDALE

Life has loveliness to sell—
All beautiful and splendid things,
Blue waves whitened on a cliff,
Climbing fire that sways and sings,
And children's faces looking up
Holding wonder like a cup.

Life has loveliness to sell—
Music like a curve of gold,
Scent of pine trees in the rain,
Eyes that love you, arms that hold,
And for your spirit's still delight,
Holy thoughts that star the night.

Spend all you have for loveliness,
Buy it and never count the cost;
For one white singing hour of peace
Count many a year of strife well lost,
And for a breath of ecstasy
Give all you have been, or could be.

L'Envoi

RUDYARD KIPLING

[Choir to be arranged in three parts: low, medium, and high.]

Medium When Earth's last picture is painted and the tubes are twisted and dried,
When the oldest colors are faded, and the youngest critic has died,
All We shall rest, and, faith, we shall need it—lie down for an aeon[1] or two,
Till the Master of all Good Workmen shall put us to work anew!

Medium And those that were good shall be happy: they shall sit in the golden chair;
High They shall splash at a ten-league canvas with brushes of comets' hair;
Medium They shall find real saints to draw from—Magdalene, Peter, and Paul;
Low They shall work for an age at a sitting and never be tired at all!

Medium And only the Master shall praise us, and only the Master shall blame;
High And no one shall work for money, and no one shall work for fame,
All But each for the joy of the working, and each, in his separate star,
Shall draw the Thing as he sees It, for the God of things as They are!

PICTURES OF THE LIFE OF CHRIST

The beauty, the sorrows, and the majesty of the life of Christ are exalted reasons for great art. Among great pictures are *The Good Samaritan*, by REMBRANDT; *The Raising of Lazarus*, by GIOTTO; *Among the Lowly*, by LHERMITTE; *The Last Supper*, by DA VINCI; *Christ in the Garden of Gethsemane*, by DELAROCHE; *The Crucifixion*, by RUBENS.

1. *aeon* (ē'ŏn): an immeasurable period of time.

Only those who have known suffering and sorrow and repentance for sins can realize what it means to find for oneself

The Fragrance of Roses

MICHAEL WILLIAMS

The Carmelite monastery was situated in the house where Robert Louis Stevenson's widow had lived after Stevenson's death in Samoa[1]; a house in which the great romancer, I am sure, would have delighted to dwell. It was perched on the steep side of Russian Hill, overlooking San Francisco Bay and facing toward Mount Tamalpais,[2] with Alcatraz[3] Island lying at the foot of the hill. It reminded you of a sympathetic picture-setting for one of Stevenson's own stories.

Passing up a short flight of stairs protected by an iron railing of peculiar beauty, I entered the door where a sign said: "Enter without knocking." I found myself in a small room with one or two bookcases, and a bell-pull hanging against the wall. I was about to ring the bell when I saw a slip of paper pinned under it saying: "Community in retreat: do not ring the bell. Leave messages and petitions at the turn."

Retreat? What was that? And "turn," what could that be? I did not know; but what I did know now was that my usual bad luck had followed me to the door of Mount Carmel. I had at last dragged myself there, ready to knock—and now I was forbidden to knock. I must go away. Would I ever try again? It was unlikely. A mood, a day, had come in which I had experimented; but the experiment had failed; I would go away; probably not to try again.

There was a large picture of Saint Teresa of Lisieux on the dusky wall of the little room. And in the bookcases were a number of booklets concerning her. There was a copy of a periodical devoted to chronicling the "favors" attributed to her intercessory power. I stopped to look these over and

1. *Samoa* (sä mō'ä): a group of islands in the Pacific Ocean. Robert Louis Stevenson spent his last days there. 2. *Mount Tamalpais* (tăm ăl pis'): a high mountain and scenic resort northwest of San Francisco. 3. *Alcatraz* (ăl kȧ träs'): an island in the harbor of San Francisco on which are located United States fortifications and a Federal prison.

wished that I could buy some of them. Then I thought: "I have come, and I am turned away; but why not leave a message?" And I drew a sheaf of paper from my pockets, and a pencil and scribbled a few words.

"To the Mother Prioress:

"I have just finished reading, at the recommendation of Bishop Hanna, the books concerning 'Sister Teresa; The Little Flower of Jesus,' and 'Sister Elizabeth: The Praise of Glory.' I am a writer, 36 years old, married, with two children. I am trying to reach Jesus Christ. I am a great sinner. I was born into the Church but have fallen away during twenty years.

"Will you pray for my conversion to Christ, dear Mother, asking Sisters Elizabeth and Teresa also to pray for me? Sister Teresa has brought about many conversions. Please pray that she may intercede for me. Surely God will grant her prayer."

As I folded the scrap of paper, suddenly in the dark doorway that led to the interior, a nun appeared, and advanced

into the room saying: "Is there anything I can do for you?" She was an Out-Sister,[4] as I learned afterward. I said, I had come to see the Prioress, if it were possible. "No, the community is in retreat," the Sister said; "no visitors are received." But it was permissible to buy books and these were selected. I gave a coin in payment and the nun said she must go inside for change. I gave her the note, then, asking her if she would deliver it to the Prioress. She bowed and withdrew.

She was gone for quite some time, and when she returned, she said to me: "Reverend Mother says if you will come to the speak-room, she will see you. Please come this way."

I followed her down a little dark passageway into a little dark room, whereupon she immediately left me and shut the door. In the wall, high up, a barred window admitted a dim light. There was a crucifix on the wall, a picture or two, and a holy water font. Two chairs stood on the bare floor in front of a grating[5] that reached from the ceiling to within two or three feet from the floor. Behind this grating, some two feet distant, was another grating, covered on the inside with a black curtain, and save for the passing of a cable car outside, now and then, there was no sound to break the silence.

Then I heard a voice: a clear-toned, energetic woman's voice out of the silence, that said, "Praised be Jesus Christ!"

Astonished, I said nothing in reply. What could I say? This Jesus whom I had denied—how could I praise Him?

Then the voice went on: "Is there somebody in the room?"

I divined that the speaker was behind the black curtain, within the second screen.

"Yes," I answered, "yes, Reverend Mother."

"Oh, yes! I am so glad. I read your note. We are in retreat, you know. We don't receive visitors while we are in retreat, but I felt I must make an exception. So you have read Sister Teresa?"

I replied—I know not what—but soon my lips were unsealed, and my heart and soul, as well.

I told the invisible listener how unhappy I was, and why;

4. *Out-Sister:* one who is not cloistered. 5. *grating:* a lattice of cross-barred wood or metal.

how I had been searching after God in strange places, and how Sister Teresa had led me to this place, where out of the surrounding darkness and out of the brooding depths of silence and mystery, the voice had spoken, which said: "Praised be Jesus Christ!"

By and by, I rose to go.

"You will please wait for a minute, while I give Sister Gertrude a relic of Sister Teresa for you," said the voice. "And the prayers will begin at once. We will storm Heaven for you. And you will come again?"

"I will."

And presently I was out in the street, walking homewards, happy with the little packet of books in my hand. The Out-Sister had said she had placed the relic of Sister Teresa in the packet.

The sun was shining as I went along, a golden, reddish sunshine of the late afternoon and I passed a little open space of greenery, a hillside park, walking like a person in a dream for whom, as the dream slowly fades, the distant horizon shines like silver, and secret stars drop down the sky, slowly, one by one, like big drops of violet rain.

And, just then, as I walked past the little green hill, feeling as if the golden-red sunshine were inside me as well as shining all about me, and upon me, there fell about me a breath from Heaven—I inhaled a potent, penetrating perfume, stronger and stranger by far than rich and subtle incense, simpler by far than the odor of yerba buena[6] or of mint or violets; sweet, most rare, and wonderful.

I remember how I lifted the bundle of books to my face thinking, with an inward smile: "The good nuns are women still. These books have been lying too near the scent bottle or the powder box." But, instantly, the perfume was gone. There was no odor, none at all, emanating from the bundle of books.

"Perhaps it was a whiff from some flowers or herb in the grass of the little park," and then I thought no more about it,

6. *yerba buena* (yĕr′bä bwā′nä): trailing mint of California with small white flowers.

but walked on, trying to retain my strange new sense of the other-world, striving not to lose it, and not to find myself back again in the gray and chilly world outside that world of warmth and light and gladness.

Then I reached the door of my apartment house, down in the heart of the city, and, as I entered it, all at once, the breath from Heaven breathed once more upon me. I was in the midst of a pulsation of perfume, more exotic than the richest incense, yet simpler and more familiar than the homeliest scents that are distilled by all sweet flowers, and rare and wonderful.

Whereupon, I remembered, and I knew. I remembered that the account of Sister Teresa's manifestations are full of such instances of psychic[7] odors. She is the Little Flower. She said just before her death: "I will let fall a shower of roses." After her death she came back to earth in vision, and said: "I will make the shower of roses a torrent." She asked God, before she died, to let her soul stay, till time is over, near the earth in order to do good for poor souls in this world.

And at my feet, even at mine, at the feet of the stained, broken, wandering writer, she had thrown a secret rose: a mystical rose, the rose of my desire.

HELPS FOR DISCUSSION

The Carmelite Sisters lead a contemplative life. Much of their time is spent in prayer in the presence of the Blessed Sacrament, and the rest is occupied with household work and other occupations. Their life is necessarily strict, their fasting is severe. They have many opportunities for increasing virtue. Because they are living solely for Christ, their lives are usually very happy.

1. Why did the writer visit Mount Carmel? What trouble of mind did his note reveal and what request did he make?

2. Why did the Reverend Mother allow the visitor to come into her unseen presence even though she was in Retreat? What was given to him and what was promised?

3. What had been Sister Teresa's prayer to God? How did the Little Flower manifest her help to a "stained, broken, wandering writer"?

7. *psychic* (sī'kĭk): pertaining to the mind.

Up-Hill

CHRISTINA ROSSETTI

Does the road wind up-hill all the way?
  Yes, to the very end.
Will the day's journey take the whole long day?
  From morn to night, my friend.

But is there for the night a resting-place?
  A roof for when the slow dark hours begin.
May not the darkness hide it from my face?
  You cannot miss that inn.

Shall I meet other wayfarers at night?
  Those who have gone before.
Then must I knock, or call when just in sight?
  They will not keep you waiting at that door.

Shall I find comfort, travel-sore and weak?
  Of labor you shall find the sum.
Will there be beds for me and all who seek?
  Yea, beds for all who come.

Literature, like a great searchlight, brings out beauties not often seen. A priest-poet found them in

Wide Vista

FREDERICK WILLIAM FABER

Let us sit down upon the top of this fair hill.

The clear sunshine and the bright air flow into us in streams of life and gladness, while our thoughts are lifted up to God, and our hearts quietly expand to love. Beneath us is that beautiful rolling plain, with its dark masses of summer foliage sleeping in the sun for miles away, in the varying shades of blue and green, according to the distance or the clouds.

There at our feet is the gigantic city, gleaming with an ivory whiteness beneath its uplifted but perpetual canopy of smoke. The villa-spotted hills beyond it, its almost countless spires, its one huge many-steepled palace, and its solemn presiding dome, its old bleached tower, and its squares of crowded shipping—it all lies below us in the peculiar sunshine of its own misty magnificence. There, in every variety of joy and misery, of elevation and depression, three million souls are working out their complicated destinies.

Close around us, the air is filled with the songs of rejoicing birds, or the pleased hum of the insects that are drinking the sunbeams, and blowing their tiny trumpets as they weave and unweave their mazy dance. The flowers breathe sweetly, and the leaves of the glossy shrubs are spotted with bright creatures in painted surcoat or gilded panoply, while the blue dome above seems both taller and bluer than common, and is ringing with the loud peals of the unseen larks, as the steeples of the city ring for the nation's victory.

Far off from the river-flat comes the booming of the cannon, and here, all unstartled, round and round the pond, a fleet of young perch are sailing in the sun, slowly and undisturbedly as if they had a very grave enjoyment of their little lives.

What a mingled scene it is of God and man! and all so bright, so beautiful, so diversified, so calm, opening out such foundations of deep reflection, and of simple-hearted gratitude to our Heavenly Father.

The custom of adding the angelic salutation, the "Ave Maria," to the Lord's Prayer was first introduced in the tenth century. By the end of the following century it had been adopted in the Office of the Church. Ever since, as reminder of the mystery of the Incarnation, we repeat at sunrise, noon, and at sunset

THE ANGELUS

The Angel of the Lord announced unto Mary, and she conceived of the Holy Ghost.
Hail, Mary, full of grace, the Lord is with thee; blessed art thou amongst women, and blessed is the fruit of thy womb, Jesus.
Behold the handmaid of the Lord: be it done unto me according to Thy word.
And the Word was made flesh, and dwelt among us.
Hail, Mary . . . . .
Pray for us, O holy Mother of God.
That we may be made worthy of the promises of Christ.

The Angelus

CARDINAL WISEMAN

The bell, at the appointed hour, gives the signal; and upon it every occupation, be it of study or recreation, is suspended. The solitary student in his cell puts down his pen, and turns to his little domestic memorials of piety, picture, or crucifix, and joins his absent brethren in prayer.

The professor pauses in his lecture, and, kneeling at the head of his class, leads the way to their responses. The little knot engaged in cheerful talk drop their mirth and contend more pleasantly in the verses of that angelic prayer. Nay, even the sport and play of youth and childhood are interrupted, to give a few moments to more serious thoughts.

Well might the Angelus bell have inscribed upon it, "At evening, morn, and noon I will call out, and give the angelic

Annunciation." For this is truly the order of the ecclesiastical day; and in southern countries of more Catholic atmosphere, of the civil. With first vespers comes in the festival; and the Ave Maria, with its clattering peal, rings in the new day. We own we like it. We love not the old day to slip away from us, and the new one to steal in, "like a thief in the night," upon our unconscious being, at the hour when ghosts walk, and when nature, abroad and within us, most awfully personates death.

We like the day to die even as a good Christian would wish, with the heavens a mild splendor above, enriched in hues as its close approaches; with golden visions and loved shapes, however fantastic, floating in clouds around; with whispered prayer, and a cheering passing bell, and the comfort that, when gloom has overspread all, a new, though unseen, day has risen to the spirit; that the vigil only has expired, that so the festival day may break.

Then, when we awake once more to sense and consciousness, let the joyful peal arouse us, with the first dawn of day and reason, to commemorate that mystery which alone has made the day worth living; and greet, with the natural, the spiritual Sun, the day-spring from on high, that rose on benighted man and chased away the darkness and the shadow of death wherein he sat.

Then will the Angelus bell call out to us aloud, and make the joyful Annunciation, speaking in angels' words and angels' tones, to the gladsome, to the anxious, and to the weary heart —gladsome at morn, anxious at noon, weary at eve.

Truly, it was a heavenly thought that suggested the appointment of both time and thing. For what can chime so well with the first of those feelings and its season as the glorious news that "the Lord's angel" hath brought to earth such tidings as his? What can suit the second better than to speak resignation in Mary's words, "Behold thy servant, or handmaid"? What can refresh the thirst, and cast forward bright rays into the gloom of approaching night, more than the thought that God's own Eternal Word dwelleth ever amongst us, our comforter and help?

Sometimes the loveliest lilies of the spirit grow in the mire of misery.
In the Second World War a young French priest volunteered to go into Germany as a workman in order that he might serve as chaplain to men of his own people imprisoned there in forced labor. Out of his sufferings came one of the finest books of wartime record, ending with the remarkable chapter he has called

Crossroads

HENRI PERRIN, S. J.

One morning, the military policeman gave me the job of drilling holes in the cement, around the edge of the terrace. I worked gently away with my pick and mallet, my legs hanging over the edge, one hundred feet from the ground, facing the crossroads between the Police Headquarters and the German Supreme Court. We often used to look at it, like children looking out of the window, when their mother has forbidden them to go out—that was always the time when the road seemed liveliest, and most full of people and adventure.

With hands in our pockets, and eyes fixed on the crossroads, we spent ages watching life rushing past us in the heart of the city. Germans in all sorts of uniforms, cartloads of Ukrainians, groups of English and Russian prisoners, French

prisoners of war singled out by their red triangles, International Red Cross cars with Swiss or Swedish soldiers in them, conscripts of every nation looking for information, every country of Europe met before us at the crossroads of peoples.

You felt that the world had suddenly shrunk, that people who were yesterday comfortably settled in their own little corners were now being hurled together and mixed up, forced to meet each other.

I remembered one Christmas night on the edge of the Lake of Tiberias,[1] several years back, when English, Germans and French all sang songs of their own countries round a lighted Christmas tree.

Crossroads, meetings; yesterday by chance on a journey, today in war, tomorrow in work. The world which used to seem so vast had now become a single work-yard, where humanity gathered together. The time was coming when everyone must think in terms of the world, leave his house, his village, his province, his country, and learn to be a brother to everyone in the world.

I refused to admit that the roads of the world must cross only in hatred, dividing peoples and classes. I was convinced that most of the national tendencies were often the result of ignorance and obstinacy. Our hearts were not Christian enough to make a social revolution in the name of the gospel, and we had failed in our mission to bring unity in the social sphere. We must not fail in the future in the international sphere.

Through His own love and the communion of saints, Christ has made men of all nations and races our brothers—brothers nearer and dearer even than our natural brothers, brothers in a far stronger sense of the word than we use in speaking of our fellow-countrymen. Could anything be sadder than the present indifference of so many Christians to the Church, which was something so much better than an international family, since we were, so to speak, her very flesh, and all our true life came through her?

1. *Lake of Tiberias:* a lake in Palestine, near the Sea of Galilee, beside the town of Tiberias, which was once the capital of King Herod.

And yet, with all the people we met, with all our intentions at prayer, it would be so easy to live with the whole Church, to force ourselves to think of the whole world, and to re-echo the world's sufferings. Masses, rosaries, prayers of every kind with so many souls rotating upon their own ego—would these souls some day reach the true dimensions of their prayer and life?

Lord Jesus Christ,

You unite in Your Body all the families and all the nations of the world; You have made us all sons of one Father, and You want us to be united to each other as You are to Him. Make us brothers of all whom You love, of all our fellow-men; teach us the truth of the Baptism we have received, of the life which unites us, of the mission which binds us still closer. Teach us to live as members of Your Body, as sons of Your Church, fearing nothing so much as wounding her unity.

Forgive us for our hatred and resentment towards men, families, castes and nations which have hurt us. Teach us to forgive them.

Forgive us for being so ready to limit our horizon to the mountains of our own village and the boundaries of our own country. Teach us to leave home with a joyful heart, and our eyes fixed on the future.

Forgive us for living so little in union with Your Church's rhythm, for not feeling the wounds which tear her. Teach us to feel Your pulse throbbing through the pages of newspapers, history and geography books, news films, radio announcements.

Cry once more in our ears that we Christians cannot have the same political principles as those who do not believe in You.

Teach us to seek in other peoples the qualities we lack, to love the men of every nation.

Teach us, You Who are abroad upon every road, You Who are the companion of every man upon every road, teach us to recognize You at every crossroads upon the whole earth.

"Oh, May I Join the Choir Invisible"

GEORGE ELIOT

Oh, may I join the choir invisible
Of those immortal dead who live again
In minds made better by their presence; live
In pulses stirred to generosity,
In deeds of daring rectitude, in scorn
For miserable aims that end with self,
In thoughts sublime that pierce the night like stars,
And with their mild persistence urge man's search
To vaster issues. . . .

. . . This is life to come,
Which martyred men have made more glorious
For us who strive to follow. May I reach
That purest heaven, be to other souls
The cup of strength in some great agony,
Enkindle generous ardour, feed pure love,
Beget the smiles that have no cruelty,
Be the sweet presence of a good diffused,
And in diffusion ever more intense.
So shall I join the choir invisible
Whose music is the gladness of the world.

A Prayer

EDWIN MARKHAM

Teach me, Father, how to go
Softly as the grasses grow;
Hush my soul to meet the shock
Of the wild world as a rock;
But my spirit, propt with power,
Make as simple as a flower.
Let the dry heart fill its cup
Like a poppy looking up;
Let life lightly wear her crown,
Like a poppy looking down.

Teach me, Father, how to be
Kind and patient as a tree.
Joyfully the crickets croon
Under shady oak at noon;
Beetle, on his mission bent,
Tarries in that cooling tent.
Let me, also, cheer a spot,
Hidden field or garden grot—
Place where passing souls can rest
On the way and be their best.

The Pillar of the Cloud

JOHN HENRY NEWMAN

Lead, Kindly Light, amid the encircling gloom,
  Lead thou me on!
The night is dark, and I am far from home,—
  Lead thou me on!
Keep thou my feet; I do not ask to see
The distant scene,—one step enough for me.

I was not ever thus, nor pray'd that thou
  Shouldst lead me on.
I lov'd to choose and see my path, but now
  Lead thou me on!
I loved the garish day, and, spite of fears,
Pride ruled my will: remember not past years.

So long thy power hath blessed me, sure it still
  Will lead me on;
O'er moor and fen, o'er crag and torrent, till
  The night is gone;
And with the morn those angel faces smile
Which I have loved long since, and lost awhile.

At High Mass

ROBERT HUGH BENSON

Thou who hast made this world so wondrous fair,—
The pomp of clouds; the glory of the sea;
Music of waters; song-birds' melody;
The organ of Thy thunder in the air;
Breath of the rose; and beauty everywhere—
Lord, take this stately service done to Thee,
The grave enactment of Thy Calvary
In jewelled pomp and splendor pictured there!

Lord, take the sounds and sights; the silk and gold;
The white and scarlet; take the reverent grace
Of ordered step; window and glowing wall—
Prophet and Prelate, holy men of old;
And teach us, children of the Holy Place
Who love Thy Courts, to love Thee best of all.

Books for Further Reading

UNIT I. BY THE FIRESIDE

ALCOTT, LOUISA MAY. *Jo's Boys.* Little, Brown.
ALCOTT, LOUISA MAY. *An Old-Fashioned Girl.* Little, Brown.
BAZIN, RENÉ. *Juniper Farm.* Macmillan.
BURNETT, FRANCES HODGSON. *The Secret Garden.* Lippincott.
CABLE, GEORGE W. *Old Creole Days.* Scribner.
CHASE, MARY ELLEN. *A Goodly Heritage.* Macmillan.
CRAIK, DINAH MARIA (MULOCK). *John Halifax, Gentleman.* Epworth.
DICKENS, CHARLES. *David Copperfield.* Ginn.
DORCY, SISTER MARY JEAN, O.P. *Our Lady's Feasts.* Sheed.
HAWTHORNE, NATHANIEL. *The House of the Seven Gables.* Houghton.
HAWTHORNE, NATHANIEL. *Tanglewood Tales.* Houghton.
KILMER, JOYCE. *Poems, Essays, and Letters.* Doubleday.
LONGFELLOW, HENRY W. *The Children's Own Longfellow.* Houghton.
MILLAY, EDNA ST. VINCENT. *Poems Selected for Young People.* Harper.
NOYES, ALFRED. *Forty Singing Seamen.* Lippincott.
PALGRAVE. F. T. *Golden Treasury of Songs and Lyrics.* Macmillan.
REPPLIER, AGNES. *Book of Famous Verse.* Houghton.
UNTERMEYER, LOUIS. *This Singing World.* Harcourt.
UNTERMEYER, LOUIS. *Stars to Steer By.* Harcourt.
UNTERMEYER, LOUIS. *The Pocket Book of Story Poems.* Pocket Books.

UNIT II. IN THE TOWN

AUSTEN, JANE. *Pride and Prejudice.* Ginn.
BARRIE, JAMES M. *Little Minister.* Scribner.
BARRIE, JAMES M. *Peter Pan in Kensington Gardens.* Scribner.
BARRIE, JAMES M. *Window in Thrums.* Scribner.
BOK, EDWARD. *A Dutch Boy Fifty Years After.* Scribner.
CHESTERTON, GILBERT K. *Saint Francis of Assisi.* Doubleday.
CLEMENS, SAMUEL L. *The Prince and the Pauper.* Harper.
DOYLE, CONAN. *The Adventures of Sherlock Holmes.* Harper.
ELIOT, GEORGE. *Silas Marner.* Ginn.
FRANKLIN, BENJAMIN. *The Autobiography of Benjamin Franklin.* Pocket Books.
GASKELL, ELIZABETH C. *Cranford.* Oxford.
GOLDSMITH, OLIVER. *Vicar of Wakefield.* Macmillan.
HÉMON, LOUIS. *Maria Chapdelaine.* Macmillan.
HUGHES, THOMAS. *Tom Brown's School Days.* Harper.
JOHNSON, JAMES WELDON. *God's Trombones.* Viking.
JOHNSON, OWEN. *The Varmint.* Little, Brown.
KING, GRACE. *New Orleans; the Place and the People.* Macmillan.
KIPLING, RUDYARD. *Stalky & Co.* Doubleday.
PUPIN, MICHAEL. *From Immigrant to Inventor.* Scribner.
READE, CHARLES. *Cloister and the Hearth.* Dutton.

REESE, LIZETTE WOODWORTH. *A Victorian Village*. Rinehart.
REPPLIER, AGNES. *In Our Convent Days*. Houghton.
RIIS, JACOB. *The Making of an American*. Macmillan.
TARKINGTON, BOOTH. *Penrod*. Doubleday.
TARKINGTON, BOOTH. *Seventeen*. Harper.

UNIT III. ON THE HIGHWAYS

ATKINSON, ELEANOR. *Greyfriars Bobby*. Harper.
BLACKMORE, R. D. *Lorna Doone*. Ginn.
BURROUGHS, JOHN. *Bird Stories from Burroughs*. Houghton.
CLEMENS, SAMUEL L. *The Adventures of Huckleberry Finn*. Harper.
ELIOT, GEORGE. *The Mill on the Floss*. Ginn.
FOX, JOHN, JR. *The Little Shepherd of Kingdom Come*. Scribner.
FOX, JOHN, JR. *The Trail of the Lonesome Pine*. Scribner.
HOUSMAN, ALFRED E. *A Shropshire Lad*. Grosset.
HUBBARD, REVEREND BERNARD, S.J. *Mush, You Malemutes*. American.
JAMES, WILL. *Smoky, The Cow Horse*. Scribner.
JEWETT, SARAH ORNE. *A White Heron*. Houghton.
KNIGHT, ERIC. *Lassie Come-Home*. Winston.
LONDON, JACK. *Call of the Wild*. Macmillan.
OLLIVANT, ALFRED. *Bob, Son of Battle*. Doubleday.
PORTER, GENE STRATTON. *Freckles*. Doubleday.
SETON, ERNEST THOMPSON. *The Biography of a Grizzly*. Appleton-Century.
STEVENSON, ROBERT L. *Kidnapped*. Macmillan.
WHITE, STEWART E. *The Blazed Trail*. Doubleday.
WISTER, OWEN. *The Virginian*. Macmillan.

UNIT IV. AT CHRISTMASTIDE

FIELD, EUGENE. *Poems of Childhood*. Scribner.
GHÉON, HENRI. *Christmas on the Village Square*. Sheed.
IRVING, WASHINGTON. *Old Christmas*. Macmillan.
JEWETT, SARAH ORNE. *Betty Leicester*. Houghton.
LAGERLÖF, SELMA. *Christ Legends*. Holt.
SMITH, ELVA S., and HAZELTINE, ALICE I. *The Christmas Books of Legends and Stories*. Lothrop.
VAN DYKE, HENRY. *Story of the Other Wise Man*. Harper.

UNIT V. IN THEIR OWN LANDS

BAZIN, RENÉ. *Children of Alsace*. Brentano's.
BENÉT, STEPHEN V. *John Brown's Body*. Rinehart.
BENSON, MONSIGNOR ROBERT H. *Come Rack! Come Rope!* Kenedy.
CHURCHILL, WINSTON. *The Crisis*. Macmillan.
CRANE, STEPHEN. *The Red Badge of Courage*. Appleton.
CRAWFORD, F. MARION. *In the Palace of the King*. Macmillan.
CURWOOD, JAMES O. *Steele of the Royal Mounted*. Burt.
DOYLE, CONAN. *The White Company*. Harper.

Fitzgerald, Brassil. *Never Surrender.* Ginn.
Garland, Hamlin. *Trail Makers of the Middle Border.* Macmillan.
Graham, Shirley, and Lipscomb, George. *Dr. George Washington Carver.* Messner.
Hough, Emerson. *The Covered Wagon.* Appleton.
Keller, Helen. *The Story of My Life.* Doubleday.
Kelly, Eric. *Blacksmith of Vilno.* Macmillan.
Macaulay, T. B. *Lays of Ancient Rome.* Oxford.
McCarthy, Justin H. *If I Were King.* Grosset.
Minnigerode, Meade. *Cockades.* Putnam.
Nazaroff, A. *The Land of the Russian People.* Lippincott.
O'Sullivan, Maurice. *Twenty Years A-Growing.* Viking.
Page, Thomas Nelson. *Red Rock.* Scribner.
Parkman, Francis. *Oregon Trail.* Little, Brown.
Pyle, Howard. *Men of Iron.* Harper.
Rostand, E. *L'Aiglon.* Harper.
Sargent, Daniel. *Our Land and Our Lady.* Longmans.
Sperry, Armstrong. *Wagons Westward.* Winston.
Thompson, Maurice. *Alice of Old Vincennes.* Bobbs.
Washington, Booker T. *Up from Slavery.* Doubleday.

UNIT VI. ON THE SEA AND IN THE SKY

Byrd, Richard E. *Skyward.* Putnam.
Colum, Padraic. *Road around Ireland.* Macmillan.
Connolly, J. B. *Book of the Gloucester Fishermen.* Day.
Connolly, J. B. *Sonnie Boy's People.* Scribner.
Cormack, Maribelle. *Wind of the Vikings.* Appleton.
Dana, R. H. *Two Years Before the Mast.* Houghton.
Duncan, Norman. *Dr. Luke of The Labrador.* Revell.
Fisher, Cyrus. *The Avion My Uncle Flew.* Appleton.
Halliburton, Richard. *The Royal Road to Romance.* Garden City.
Hodges, C. Walter. *Columbus Sails.* Coward.
Ingelow, Jean. *High Tide on the Coast of Lincolnshire.* Collins.
Lindbergh, Anne M. *North to the Orient.* Harcourt.
Masefield, John. *Salt-Water Poems and Ballads.* Macmillan.
Marryat, Frederick. *Mr. Midshipman Easy.* Macmillan.
Melville, H. *Moby Dick.* Oxford.
Ransome, Arthur. *Pigeon Post.* Lippincott.
Saint-Exupéry, Antoine de. *Flight to Arras.* Reynal.
Saint-Exupéry, Antoine de. *Night Flight.* Reynal.
Saint-Exupéry, Antoine de. *Wind, Sand and Stars.* Reynal.
Shore, Maxine, and Oblinger, M. *Hero of Darien.* Longmans.
Stevenson, R. L. *Treasure Island.* Ginn.
Stockton, Frank R. *The Casting Away of Mrs. Lecks and Mrs. Aleshine.* Appleton.
Stockton, Frank R. *The Reformed Pirate.* Scribner.
Verne, Jules. *Twenty Thousand Leagues under the Sea.* Scribner.

UNIT VII. AMONG THE NATIONS

BOUTET DE MONVEL, L. M. *Joan of Arc.* Appleton.
BUCHAN, JOHN. *Mountain Meadow.* Houghton.
BULWER-LYTTON, EDWARD. *The Last Days of Pompeii.* Scribner.
BYRNE, DONN. *Messer Marco Polo.* Appleton.
COE, DOUGLAS. *Marconi, Pioneer of Radio.* Messner.
DICKENS, CHARLES. *A Tale of Two Cities.* Ginn.
DU CHAILLU, PAUL B. *Land of the Long Night.* Scribner.
FARROW, JOHN. *Damien the Leper.* Sheed.
HAWES, CHARLES B. *The Dark Frigate.* Little, Brown.
KELLER, REVEREND JAMES, M.M., and BERGER, MEYER. *Men of Maryknoll.* Scribner.
KELLY, ERIC. *The Land of the Polish People.* Lippincott.
LAMB, CHARLES and MARY. *Tales from Shakespeare.* Ginn.
MAGNER, REVEREND JAMES A. *Latin American Pattern.* Catholic Students' Mission Press.
NEWCOMB, COVELLE. *Black Fire.* Longmans.
SARGENT, DANIEL. *Mitri: Life of Prince Gallitzin.* Longmans.
SCOTT, WALTER. *The Talisman.* Houghton.

UNIT VIII. IN CHRIST OUR LORD

BENSON, ROBERT H. *Lourdes.* Herder.
COFFEY, REGINALD M., O.P. *The Man from Rocca Sicca.* Bruce.
CONSIDINE, REVEREND J. J., M.M. *Across a World.* Longmans.
CONSIDINE, REVEREND J. J., M.M. *When the Sorghum Was High.* Longmans.
DORCY, SISTER MARY JEAN, O.P. *A Crown for Joanna.* Sheed.
GHÉON, HENRI. *Secrets of the Saints.* Sheed.
KILMER, JOYCE. *Dreams and Images.* Halcyon House.
MARITAIN, RAISSA, and MARITAIN, JACQUES. *Saint Thomas Aquinas.* Sheed.
MARY ELEANORE, C.S.C., SISTER. *Troubadours of Paradise.* Appleton.
MAYNARD, SARA. *Rose of America.* Sheed.
NOYES, ALFRED. *The Golden Book of Catholic Poetry.* Lippincott.
PAPINI, GIOVANNI. *Life of Christ.* Harcourt.
SIENKIEWICZ, HENRYK. "*Quo Vadis.*" Little, Brown.
VAN DER VELDT, REVEREND JAMES A., O.F.M. *City Set on a Hill.* Dodd.
VAN DYKE, HENRY. *The Mansion.* Harper.
WALSH, THOMAS. *Catholic Anthology.* Macmillan.
WILLIAMS, MICHAEL. *Little Brother Francis of Assisi.* Macmillan.

Biographical Index

ADAMS, HENRY (1838–1918), Boston-born patron of the arts, teacher, and philosopher. He viewed life with the eyes of a critic, but he found in the cathedrals of France the closest approach to inner peace he had ever known. Out of this setting he wrote *Mont-Saint-Michel and Chartres.*

ALLEN, JAMES LANE (1849–1925), American novelist. Among his books are *Flute and Violin, The Choir Invisible, A Kentucky Summer in Arcady,* and *The Landmark.*

ANGELA, MOTHER MARY (1824–1887), a Superior of the Congregation of the Holy Cross. Born in Pennsylvania, the descendant of one of America's earliest pioneers, she became a nurse and teacher and organizer. She joined the Sisters of the Holy Cross in 1853.

BAKER, KARLE WILSON (1878–), American poet. Born at Little Rock, Arkansas, she now lives in Texas. In addition to poetry she has written children's books, prose tales, essays, and novels.

BARING, MAURICE (1874–1948), English novelist, essayist, poet, and journalist. A graduate of Cambridge, he served in the British diplomatic corps, then became a war correspondent in Russia in 1905. In the First World War he was a wing commander in the Royal Air Force.

BEECHING, HENRY C. (1859–1919), English writer, born in London and educated at Oxford. Taking holy orders in 1882, he devoted the major part of his life to religious work.

BELLOC, HILAIRE (1870–), English author. Born in France in 1870, the son of a French lawyer and a literary Englishwoman, he was educated in England and later naturalized there. He has written histories, military studies, satires, even nonsense rhymes. As an upholder of his Catholicism he wrote *Europe and the Faith* and *How the Reformation Happened.*

BENÉT (bĕ nā'), STEPHEN VINCENT (1898–1943), storyteller, novelist, and poet. His boyhood reading of records kept by his father, who had been an officer in the Civil War, gave him the basis for his long narrative poem *John Brown's Body,* which some critics have called the great American epic. Benét had a wide range of interests and methods in his poetry. He wrote with high sincerity, and his influence on modern American poetry has been far-reaching.

BENSON, ROBERT HUGH (1871–1914), born in England, the son of an Anglican archbishop of Canterbury. Monsignor Benson was a convert to Roman Catholicism. Eleven years of his Catholic life were noted for the influence he exerted in the pulpit and for the novels which he wrote. Among these latter are *By What Authority* and *Come Rack! Come Rope!*

BRAITHWAITE, WILLIAM STANLEY, (1878–), American Negro poet and editor. Mainly self-educated, he has been given honorary degrees in recognition of his work in the field of poetry.

BRANCH, ANNA HEMPSTEAD (1875–1937), American poet. She was the author of poems, plays, and ceremonies used by the Girl Scouts.

BROOKE, RUPERT (1887–1915), English poet, son of a master at Rugby. Out of Cambridge University but a few short years before the outbreak of the First World War, he served in the British navy with the Mediterranean Expeditionary Force. He died at the Dardanelles and lies buried on the island of Skyros.

BROWN, JOHN (1810–1882), Scottish physician and author. Though Doctor Brown wrote many volumes dealing with the duties and responsibilities of a physician, he is better known as the author of *Rab and His Friends*.

BROWNING, ROBERT (1812–1889), born in London and privately educated. Married to Elizabeth Barrett, a poet whose name was far better known than his, the Brownings lived much of their lives in Italy. After Elizabeth's death, Browning returned to London, where he took his place, with Tennyson, as a leading poet of England.

BRYANT, WILLIAM CULLEN (1794–1878), poet and lover of nature. He published his first poem when he was only thirteen years old. When he was twenty-one he began to interpret the beauties of nature and he became the renowned editor of the New York *Evening Post*, a great traveler, and a noted poet. His poems of nature were notably successful, some of them remaining classics of American literature.

BURNS, ROBERT (1759–1796), the greatest of Scottish poets. He received little formal education, but was taught by his father, a hard-working farmer. Burns always wrote of the simple things of life. In spite of his tremendous popularity, he himself remained unchanged and continued to interpret not only his own people but the basic values of life.

BURT, MAXWELL STRUTHERS (1882–), born in Baltimore. A graduate of Princeton University, he has been a cattle ranchman in Wyoming since 1908.

CALIFANO, HELEN, teacher in the public schools of Philadelphia. She is a frequent contributor to Catholic periodicals.

CARMAN, (WILLIAM) BLISS (1861–1929), Canadian poet, born in New Brunswick. He is best known for his many volumes of verse, including *Songs from Vagabondia*, written with Richard Hovey.

CHANNING, WILLIAM ELLERY (1780–1842), noted American Unitarian clergyman. He was a friend of poets, a fearless defender of freedom, a social reformer, and an ardent anti-slavery agitator.

CHASE, MARY ELLEN (1887–), author and educator. Born in Maine, she taught at the University of Minnesota and later at Smith College. Contributor of short stories, essays, and reviews in leading American magazines, she has also written many charming books.

CHAVEZ, FRAY ANGELICO (chä′vās, frā än jĕl′ê kō), a member of the Order of Friars Minor. A resident of New Mexico, he writes with fervor and understanding of Spanish and Indian lore. The vivid imagery and deep spirituality of his poetry have brought him quickly into the front rank of American poets.

CHESTERTON, GILBERT KEITH (1874–1936), English journalist and writer. He was a journalist, editor, poet, and author of more than a hundred volumes, ranging from the popular detective novel about Father Brown to the most learned histories. He became a stanch crusader for the teachings of Roman Catholicism during those few years just before and after the First World War, when so many intellectual leaders of England joined the Church.

CLARKE, JOSEPH I. C. (1846–1925), Irish editor and playwright. In 1868 he came to the United States, where he gained recognition as a newspaperman.

CLAUDEL, PAUL (1868–), French poet, dramatist, and diplomat. He served as Ambassador from France to the United States in 1927. He is the noted author of many volumes of poetry and prose.

COLERIDGE, MARY ELIZABETH (1861–1907), English poet, novelist, and critic. Her reputation in literature rests upon her poems, which are spontaneous and imaginative.

COLUMBUS, CHRISTOPHER (1446–1506), discoverer of America. He was not only a great explorer, but he was also the first writer to publish an account of his findings in the Western Hemisphere.

CONSIDINE, REVEREND JOHN JOSEPH, M.M. (1897–), born in New Bedford, Massachusetts. He entered Maryknoll in 1915, was ordained in 1923, and is now the Assistant-General of Maryknoll. Father Considine journeyed from Rome through Asia and then across the dark continent of Africa. He has written many stirring accounts of the Maryknoll Missions in foreign lands.

CURIE, EVE DENISE (1904–   ), musician and playwright. The daughter of distinguished parents, she went to London from France in 1940. Since then she has been a war correspondent and author of *Journey among Warriors* and *Madame Curie*.

DALY, THOMAS AUGUSTINE (1871–1948), American journalist and poet. Born in Philadelphia, he was educated at Villanova and Fordham universities. Famous for his dialect poems, which have serious undertones in spite of their lightness of mood, he is the author of several volumes of verse.

DAUDET (dō dĕ'), ALPHONSE (1840–1897), born at Nîmes, France. For a while he taught, then went to Paris, where his poetry brought him swift academic recognition.

DAY, THOMAS FLEMING (1861–1927), English writer of prose and verse. He is especially known as a writer on yachting.

DE ANDREA, MOST REVEREND MIGUEL, pastor of the Church of Saint Michael the Archangel in Buenos Aires, the titular Bishop of Temno. He is a noted social reformer in his country.

DICKENS, CHARLES (1812–1870), English novelist. He grew up in London, where, when his father was thrown into a debtor's prison, he went to work in a warehouse. Neither loneliness nor poverty, however, could thwart his love of the city, the river, the ships, the shabby, hopeless poor. Because of some of his novels—*Oliver Twist, Nicholas Nickleby, Little Dorrit*—the laws of England that affected the oppressed were gradually changed. After he died, the English people requested that he be buried in Westminster Abbey.

DICKINSON, EMILY (1830–1886), American poet, perhaps one of the greatest of women poets. Her life was spent in Amherst, Massachusetts, where she was born. She had little contact with the life around her, but her inner life was rich and intense. Not until after her death were the first volumes of her verses published. Then the world discovered the rich heritage she had left it.

DO CEO, SISTER VIOLANTE (1601–1693), lyric poet. Born in Lisbon, she spent sixty years in a Dominican Convent there. She was famous as a musician as well as a poet.

DONNE (dŏn), JOHN (1573–1631), often called the father of modern poets. He was the first to rebel against the style of the Elizabethan form of poetry.

DORCY, SISTER MARY JEAN, O.P., born in Anacortes, Washington. She entered the Novitiate of the Dominican Sisters at Everett, Washington, in 1932. Both an artist and a writer, she has contributed many illustrations to national magazines. She also has written several books on religious subjects for children.

DU CHAILLU (dü shȧ'yü'), PAUL (1831–1903), explorer, novelist, authority on Africa. He led his first hunting expedition into the wilds of Central Africa when he was twenty-four years old. Born in France, but a naturalized American citizen, he is buried in New York.

EASTMAN, CHARLES (1858–1939), an American physician of Sioux Indian parentage. As a member of the National Council of Boy Scouts he took an active interest in modern youth. He wrote many books dealing with the Indian, the best known being *Indian Boyhood*.

EDELMAN, KATHERINE, poet and composer. She was born in Ireland but is married to an American and has lived in Kansas City since 1909.

ELIOT, GEORGE (1819–1880), the pseudonym of Mary Ann Evans, English novelist and poet. She wrote *Silas Mar-*

ner, Adam Bede, The Mill on the Floss, Middlemarch, many other stories, and two volumes of poems.

FABER, REVEREND FREDERICK WILLIAM (1814–1863), born in England. Educated at Harrow and Baliol colleges, he became an Anglican minister, a convert to Catholicism, a priest, and a friend of Cardinal Newman. He wrote many fine devotional works, poems, and hymns.

FEENEY, REVEREND LEONARD, S.J. (1897–), literary editor of the Jesuit magazine *America.* He is well known for the warm tenderness and whimsicality of his prose and verse.

FINN, REVEREND JOHN J., a secular priest from Brooklyn. A chaplain in the First World War, he was wounded while serving in France. Praying for peace on the eve of the Second World War, he collapsed and died.

FITZGERALD, BRASSIL (1896–), educator and writer. He is a contributor to Catholic and secular magazines.

FOSS, SAM WALTER (1858–1911), American editor and humorist. He is the author of several volumes of poetry.

FROST, ROBERT (1875–), born in San Francisco and educated at Dartmouth. He is identified with New England because he lives there, as did eight generations of his ancestors, and because the subject matter of his poetry deals with New England country life. Twice winner of the Pulitzer prize, he is one of the outstanding poets of the present.

FULLER, ETHEL ROMIG, poet, born in Big Rapids, Michigan. She has written *White Peaks and Green* and *Kitchen Sonnets.*

GARESCHÉ, REVEREND EDWARD F., S.J. (1876–), born in St. Louis. He is the author of several volumes of poetry and numerous devotional works. He writes with eagerness and with rich depth of understanding.

GINSBERG, LOUIS (1896–), poet and teacher. Though his themes suggest present-day backgrounds, the general effect is deeply spiritual.

GORE-BOOTH, EVA (1872–1926), Irish lyric poet. She descends from a famous Irish family of whom one of the members was the Countess Markiewicz, the heroine of the Irish Easter Week rebellion.

HALLACK, CECILY (1898–1938), English poet. A convert to Catholicism, she became a member of the Third Order of Saint Francis and took the name of Sister Mary Easter. The charm of her personality and the enthusiasm of her faith are shown in all her writings.

HANNUM, ANNA P., author of *The Christ of the Andes.* She has written other articles in the same hope of promoting world peace.

HENDERSON, ALICE CORBIN (1881–), poet and editor. She has written several volumes of verse.

HICKY, DANIEL WHITEHEAD (1900–), lyric poet. He has been a lifelong resident of Georgia.

HINKSON, KATHARINE TYNAN (1861–1931), Irish poet and novelist. She wrote novels, miracle plays, and many books for children. Her best work is her poetry, which expresses her deep religious feeling. She was the first Catholic poet of the Irish revival to win general acknowledgment.

HOLMES, OLIVER WENDELL (1809–1894), American poet and wit. In addition to his many activities he published many essays and poems while teaching medicine in Boston.

HOUSMAN, ALFRED EDWARD (1859–1936), English scholar and poet. After failure in his final examinations at Oxford University diligent study of the classics made him not only a distinguished scholar but a noted professor and poet.

HOVEY, RICHARD (1864–1900), American poet. He was theologian, actor, journalist, lecturer, and teacher before he collaborated with Bliss Carman to write the most spirited verse of his day.

IRVING, WASHINGTON (1783–1859), first American novelist. He was born just as the British soldiers were leaving New York at the close of the War for Independence. In addition to his novels he wrote many fine essays and travel journals. He also wrote *Knickerbocker's History of New York.* His deep interest in the traditions of the Hudson River Valley led him to the writing of some of his most famous stories, "Rip Van Winkle" and "The Legend of Sleepy Hollow."

JAMMES, FRANCIS (1868–1938), French poet and novelist. His works are characterized by great simplicity and a profound Catholic attitude.

JOHNSON, RIGHT REVEREND GEORGE (1889–1944), Catholic educator and outstanding essayist. As head of the Department of Education at The Catholic University of America and director of the Commission on American Citizenship, he wrote *Better Men for Better Times,* supervised the construction of the curriculum, *Guiding Growth in Christian Social Living,* and the writing of the Faith and Freedom Readers.

JOHNSON, OWEN (MCMAHON) (1878–), writer of novels and short stories. Born in New York, he studied at Lawrenceville and Yale. He wrote *The Varmint, The Tennessee Shad, Stover at Yale,* and many short stories.

JONES, EDWARD SMYTH, noted Negro poet. He attracted national attention by walking some hundreds of miles from his home in the South to Harvard University.

KEELER, HARRY STEPHEN (1894–), writer of mystery novels.

KELLER, REVEREND JAMES, M.M., a Californian ordained at Maryknoll in 1925. He is director of the New York City headquarters of the Maryknoll Fathers and managing editor of *The Field Afar.*

KELLY, ERIC (1884–), educator, novelist, and college professor. In 1919 he went to Poland with the Polish legions as they departed from France and received the Chevalier Order of Polonia Restituta in 1934. He was awarded the Newbery Medal of the American Library Association in 1929 for the most distinguished contribution to American literature for children in that year.

KILMER, JOYCE (1886–1918), an outstanding Catholic poet of this century. Born in New Jersey, he became a newspaper reporter after he graduated from Rutgers University, but soon made his fame as a writer of poetry. His best-known verses are "Trees," "Main Street," "The House with Nobody in It," "A Blue Valentine," and "Rouge Bouquet." Kilmer enlisted as a private soldier in the First World War and was killed on a battlefield in France. His poetry retains the appeal which made it instantly popular upon its first publication.

KINGSLEY, CHARLES (1819–1875), an English clergyman and novelist. He graduated from Cambridge University and became a clergyman of the Church of England, a poet, and a novelist.

KIPLING, RUDYARD (1865–1936), English author and poet. His works deal chiefly with life in India, where he was born. His wide knowledge of the British Empire, particularly of India, went into *Barrack Room Ballads, Plain Tales from the Hills, The Man Who Would Be King,* and *Stalky & Co.* Master of the short story, Kipling wrote of British soldiers, of Indian paupers and princes, and of the whole sweep of empire.

LAVIGERIE, CARDINAL CHARLES MARTIAL ALLEMAND (1825–1892), born near Bayonne, in France. Ordained in 1849, he showed a true genius for organization and was sent to Africa where, with the help of the White Fathers and the White Sisters, whom he founded for the purpose, he began his great work of expanding the Church into the very heart of Africa. In 1890 the Conference of Brussels practically adopted Cardinal Lavigerie's plan to abolish slavery in the Congo.

LEACOCK, STEPHEN BUTLER (1869–1944), famous Canadian economist and humorist. Born in England, he received his education in Canada and the United States. His writings cover a wide range—from works on political science to essays and novels in a light and fanciful vein.

LEAR, EDWARD (1812–1888), English painter and poet. Although best known for nonsense rhymes, he first specialized in portrayal of birds and later in landscapes.

LESLIE, SHANE (1885–), Irish poet. Educated at Cambridge University in England, he spent some years in the United States, then returned to London to edit *The Dublin Review* and to write poetry and biography.

LETTS, WINIFRED M. (1887–), a poet who writes of the western counties of her native Ireland. During the First World War she served as a volunteer nurse, and many of her poems reflect her experiences and her sympathy.

LINCOLN, ABRAHAM (1809–1865), a great leader, not only in his nation's history, but also in its literature. His "Gettysburg Address" and "Second Inaugural Address," given while he was President of the United States, are masterpieces of logic and simplicity.

LINDBERGH, ANNE MORROW (1907–), born in Englewood, New Jersey, the daughter of Dwight Morrow, late United States ambassador to Mexico. She was married to Charles Lindbergh soon after his famed solo flight across the Atlantic to France. Mrs. Lindbergh is an accredited pilot, a licensed radio operator, and a writer of great literary beauty and distinction.

LINDSAY, VACHEL (1879–1931), born in Illinois, wrote democratically of the American scene. His poems are particularly appealing to young people because of their spirit and vigor.

LONGFELLOW, HENRY WADSWORTH (1807–1882), probably the best known and loved of American poets. Born in Maine, he went to Bowdoin College at the same time as Nathaniel Hawthorne. He studied modern languages in France, Italy, Spain, and Germany. He brought much of the culture of these lands into his later verse. He became professor of modern languages at Harvard University. He began writing poetry while still a student at Bowdoin and continued throughout his lifetime to produce poems of great popularity. His best-known long poems are *Evangeline, The Courtship of Miles Standish, The Song of Hiawatha,* and *Tales of a Wayside Inn.* Some of his best-known shorter poems are "A Psalm of Life," "The Village Blacksmith," "The Skeleton in Armor," "The Arrow and the Song," "The Bridge," "The Children's Hour," and "My Lost Youth." Longfellow had a notable influence upon American literature during the long years of his active career as a writer.

LOWELL, AMY (1874–1925), born in Brookline, Massachusetts, of a family distinguished in New England for more than two hundred years. During her lifetime she was a critic, a lecturer, and author of many books of verses, including *A Dome of Many-Coloured Glass, Sword Blades and Poppy-Seeds,* and *Poems Translated from the Chinese.*

LOWELL, JAMES RUSSELL (1819–1891), American poet and essayist. He was one of the first American poets to use Yankee dialect successfully and one of the most vigorous in defending human liberty during the Mexican and Civil wars.

MCCRAE, JOHN (1872–1918), a Canadian physician, soldier, and poet. He served in the Boer War and joined the Canadian forces in the First World War with the rank of lieutenant colonel. He served at the great battle of Ypres and died in January of 1918.

MACDONAGH, THOMAS (1878–1916), Gaelic scholar, playwright, poet, and editor. Born in County Tipperary in Ireland, he became a teacher in the famous Saint Enda's School in Dublin. A leader in the Easter Rebellion of 1916, he died for the freedom of Ireland.

McKAY, CLAUDE (1890–1946), poet and novelist. He came to the United States in 1912 from his birthplace in Jamaica, West Indies. He studied at Tuskegee University and Kansas State College. A Catholic poet, he became associate editor of *The Liberator* and author of a number of volumes of poetry.

MACMANUS, SEUMAS (1869–), Irish storyteller. Born in the County Donegal, of which he wrote in *Dark Patrick*. Author of many plays, stories, and fairy tales of Ireland, he once was a barefoot boy who herded cattle.

MADELEVA, SISTER M. (1887–), a member of the Congregation of the Holy Cross, now president of Saint Mary's College at Notre Dame, Indiana. She is noted for the perfection and purity of her style.

MARKHAM, EDWIN (1852–1940), American poet, writer, and lecturer. His poem "The Man with the Hoe" won worldwide attention. Besides his books and lectures on labor and child-labor problems, he published several volumes of verse.

MASEFIELD, JOHN (1875–), poet laureate of England from 1930. Going to sea as a boy and sailing through hardship and dangers for many years, he returned in 1897 to England. Since 1911 he has been considered one of the most important poets of our time.

MEYNELL, ALICE (1847–1922), poet and essayist. One of the leaders in the revival of English Catholic literature, she published many books and verses.

MILLAY, EDNA ST. VINCENT (1892–), American poet. A native of Maine, graduate of Vassar, Pulitzer prize winner, she is considered the outstanding American woman poet of our time. She has written *A Few Figs from Thistles*, *Second April*, *The Harp Weaver*, and the libretto for an American opera, *The King's Henchman*.

MITCHELL, RUTH COMFORT (1882–), a writer of plays, novels, short stories, and verse.

MOHR, JOSEPH (1792–1848), born in Austria. He is remembered today as the author of the beloved Christmas song "Silent Night, Holy Night."

MUNKITTRICK, RICHARD KENDALL, born in England. He came to the United States in childhood and received his education here.

MÜNSTERBERG, MARGARET, poet and essayist. She is the daughter of Hugo Münsterberg, formerly noted psychologist and professor at Harvard University.

NESBIT, WILBUR (1871–1927), contributor to popular magazines and a staff writer on a Chicago newspaper.

NEWMAN, CARDINAL JOHN HENRY (1801–1890), an Anglican minister who became a Catholic priest, later made Cardinal. A master of language, an ardent educator, a crusader for sound spiritual principles, he dedicated his life to the highest culture of spiritual values.

NOEL, SISTER M. (METCALFE), a Sister of the Congregation of the Holy Cross at Notre Dame, Indiana. She was one of a group of Sisters of her community who wrote the poems which were collected and published as *Songs of the Rood*.

NOYES, ALFRED (1880–), one of the best known of modern English poets in America. Born in England, he now lives in the United States. After the First World War he was among the distinguished men and women of letters who entered the Church in large numbers. His poetry has achieved greatness chiefly because of its musical rhythms and rhymes.

O'HIGGINS, BRIAN (1882–), Irish poet. He has been a member of the *Dail* (Parliament) for County Clare. He is the author of *Hearts of Gold* and other sketches of life in Ireland.

O'SHAUGHNESSY, ARTHUR (1844–1881), born in London of Irish parents. His poems, touched with melancholy, are rich in imagination and color.

OTERO REICHE, RAUL (ō tā'rō rī'kĕ, rä o͝ol'), well-known poet of Bolivia. His poems are noted for their beauty of imagery.

PARKER, SIR GILBERT (1862–1932), Canadian novelist. In 1900 he settled in London, where he became recognized as a champion of British imperialism. His writings include plays, poems, short stories, and novels. Many of them reflect his interest in Canadian life and character.

PERRIN, HENRI, S. J., who went into slave labor in Germany with thousands of conscripted Frenchmen so that he might serve there as their chaplain.

POE, EDGAR ALLAN (1809–1849), poet and writer of rare genius. In his extraordinary but short life he produced many volumes of poetry and short stories, all of them distinctive in charm and wonder. His unhappy life undoubtedly was the source of much of the "mood poetry" for which he is most famous. His prose, including mystery stories which were the forerunners of the modern school of mystery writing, still serves as a model for writers.

POPE PIUS XI (1857–1939), born in Milan. His family name was Achelle Ambrogio Damiano Ratti. It was probably in his father's silk factory that the future pope learned much about the problems of the factory worker and the wage earner which he discussed later in his encyclical on *Reconstructing the Social Order* (1931).

Ordained to the priesthood in 1879, he was created Cardinal in 1921, and in 1922 was elected to the Papacy.

Among his better-known encyclicals are *Christian Education of Youth* (1929), *Christian Marriage* (1930), and *Atheistic Communism* (1937).

POPE PIUS XII (1876–), born in Rome. His family name is Eugene Pacelli. Ordained to the priesthood in 1899, he was made Cardinal in 1929. In 1936 he made an airplane tour of the United States, thereby becoming the first pope ever to visit America.

PUPIN, MICHAEL (1858–1935), physicist and inventor. Born in Hungary, he came to America with nothing but youth and hope and lived to achieve all his dreams. He was educated at Columbia University and at Johns Hopkins University, then taught science at Columbia, and received high honors for his contributions to scientific knowledge.

RANKIN, KATHERINE, born in Chicago, Illinois, magazine writer and a newspaper reporter. She has written "The Road to Vaux," "Roll Call," "Quincy, Illinois," and many other popular verses.

RICE, ALICE HEGAN (1876–1942), born in Shelbyville, Kentucky. Her two very popular books, *Mrs. Wiggs of the Cabbage Patch* and *Lovey Mary*, grew out of her interest in charitable work among the poor of Louisville.

ROOS, ANN, born in Brooklyn, New York. She was trained in Girl Scout organization, and lives on Long Island.

ROSSETTI, CHRISTINA (1830–1894), sister of the British poet and artist, Dante Gabriel Rossetti. Many of her poems are serious in nature, but she will be long remembered for the charming verses in *Sing-Song*, a volume of poems for children.

SAINT-EXUPÉRY, ANTOINE DE (săn-tāg' zü'pā rē', ȧn twän' dē), (1900–1944), French novelist and essayist and internationally known airman, reported missing in August, 1944, after a reconnaissance mission over southern France. He served as a pilot with the French air forces in the Second World War. From his earlier experiences he wrote *Night Flight* and *Wind, Sand and Stars*; from his later war experiences, *Flight to Arras*.

SANDBURG, CARL (1878–), Chicago journalist and poet. He is recognized as one of the most successful poets in portraying modern American industrial life.

SARETT, LEW (1888–   ), author, lecturer, and poet. He has for years had as an avocation vacationing as woodsman and guide and United States ranger in the Northwest.

SAWYER, RUTH (1880–   ), writer for young folk, specializing in Irish folk stories. Her books for boys and girls have become increasingly popular.

SCHULTE, REVEREND PAUL, O.M.I., often called the Flying Priest. Interested in the problems of the missionaries whose work had taken them to the Arctic, he founded the MIVA,—the Missionary International Vehicular Association,—an organization devoted to bringing comfort and aid to the far-flung missions of the Church.

SCOTT, SIR WALTER (1771–1832), born in Edinburgh, Scotland. His childhood gave him a thorough knowledge of the ancient folk stories of his people. It was only natural that his writings should follow in this direction. He was one of the leaders in the English Romantic movement in literature.

SEEGER, ALAN (1888–1916), American poet. Born in New York City he was educated at Harvard. After graduation he spent four years in France; then, during the third week of the First World War, he enlisted in the French Foreign Legion and was killed in action.

SHAKESPEARE, WILLIAM (1564–1616), the greatest of the English dramatists. He was born at Stratford-on-Avon and died there. Little is known about his life. He had meager formal education; he learned the craft of the playwright as an actor and manager in London theaters.

SHELLEY, PERCY BYSSHE (1792–1822), English poet. He was a timid boy in school and a wild experimenter in college, where his eccentricity won him the name of "mad Shelley." Later, though a victim of emotional and financial distress, he became England's great lyric poet. He wrote several romantic dramas, but he will be longest remembered for "To a Skylark" and "To the West Wind."

SHEPARD, ODELL (1884–   ), teacher and writer. Born in Illinois, he now teaches at Trinity College in Connecticut. His biography of Bronson Alcott, *Pedlar's Progress*, was awarded the Pulitzer prize.

SHUSTER, GEORGE N. (1894–   ), a noted Catholic educator, journalist, and critic. He is now president of Hunter College in New York City.

SIENKIEWICZ (shĕn kyā'vĭch), HENRYK, (1846–1916), Polish novelist. He wrote "*Quo Vadis*" as the result of an intensive study of the Latin writers of the first few Christian centuries. In 1905 he received the Nobel prize in literature.

SILL, EDWARD ROWLAND (1841–1887), American poet and essayist. He was a teacher for several years and author of many essays and poems.

SILVER, ABBA HILLEL (1893–   ), rabbi at the Cleveland Temple. Born in Lithuania, he is a graduate of the University of Cincinnati, a civic leader, war veteran, preacher, and author.

SMITH, ARCHIBALD WILLIAM (1897–   ), born in Spain of British parents. After several years of service in the British army he joined an Indian trading corporation. At Bombay he found time to observe the work of the Little Sisters of the Poor, and of them wrote "A Bountiful Providence."

SPRING-RICE, SIR CECIL ARTHUR (1859–1918), English diplomat. Born in London, educated at Oxford, entered the British foreign service. In 1912 he was Ambassador to the United States.

STEVENSON, ROBERT LOUIS (1850–1894), born in Edinburgh, Scotland. Because of illness he lived in many places—California, Saranac Lake, Switzerland, and the South Sea Islands. His courageous spirit kept him at work. His romances and poems include *Treasure Island* and *A Child's Garden of Verses.*

He died in Samoa in the South Seas, where he is buried.

STUART, MARY, QUEEN OF SCOTS (1542–1587), unhappy ruler of whom poets have sung through the years. Her heritage was religious and national turmoil. She was accused of conspiracy, tried, found guilty, and executed.

SWINBURNE, ALGERNON CHARLES (1837–1909), English poet. A rebel against all established authority, he was a writer of poetry, drama, and prose.

TABB, REVEREND JOHN BANISTER (1845–1909), an American poet and educator. A convert to Roman Catholicism, after his ordination he taught English at Saint Charles' College in Maryland. His poems have long endured because of their lyric beauty.

TARKINGTON, BOOTH (1869–1946), American novelist. His first literary success came in 1899 with the publication of *The Gentleman from Indiana.* In his lifetime he became one of the most popular writers in America. Of particular interest to young people are ***Penrod, Penrod and Sam,*** and ***Seventeen.***

TEASDALE, SARA (1884–1933), American poet. Born in St. Louis, she possessed a rare gift for expressing poignant emotion in a few brief lines of verse.

TENNYSON, ALFRED, LORD (1809–1892), English poet. Baron of Aldsworth and Farringford, he won honors in poetry even while he was a student at Cambridge University in England. In 1850 he was made poet laureate of England. Although many of his shorter poems are still enjoyed today, Tennyson is best remembered for his two long poems, ***In Memoriam*** and *Idylls of the King.*

THACKERAY, WILLIAM M. (1811–1863) English satirist and humorist. With sharp powers of characterization of English society, he had an easy urbane style. His best-known novels are ***Vanity Fair*** and *Henry Esmond.*

THOMAS À KEMPIS (1380–1471), author of *The Imitation of Christ.* Born in Germany and educated in Holland, he became a Brother of the Canons Regular at Mount Saint Agnes. Over his tomb, which was built by subscriptions from all over the world at Saint Michael's church in Zwolle, Holland, is this inscription: *To the honor, not to the memory, of Thomas à Kempis, whose name is more enduring than any monument.*

WALSH, THOMAS J. (1875–1928), authority on Spanish and Latin literature. He was a poet, an editor of an Hispanic anthology and a Catholic book of verse.

WHITMAN, WALT (1819–1892), often acclaimed the most distinctively American poet. His use of flexible rhythm in verse led to a greater freedom of expression. This has increased his importance in American literature.

WILLIAMS, MICHAEL (1878–), founder and first editor of *Commonweal,* author of *Little Brother Francis of Assisi* and *The Book of High Romance.* His very short booklet, *The Road Mender,* established his position in American letters as a writer of exquisite prose.

WISEMAN, CARDINAL NICHOLAS PATRICK (1802–1865), born in Spain and died in London. He was educated in Ireland and in Rome. After many years' residence in Italy, where he wrote *Fabiola,* he returned to England. There, as Cardinal, he fought and won the bitter though short-lived agitation against the Catholic Church.

WORDSWORTH, WILLIAM (1770–1850), English poet. His poems glorified the commonplace and found spiritual beauty in the sights and sounds of nature. He was made poet laureate of England in 1843.

Audio-Visual Aids

The tremendous increase in the use of audio-visual aids in education has developed along artistic as well as informational lines. Thousands of films and recordings have been made to aid in the teaching of art, music, and literature. Many of these are related to the selections used in this book. The following list, indicative rather than comprehensive, has been made to aid the teacher in choosing material.

Most of the films and records set down here have direct relationship to the select tions in the units of the book. Recordings of music with less direct but with general cultural associations have been added. Here are some of the films and recordings which may be used as aids in the teaching of *A Book of Friendliness*:

Unit I · By the Fireside

Films

Boyhood of Jesus (LF)
Faith of Jairus (LF)
Little Women (RKO)
David Copperfield the Boy (TFC)
Maria Chapdelaine (BraF)
Family Teamwork (FF)

Recordings

Golden Jubilee (CER–RCAV)
Charles Dickens (DV)
Cotter's Saturday Night (T–O–D)
Old Folks at Home (RCAV)

Unit II · In the Town

Films

Story of Zaccheus (LF)
The Rich Young Man (LF)
Miracle of Blind Beggar (LF)
Greater Victory (Fm)
Tale of Two Cities (TFC)
Drama of Steel (USM)
Furnaces of Industry (UWF)
Communications and Our Town (TFC)
Transportation and Our Community (TFC)
Immigration (EBF)
Main Street on the March (TFC)

Recordings

Day Will Come (CER–RCAV)
Ballad Told at Candlelight (RCAV)
Carnival, Schumann (RCAV)
Street Boys' Parade, Bizet (RCAV)

Unit III · On the Highways

Films

The Good Samaritan (LF)
The Prodigal Son (LF)
Saint Francis of Assisi (ITTCO)
The River (USTF)
George Washington Carver (TFC)
The Wonder Trail (TFC)
Yellowstone National Park (FM)
Canoe Trails through Mooseland (CGMPB)
Girl of the Limberlost (ITTCO)
The Biscuit Eater (Fi)

Recordings

Legend of Sleepy Hollow (T–O–D)
Evangeline (T–O–D)
Country Dance, Weber (RCAV)
Country Dance, Beethoven (RCAV)
Shepherds Dance, German (RCAV)
Country Gardens, Granger (RCAV)

Unit IV · At Christmastide

Films

Starlight Night (Hf)
Night before Christmas (TFC)
It Came upon a Midnight Clear (PPC)
Little Town of Bethlehem (PPC)
Silent Night (PPC)

Recordings

Candle for Christmas (CER–RCAV)
Hark the Herald Angels Sing (CER–RCAV)
A Christmas Carol, Dickens (Col)
Christmas Gift (Decca)
David Copperfield (T–O–D)
To Bethlehem, Singing (Puerto Rico) (RCAV)
We Three Kings of Orient Are (RCAV)
O Come, All Ye Faithful (RCAV)
While Shepherds Watched (RCAV)

Unit V · In Their Own Lands

Films

America the Beautiful (USTF)
Man Without a Country (UWF)
The Greater Victory (Fm)
Land of Liberty (TFC)
Story of Our Flag (DV)
Star-Spangled Banner (DV)
Canada (ITTCO)
Province of Quebec (EBF)
Last Lesson (TFC)
Land of My Mother (PIC)
Irish Pastoral (TFC)
Village in India (TFC)

Recordings

Jasmine and General Jackson (CER–RCAV)
North Atlantic Testament (CER–RCAV)
The Lexington (CER–RCAV)
Mine Eyes Have Seen the Glory (RCAV)
Star-Spangled Banner (RCAV)
America (RCAV)

Unit VI · On the Sea and in the Sky

Films

Treasure Island (TFC)
Sindbad the Sailor (CF)
Swiss Family Robinson (Fi)
The Ship that Died (TFC)
Mutiny on the Bounty (TFC)
Flight Six (BraF) (NFBC)
The Mail (UWF)

Recordings

Treasure Island (T–O–D)
Where the Typhoon Blows (GCR)
Rime of the Ancient Mariner (T–O–D)
Blow the Man Down (Chantey) (RCAV)
Duna (RCAV)
Crossing the Bar (T–O–D)

Unit VII · Among the Nations

Films

Story of the Vatican (March of Time) (ITTCO)
Palestine (DV)
Holy Land (UWF)
Frontiers of the North (CGMPB)
Story of Alfred Nobel (TFC)

Recordings

Crown of Glory (CER–RCAV)
Bell of Canterbury (CER–RCAV)
Sanctuary (CER–RCAV)
Knowest Thou the Land, Thomas (RCAV)

Unit VIII · In Christ Our Lord

Films

John the Baptist (LF)
Conversion of Matthew (LF)
Disciples at Emmaus (LF)
The Rich Young Man (LF)
The Unmerciful Servant (LF)
Sacrifice of the Mass (EBF)

Recordings

He Shall Feed His Flock, Handel (RCAV)
Ave Maria, Schubert (RCAV)
Ave Maria, Gounod (RCAV)
Gregorian Chant Series (CEP)
Saint Francis Xavier Cabrini (CER–RCAV)
Saint John Vianney, the Curé of Ars (CER–RCAV)
Saint Rose of Lima (CER–RCAV)
Our Lady of Fatima (CER–RCAV)

Abbreviations

BraF: Brandon Films
CEP: Catholic Education Press
CER: Catholic Educational Recordings
CF: Castle Films (Distributed by RCAV)
CGMPB: Canadian Government Motion Picture Bureau
Col: Columbia
DV: De Vry
EBF: Encyclopedia Britannica Films
FF: Frith Films
Fi: Films Incorporated
Fm: Filmedia
FM: Ford Motor Company
GCR: Gloria Chandler Recordings
Hf: Hoffberg
ITTCO: International Theatrical and Television Company
LF: Loyola Films
NFBC: National Film Board of Canada
PIC: Polish Information Service
PPC: Post Pictures Corporation
RCAV: Radio Corporation of America–Victor
TFC: Teaching Film Custodians, Inc.
T–O–D: Teach-O-Disc
USM: United States Mines
USTF: United States Treasury Films
UWF: United World Films

Index

PRINTED IN THE UNITED STATES OF AMERICA